Military Role and Rule

Want to get ahead faster?

Yes, it's true! A few short years ago, Idi Amin of 10 Prince Charles Drive, Kampala, was a humble sergeant drawing £14 7s. 8d. per week. Today, he's in charge of a £100,000,000 country, involved in top decision-making, and clearly having a wonderful time, with marvellous opportunities to travel, water-ski, and shoot people. "I owe it all to the British Army," says Idi. "Without them, I might have ended up singing 'Ol' Man River' at the Finsbury Park Empire like my parents always wanted. You were wrong, Mummy and Daddy!"

You don't have to wait around hoping something better will turn up! You can go where there's real opportunity to make it while you're still young! The Army offers you the chance to get ahead faster than you will anywhere else, whatever your interests are. The Army will develop your abilities, train you for a skilled job, give you big responsibility— *and* pay you the sort of money you're really worth!

A group of REME privates somewhere on Salisbury Plain, training to be the next Tanzanian Government. "Starting pay is a generous £17 17s. per week," says nineteen-year-old Ngo Mbabwi, "plus uniform allowance, and the food is spiffin'. And as soon as my basic training's over, I hope to be Foreign Secretary, a job with status and prospects and £2,000 a month, free of tax."

Yakubu Gowon joined the British Army to see the world, and now owns 357,000 square miles of it! Sandhurst-trained, Yakubu first thought he'd like a career in signals, then he thought of the Catering Corps, but finally he plumped for taking over Nigeria. "Yes, the range of trades is enormous if you're a Professional," he says, "and promotion is very quick for the right man."

Find out about the Professionals

For FREE Army leaflet post the coupon to Army Careers MP6 (A), Lansdowne House, Berkeley Square, London W1X 6AA.

NAME

ADDRESS

TOWN

COUNTY

AGE

M004-307-01

THIS IS THE ARMY

ARMY

Military Role and Rule

Perspectives on Civil-Military Relations

Claude E. Welch, Jr.
*State University of New York
at Buffalo*

Arthur K. Smith
*State University of New York
at Binghamton*

Duxbury Press
North Scituate, Massachusetts
A division of Wadsworth Publishing Company, Inc., Belmont, California

Duxbury Press
A Division of Wadsworth Publishing Company, Inc.

ISBN-0-87872-054-5

L. C. Cat. Card No. 73-80877

Printed in the United States of America

1 2 3 4 5 6 7 8 9 10 - - - 76 75 74 73

Table of Contents

Preface

No political group is more influential and less studied than the armed forces.

In the early 1970's, national governments have been spending more than $200 billion annually on their armed forces. No other institution receives such extensive financial support. According to figures compiled by the United States Arms Control and Disarmament Agency, our federal government spends approximately as much on the military as on education and public health combined.* Sophisticated equipment, such as a single supersonic aircraft, may cost several million dollars; standing armies can easily absorb half a government's revenues.

But the political impact of the military is even more profound than its economic weight. More than a third of the member states of the United Nations are headed by individuals who seized power in coups d'etat—the classic means by which members of the armed forces move from their barracks into presidential palaces. Despite extensive efforts to subordinate the military to civilian control, the failures have been more pronounced than the successes. The number of governments under military

*World Military Expenditures 1970 (Washington: United States Arms Control and Disarmament Agency, 1972), p. 10.

leadership has recently increased: in Latin America, the total rose from one in early 1962 to ten by mid-1973; in Africa, the total jumped from two to fifteen in the same period.

Military involvement in politics takes many forms. It may be expressed as *influence,* in which the armed forces act as a particularly powerful pressure group or segment of the bureaucracy. This influence exists even in states in which the civilian control over the armed forces is strong and stable. Less common, but still widespread, is military *participation* in politics. In its indirect form, the military participation is exercised in vetoes of policy choices or of individual candidates seeking office; direct participation is less subtle, sometimes culminating in the ouster of elected officials. Military *control* of politics represents the most extensive form of involvement. Members of the armed forces decide who will hold leadership positions, what policies will be followed, and how government resources will be divided among contending groups. In nations where coups d'etat change government personnel more often than elections, the armed forces serve as the supreme political arbiters—and as the foundation for military regimes.

Military control of politics characterizes four states we examine in *Military Role and Rule.* In these states, the responsibilities of the armed forces encompass far more than the traditional defense of borders; these responsibilities spread through the entire political system. Military regimes are the consequence—and the rule of officers is a fact—where members of the armed forces see their roles as requiring them to exercise direct political leadership.

Military Role and Rule sprang from the authors' mutual interest in members of the armed forces who thrust themselves to the center of the political stage. We drew upon different regional specialties, constructing from them a common framework for analyzing the political roles of armed forces. We chose to complement our theoretical framework with case studies. The chapters on Egypt, France, Nigeria, Peru, and Thailand illustrate different varieties of military involvement in politics, ranging from the military's acceptance of civilian control to its unchallenged displacement of the elected government.

The lessons of our inquiry go far beyond the countries examined in the case studies, however. The wide-ranging political responsibilities exercised by officers in other nations indicate that civilian control as it exists in the United States characterizes only a small fraction of nations. Even in the United States, the political and economic impacts of the military are vast. Debates rage over what former President Eisenhower termed the "military–industrial complex," over the all-volunteer armed forces, and over defense expenditures—for the United States spends as much on its armed forces as the *combined* gross national products of all countries in the Middle East and South Asia, some sixteen states with a total population of close to 800 million. Underlying all these areas of heated controversy are two fundamental questions. How much power should be allotted to the armed forces? Can states in which military *control* of politics exists move toward military *influence* in politics?

The importance of *Military Role and Rule* lies in responses to these questions. Unlike other studies of civil–military relations that have concentrated on the so-called developing countries, this book develops a framework applicable to all states—modern, industrialized, and urbanized; transitional, partially industrialized, and urbanizing; traditional, agricultural, and rural. The combination of case studies with an overall analytical framework permits comparison with countries other than the five described in Part II. Readers interested in these states may wish to turn directly to the relevant chapters, then return to the framework presented in Part I; readers interested in the overall political impact of the armed forces may choose to look first at Part III, in which the implications of the case studies are extrapolated into general conclusions. Whatever the background of the individual reader, *Military Role and Rule* should help him better understand the undoubted political prominence of the military throughout the world.

The Research Foundation of the State University of New York provided fellowships to abet preparation of the manuscript. We wish to give special thanks to Robin Luckham of Harvard and Robert Price of Berkeley for their detailed critiques of earlier drafts. Many colleagues at Binghamton and Buffalo commented on our labors, including Richard H. Dekmejian, Walter O. Filley, Joseph M. Firestone, Edwin M. Rutkowski, Jerome N. Slater, William Stover, and Mavis B. Taintor. We also thank David Morell and Douglas Paradis for helping us through the complexities of Thai politics. Our families endured the travails of research and writing, and to them goes the special recognition they deserve. For the accuracy of the data and interpretations presented on subsequent pages, we take full responsibility.

C. E. W.

A. K. S.

Political Involvement of the Military:
An Overview

Throughout time, philosophers and politicians alike have grappled with the problem of how to secure compliance to the laws of the body politic; and consideration of this problem has always led to the related study of the political functions of coercion. How can a political system protect itself from domestic lawlessness and external encroachment?

In small-scale societies, individuals have often banded together, ensuring protection collectively—for example, the posse of American frontier society, or the *pao-chia* system of Imperial China. But in most contemporary societies and in the large-scale societies of the past as well, protection has been furnished by formally constituted branches of the government. Police and armed forces are integral parts of most modern political systems.

Can the obedience of the military and its subordination to civilian authority be compelled? What happens when members of the armed forces take power into their own hands? These problems are as ancient as the protection agencies themselves. The Roman poet Juvenal posed the problem succinctly: "Who is to guard the guards themselves?" The sweep of history suggests that military dominance in politics is far

more common than civilian control over the armed forces. A frequent
consequence of military disenchantment with a government is the coup
d'etat—a direct seizure of political control by members of the armed
forces, who may be acting in concert with civilian allies.

Civilian control of the armed forces cannot be achieved without understanding why, and how, military influence in politics becomes
transformed into military intervention in politics. Who is to guard the
guards remains as apt a question now as for Juvenal 1900 years ago. The
pages that follow derive from our concern, as citizens and as political
scientists, about what has loosely been deemed the "military–industrial
complex." Our emphasis on military regimes, the most obvious form of
military involvement in politics, is intended to provide a theoretical
and factual foundation on which to construct an understanding of why
politically subordinated armed forces have been historical exceptions
rather than historical rule.

The problems we examine in *Military Role and Rule* are by
no means new: How can a government keep the political influence of its
military within established channels? What means can be employed to
ensure that the armed forces will direct their "might" in accord with the
"right" the government should embody? What steps can be taken to preclude coups d'etat? How, in short, can the influence of this particularly
powerful institution, the military, be halted short of policy vetoes, or of
total usurpation?

Part I of *Military Role and Rule* presents a format for analyzing military involvement in politics. The material in Part I describes the
kinds and degrees of military influence, the factors that encourage military intervention, and the types of military regimes that result from
intervention. Throughout the book, we attempt to relate the general
arguments presented in Part I to specific military regimes. Hence, Part II
examines five countries in detail, using them as case studies of military
involvement in politics. The observations in Part III unite the general
and specific material in an attempt to determine whether the current
plethora of military regimes augurs for increased involvement of armed
forces in politics.

Analysis of the Military's Role in Politics

Part I approaches the complex question of how armed forces are involved in politics. We shall first assess the spectrum of the political influence wielded by armed forces—from that minimal influence inherent in their responsibilities, perceptions, and costliness to the other extreme of overt intervention in politics. Next we consider the factors that affect the probability of intervention; and last we turn to the natural consequence of coups d'etat, military regimes and the numerous differences among them. The most important variables that affect civil–military relations will be discussed and illustrated; they are: political participation, civil institutions, military strength, and the institutional boundaries between the armed forces and other groups.

Our essential arguments in the three chapters of Part I are summarized in the following statements:

1.   The political roles of the armed forces vary in accordance with factors peculiar to each state. These factors, which we call environmental, include the nature and extent of political participation within the society, the relative isolation of the armed forces from social and political currents, the extent to which the military serves as a direct support for the government, and the legitimacy enjoyed by the government.

2.   Variations in the organization of the armed forces, which we call internal factors, interact with environmental variables. Among the internal variables are mission, political awareness, level of cohesion, technological proficiency, the nature and extent of military professionalism, and the values espoused by the military, particularly values reinforcing or undercutting political subordination.

3.   Outright military intervention in politics arises primarily from the limited or declining legitimacy of civilian political institutions and is particularly likely to occur during periods of rapidly changing norms and rising political participation.

4.   Strong civilian control over the armed forces emerges gradually through complex historical processes, reaching its fullest expression in the military's voluntary acceptance of subordination. This acceptance can be fostered by the growth of civilian political institutions (such as political parties) that enjoy wide popular support, by recognition of agreed-upon spheres of military autonomy in technical decisions, and by the successful and peaceful transfer of political power among contending civilian groups in ways that enhance government legitimacy.

1

Military Influence and Military Intervention

No nation's armed forces remain apart from politics. Politics is concerned with the distribution of values and power within a society—and the military can hardly be prevented from participating in that process in some manner.

Almost every state has a standing army, and quite possibly a navy, air force, and paramilitary groups such as a gendarmerie. These forces consume resources. They also serve as major purveyors of political values such as security, public order, and national prestige. Accordingly the armed forces' need for resources and their responsibilities make them powerful political actors.

The military traditionally has defended against external encroachments and on occasion has enforced government decisions domestically. To fulfill these roles, a military organization must be cohesive and hierarchical. The armed forces often are the most structurally differentiated and functionally specific branch of government bureaucracy. Members of the military profession may develop a strong sense of professional identity. They may also make a claim for institutional autonomy in their area of expertise, the management of violence, for the military must control or even monopolize organized violence within its society. The implications of this organizational identity, autonomy, and functional specialization are enormous.

The influence of the military on important policy decisions differs from society to society. Such factors as the officers' image within the society, the prevailing state of public order, the perceived seriousness of foreign threats to national security, and the confidence political leaders have in their hold on power naturally affect the military's political impact. It is easy to envisage situations in which this impact might increase—particularly if the military profession enjoys high public esteem, if public order is threatened by acute unrest, if war seems a strong possibility, or if incumbent political leaders feel threatened by challenges to their position. Thus, the military's political role is a question not of *whether* but of *how much* and *of what kind*.

Many variations exist in the political perceptions and ambitions of national armies. In some states, the military strives to exert a dominant political influence; in others, it remains on the sidelines, a mute servant of the government in control; in yet others, it periodically pressures the government to carry out the armed forces' will. The armed forces, or factions within them, may be aligned with existing political or social groups; they may stand aloof from partisan strife to protect their own organizational integrity; or they may be solicited by contending groups for support in struggles for power.

In the United States and a few other societies, the participation of the military in the policy process is a fact. Organized military sanctions against civilian authority, on the other hand, are not part of the political equation; they would violate the fundamental political values of these societies. Such societies, which we term "civic," enjoy civilian control. Civilian control is not a matter of levels of social and economic development, nor of maximizing the professionalism of the military, nor even of a distribution of political power overwhelmingly favorable to civilian groups. Civilian control exists if the officer corps has internalized the value of civilian supremacy as part of its ethical makeup. (Even in contemporary industrialized states, the military's acceptance of civilian supremacy may be tenuous: witness the problems of France in wrestling with the issue of Algeria, or the central role played by the General Staff in pre-1945 German politics.)

In the developing societies of Africa, Asia, and Latin America, civilian supremacy is rare indeed. Here the military's role in politics knows few bounds. The norm of civilian control may not have entered the military ethic. Leaders of the armed forces may exercise an effective veto over certain policy options and may even bar from high office politicians they deem inimical to their interests. In such settings, outright usurpation of power and the establishment of military regimes become possible. Such are "praetorian" socieites, those in which the military does not play a subordinate role to that of the civilian authority. The bulk of this book is devoted to the study of praetorian societies.

In the perspective of recent years, it seems that little progress has been made in enhancing civilian control. In early 1962, military regimes governed but one (Paraguay) of the twenty-one Latin American republics then independent; a decade later, eleven of these countries had fallen under military sway. Only a few small, isolated states—some island republics, a few African ministates, Costa Rica—did not maintain standing armies in the early 1970's. They were far outnumbered by 118 countries with such forces. Military expenditures weighed heavily on national budgets. In 1970, an average of $57 per inhabitant was expended on armed forces around the earth, for a total of more than $208 billion; by 1972, the total was estimated at more than $220 billion. [1] Nearly half the member states of the United Nations are ruled by outright military regimes, in which officers fill senior political positions; or by military–civilian coalitions, in which officers exercise paramount influence behind a facade of civilian control.

The reasons for military usurpation of political primacy form the subject of the next chapter.

References

1. *World Military Expenditures, 1970* (Washington: U.S. Arms Control and Disarmament Agency, 1972), p. 10. See Appendix for details on military expenditures.

2

Factors in Intervention: Stimulants and Deterrents

Military dominance in politics is far from an unusual phenomenon. In the judgment of Gaetano Mosca, a nineteenth-century Italian political scientist, "the class that bears the lance or holds the musket regularly forces its rule upon the class that handles the spade or pushes the shuttle."[1]

The most dramatic contemporary form of military dominance in politics is the coup d'etat. A coup installs new persons in the corridors of power. In a country like Honduras, which experienced 115 changes of executive in 125 years, military uprisings change the political personnel far more commonly than do elections.[2] Coups seem to follow a time-honored format. Popular discontent with the government increases, marked by sporadic strikes, rioting, or other forms of domestic violence. If an election is in the offing, tempers and political promises run high. The incumbent president eventually must call on the armed forces to maintain order. Not wanting to besmirch themselves by propping up a tottering government, and probably incensed by efforts to diminish the institutional prerogatives of the military, officers choose a more attractive course: dismiss the current government and draw a new cabinet substantially from within the military and its civilian supporters.

8

The frequency of military seizures of power has spawned many divergent interpretations concerning their causes. Some political scientists feel that the most significant factor is the organization of the armed forces and their recruitment patterns. Mosca, for example, wrote in this vein, asserting that "the standing army will absorb all the more belligerent elements, and, being readily capable of prompt obedience to a single impulse, it will have no difficulty in dictating to the rest of society."[3] Others feel that far more significance inheres in the total political context. The environment, in their view, more directly affects the likelihood of coups d'etat than do the organizational characteristics of the military.

We do not intend in this chapter to find The Cause of military intervention, for coups usually are engendered by several factors. However, by classifying what are asserted to be causes of individual seizures of control, we hope to illustrate some of the contributing elements of coups d'etat.

Internal Factors Affecting Military Intervention

Many aspects of military organization affect the possibility of coups d'etat. For example, what purposes do officers see as appropriate for the armed forces? If they view their mission as protecting the nation from the machinations of corrupt politicians, even if these politicians are popularly elected, then it is certain that the officers are willing to shoulder aside civilian control when necessary. What cleavages exist within the armed forces? Whether the cleavages are founded in class or ethnic origins, in the differences inherent in specialized branches of the military, in types of professional training, or in some other factor, they may become so divisive that they result in intervention. Do members of the armed forces exhibit types of political awareness that draw them toward active involvement in politics? The nature and extent of political awareness also clearly figures among the underlying factors in coups d'etat.

The propositions in this section concentrate on factors such as the preceding, those *internal* to the armed forces. In the following section, we shall turn to factors *external* to the armed forces, namely, to the social and political contexts within which the armed forces exist.

Mission

The responsibilities of the armed forces are unique. Theirs is the burden of protecting the state, their sole patron. Unlike the police, who are oriented toward domestic duties, the armed forces tend to look outward: to border defense, to prevention of attack.

The mission of the police involves maintaining tranquility. Most organized enforcement groups can influence decisions made by political leaders, but the police do not; rather, they usually carry out decisions of others.[4] Police forces are almost never heavily armed, even those that are paramilitary units. Their effectiveness depends instead on close ties with the populace; as a result, policemen generally are both recruited and stationed locally.

By contrast, military units are usually deployed along frontiers, or in garrisons substantially removed from civilian influence. Recruitment is commonly carried out on a national basis; units are regularly rotated, to reduce ties with the local populace. The military is particularly concerned with foreign policy decisions; the police, with domestic policy decisions.

Involvement of the armed forces in internal pacification—in short, in duties usually assigned to the police—inherently and inevitably brings the military into political disputes. As S. E. Finer comments, "The professional army sees itself as the nation's custodian against foreign foes. . . . It also sees itself as a fighting force, not as a body of policemen."[5] Military neutrality and subordination to the government are strained when the armed forces are called on to enforce unpopular governmental decisions. Accordingly, we suggest:

> 1. *The likelihood of military intervention rises should the armed forces become heavily involved in primarily domestic, police-type or counterinsurgency activities.*
>
> 2. *The likelihood of military intervention rises should the armed forces be ordered, contrary to the advice of the officer corps, to use coercion against domestic opponents of the government.*

Apparent confirmation of these propositions comes from the detailed analytical study of Egil Fossum. Fossum examined 105 successful coups d'etat in Latin America between 1907 and 1966. Nearly two-thirds were undertaken at times of public disorder. However, correlation must not be construed as causation. Do coups spring from popular unrest? Fossum indicates that disorder may "serve as a pretext to intervene," or conversely that the military "may have a real desire to reestablish public order without further motives. . . ."[6]

Let us shift our attention from an internal to an international mission. What happens when armed forces are commanded to use their coercive strength against external opponents?

Scattered evidence suggests that military intervention in the government rarely occurs in the *early* stages of a nation's involvement in international conflict. The advent of war, or the exacerbation of international crises, may be accompanied by outbursts of patriotism. An infringement of national territory, or a slap at national "honor," can help mobilize support for both the armed forces and the government. The military's mission stands out with stark clarity: repel the threat. An army devoting its attention to external crises has responsibilities well removed from domestic politics. As a result:

> 3. *The likelihood of military intervention diminishes with the emergence of a clear-cut, external focus for national defense.*

Indirect support for this proposition comes from Fossum. The 1940–1942 period was the sole three-year span unpunctuated by a Latin American coup in this century. Although only Brazil entered World War II, the conflict initially may have muted the domestic antagonisms in other Latin American nations. As the war dragged on, however, domestic issues intensified. The 1943–1945 period witnessed nine coups, the second highest number of any period in Fossum's study.[7] Hence, we must conclude that the unifying effect of international crises may be temporary. Protracted conflict or defeat in war serves to increase the likelihood of a coup d'etat. (See proposition 13 below.)

To define a clear mission for the armed forces when they are not involved in external conflict and (not incidentally) to reduce the possibility of intervention, many governments have turned to civic action programs, which involve the military directly in national development. Such programs absorb the military's attention and expertise; by using the armed forces in national construction, the government hopes to thwart, or at least channel, the military's political ambitions. An example frequently cited, though not necessarily an accurate parallel for contemporary civic action programs, is the nineteenth-century history of the American armed forces. West Point was founded as a school of engineering, not as a standard military academy. Until after the Civil War, West Point remained part of the Corps of Engineers, producing (in Samuel Huntington's words) "more railroad presidents than generals."[8] The armed forces enjoyed a clear domestic mission: open the West for settlement. The absence of major international threats to the United States during most of the century enabled the military to concentrate on the simple, bloody crushing of Indian resistance. Similarly, the Israeli military has taken responsibility for *kibbutzim* in strategic areas, thereby coupling development with border defense. Largely through American prodding, the armed forces of several Latin American and Southeast Asian states have also embarked on civic action.[9] We suggest:

4.   The likelihood of military intervention diminishes if the armed forces undertake civic action programs.

The propositions thus far have assumed that the mission of the armed forces is defined by civilians: subdue domestic opposition, undertake civic action. However, the military may have its own very different definition of its mission. Coups have been mounted by officers who view their responsibility as safeguarding the entire state from the machinations of political leaders. A mission making the armed forces the guarantor of national institutions leads directly to intervention:

5.   A mission that differentiates between service to "the government" and service to "the nation" encourages the armed forces to move directly into politics.

A clear example of this perspective comes from Gamal Abdel Nasser, who explained the intervention of Egyptian Free Officers in mid-1952:

> *The state of affairs singled out the armed forces as the force to do the job. The situation demanded the existence of a force set in one cohesive framework, far removed from the conflict between individual and classes, and drawn from the heart of the people: a force composed of men able to trust each other, a force with enough material support at its disposal to guarantee swift and decisive action. These conditions could be met only by the army.*[10]

Nasser's voice is but one of many. The belief of officers that the military alone can "save" the country from certain perils figures prominently in the rationalizations of coups, both successful and abortive, and in rationalizations for substantially expanding the military's political influence. For example, the French generals who took up arms against President de Gaulle in April 1961 were convinced that the citizens of France had been tricked into an acceptance of Algerian autonomy which counteracted the true interests of France. General Douglas MacArthur, after being relieved of his command by President Truman in 1952, gave voice to a similar attitude. In MacArthur's words, "I find in existence a new and heretofore unknown and dangerous concept that the members of our armed forces owe primary allegiance or loyalty to those who temporarily exercise the authority of the Executive Branch of Government rather than to the country and its constitution which they are sworn to defend. No proposition could be more dangerous."[11] The General's assertions were far removed from the American conception of civil–military relations, which makes the President not only head of the Executive Branch but also Commander-in-Chief of the armed forces.

We have seen that significant differences between the policies espoused by the government in power and the self-conceived mission of the military account for many attempts to seize power, or to effect a dramatic expansion of political influence. However, the mission must be viewed in terms of two other factors internal to the military: organizational characteristics and the officers' political awareness.

Organizational Characteristics

One of the most significant aspects of the military is its organization. Several distinctive attributes of this organization strongly affect the military's propensity to intervene or abstain from intervention in the government. These include centralized command, discipline, hierarchy, formalized internal communication, esprit de corps, and a corresponding concept of self-sufficiency.[12] All these attributes, the last two in particular, tend to enhance the cohesion of the armed forces and to isolate them from society as a whole.

Cohesion   Probably no institution can match the solidarity developed within a modern army. All the organizational attributes cited above contribute greatly to the cohesion of the institution. In addition, a host of long-standing army practices stress the totality of the institution and diminish the uniqueness of the individual. Consider the basic training given a raw recruit in the American army. He is stripped of his civilian clothing, his hair, even his first name (Joe Jones becomes Private Jones); incorporated into a large, impersonal organization; severed for several weeks from friends and family. The uniform, salute, PX, and clubs provide new forms of identification and stratification.

Cohesion must be maintained in the stress of battle, hence the emphasis on solidarity found within armed forces. Paradoxically, however, a high degree of cohesion may encourage coups d'etat. Emphasis on the military as a total and unique institution can result in its members' believing they hold special responsibilities for "the nation," as noted in the preceding proposition. The soldiers' training to follow commands quickly, efficiently, and without questions—an asset in times of conflict—may make them a threatening force to civilian leaders. In theory, a disciplined, cohesive army would unhesitatingly obey any order received through the appropriate channels, even if that order were a command to march on the presidential palace and eliminate its occupants. We thus suggest, following Morris Janowitz: [13]

6. *Armed forces with high internal cohesion have a greater capacity to intervene in domestic politics than armed forces with lesser cohesion; countercoups after the seizure of power are more likely to occur if the new military regime is one of low internal cohesion.*

Autonomy   Armies throughout history have claimed the right to exercise autonomy in internal organization and operations. In fact, military independence from civilian control represents a more common historical phenomenon than subordination to civilian authority. Does a relatively wide sphere of military decision making increase the likelihood of military intervention? Attempts to alter the policy prerogatives of the armed forces, it is often hypothesized, encourage coups d'etat. Finer puts the case bluntly. "The military is jealous of its corporate status and privileges. Anxiety to preserve its autonomy provides one of the most widespread and powerful of the motives for intervention." [14]

One antidote to civil–military tensions, it stands to reason, is the recruitment of officers sharing the backgrounds and outlooks of political leaders. Historically, perhaps the most common form of this homogeneity, at least in the European context, was the prevalence of aristocrats in top military and political positions. In 1865, more than eighty percent of the colonels and generals in the Prussian army were drawn from the aristocracy.[15] In Great Britain, the officer's code of conduct emphasized his status as a gentleman, hence his status as a privileged individual occupying a particular niche in the class structure.[16] In France, as Raoul Giradet observed, an officer was conscious of "belonging to a privileged group, to a particular order, clearly distinct from the rest of national society. . . ."[17]

Mosca argued that civilian control over the military, though a "most fortunate exception" to the usual civil–military relationship, could result from the recruitment of officers from the "politically dominant ranks of society."[18] In other words, from the nobility.

Mosca's thesis is bounded, however, in both time and space. His observations applied to Western Europe in the middle to late nineteenth century; the wholesale slaughter of officers during World War I ended the dominance of aristocrats. The "ruling class" concept also breaks down when applied in non-European contexts, for example in Latin America. During the nineteenth century, most Latin American officers were drawn from large, land-owning families, not from Indian or *mestizo* families, yet these traditional oligarchs regularly overthrew governments by coups d'etat. We must recognize, as did Stanislav Andreski, that "the integration of the officers' corps in the ruling layer appears to be a necessary condition of some measure of political neutralization; but the evidence from Latin America shows that it is not a sufficient condition. . . ."[19] Andreski offers two explanations, both of which involve environmental rather than internal factors: (1) bitter class warfare throughout the society; (2) a political order marked by the lack of widely accepted codes of political behavior, by disorderly administration, and by the absence of well-organized political parties—all of which ensured violent overthrows of governments.

Issues of social class may be overshadowed in ethnically pluralistic states by issues of "tribalism," but both are concerned with the dominance of some individuals over others. The officer corps may be dominated by members of one ethnic group, the rank and file by another, and the government by a third. Differences among them can explode into unrest and intervention, as occurred in Nigeria.

Recognizing the complex functions of class and ethnic factors, we suggest:

> 7. *The likelihood of military intervention diminishes if officers are drawn from or incorporated into the same social strata as the governing elite, and rises if the two groups are drawn from different strata.*

In the study of autonomy, the usual distinction, drawn by Clausewitz [20] and many others, separates "technical" from "policy" matters. The latter represent objectives, the ends for which military strength is to be employed; the former represent means, the steps necessary to achieve goals. A few, simple illustrations from the United States will clarify the distinction. The power to declare war rests with Congress; the tactics to be pursued, within overall strategic aims, rest with the military. Appropriations for the armed forces must be approved by Congress and the President; the professional assessment of different weapons systems rests primarily with officers. Promotions into the highest ranks must be scrutinized and formally approved by civilians; promotions at lower levels remain essentially under the military's control, though formally made on behalf of the government.

An end–means separation is easy in theory, difficult in reality. The dividing line shifts from issue to issue, and clearly differs from country to country. Tasks that are under exclusive military jurisdiction in one nation (for example, weapons procurement) may in another nation be shared by civilian and military authorities, and elsewhere reside totally with civilians.

A more crucial distinction lies between "professional" decisions, vested in the military, and "political" decisions, vested in elected officials. The distinction is a finer one than that between know-how and rationale. This one is more a question of degree. Let us consider the French embroilment in Algeria. French commanders embarked on a policy of *quadrillage* (literally, dividing the countryside into squares) that required moving more than two million Algerians from their homes.[21] To French generals, such efforts stemmed from military necessity, from the need to counter-act Algerian guerrillas. To leaders of the Fourth Republic, however, these policies suggested that the armed forces had overstepped their role as im-plementors of policy and had assumed the role of formulators. When Premier Pierre Pflimlin favored a settlement with the Algerian national-ists, he faced military insurrection that forced his resignation and brought the collapse of the French government.

A second example of disagreement over professional and political arenas concerns the self-regulatory powers of the Peruvian armed forces. The *estado militar* denotes the policy of autonomy of the armed forces.

> *By law and convention, [the Peruvian armed forces] constitute a corporate entity separated from the general society by well-defined boundaries; they enjoy a substantial measure of self-regulatory power; and they possess a collective set of attitudes, values, and interests. These attributes affect directly their motivation and capacity for political action.*[22]

Powers granted under the *estado militar* cover a wide range, including standards of performance, recruitment and promotion, exclusive juris-diction over service personnel in military and occasionally in civil offenses, internal budget priorities, pay scales, and a host of benefits, including retirement, housing, medical, and educational perquisites. These far-reaching prerogatives, it stands to reason, give the military wide areas of autonomy that are jealously guarded from politicians who might seek to upset the balance—and in so doing, court intervention. As Victor Villaneuva observed, since 1912 no Peruvian government that has attempt-ed to reduce military expenditures has completed its term in office.[23]

The vital necessity for both officers and politicians, we suggest, is mutual recognition—that is, awareness by military as well as civilian leaders—of (a) the areas of *exclusive* policy authority for each, and (b) the areas of *shared* policy authority. The balance between these authori-ties constitutes civil–military relations. Abrupt shifts in the nature of policy, particularly alterations that seem to threaten the armed forces' purported prerogatives, may encourage intervention. The coups discuss-ed in the subsequent case studies were sparked by a variety of steps taken by civilians which the military perceived as reducing its responsibilities: announcement of plans for a popular militia; drastic reduction in military budgets; denial of new weapons; "interference" in promotions or elections to the officers' club; early retirement of leading officers. Hence:

8. *Changes or intentions to alter the armed forces' areas of decision making against their advice or desires increase the likelihood of military intervention.*

Structural Differentiation and Functional Specialization   A clear trend in military organization has been toward increased structural differentiation. Complex weaponry has led to the multiplication of service branches. Though the infantry remains the largest and most costly branch of the military in almost all states, the claims of navies, air forces, and special or civic action units cannot be ignored. Such complexity makes it more difficult today to plan and mount a successful coup d'etat. Intelligence units, alert to conspiracy, may rout out plotters; governments without these units can be readily toppled.

Another marked trend in military organization is that of functional specialization. The trend was set in motion by the Industrial Revolution and is kept moving by both technological advances and the spread of democratic ideals. Functional specialization also serves to deter military intervention in government. It obliges the would-be coup maker to build a coalition of divergent interests, for each branch of the armed forces has its own perspective on national priorities.

Under certain conditions, to be sure, interservice rivalries may encourage intervention. The most noteworthy condition is the creation of a paramilitary organization as a deliberate counterweight to the armed forces. The histories of two African states support this observation. In Ghana, the creation of the President's Own Guard Regiment led to resentment among "regular" officers, who joined in ousting the civilian government in 1966. Two years later, officers of Mali, resenting the paramilitary activities of the government-sponsored *Brigades de Vigilance,* staged a successful coup. Both coups stemmed from the perceived abridgement of military authority, which we examined in a preceding proposition.

Functional specialization and structural differentiation characterize the overall process of bureaucratization of the military. Its impact has been noted by all students of civil–military relations. Janowitz, for example, has described the shift from "heroic" to "managerial" skills within the armed forces:

The basis of authority and discipline in the military establishment [has shifted] from authoritarian domination to greater reliance on manipulation, persuasion, and group consensus. . . . The new skills of the military require that the professional officer develop more and more of the skills and orientations common to civilian administrators and civilian leaders. The narrowing difference in skill between military and civilian society is an outgrowth of the increasing concentration of technical specialists in the military.[24]

In other words, to the degree that officers acquire civilian-type skills and orientations, they are able to pursue goals through influence, not through overt intervention. We propose:

9.   The likelihood of military intervention is reduced by structural differentiation and functional specialization within the armed forces.

Key among the stimuli for structural differentiation and functional specialization is the example of other states. All armies share the same manifest function, serving as the coercive branch of the state against external opponents; and the basic characteristics of military organization exhibit relatively little variation. As Lucian Pye has asserted, comparisons are regularly drawn: "The soldier . . . is constantly called upon to look abroad and to compare his organization with foreign ones."[25] But can such comparisons enhance civilian control over the armed forces? Arguments have been made to the effect that military assistance from industrialized countries, such as the United States, can inspire the armed forces of developing countries to undertake disinterested public service, and possibly to incorporate as well the self-concept of a military that is subordinate to the government.[26] On the other hand, expertise brought by foreign aid may whet rather than mute the armed forces' desire for a broader political role. Should the military consitute the most "modern" sector, or view itself as the most "progressive" and the best equipped to protect the state, its political ambitions may soar. Hence, aid that encourages the armed forces to undertake new responsibilities may undercut civilian control. We suggest:

10.   The likelihood of domestic military intervention rises to the extent that external military assistance facilitates role expansion and greater autonomy for the armed forces.

This proposition, it should be noted, partially contradicts proposition 4, which suggested that civic action programs could reduce the likelihood of coups. Civic action involves members of the armed forces more deeply with domestic issues. Such involvement may in fact encourage intervention. In Argentina, as Jose Luis de Imaz has noted, the military's counterinsurgency actions have led the army "to assume *de facto* a new guardianship function . . . of guaranteeing the continuity of formal democracy, the solidarity of the Western world, and individual liberties";[27] this development has been marked by increasingly overt military involvement in politics. In Peru, American assistance through the Alliance for Progress, intended to stave off a Castroite social revolution, helped encourage the armed forces to impose their own program of radical modernization (see the chapter on Peru in Part II). Civic action is no panacea for military intervention. In fact, a government may expand the role of the military and give it greater autonomy because it wishes the military to function, in Henry Bienen's words, "as a surrogate for a civilian government that will not or cannot engage in social and economic reform and cannot hold the fort against insurgency, *whether the military takes over or not.*"[28] Coups d'etat may thus come as a consequence of military assistance that expands the political awareness and the organizational responsibilities of the armed forces.

Professionalism   Members of a profession, according to Huntington, combine expertise, corporate solidarity, and social responsibility. These attributes, collectively called professionalism, make the officer corps more than just an assemblage of competent job-holders.[29] Professionalization is the process by which professionalism is achieved. It is an increasingly elaborate process because the armed forces are constantly growing more complex. Both functional specialization and structural differentiation contribute significantly to professionalization in the modern military.

The professionalization of the armed forces refers to two processes: one corporate, the other individual. The corporate process of professionalization, according to Bengt Abrahamsson, occurred historically in four areas: (1) state centralization, leading to the domestic recruitment of cheap military labor for mass armies; (2) industrialization, making possible the equipment of large armies and creating ties between the officer corps and the bourgeois class; (3) the decline of the nobility as a source for officer recruitment; and (4) technological innovations.[30] Advanced training for officers became necessary, and thus military academies were established early in the nineteenth century.

The individual process of professionalization occurs through the indoctrination of values and goals peculiar to the military institution. The values and goals characteristic of a small, privileged, aristocratic group of officers have been essentially supplanted by (again, according to Abrahamsson) nationalism, pessimistic beliefs about human nature and the probability of war, political conservatism, and authoritarianism.[31]

The crucial issue, then, is the determination of the relationships among corporate professionalization, individual professionalization, and the establishment and maintenance of civilian control over the military. Heated scholarly debate has yet to produce agreement on the role of professionalism in subordinating the military to civilian authority.

One school of thought is represented by Huntington, author of *The Soldier and the State.* Civilian control, according to Huntington, exists in two forms. "Subjective" civilian control is by far the more common; no clear line exists between military and civilian groups, or between military and civilian values; civilian control is "the product of identity of thought and outlook between civilian and military groups."[32] "Objective" civilian control depends on clear-cut boundaries between civilian and military authority. More important, it requires "the recognition of autonomous military professionalism."[33] "A highly professional officer corps stands ready to carry out the wishes of any civilian group which secures legitimate authority within the state."[34] Yet Huntington concedes that "professional success breeds its own downfall by stimulating political involvement."[35] Hence, the conditions that favor objective civilian control may be fleeting, and in fact provide little restraint to the ambitions of officers.

A second school of thought, led by Finer and Abrahamsson, takes an unequivocally dark view of the role of professionalization in military intervention. The greater the responsibilities of the military and the more advanced the training of officers, the more insistent will be the pressures on members of the armed forces to entangle themselves in politics. Officers, as part of their academy background, are encouraged to make political decisions. Janowitz' "narrowing difference in skill" between officers and civilian elites may bear bitter fruit. Professionalization may thus, contrary to our argument in proposition 9, enhance the possibility of undue military influence or even overt military intervention in politics. We return to this issue in the concluding chapter, and in the propositions concerning political awareness.

Political Awareness

Military intervention means that members of the armed forces make themselves, or their chosen front-men, the supreme political arbiters within a state. The third set of internal variables to consider is the political awareness of the armed forces. What is the nature and extent of this awareness? What means will the military employ to press for goals it favors, or to alter policies it dislikes? The gamut of political awareness runs from total disinvolvement (the armed forces are willingly or necessarily on the political sidelines) to total involvement (the armed forces create military regimes drawn from within their own ranks). The lower the political awareness and involvement of the military, the less likely is military intervention.

History is studded with serious attempts to ensure the political neutrality of the armed forces. For example, French theorists of civil–military relations frequently eulogized the armed forces of the Third Republic (1875–1940) as *la grande muette,* the great mute force. A mute force does not speak; it obeys. It concerns itself with professional questions of military tactics, leaving to civilians the broader issues involved in financing and utilizing the military. Obedience becomes an end in itself.

In reality, however, no army can be fully divorced from political considerations, nor its members from political awareness. Both are questions of degree: more or less awareness, more or less willingness to accept government directives. (On the civilian side, to be certain, there are corresponding degrees of awareness of military considerations, and of willingness to issue clear government directives. The weakness of civilian control during the war in Algeria encouraged the French army to cast aside its nonpolitical presumptions and depose the Fourth Republic.)

The nature of political awareness and involvement appears to differ with the rank of the individual soldiers concerned. Highest ranking officers, it seems, generally work within existing political structures. Able to use influence in wheedling budgets or advising on policy matters, they can achieve their ends by pressuring the government, not by ousting it. A senior officer rarely is the active leader of a coup d'etat; it is more likely that he will be brought in as a figurehead when ambitious junior officers seize control (witness General Naguib of Egypt) or as a "swingman" intended to lend an aura of military legitimacy to a coup.[36] At the bottom of the military hierarchy are recent recruits, volunteers or draftees, who may wish strongly to return to civilian life. They do not initiate intervention, save possibly when a collapse of military discipline brings mutiny.[37] Most coups in fact spring from the ranks of commissioned officers (usually at the level of major or lieutenant colonel) who do not fully participate in the usual channels of decision making, or who may face pressure for retirement, or who feel grievances against the "brass" or political leaders. Thus, we suggest, subject to further analysis in the case studies:

> 11. *Military intervention is more likely to be planned and executed by field-grade officers than by commanding officers, noncommissioned officers, or the rank and file.*

The political neutralization of the military explicit in the concept of *la grande muette* depends substantially on officers' shunning "politics" and on the self-restraint of individual politicians or groups. Civilian attempts to utilize the armed forces, or a segment of them, for partisan ends certainly contribute to political awareness among the military. In short, if officers have a high degree of political awareness, it may reflect a combination of grievances internal to the armed forces and issues affecting the society as a whole. The ambitions that lead to coups are not only concentrated at specific levels of the military hierarchy; they are also concentrated among officers linked to social forces opposed to the government. "Almost invariably, the conspirators are in touch with civilian politicians and respond to their advice, counting on their assistance in justifying the coup to public opinion and helping to run the country afterwards."[38]

A standard government ploy to reduce political awareness within the military involves isolating its members in essentially self-contained bases or garrisons. Isolation fosters efficiency and esprit de corps, and not incidentally limits the contacts with civilians which could erode the armed forces' support for the government. The location of garrisons (how close are they to the capital?) affects the likelihood of individual units' joining coup attempts. The commander of a strategically situated base, such as a garrison in the capital city, must support intervention if it is to succeed.

Political awareness thus varies with locale; it also varies with the means of entry into the officer corps. Officers who enter by commission after short-term training, rather than by promotion from the ranks, may be far less socialized into the norms of the military, and far more likely to maintain contacts with civilians. The handful of university graduates in the Nigerian armed forces in 1966 figured prominently in the first coup, for they shared the discontent of most Nigerian intellectuals with the political system as a whole. Hence, it seems reasonable to suggest:

> 12.   Officers with close ties to individuals or groups that are opposed to government policies form the nucleus of conspiracies aimed at military intervention.

There is nothing more destructive of military cohesion and discipline than unsuccessful war. Victory knows many fathers; defeat knows none. Fixing the blame for loss heightens tensions between civilian and military leaders, and brings recriminations within the armed forces themselves. These tensions and recriminations increase political awareness within the military. Take, for example, Egypt following its 1948 defeat by Israel. The loss led to widespread disillusionment with King Farouk and his entourage, which included some leading members of the armed forces. Some officers felt that civilian machinations had negated possible victory; they created widespread resentment against the monarchy, thereby helping prepare for the 1952 coup d'etat. Hence, we propose:

> 13.   Defeat in war, particularly if accompanied by a belief that the government failed to give the armed forces sufficient support, increases the likelihood of military intervention.

The nature and scale of intervention will vary to some extent with the grievances involved. Coups are often prompted by disgruntlement over issues essentially internal to the armed forces, such as salaries, promotions, or (more broadly) "political interference" with military prerogatives. But these coups may not alter basic political structures; instead, they bring changes of personnel or policy. The more specific the grievance, the easier the return to the barracks when new leaders have been installed, or new policies instituted. By contrast, intervention springing from widespread, diffuse alienation from "the system" lacks specific targets. The impact of such a coup will not be confined to rectifying a few specific grievances that affect primarily the armed forces. Instead, the coup will attempt to recast the entire political system—and with attempts of this scope, military regimes are born. Thus, we suggest:

> *14. Military intervention resulting from specific policy grievances may lead to the restoration of civilian rule when the grievances have been rectified; military intervention resulting from distrust of the total political system leads to the establishment of a military regime of long duration.*

Finally, the content of military education affects the political awareness of members of the armed forces.

It can be argued that the curricula of service academies should include extensive attention to political matters, as a means of bolstering civilian control. Officers acquainted only with military techniques—who understand the means but not the objective of coercive strength—may concern themselves with narrowly defined corporate interests that, if abridged, might encourage intervention. They might fail to consider the broader interests of the society, or might pose demands far beyond the government's fiscal capabilities. Under certain conditions, however, a high level of political awareness could increase rather than diminish the military's potential for overthrowing the government. Recall proposition 5, which noted the distinction between "government" and "nation" frequently drawn by instigators of intervention. The "disposition to intervene" rises when officers who believe they bear responsibility for the health of the whole political system discover that civilians have neglected or botched their duties. With reference to the Argentinian military, Imaz suggests its members "see themselves as the guarantors of the continuity of the spirit of their fatherland, as the legatees of historical tradition and of the heroic virtues of their ancestors, and as the custodians of national values."[39] Training that emphasizes such broad-gauge responsibilities inherently boosts the political awareness of the military. If linked with organizational changes (see propositions 9 and 10), and if linked with inadequacies of the political system as a whole (see propositions 18, 19, and 20), a broadening of military education (a part of individual professionalization) may lead toward intervention.

> *15.   The likelihood of military intervention rises as the content of officer education is expanded to encompass political issues customarily resolved by civilians.*

Environmental Factors Affecting Military Intervention

There are many factors that can reduce the legitimacy enjoyed by a government; and when legitimacy is reduced, the government is in danger of being toppled. What, then, is this important variable of legitimacy? It is the widespread popular belief that political decisions are being made in accordance with popularly accepted legal and moral principles.

How is the legitimacy of the government diminished? The environment abounds with potential explanations: Social cleavages may perilously divide the state, negating the possibility of any widespread support for the civilian authority. Or economic collapse may threaten many citizens and encourage members of the armed forces to step in and try their hand at planning. Sometimes, the success of intervention in a few countries may touch off a chain reaction in other nations with similarly dissatisfied armed forces.

The propositions in this section view intervention as the dependent variable, as the outcome of specific factors in the environment.

Social and Economic Factors

Central to the relationship between military intervention and social and economic factors are the links forged between disaffected groups within the civilian population and members of the armed forces. Gino Germani and Kalman Silvert have suggested a direct relationship: the greater the cleavages and the lesser the consensus in a society, the greater the likelihood of military intervention.[40]

In a period in which social conflicts are becoming more intense and numerous, social mobilization is taking place; this is the process by which individuals and groups gain social and political awareness. It can be measured, and accordingly can be correlated with various types of military influence or intervention. Robert Putnam carried out such an analysis for Latin America in the 1956–1965 period. He linked the extent of military influence in politics with five indicators of social mobilization (urbanization, literacy, newspaper circulation, higher education, and the distribution of radios) and found a negative correlation (–0.53) between the two.[41] Thus, it seems that the higher the level of social mobilization, the greater the restraints on the political ambitions of the armed forces.

Huntington, however, has presented a cogent argument that, in some instances, can contradict Putnam's findings. He suggests that the significant factor affecting the military's propensity to intervene is not social mobilization per se; rather, it is the political institutions' competence in meeting the expectations engendered by rapid social mobilization which is the key factor influencing the possibility of intervention. Thus, Huntington would consider it possible that both social mobilization and the likelihood of military intervention could be high simultaneously.

A full list of divisive social factors could extend over many pages. Class divisions; ethnic tensions; regional differences; cleavages based on education, language, or age: these are illustrations. With deep splits in the society, the legitimacy of the government remains low—simply because no government is likely to be satisfactory to two or more groups with widely varying goals or values. Political issues may be resolved more by force than by a reasoned-out compromise. Take, for example, the island of Zanzibar. Its government was among the first in independent tropical Africa to be brought down by violence. The armed insurrection had grown from social antagonisms. The Arab-dominated government, as Michael Lofchie noted, was presiding over a state that had shown ominous portents of instability.[42] Extreme socioeconomic disparities sundered Africans from Arabs, and race had become the paramount issue. Compromise and accommodation proved impossible. In January 1964, African insurgents (including many recently fired members of the police force) seized the police armory and rapidly deposed the ruling Arab minority. Violent seizure of control was followed by the expropriation of Arab property and the expulsion of the sultan and hundreds of his followers. Because race had become so divisive an issue, force became paramount. The suppressed majority turned to violence to achieve control.

Nineteenth-century Latin America offers a host of examples in which the military threw their coercive strength behind the landed oligarchy. Often closely linked by kinship to the large landowners, army officers, in John Johnson's judgment, "began to intrude seriously in civilian affairs when they used the forces at their command in order to tip the balance of power away from the liberal intellectuals and toward the conservative landed oligarchies, who already had the blessing of the Catholic Church."[43] The predatory military regimes of nineteenth-century Latin America, discussed in greater detail in the next chapter, reflected an alliance of conservative groups against the emergence of middle-class interests.

In both Zanzibar and Latin America, increasing popular resentment of minority control could not be assuaged because, until violence unseated them, those atop the social pyramid had remained unmovable. Social antagonisms were bottled up, then exploded in conflict. But the outcomes were quite different. Disgruntled policemen took the initiative into their own hands in Zanzibar, for electoral politics had not responded to the African majority; hence, violence in that state assisted in bringing overdue reform. The reverse occurred in nineteenth-century Latin America. Military leaders stood, together with the landed oligarchs and the church, against reform. Intervention in these countries served to forestall further alteration. Both examples testify to the ease with which the armed forces can be drawn into the political arena. It happens when boundaries between social groups and the military become fragmented (that is, when the military finds it is in its interest to become involved in the political process), and when peaceful change cannot readily be carried out. We accordingly suggest:

> *16. The likelihood of military intervention rises as the intensification of conflicts arising from ethnic and/or class cleavages threatens the status and power of the dominant group or class.*

Does economic recession help prompt military intervention? Gurr has suggested that coups d'etat may spring from a feeling among military leaders that their position is threatened.[44] Cuts in the military's budget, necessitated perhaps by economic downswings, may be interpreted as threats to the armed forces' prerogatives, further enhancing the possibility of intervention.

The impact of economic decline on the frequency of military intervention has been demonstrated by Fossum and Needler. According to Fossum, the frequency of coups d'etat in Latin America was twice as great in years of economic deterioration (2.6 coups annually) as in years of economic improvement (1.3 coups annually).[45] Needler noted that between 1938 and 1942, a time of increased prosperity in Latin America, only one successful military seizure of power was carried out, contrasted with six triumphant coups in 1944.[46] With economic downturn, support for any government ebbs. Unemployment, reduced government revenues which can lead to drastic slashes in domestic budgets, and general social suffering all suggest that the government no longer merits support, for it cannot discharge its responsibilities and should itself be discharged. As a proposition, we suggest:

> *17. The likelihood of military intervention rises with a perceived deterioration of economic conditions, especially if accompanied by a belief that the government cannot resolve, or is responsible for, this deterioration.*

Political Factors

Among all the environmental factors that affect the likelihood of overt military intervention, the most crucial and the most difficult to analyze is legitimacy.

Military intervention rarely occurs in countries marked by a high degree of legitimacy. Although the armed forces possess influence, they try in these nations to achieve their goals through bargaining rather than ostentatious pressure or coups. Establishment of a military regime would run counter to popular sentiment. In the face of articulate, mobilized public opinion, officers would find their attempt at seizing power greeted not with gratitude for salvation but with sullen resentment.

Coups d'etat characteristically occur in states marked by low levels of legitimacy. When there is no agreement among politically relevant groups on the ways of resolving political conflict, the governing element will eagerly solicit the support of those holding coercive power. But so will other groups. Why prop up a government lacking public approval? Why support a government incapable of meeting its basic responsibilities?

One powerful corrosive of legitimacy is protracted, unsuccessful war. Proposition 13 suggested that military defeat increases the likelihood of intervention—by reducing the military's cohesion and by undercutting the government's legitimacy. Two of the most sweeping political revolutions of the twentieth century followed military setbacks. In Russia, soldiers "voted with their feet" against the inadequacies of the Czarist government and its successor, the Provisional Government; between one and a half and three million soldiers deserted in 1917 alone, testifying to the erosion of military cohesion that helped make the Bolshevik revolution successful. In China, the Nationalist forces of Chiang Kai-shek seemed to melt away from Japanese invaders. According to one distinguished student of Chinese Communism, "Defeat in war . . . is the one occurrence that dissolves even well-trained military formations, and from a restricted perspective revolution in modern times can almost be considered an invariable complication of international conflict."[47] Unsuccessful war breaks down the discipline officers use to maintain control; in addition, mutual deprivations link civilians and soldiers. As Katharine Chorley observed,

> *The policy of those who plan revolutions is therefore clear. They will work for a close tie-up between the armed forces and the civil population and, alternatively or in addition, they will bid for the future support of the troops by linking their grievances to revolutionary propaganda during the period of education and preparation for a revolt.*[48]

Revolutions break out in those rare cases in which the *ancien régime* has withstood efforts at reform, thereby bottling up resentment, and in which almost all segments of the population join in the quest for a new basis for political legitimacy. Both coups and revolutions manifest weaknesses in legitimacy, as well as the pervasiveness of violence within the political system as a whole. Military intervention springs from conditions that encourage the widespread use of force. All governments employ coercion against those who break laws. However, the most "efficient" government is that enjoying a high degree of authority, in which individuals accept laws voluntarily; their acquiescence is self-imposed, not necessitated by threat or overt violence. In a government lacking legitimacy, force is used disproportionately to consent. Where agreement on the means of changing policies and personnel is lacking, violence becomes politically prominent. A government without legitimacy must rely on its police and military to maintain order. Unless the armed forces accept the right of the government to issue orders, a command to soldiers to disperse demonstrators may culminate instead in the troops' fraternizing with the protesters, then turning their guns against the government.

The most detailed considerations of the relationships between legitimacy and the political roles of the military have been published by Finer and Huntington. Finer's concept of "political culture" is analogous to our concept of legitimacy.[49] He classifies four degrees of political culture.

In countries of "minimal" political culture, the government can be readily toppled by the use, or threatened use, of coercion. The armed forces may press their intervention beyond ouster to supplantment: officers assume governmental positions, in the apparent presumption they will continue in these offices for an indefinite period. The "minimal" political culture has few, if any, barriers to the use of force. In essence, the legitimacy enjoyed by the men in power and by the political system as a whole is so slight as to present no check on the ambitions of contending groups.

In countries of "low" political culture, legitimacy assumes somewhat greater importance: intervention (though rarely precluded) must include a justification for its occurrence. Although the government can be supplanted totally by a military junta, it is more likely to be displaced temporarily by a military-based regime, or by a coalition drawn from civilian and military elements. Legitimacy is fluid, Finer asserts, ebbing and flowing from one government to the next.

"Developed" political culture entails a high degree of government legitimacy—that is to say, accepted procedures for the transfer of political power, legitimacy for the holders of public office, and large and well-mobilized nongovernmental associations. Total supplantment or

partial displacement of the government by the armed forces, either directly or by a civilian–military coalition, rarely occurs. Nonetheless, the armed
forces can exert strong, behind-the-scenes pressures that Finer equates
with blackmail. For example, in the waning days of the Fourth Republic
of France, the military used its influence to hasten the installation of a
new political order.

Only in a "mature" political culture does military influence
rather than intervention become the normal avenue, the legitimacy of
the government being sufficiently strong to ward off threats from the
armed forces.

For Huntington, coups d'etat result from "the general politicization of social forces and institutions. . . . No political institutions, no
corps of professional political leaders are recognized or accepted as
legitimate intermediaries to moderate group conflict."[50] The praetorian society, one in which the military can intervene at will, manifests
political decay, not political order. "The wealthy bribe; students riot;
workers strike; mobs demonstrate; and the military coup."[51]

Huntington differentiates three types of praetorian society—
oligarchical, radical, and mass—on the basis of political participation.[52]
Oligarchical praetorianism witnesses political struggles among personal
and family cliques; radical praetorianism manifests competition among
institutional and occupational groups; mass praetorianism is characterized by the domination of social classes and movements in politics.
Tension rises and the longevity of governments decreases as political
participation increases. In a praetorian society, coups need not emanate
from the armed forces; since regularized widely accepted means for
transferring control do not exist, force becomes the "normal" way of
changing government personnel.

A prevalent theme in Huntington's observations about the
praetorian society is that its civilian political institutions are always weak.
A vacuum in institutions and leadership impels groups to arrogate control for their own ends, and the armed forces count among many
potential contenders for power.

The political role of the armed forces thus should be viewed
from the perspective of legitimacy. Do civilian institutions enjoy the authority to which Finer and Huntington refer? If so, military intervention
(as in France in 1961) would be viewed as usurpation—and soldiers cannot successfully usurp control, over an extended period, from a government considered legitimate by the populace.[53] Have civilian institutions
squandered, or failed to build, a foundation of legitimacy? If so, military intervention (as in Nigeria in 1966) will result in public rejoicing.
The legitimacy enjoyed by a government affects the political role of its
armed forces far more than any other environmental or internal factor.

For our concluding propositions, we suggest:

18.   The likelihood of military intervention rises in the absence or weakness of agreed-upon procedures for peaceful political change.

19.   The likelihood of military intervention rises as contending civilian groups solicit support from the armed forces in order to achieve political power.

20.   The ease with which the armed forces assume political power varies inversely with the legitimacy enjoyed by the existing civilian government.

A brief summary seems appropriate at this point. The political roles filled by members of the armed forces cover a wide range: (a) total subordination to civilian rule (*la grande muette*); (b) willing or not-so-willing acceptance of civilian supremacy, coupled with varying degrees of political influence; (c) outright displacement of civilian governments. A totally apolitical military does not, and cannot, exist. Armed forces are created by states to carry out coercion; pressing for recognition, responsibility, and recompense brings members of the military into the political arena.

The propositions suggested in this chapter have stressed military intervention, for military regimes necessarily begin with the seizure of political control. However, our discussion of internal and environmental factors requires extension. How do these factors affect the functioning of military regimes? The final chapter in Part I turns to the results of successful coups, governments over which the armed forces hold sway.

References

1. Gaetano Mosca, *The Ruling Class,* ed. Arthur Livingston (New York: McGraw-Hill, 1939), p. 228.
2. John J. Johnson, *The Military and Society in Latin America* (Stanford: Stanford University Press, 1964), p. 4.
3. Mosca, *The Ruling Class,* p. 228.
4. Christian P. Potholm, "The Multiple Roles of the Police as Seen in the Africa Context," *Journal of Developing Areas,* III, 2 (1969), p. 142.
5. S.E. Finer, *The Man on Horseback: The Role of the Military in Politics* (New York: Praeger, 1962), p. 27. Janowitz concurs: "The professional soldier resists identifying himself with the 'police,' and the military profession has struggled to distinguish itself from the internal police force. In this sense, civilian supremacy in the United States has rested on the assump-

tion that its national military forces were organized and controlled separately from the local and more decentralized police forces." Morris Janowitz, *The Professional Soldier: A Social and Political Portrait* (New York: Free Press of Glencoe, 1960), p. 435. Also see proposition 9.

6. Egil Fossum, "Factors Influencing the Occurrence of Military Coups d'Etat in Latin America," *Journal of Peace Research*, 3 (1967), p. 236.

7. Ibid., p. 237. It should be noted, however, that Fossum attributes the upsurge in the number of coups to declining economic conditions. See proposition 17.

8. Samuel P. Huntington, *The Soldier and the State: The Theory and Politics of Civil–Military Relations* (New York: Vintage, 1957), p. 199.

9. Hugh Hanning, *The Peaceful Uses of Military Forces* (New York: Praeger, 1967).

10. Gamal Abdel Nasser, *Egypt's Liberation: The Philosophy of the Revolution* (Washington: Public Affairs Press, 1955), pp. 42–43.

11. Quoted in Finer, *The Man on Horseback*, p. 26.

12. Finer, *The Man on Horseback*, p. 7.

13. Morris Janowitz, *The Military in the Political Development of New Nations* (Chicago: University of Chicago Press, 1964), p. 68.

14. Finer, *The Man on Horseback*, p. 72.

15. Gordon A. Craig, *The Politics of the Prussian Army 1640–1945* (New York: Oxford University Press, 1964), p. 233. Craig does note, however, that the growing need for officers outstripped the number available with aristocratic backgrounds, so that by 1913, seventy percent of the officer corps was of bourgeois origin (p. 235).

16. C.B. Otley, "The Origins and Recruitment of the British Army Elite," Ph.D. diss., quoted in Robin Luckham, *The Nigerian Military: A Sociological Analysis of Authority and Revolt 1960–67* (Cambridge: Cambridge University Press, 1971), p. 127n.

17. Raoul Giradet, *La société militaire dans la France contemporaine 1885–1939* (Paris: Plon, 1953), p. 255.

18. Mosca, *The Ruling Class*, p. 235.

19. Stanislav Andreski, *Military Organization and Society* (Berkeley and Los Angeles: University of California Press, 1968), p. 198.

20. General Carl Maria von Clausewitz was director of the Prussian Military Academy in the early nineteenth century, when he penned his noted work, *On War*. He stressed the division of responsibilities between politician and officer, the former determining objectives, the latter determining tactics. "The subordination of the military point of view to the political is, therefore, the only thing which is possible." Carl von Clausewitz, *On War* (London: Routledge and Kegan Paul, 1966), Vol. III, p. 125.

21. George Armstrong Kelly, *Lost Soldiers: The French Army and Empire in Crisis 1947–1962* (Cambridge: M.I.T. Press, 1965), p. 188.

22. Lyle N. McAlister et al., *The Military in Latin American Socio-Political Evolution* (Washington: National Technical Information Service, 1970), p. 38.

23. Victor Villeneuva, *¿Nueva Mentalidad Militar en el Peru?* (Lima: Editorial Juan Mejía, 1969), p. 194.

24. Morris Janowitz, *The Professional Soldier: A Social and Political Portrait* (New York: Free Press of Glencoe, 1960), pp. 8–9.

25. Lucian W. Pye, *Aspects of Political Development* (Boston: Little, Brown, 1966), p. 178.

26. See, for example, Guy J. Pauker, "Southeast Asia as a Problem Area in the Next Decade," *World Politics,* XI, 3 (April 1959), pp. 325–345.

27. Jose Luis de Imaz, *Los Que Mandan (Those Who Rule)* (Albany: State University of New York, 1970), p. 87.

28. Henry Bienen, ed., *The Military and Modernization* (Chicago: Aldine-Atherton, 1971), p. 27; italics added.

29. Huntington, *The Soldier and the State,* pp. 8–18.

30. Bengt Abrahamsson, *Military Professionalization and Political Power* (Beverly Hills: Sage, 1972), p. 37.

31. Ibid., p. 99.

32. Samuel P. Huntington, "Civilian Control of the Military: A Theoretical Statement," Heinz Eulau, Samuel J. Eldersveld, and Morris Janowitz, eds. *Political Behavior: A Reader in Theory and Research* (Glencoe: The Free Press, 1956), p. 380.

33. Huntington, *The Soldier and the State,* p. 83.

34. Ibid., p. 84.

35. Ibid., p. 95.

36. Martin C. Needler, "Political Development and Military Intervention in Latin America," *American Political Science Review,* LX, 3 (1966), p. 621.

37. Possibly the most striking recent example came in the Republic of Zaire (formerly the Belgian Congo), in which a mutiny of the armed forces five days after independence unleashed close to five years of widespread anarchy. The armed forces were splintered into various private armies. Jean-Claude Willame, *Patrimonialism and Political Change in the Congo* (Stanford: Stanford University Press, 1972), pp. 57–76.

38. Needler, "Political Development and Military Intervention," p. 618.

39. Imaz, *Los Que Mandan,* p. 82.

40. Gino Germani and Kalman Silvert, "Politics, Social Structure and Military Intervention in Latin America," *Archives Européennes de Sociologie,* II, (1961), pp. 62–81.

41. Robert D. Putnam, "Toward Explaining Military Intervention in Latin American Politics," *World Politics,* XX, 1 (1967), p. 96.

42. Michael F. Lofchie, *Zanzibar: Background to Revolution* (Princeton: Princeton University Press, 1965), p. 268.

43. Johnson, *Military in Latin America,* pp. 47–48.

44. Ted Robert Gurr, *Why Men Rebel* (Princeton: Princeton University Press, 1970), p. 335.

45. Fossum, "Factors Influencing Coups," p. 237.

46. Needler, "Political Development and Military Intervention," pp. 617–618.
47. Chalmers Johnson, *Revolutionary Change* (Boston: Little, Brown, 1966), p. 104.
48. Katharine Chorley, *Armies and the Art of Revolution* (London: Faber, 1943), p. 136.
49. Finer, *The Man on Horseback,* pp. 86–163. Three criteria enter in Finer's concept of high political culture: (1) general acceptance of the "political formula," or in other words, the belief or emotion by virtue of which rulers claim the moral right to govern and be obeyed; (2) the various civil procedures and organs of the political system are recognized as authoritative; (3) public involvement in and attachment to civil institutions are strong and widespread (p. 87).
50. Samuel P. Huntington, *Political Order in Changing Societies* (New Haven: Yale University Press, 1968), pp. 194, 196.
51. Ibid., p. 196.
52. Ibid., pp. 198–237.
53. David C. Rapoport, "The Political Dimensions of Military Usurpation," *Political Science Quarterly,* LXXXIII, 4 (1968), p. 569.

3

Civil-Military Relations: A Typology of Civic and Praetorian Systems

Military intervention in politics, as contrasted with military influence in politics, characterizes political systems which we deem praetorian.[1] The praetorian condition exists before intervention occurs; thus it is necessary to understand the overall framework of a praetorian system in order to understand the rationale for and mechanics of military intervention. Praetorianism exists in a state in which institutions are weak and the basis for legitimizing political authority is uncertain.

The factors most important in coups d'etat derive from the societal environment: the extent and nature of class or ethnic cleavages; the effectiveness and stability of political organizations and procedures; the extent of public support for political institutions staffed by civilians. The propensity of military leaders to usurp governmental roles is also affected by factors internal to the military: its sense of mission; the nature and depth of its political awareness; the degree of organizational complexity and the level of autonomy attained by military institutions; the recruitment patterns and cohesion of the officer corps. Environmental variables must not be emphasized to the exclusion of internal variables.[2]

In the following typology, we attempt to incorporate the most significant environmental and internal factors, thereby illustrating the

various roles the armed forces can play in politics. To simplify consideration, we have combined the factors suggested in the twenty propositions
into four "summary variables."[3] The first two variables summarize the
sociopolitical characteristics of the civilian sphere, the third describes the
military in terms of the politically relevant resources it controls, and the
fourth denotes the relationship between civilian and military institutions:

    *a. the extent and nature of political participation of the
    populace;*
    b. the strength of civil institutions;
    c. military strength; and
    d. the nature of military institutional boundaries.

Political Participation

All political systems include structural frameworks through
which public policy decisions are made. In some cases, these frameworks
or institutions may be obvious and formal—for example, a parliamentary
or presidential format for decision making. In other situations, these
institutions may be less open to public influence and scrutiny, as when
pressure groups or informal advisors wield a great deal of influence. In
still others, policy decisions may be virtually dictated by a small ruling
elite who are unresponsive to public opinion. The question becomes one
of who participates in the making of political decisions, and in what
fashion.

The extent of participation in national political processes and
its rate of change over time both vary widely from society to society.
At the lowest levels of participation, national politics may be dominated
by a small aristocratic or bureaucratic elite. Before the overthrow of
Thailand's absolute monarchy in 1932, the king and his advisors were able
to make policy with sovereign disregard for public preferences. After the
1932 "Revolution," a new elite composed of military and civilian officials
assumed the monarch's policy-making prerogatives; rarely, however, have
Thai businessmen or farmers exerted a significant influence over government decisions. At medium levels of participation, members of the urban
middle classes enter the political arena. Their voices begin to affect major
decisions, imposing a constraint on the freedom of action of governing
elites. These new "middle sectors" reflect the increased socioeconomic
differentiation that is part of the modernization process, and their appearance—as in Nigeria, Egypt, and Peru—may herald a challenge to rule by
landed elites or a colonial power.[4] High levels of participation, finally,
signify that the mass of the populace has become an important factor in
national politics. As in France, public opinion and modern political

parties impose broad limitations on the actions of official decision makers. Obviously, the political appeals and techniques employed to influence decisions differ widely from low to high levels of participation.

The rate at which political participation expands to encompass new groups in the policy process helps determine the stability and effectiveness of national political institutions. High rates of change signify the rapid mobilization of new groups into politics. Their demands for social reform may strain the capacity of existing institutions. The result may well be political decay and system breakdown, producing the conditions of public disorder and instability that often herald military intervention. However, a more gradual expansion of participation may have the opposite effect. The demands of new groups may be taken up by existing political parties or other institutions, and the system may actually be strengthened by broadening its base of support among the people.

Strength of Civil Institutions

To invert Clausewitz's famous dictum, politics may be war carried out by other means. The "other means" are, of course, political institutions. Political institutions serve to integrate the demands and channel the energies of conflicting groups, making it possible for government to formulate and carry out policy decisions on behalf of the society as a whole.

The strength of political institutions is affected by many factors. One criterion of strength is the effectiveness with which these institutions carry out their functions. A society in which groups and individuals have recourse to a framework in which disputes can be resolved and decisions can be made has established the vital basis necessary for the attainment of "political goods" such as security, liberty, social justice, and welfare.[5]

A second factor affecting the strength of political institutions is their legitimacy. The concept of political authority refers to the right of certain office holders or individual citizens to exercise power and use resources in the name of the society; political legitimacy refers to the moral validation of that right by those who are the governed. It measures the extent and depth of public support for the political rules and procedures of the society.

Political instability reflects, in large measure, an imbalance between socioeconomic change (which generates new policy issues) and political institutionalization, the development of effective political institutions (by means of which these issues may be resolved). The disjuncture between these two processes may be especially marked in the less developed states of Africa, Asia and Latin America—states in which the armed forces may play leading political roles. Social and economic changes—urbanization, mass education and communications, industrialization—have undermined traditional values and behavior patterns. Individuals find themselves torn from their settled roles in the traditional rural segment of society, and drawn to the more modern urban centers and the possibility of a better life. This "social mobilization" may generate high personal expectations, in other words, a situation of widespread social frustration and unrest caused by the inability of the society to meet its citizens' rising aspirations.[6] People become rootless, uncertain about the ways and means of politics, yet anxious to make their voices heard. This social frustration, if unmoderated by the creation of new opportunities for social and economic mobility or by political institutions capable of absorbing and channeling its energy, may lead to a rapid expansion of demands on government and a concomitant rapid mobilization of new social forces seeking to press those demands.

Existing political institutions in many of the less developed countries have proved inadequate to the challenge of modernization. As their effectiveness in resolving conflicts and finding solutions to social problems declines, their legitimacy is eroded. The result is political decay, a deterioration in the general level of political institutionalization relative to participation.[7] Political decay marks the praetorian polity. The failure of the polity's integrative and conflict-resolving institutions causes various social forces—workers, students, landowners, businessmen, the military—to act directly in the political arena, bypassing established rules and procedures in favor of their own particular resources and methods. Political decay inevitably involves a general increase in the use of coercive political resources, with the result that the military is drawn into the political process.

Political systems with high ratios of institutionalization to participation and high degrees of legitimacy thus have relatively strong civil institutions. Irrespective of their variations in governmental forms—monarchy or republic, democracy or dictatorship—these systems have the power to innovate and implement policy decisions for their societies. Such systems may be called *civic* polities. Conversely, systems with low ratios of institutionalization to participation and low legitimacy have relatively weak civil institutions. These are *praetorian* polities, characterized by varying degrees of overt class and ethnic conflicts, student rioting and mob violence, unstable and erratic political leadership, bureaucratic inefficiency and corruption, government infringement of civil liberties, individual and group alienation, and military coups d'etat.[8] Both civic and praetorian polities may be found in conjunction with any of the three levels of political participation discussed previously. Moreover, although some political systems that are manifestly praetorian may also have armed forces who resolutely subordinate themselves to civilian control, the occurrence of this pattern is increasingly rare. Since World War II, political decay in the new states of Africa and Asia has tended to breed military intervention in politics along lines broadly similar to the historical pattern of praetorianism in Latin America.

Military Strength

The potential political strength of any nation's military establishment is dependent primarily on its size (both in absolute terms and in relation to population), its share of the national budget (both absolute and in relation to gross national product), the extent and variety of the coercive resources it controls, and the organizational effectiveness with which it can apply those resources under different circumstances.[9] The crucial question is not the absolute measures of these factors but rather how they are weighed within a particular sociopolitical context. In a modern industrialized society, for example, the armed forces may be large in size, organizationally cohesive and effective, and in control of the most sophisticated weapons systems. Yet the potential *political* strength of these armed forces may be relatively low if the government enjoys high legitimacy and is only minimally dependent on coercion to secure obedience to its laws. Political strength of the military is also low if its weaponry does not readily lend itself to use in domestic politics; for example, neither strategic nuclear weapons nor aircraft carrier task forces can be deployed with effectiveness to quell mob violence or to threaten credibly a president who has lost favor in the eyes of the military. In most countries the resources that are potentially most effective are army infantry and tank battalions, but even these may be of little political value against civilian politicians when the army is so complex and widely deployed, as in the United States, as to render virtually insurmountable the logistical problems of staging a coup. Conversely a much smaller military establishment, such as the 1500-man army of Togo with its comparatively primitive conventional weaponry, can, in the setting of a much more traditional society, exercise decisive power over civilian authorities.

Effective internal organization of the military has political relevance not only with respect to the management of coercive resources, but also to the extent that it provides a reservoir of manpower and differentiated skills that are potentially reassignable to nonmilitary tasks. Important in this sense are the general educational level, experience, and world view of the officer corps, its degree of professionalization, and its capacity and willingness to divert some of its members to political and administrative roles in the government.

Cyclical patterns of military intervention or prolonged periods of military rule may seriously undermine the cohesion of the officer corps, creating a breach between those officers who remain dedicated to intramilitary pursuits and those who must deal directly with public policy making. In Brazil, for example, where the armed forces have ruled since the April 1964 coup, the military politicians have apparently been successful in countering the urban terrorist tactics of their leftist opposition. They appear to have the support of the middle classes by virtue of their restoration of health to the Brazilian economy and their repression of populist pressures. Yet serious internal disagreements over national goals and the means to attain them continue to simmer behind the military's facade of unity, raising the possibility of a countercoup from within the armed forces.[10]

The military's strength as a political actor is also affected by other factors: the prevailing levels of political institutionalization and participation in the society, the social stratification patterns and value systems, and the historical role and mission of the armed forces. The prestige of the military and of its leaders is important in estimating the probability of public acceptance of military intervention and rule.[11] The attitudes and actions of powerful foreign governments may also become a factor. Military aid from outside increases the coercive strength of the armed forces. At the same time, it undermines the relationship of budgetary dependence that is part of the military's subordination to civilian authority. On some occasions, however, foreign influence may be used to discourage an attempt at a coup and may thus uphold constitutionalism. During the Kennedy administration, for example, the United States threatened diplomatic and economic sanctions against Latin American military juntas who deposed constitutionally elected presidents.[12] Finally, the political strength of the military and the character of its political role are considerably affected by the interaction between military and civilian institutions. We shall next consider the relative integrity of the organizational boundaries separating these two spheres, which is a major determinant of civil–military relationships.

Military–Institutional Boundaries

Armed forces are social organizations made up, analytically speaking, of roles. The sociological concept of role forms the basic unit of all social systems. It refers to the attitudes and behaviors of the individual member of society, each of whom usually belongs to a variety of social organizations—for example, a family, a church, social clubs, a business, a union, a profession. A military officer can be expected to share certain attitudes and values common to members of his profession (e.g., discipline, hierarchy, and service pride). But as an individual, he will harbor other attitudes and values in keeping with his other roles as a member of an ethnic or religious group, a political party, or other interest associations. The resultant complex of attitudes and values may produce conflicting behavioral tendencies in the officer. Thus, a Ghanaian army officer in 1966 might have been torn between taking part in the conspiracy to overthrow President Kwame Nkrumah, a course dictated by concern for the military's institutional interests, and continuing to uphold Nkrumah's authority, a conflicting course dictated by other values (e.g., a citizen's belief in civilian supremacy or perhaps, in this case, loyalty to Nkrumah as a fellow tribesman).[13]

Social organizations are made up of structures (or institutions), which are patterns of interacting roles. For purposes of analysis, we can conceptualize "boundaries" separating the structures of one organization from the structures of others within a particular political system. Thus, for example, a military organization is made up of roles and structures of roles. We could, if we wished, analyze the internal structures of the military as if they constituted a closed system, but the disadvantages of this would obviously be great. The military does not exist in a vacuum. It is a part of the larger social system, and both affects and is affected by the role structures of other organizations. Some military organizations, however, are more autonomous and coherent than others. That is, they are less affected by (and may have less impact on) the other social institutions and organizations that make up their societal environments. We employ the concept of "boundary" to describe the interchanges that take place between a military role or structure and a role or structure of the environment; in particular, we are concerned with the volume and character of these interchanges, which signify the clarity and impermeability of the boundary.[14]

Armed forces that are highly institutionalized can be said to have *integral* boundaries, meaning that their roles and structures are sharply differentiated from those of other organizations making up the total social system. Integral boundaries imply high levels of coherence and autonomy. Their existence suggests that the military institutions have acquired identity, value, and permanence, both within themselves and with respect to the wider society. Interchanges across integral boundaries are limited in volume and are controlled according to established rules and procedures. By contrast, armed forces organizations that are considerably less institutionalized are said to have *fragmented* boundaries. Such organizations have less coherence and autonomy, and their interchanges with the roles and structures of the wider society are comparatively numerous and unregulated.[15]

Our particular focus is on military organizations established as the coercive arm of the state; i.e., regular armed forces on active duty, not paramilitary or police forces. In general, the more professionalized a military organization is, the more likely it is that the boundaries it shares with its environment will be integral rather than fragmented. Professional armies have officer corps that are expert in the management of violence, highly coherent and autonomous as corporate bureaucracies, and attuned to the social responsibilities imposed by their profession. These armies tend to have clearly defined functions focusing on external defense, leaving the maintenance of domestic peace and tranquility to separately organized police or militia forces. They are autonomous, in the sense that the armed forces are an organization of national scope which is not subordinated to the interests of any particularistic social force (such as a landowning oligarchy, ethnic group, or political party). Organizational autonomy in this sociological sense does not, of course, preclude effective civilian control exercised through the formal institutions of government. Finally, integral boundaries also imply that transactions (e.g., information flows and structural linkages) between the various levels of the armed forces hierarchy and other social or political organizations would be channeled primarily through the military command structure. The greatest volume of contacts with the environment would take place through access points provided by the highest military leadership roles, filtering upward or downward through the rank structure.

Military establishments with fragmented boundaries are generally less professionalized overall, but are especially so in terms of their coherence and corporateness. In terms of function, the armed forces may have no clear-cut external competitive focus for their activity, no foreign adversary power against which their mission can be defined. Instead, they may be directed primarily into domestic police or counterinsurgency functions, or perhaps into civic action programs, all of which tend to exacerbate boundary fragmentation by thrusting the armed forces into the domestic political arena. Fragmented boundaries imply that the institutional roles and values of the military are relatively undifferentiated from those found in the environment. In other words, the loyalties of officers and enlisted men to the military institution may be undermined by their other loyalties as members of certain social classes, ethnic or interest groups, or political parties. In these circumstances the institutional autonomy of the military is low, with the result that the armed forces may disintegrate in time of domestic crisis or possibly become the servants, not of the nation as a whole, but of some particularistic political faction. The corporate cohesiveness of the officer corps may become fragile, with underlying strains of disunity that reflect the fundamental conflicts and cleavages present in the wider society. Many French officers, for example, were severely torn by the conflict between their sympathies for the besieged French settlers in Algeria and their duty to comply with President de Gaulle's order to respect the independence of Algeria (see the chapter on France).

In some countries, the military's boundaries have been fragmented by the consensus among civilians that it is either acceptable or desirable for the military to play an active role in domestic politics. In Latin America, civilians opposed to a particular government have frequently sought to overthrow it by subverting the loyalties of army officers. The Aprista party in Peru has resorted on several occasions to fomenting revolts among enlisted men, as a way of neutralizing the deeprooted opposition of the officer corps to Aprista political ambitions (see the chapter on Peru). Under circumstances such as these, the achievement of institutionalized civilian control over the military is made difficult indeed.

Comparative Military Political Roles

The interrelationships among the four summary variables may now be used to define a number of possible roles for the military in politics, as shown in Table 3.1. As we have seen, all military organizations take part in politics in some way or other, if only as bureaucratic pressure groups competing for shares of scarce budgetary resources. Civilian control over the military is never absolute. The military's political activity may be openly interventionist, or it may take relatively subtle or covert forms. Still, however, as long as its participation in politics does not extend to the exercise of veto power over the policy choices open to civilian officials, or to outright usurpation of political authority by coup d'etat, a practical case for the existence of civilian control can be made. The interrelationships expressed in this typology provide a framework for analysis of various forms of civil–military relations, including those that fall under the general rubric of civilian control. These are shown in the two columns in the center of the table, denoting the variety of military political roles found in *civic* polities.

The two right-hand columns of the table depict the variety of military political roles found in *praetorian* polities, where civilian control is likely to be highly tenuous or even nonexistent. In a praetorian system the military's participation in politics may extend far beyond that of a bureaucratic pressure group. Its leaders may not only influence but actually exercise a veto over certain government policies, especially in the areas of defense appropriations and foreign policy. They may use their power to bar certain civilian politicians from holding government office. They may, in the extreme case, overthrow the civilian authorities by force and

TABLE 3.1
Comparative Military Political Roles and Regimes

Extent of Political Participation	Political Strength of the Military	Civic Polity		Praetorian Polity	
		Boundaries		Boundaries	
		Integral	Fragmented	Integral	Fragmented
High	High	United States	USSR	Greece	France (late 4th Republic)
	Medium	Sweden	Israel	Turkey (1954–1963)	Argentina
	Low	Japan	Finland	Germany (c. 1920)	Austria (c. 1934)
Medium	High	India	Cuba	Brazil	Egypt
	Medium	Chile (1926–1972)	Mexico	Peru	Ghana
	Low	Costa Rica	Guyana	Burma (c. 1957)	Dominican Republic (c. 1965)
Low	High	Senegal	Iran	El Salvador	Thailand
	Medium	Ivory Coast	Ehtiopia	Malagasy Republic	Nigeria
	Low	Zambia	Nepal	Haiti	Congo (Brazzaville)
		Objective Civilian Control	Subjective Civilian Control	Military as Independent Political Actor	Military as Coalitional Actor

establish a military dictatorship. Among praetorian polities our primary interest is in the variety of military regimes, and on the socioeconomic and political consequences of military rule for these societies.

Civic Polities and Civilian Control

Two principal types of civilian control may be distinguished in civic polities, depending primarily on the character of the boundaries separating military institutions from the nonmilitary organizations, interests, and values of the society.

Integral Boundaries and Objective Civilian Control

Here, we return to the distinction drawn earlier between "objective" and "subjective" civilian control.[16] "Objective" civilian control prevails in those civic polities where military boundaries are integral, i.e., where professionalization of the officer corps is maximized. High degrees of professionalism are encouraged by civilian acceptance of a narrowly defined but independent sphere of activity reserved for the military. In other words, the military as a professional body exercises a high degree of autonomy over its internal matters, such as training, discipline and standards of professional conduct. With integral institutional boundaries, the degree of interpenetration between military and civilian authority structures is low and civilian control is exercised through the military chain of command. The officer corps is therefore conceded a considerable degree of autonomy in the management (but not the ultimate command control) of the formally organized resources of coercion available to the state. By various mechanisms, however, military officers are constrained from participating as a group in spheres of political activity not directly associated with the management of coercion.

Although in a civic polity the coercive power of the armed forces may be great, military *political* power is minimized by a complex of factors that inhibits the military's employment of coercion independent of civilian direction. The principal limiting factor, of course, is the very effectiveness and legitimacy of the civilian political institutions. Other elements which may reinforce objective civilian control are: (1) a high degree of shared class origins and group affiliations between the officer corps and the civilian political elite; (2) a military establishment of relatively small size with a correspondingly small share of the national budget (but not *too* small in either dimension, since this would tend to preclude the development of military professionalism); (3) a clearly defined competitive focus for military activity represented by an external threat to national security; (4) levels of prestige for the armed forces and of popularity for individual military leaders that are not inordinately high compared to those of civilian institutions and leaders; and (5) a basically conservative national ideology that is compatible with the professional military ethic.[17]

Examples of political systems with broadly defined objective civilian control over the military are the United States, Sweden, and Japan (among countries with high levels of political participation); India, Chile, and Costa Rica (at medium levels); and Senegal, Ivory Coast, and Zambia (at low levels). As this disparate grouping suggests, objective civilian control is possible in lesser developed as well as modern industrialized systems.

Senegal's 7500-man armed forces (including the 1600-man National Gendarmerie) put down minor domestic disturbances in 1962, 1967, and 1968. Senegalese troops were considered among the best of the old French Colonial Army, and a French garrison of some 2000 men remains in Dakar. Despite economic difficulties, high population growth, and the presence of a multiplicity of tribal groups, the elected president directs national policy and exercises control over the military. Similarly, the elected president of the Ivory Coast, Felix Houphouet-Boigny, has successfully controlled his country's 6400-man armed forces. A small group of civilian cabinet ministers and army officers was arrested in 1963 for plotting to overthrow the government, but there have been no overt rebellious acts. The army maintains close ties with the French, who maintain a 600-man regimental combat group in the country. In Zambia, the 7600-man Defence Force has until recently been led largely by British officers and NCO's. Zambianization, however, has been a matter of national policy and has been vigorously pressed since 1970. Shared borders with Portuguese Angola and Mozambique, not to omit Rhodesia and South Africa, have made Zambia something of a haven for guerrilla liberation movements. With Zambia's large size and rugged terrain, the Defence Force has been unable to fully control these guerrillas, and the threat of counterinsurgency invasions from neighboring countries has provided a real external focus for military activity.[18]

Civil—military relations in Costa Rica are of a pattern decidedly uncharacteristic of Latin America as a whole. In 1948 the country's military establishment was permanently disbanded by President Figueres, and since that time the specter of military intervention has not haunted Costa Rican presidents. Although a 1500-man Civil Guard remains, a noticeable spirit of civilianism pervades this functioning democracy.[19] The time-honored political neutrality of Chile's armed forces has been sorely tested since the 1970 election of Dr. Salvador Allende Gossens, a professed Marxist bent on socializing the country's economy. Allende's election was by a narrow plurality in a tight three-way race. Despite strong anti-Communist predispositions within the officer corps, Chile's military leaders held firm in their resolve not to contravene their country's democratic traditions, even in the face of the assassination of Army Chief of Staff Rene Schneider (apparently by right-wing extremists seeking to provoke a military takeover to thwart Allende's accession to office).[20] A national strike of transport workers and small businessmen in late 1972 nearly brought the economy to a halt, but was ended when military leaders made it clear that they would continue to support Allende. India's political system, like those of Chile and Costa Rica, is dominated by middle-class politics characteristic of medium levels of political participation. The Indian Army has undergone a dramatic expansion since the border wars with China in 1962 and with Pakistan in 1965 and 1971. However, the professionalization of its officer corps along British lines and the continued legitimacy of Congress Party stewardship have served to sustain the principle of civilian control even during these periods of severe national crisis.[21]

Among the more industrialized countries represented by Japan, Sweden, and the United States, objective civilian control is founded even more firmly through political institutions that have demonstrated their effectiveness and legitimacy under conditions of mass participation. In these systems the extent of popular support for civilian organizations and procedures imposes severe limitations on the political efficacy of coercion. By contrast, at low and medium levels of political participation (for example, in Zambia or Chile) the institutionalization of civilian control is much less secure. In a situation of domestic crisis, it would be a relatively simple matter for the military in Zambia to expand their political role. Key civilian institutions are few and narrowly based, with civilian control heavily dependent on the political skills of President Kaunda. Even in Chile, a military overthrow of President Allende remains a distinct possibility.* In civic polities with mass participation, however, the spread of mass education and communications has produced an articulate and informed citizenry supporting complex and adaptable political institutions. Under these circumstances it is a far more difficult matter for military elites to convert coercive power into political influence.

Such is the situation of civil–military relations in the United States, despite the vast resources of coercion deployed by the several branches of the armed forces. The imperatives of national defense and the acceptance of worldwide military responsibilities in the years since World War II have sharply increased the role of military interests and values in American society. Global security considerations and the emergence of the "military–industrial complex" have clearly facilitated military role expansion, but only as a bureaucratic interest group competing for resources within well-defined rules and limits.[22] By no means has postwar expansion provided military leaders with veto power over the civilian decision-making process, a power position enjoyed, for example, over extended intervals by high-ranking officers of the German General Staff during the interwar period. One potentially dangerous aspect of the military–industrial complex has been the increasing hierarchical interpenetration of military institutions with civilian economic structures, as officers retiring from active duty accept executive positions with corporations seeking Defense Department contracts. But on the whole, the integrity of military institutional boundaries remains relatively high. This is so in part because of deep-rooted American opposition to any role for the military in politics. Even the legitimate advisory role of the Joint Chiefs of Staff in presenting policy options to the President is widely resented, out of fear

*A possibility that was realized on September 11, 1973, while this book was in press.

that the closed nature of security debates may tip the scale unduly in favor of military alternatives.

Objective civilian control in the United States is founded primarily in the strength of countervailing civilian institutions and in the value structure of liberalism, the dominant national ideology. However, the political neutrality of the professional officer corps has also been the result of its deep internalization of the principle of civilian supremacy within its own value structure. The rightness of the concept of civilian control of the military is basic to the education received by officers at the service academies and war colleges. To the overwhelming majority of officers, the act of overthrowing the President of the United States is simply unthinkable, totally apart from the formidable logistical challenges that would have to be surmounted. Moreover, there is considerable truth in the argument that such erosion as has occurred in civilian control during the postwar period has been the result of civilian, more than military, pressures for greater preparedness and for reliance on military solutions to foreign policy problems.[23]

In contrast with the pattern of civil–military relations prevailing in the United States, a somewhat different form of objective civilian control has been institutionalized in the civic polities of Sweden and Japan. The armed forces in these countries are highly professionalized, yet have no clearly defined external competitive focus for their activity. The coercive resources they manage are more moderate in size, both in absolute terms and relative to their respective populations. Of the two, the Swedish armed forces constitute the more significant bureaucratic pressure group, given Sweden's long tradition of armed neutrality.[24] Japan's defense imperatives have been moderated by United States security guarantees, and her small but highly professional armed forces are further restrained by the deep antimilitaristic feelings that have prevailed in Japanese society since World War II. The strength of the military in these countries is far exceeded by that of the civilian political institutions. Janowitz refers to these as military forces organized under a "constabulary concept": small in size and posing little threat to civilian control, and justified by limited functions in policing frontiers and in external peace-keeping operations.[25]

In all of these civic polities, the legitimacy of the civilian political order together with the professionalization of the military have established potent constraints against overt military participation in partisan struggles for power. Still, in none of these has objective civilian control been perfected, nor is it likely to be. Completely integral institutional boundaries for any nation's military establishment are probably unattainable, just as the military's participation in politics as a bureaucratic pressure group will not likely be eradicated short of the complete abolition of organized coercive forces in human society. Objective civilian control is encouraged and indeed made possible by military professionalization. It is buttressed by effective and legitimate civilian institutions. It may be reinforced by other factors, such as the world-view of the officer corps, a history of successful civilian resolutions of major political issues, and popular attitudes concerning the appropriate functions of the military. All of these factors are important, but the *sine qua non* of effective checks on the military's political strength remains the acceptance by the officers themselves of the principle of civilian supremacy.

Fragmented Boundaries and Subjective Civilian Control

The second general pattern of civil–military relations in civic polities is one in which the boundaries separating military institutions from those of society are substantially fragmented. In these systems military institutions lack autonomy. This may be because civil authorities do not recognize the existence of an independent sphere of activity for the military and hence seek to subordinate military values and interests within those of the larger society. This appears to be the general case in the People's Republic of China after the Great Proletarian Cultural Revolution. Chinese military boundaries have been virtually permeated by party controls, and distinctions of rank have been abolished in deference to Maoist concepts of revolutionary egalitarianism.[26] In Australia, as a further example, a small military establishment with professional aspirations has been hard pressed to maintain military autonomy and integral boundaries in the face of the liberal egalitarianism of "Aussie" political culture.[27] The Australian military is highly expert in the management of coercive resources and clearly recognizes and accepts its professional responsibilities to society. However, the relatively low institutional autonomy that accompanies fragmented boundaries means that the third dimension of professional development—corporateness—is stunted.

Military institutional boundaries may be fragmented as a result of one of several conditions (or their combination). The hierarchical structure of the officer corps may be penetrated by individuals whose primary loyalties are owed to some nonmilitary organization (for example, to a communist party). The social origins and group affiliations of officers may be relatively undifferentiated from those of certain subnational civilian elites, raising the possibility that officers may place ethnic, regional, or other group interests above those of the nation as a whole. The military values—hierarchical organization, discipline, and expertise in the application of force—may be fundamentally incompatible with the dominant values of the society (e.g., egalitarianism or pacifism). These or similar conditions may prevail even in countries where national security demands the maintenance of a large military establishment. Their effect is to undermine the autonomy of the military institution. The coercive resources of the army may thus be politically neutralized by the strength of other social institutions. As in Israel, this may be because coercion itself is low in domestic political value as a result of the effectiveness and legitimacy of the civilian government. In other countries the domestic political uses of coercion may be more prevalent, but the military may nevertheless have little opportunity to act independently in politics because of its heavily penetrated institutional boundaries. An example of this might be the Soviet Union. Other civic polities with subjective civilian control over their armed forces include Finland, Cuba, Mexico, Guyana, Iran, Ethiopia, and Nepal.

Civilian control exercised through a political party is exemplified here in three variations: the Soviet Union, Cuba, and Mexico. In the Soviet Union, military power is extremely high and coercion is relatively salient to domestic political life. However, the domestic uses of coercion are reserved by the Communist Party leadership to groups other than the army, i.e., the police and secret police apparatus (KGB). The potential for the Soviet military to convert coercive resources into domestic political influence appears to be effectively checked by the Communist Party bureaucracy. The military's institutional boundaries have been penetrated at virtually all levels of command according to a purposeful design on the part of the CPSU (Communist Party of the Soviet Union). The Communist Party ensures the political loyalty of the officer corps by establishing surveillance over the full range of military activities, and by an elaborate system of political indoctrination for both officers and enlisted men. In effect, party controls have atomized the officer corps so as to impair the development of an autonomous corporate identity within it. Students of Marxism–Leninism have observed that its success as a totalitarian system depends on the extent to which individuals throughout the society are psychologically isolated from one another, thus preventing the emergence of autonomous social organizations that might intervene between the regime and its subjects.[28] Full party control would therefore imply the complete permeation of the military's boundaries by the CPSU, producing a virtual identity of values and interests between these two organizations. As a practical matter, this ideal has fallen short of achievement. For foreign policy purposes, the Soviet government has accepted the need for maintaining a vast, highly modern, technologically advanced military establishment. This functional role in defense has allowed the Soviet military a much greater latitude for professional development and institutional autonomy than Marxist–Leninist ideology would legitimate. As a result, relations between the party and the military remain an area of uneasiness and suspicion.[29]

Cuba offers several interesting contrasts with the Soviet pattern of civil–military relations. Neither the Cuban Communist Party nor the Revolutionary Armed Forces has been allowed much latitude for development as an autonomous organization. Both have been penetrated and dominated by the closely knit circle of Fidel Castro's old-line associates, who respond to his personal leadership rather than to the dictates of Marxism–Leninism or to military institutional concerns. The role of the Communist Party—which has no formal bylaws and has never held a party congress—appears negligible. Two-thirds of the membership of its Central Committee are military men, as are six of the eight members of the Politburo.[30] Major Raul Castro, Fidel's brother, is a member of both bodies and also commands the armed forces. Military and political elite roles in Cuba have become virtually interchangeable. Officers simultaneously hold diverse political and administrative responsibilities along with their military duties. The unique blend of Cuban revolutionary pragmatism, guerrilla egalitarianism, and Castro's charisma has left little scope for an independent sphere of military activity or for the development of a corporate professional identity among officers.[31]

In Mexico, control over the military appears to be in the hands of a particular political party, but the armed forces are relatively professionalized with fairly integral institutional boundaries. Should we consider the Mexican pattern of civil–military relations under the rubric of objective or subjective civilian control? Mexico is ruled by a cohesive elite— the so-called "Revolutionary Family"—which implements a significant measure of its control through the official Institutional Revolutionary Party (PRI).[32] However, the PRI neither exercises nor aspires to totalitarian control over Mexican society. A considerable degree of subsystem autonomy is permitted, even to opposition political movements. But military institutional boundaries are indeed fragmented at the higher command levels, since top-ranking officers are integrated within the Revolutionary Family and have a role in PRI policy making in nonmilitary as well as military areas. The Mexican army remains a powerful bureaucratic interest group. Its role in the October 1968 rioting in Mexico City suggests that, under certain conditions, the armed forces are still capable of coercive actions independent of civilian direction.[33] But in general, effective civilian control is buttressed by the legitimacy of Mexico's political institutions, their identification in the public mind with the country's revolutionary tradition, and their effectiveness in promoting sustained economic growth over the past three decades.

Still another variation of subjective civilian control is that found in Israel, and to a lesser extent in Finland. In both of these systems the military's institutional boundaries are fragmented by general societal acceptance of the "citizen soldier" principle, and in Israel's case by the imperative of total mobilization for national defense. Civilian values and purposes are so powerful as to impede the development of a professional outlook and institutional role within the armed forces.[34] Despite the extraordinary role played by the Israel Defense Forces, especially since the Six-Day War of June 1967, civilian control over the military remains firm. It is sustained by Israel's civic political culture, its strong though fragmented party system, the depoliticization of the small professional officer corps, and the virtually unquestioned acceptance among citizen soldiers of the principle of civilian supremacy.[35] Similar factors operate to the same effect in Finland where, by contrast, substantial differences in the size of the military establishment leave far less potential scope for independent military influence in politics.[36]

Guyana's tiny Defence Force numbers some 1300 troops organized in two infantry battalions. Border disputes with Surinam and Venezuela have provided an external focus for the military, whose subordination to civilian control is reinforced by British colonial experience. The remaining countries cited previously—Iran, Ethiopia, and Nepal—have broadly similar patterns of civil—military relations. In each of these three, dynastic authority provides a traditional basis of legitimacy, and political participation is low. The potential instability of traditional legitimation, and hence the tenuousness of subjective civilian control in these systems, is illustrated by the case of Ethiopia. Emperor Haile Selassie's army is drawn primarily from the dominant Amhara group and functions as a subservient instrument of the dynasty.[37] His country, however, is split ethnically among some forty different groups and religiously between Coptic Christians and Muslims. The Emperor's personal authority tends to smooth over these cleavages, but peaceful succession upon his death is not assured. He narrowly escaped deposition by an abortive military coup in 1960, and the army may well move into power when his rule is ended. To some extent, Haile Selassie's dilemma is shared by the Shah of Iran and the King of Nepal. The efforts of these and other surviving monarchs to modernize their countries will surely, in the long run, unleash forces of change that will undermine the legitimacy of royal authority. In all three countries, the army is well placed politically to assume power should the monarchs or their successors falter.

Because military boundaries in these systems are relatively fragmented and professionalization is correspondingly reduced, subjective forms of civilian control may be viewed as less reliable to ensure subordination of the military than objective control. For some of our examples—the Soviet Union, Cuba, Mexico, Ethiopia—it is the strength of existing civilian institutions that holds the military in check, not acceptance by the military themselves of the principle of civilian supremacy. (Objective control combines both these constraints.) In countries with subjective control of the armed forces, it is highly probable that the armed forces would quickly expand their political role if social crises should seriously undermine the effectiveness and legitimacy of civil authority.

Praetorian Polities and Military Rule

Praetorian polities tend to be marked by insecure civilian control over the military. As a result, the political role of the armed forces may more readily expand beyond the bounds of participation acceptable for a bureaucratic interest group. These are systems in which participation in the political process is not moderated and channeled toward common goals by the reliable functioning of political institutions. The institutions that do exist are weak, lacking in the moral authority necessary to work out binding, allocative decisions that will be regarded as legitimate by the society as a whole. Governments are rendered ineffective by their inability to aggregate mass support. This "political decay" opens the way for the more violent and coercive forms of political interaction, and thus increases the potential influence of the armed forces as it weakens the constraints that hold them apart from politics.

This general decay in political institutionalization is basically a crisis of legitimacy.[38] Whether political legitimacy in a particular system derives from rational–legal sources, or from tradition, or from the charisma of a magnetic unifying leader, it refers to the establishment of political authority that is ultimately dependent on the consent of the governed.[39] Consent may thus be thought of as a mobilizable political resource, a reserve of potential energy on which all governments must depend for the effective formulation and efficient implementation of policy. Popular consent may also be thought of as a political currency, a means of exchange that operates in the political marketplace in a way analogous to the function of money in facilitating economic transactions. [40] As a political currency, consent is amenable to measurement (for example, the tally of votes in elections, or the use of modern survey techniques to sample opinion). Consent may be used as a standard for judging among conflicting claims to political authority (the very basis of elections) or to legitimize a particular policy alternative (as with President de Gaulle's occasional resort to the use of the referendum in the French Fifth Republic). Consent is the currency of modern political parties. The capacity to aggregate a preponderance of consent makes effective government possible, but by itself it is not sufficient to assure effectiveness. A second important currency, coercion, may also be used to restructure political interrelationships in a society, and effective rule hinges on the ability of a government to command a preponderance of both. Since the military and police forces of any society normally manage a near monopoly of organized coercion, control over these forces is an indispensable condition of effective rule.[41]

Because political power and resources are dispersed among numerous groups in praetorian polities, and political parties are usually identified with particular social forces rather than aggregating the interests of a broad range of groups, governments tend to be formed by coalitions of various interests. Often these coalitions are unstable and short lived, owing to the diversity of policy goals pursued by the different groups represented within them and to the low level of mutual trust that is a characteristic of the praetorian political process. Confronting the challenges of modernization requires governments capable of bringing about fundamental social and economic change, of finding solutions to the problems of inequality, low productivity, and social disintegration. The power to effect basic change, to formulate and implement policy decisions that affect the basic values and resources of a society, is a definitive property of a *ruling* coalition in government. Ruling requires political authority that is based on effective control over both major currencies, consent and coercion. Such is the nature of authority in a civic polity. The incapacity to promote basic change, on the other hand, defines a *reigning* regime. The reigning coalitions of praetorian polities may claim a preponderance of either the consent or the coercion currency, but inability to combine the two means that government will tend to drift into ineffectiveness and instability despite the urgency of demands for change.[42]

The establishment of effective political authority thus requires (1) the aggregation of consent, and (2) control over the means to organized coercion. The first is essentially a matter of political organization and legitimacy; the second, a question of subordinating the armed forces to the direction of the state, i.e., the constituted government.

In praetorian societies the military acts in the political arena independently of government control, preserving for itself the right to determine the political uses of coercive resources. Civilian political institutions, as a result of their ineffectiveness and narrow bases of support, are not strong enough to assert control over the armed forces. Military leaders may remain aloof from coalition politics or may choose to align themselves from time to time with certain civilian groups, depending on the overall strength of the armed forces and their degree of professionalization. Essentially, however, their participation in coalitions does not mean that they surrender their independence of control over the means to organized coercion. If the armed forces thus exercise nearly total autonomy over their internal organization and, in time of crisis, over the decision to support or not support the civil government, then civilian control clearly does not exist.

Civilian coalition governments in praetorian polities may therefore reign but cannot rule. Their policies are not accepted as binding by all political actors, partly because it is apparent that policy is made and implemented, in effect, subject to the independent approval or disapproval of the military. Unlike the American President or the British Prime Minister, chief executives in praetorian systems are not masters in their own houses. The shadow of military intervention hovers over them, circumscribing the policy choices open to them. Policy decisions and even elections take on a tentative quality, with important political actors waiting to see how military leaders may react before determining their own actions.

In many countries, civil–military relations has become the Achilles heel of incumbent regimes. Indeed, given the tendency of governments in praetorian polities to attempt to perpetuate themselves in power, a military coup d'etat may be the only effective route to power that remains open to opposition elites. Military leaders are thus wooed not only by incumbent elites but also by their oppositions, each group seeking to advance its own interests by allying to itself the managers of organized coercion. Charges of administrative corruption, acts of civil disobedience, general strikes, the withholding of investments and the flight of capital, even student riots are often little more than attempts by opposition groups to demonstrate the incapacity of an incumbent government to govern, and thus to terminate it by precipitating a military coup. It is this endemic political instability resulting from the general weakness of civilian political institutions that tends to draw the military into the more overt forms of action encompassed by the term "military intervention in politics."

Referring again to the typology shown in Table 3.1, we can see that the interrelationships among the four summary variables define a number of possible patterns of civil–military relations in praetorian polities. Even the most superficial comparisons among military-based regimes suggest that there are substantial differences in their political styles and in their orientations to major questions of public policy. Military intervention has clearly had different historical meanings and consequences in Turkey, for example, as compared with Peru or Nigeria. In some countries the armed forces have intervened in politics on the side of modernizing social change and economic progress. In others it appears that military rule serves the interests of conservative social forces in preservation of the status quo. Military intervention occurs in the less developed countries of Africa, Asia, and Latin America, and also has taken place in more modern European societies that are characterized by mass participation in politics. The path of intervention has been followed by highly professional armed forces, as well as by those with severely fragmented institutional boundaries. In the remainder of this chapter we shall consider four principal types of military-based regimes: predatory, reformist, radical, and guardian.

Predatory Military Regimes

This particular category, though now largely of historical interest, arose in pre-industrial societies where the traditional political institutions had decayed and where social mobilization and economic development were in their early stages. These societies were sharply divided by the initial impact of modernizing change.[43] On the one hand, agrarian social structures remained predominantly traditional. A small aristocratic landholding class held an overwhelming share of both wealth and political power, while the unmobilized peasant masses remained in a state of quasi-feudal subjugation. By contrast, urban centers began to develop and modernize through contacts with the economically advanced countries of the West. In these urban areas a new middle class took form among indigenous entrepreneurs and managers, professional elites and bureaucrats, technicians, and others exposed to modern knowledge and skills. Although the interests of the new urban elites were in fundamental conflict with those of the rural aristocracy, often the latter was able to preserve its control over national politics by forging a conservative alliance with religious elites and the armed forces. Such was the pattern of development, for example, in nineteenth-century Spain and Portugal, in Turkey, and in much of Latin America. The historic triumvirate of rural oligarchy, Church, and military-dominated Latin America throughout most of the nineteenth century, and in some instances well into the twentieth. It was in these nations that the personalistic military style in politics found its most pronounced expressions.

The roots of the military's central political role in Latin America extend deeply into the institutional and cultural legacy of Iberian colonialism and into the circumstances of the wars of independence of the early nineteenth century. The colonial systems established by Spain and Portugal after the discovery and conquest of America were profoundly authoritarian, based on the divine right of monarchs to dominate all social, economic, and political relationships within their realms. The legitimacy of the political order was founded on this monarchical absolutism, and His Hispanic Majesty's viceroys in the new world exercised virtually unchallenged authority in his name. In practice Spain and Portugal were tempered in their administrative control over the colonies by the great distances involved and by the slowness of communications, although the Iberian rulers viewed these areas as extensions of the homeland and wished to exploit them for the enrichment of the crown. The Church reinforced this autocratic system of rule by teaching fatalism and deference to authority to the conquered Indians and imported African slaves. Little or no attention was paid to the indigenous economic development of the colonies, and standards of conduct among the colonial administrators were low. Officials on temporary assignment from the mother countries exploited their authority for personal gain and enrichment. Personal loyalties were the primary basis of political interaction. Virtually the entire system was exploitative, with the armed forces providing the vital coercive bases to sustain the dominance of the propertied few. In short, the colonial heritage of Latin America institutionalized

(1) authoritarian modes of behavior, (2) reliance on ascriptive and particularistic norms rather than norms of achievement and universalism, and (3) venality and corruption as the prevailing standards of public administration.

Latin America's wars of independence resulted in severing the political ties with Spain and Portugal but, in terms of social and economic reforms for the newly formed states, they actually changed little of the way of life for the populace. The various independence movements had been initiated primarily because the colonists resented the imposition of a Bonaparte on the throne of Spain, not out of popular aspirations for self-determination and republican government. Independence thus destroyed the monarchy as the legitimator of political authority, but failed to substitute a viable alternative. The republican institutional models borrowed from Europe and North America were merely imposed on the traditional social structure. The new states adopted democratic constitutional forms but the underlying complex of attitudes, values, and social relationships required for the proper functioning of democracy was absent. In a real sense, then, the new national governments in Latin America were irrelevant. They could hardly respond to the unarticulated demands of the great mass of their citizenry, and they commanded only a minimal capacity to penetrate and regulate their societies. The traditional rural oligarchies remained secure because public policy rarely affected their vital economic and social interests.

The imported institutional models suggested a strong economic role for the state, but in Latin America the system of private economic transactions required to give meaning to that role remained quite underdeveloped. Since the only available and significant source of government revenue was regulation of foreign trade and investment, the economic institutions of the Latin American states became much more attuned to integration with the international economic system than with their own national economies. As Charles Anderson points out in a perceptive essay, the "modern men" of these societies—those with managerial and technical skills—were really social misfits. Unable to realize their aspirations for upward mobility in the established elite systems, they were drawn into the small modernizing sector of society that was affected by government. [44] Control over the limited resources disposed of by the state became their objective. The stakes of politics were high within this modern sector because other avenues of social mobility were virtually closed. The colonial patterns of official corruption were continued, and public service remained essentially a means of self-enrichment. The constitutional rules adopted to regulate political competition were most often ignored. In this "legitimacy vacuum," coercion and violence became the dominant means of changing governments. [45]

In a certain sense, the Latin American armed forces became established in politics during the formative years of these republics and never really withdrew. It was the military who wrested independence from Spain under the leadership of Simon Bolívar, José de San Martín and others. Having been midwives at the births of their countries, they were naturally inclined to exercise a protective interest over the later development of their fosterlings. Indeed, there proved to be virtually no other outlet through which they could justify their continued existence once independence had been won. Latin America remained remarkably free of international wars during the nineteenth century. The military's role in providing for national defense had to become subordinated to its role as guardian of domestic order. Civilian political institutions remained far too weak and narrowly based, and from the outset the Latin American military found its main institutional role as an independent actor in political life.

There was no tradition of separate spheres of authority for civil and military power to inhibit the participation of military men in politics. The borrowed constitutional models stipulated that elected presidents of these republics should also act as commanders-in-chief of the armed forces, but military leaders refused to accept in principle this subordinate role. They defined their allegiance as owed first to the national interest, and only secondly to the civilian *político* who happened to be exercising a temporary proprietorship over the presidential palace. To some extent the prestige gained by the armed forces as a result of the wars of independence served to legitimate their claim to be the institutional expression of the national honor. Throughout most of Latin America the military thus became the arbiter of national political life. Simply stated, the military had the lion's share of the resources necessary to gain and hold power in societies where both political participation and institutionalization were low.

Even allowing for some variation from country to country, we can safely observe that standards of military professionalism remained low during this era of Latin American history. The *personalismo* that pervaded social and political relationships was also evident within the armed forces. Generals tended to regard their troops as belonging to them personally, since it was they who were often financially responsible for recruiting, training, and equipping their men. Rotation of officers from command to command was minimal. Military discipline was cultivated on the basis of personal loyalty rather than professional values. The administrative corruption of the civil bureaucracy was mirrored in the armed forces, with generals commonly pocketing a major portion of the government's allowance for their troops. The rank-and-file soldiers were often left poorly armed and little disciplined, forced to live off the countryside. Military establishments became top-heavy with brass. National budgets were overburdened with huge expenditures for defense which the generals demanded and the civilian politicians granted because they feared for their own tenure in office. It would hardly be overstating the situation to observe that in some countries a successful military career was defined as one that culminated in a term in the presidential palace. [46]

Nineteenth-century Latin American militarism was mainly predatory, in the sense that military institutions occupied a marginally functional role in their societies but claimed an extravagant share of scarce resources. Lieuwen's observations of Mexican politics after 1821 portray this era well:

> *For nearly sixty years political processes in Mexico were domi-nated by military violence. Hundreds of barracks uprisings and rebellions were led by army officers and backed by the politi-cal out-groups. Incumbent regimes were toppled at an average of better than one a year. In 1821 there were nearly five thou-sand officers for the eight thousand enlisted men stationed in the capital. In 1823, when total government revenues were five million dollars, the budget of the armed forces was nine mil-lion. During Mexico's first quarter-century of independence, the military budget exceeded government revenues two out of every three years.* [47]

Military coups seldom resulted in significant changes in the socioeconomic status quo. More often, they produced a further feathering of the mili-tary's own institutional nest or merely served the personal ambitions of individual officers. In Bolivia, for example, the regime of General Mariano Melgarejo (1864–1871) marked a particularly low point. Melgarejo, back-ed by his private army, was a tyrant who sold border lands to Brazil, ille-gally disposed of communal Indian lands, and presided over a presidential court noted for its debauchery and sordidness. In Venezuela the twenty-seven-year dictatorship of Juan Vicente Gomez (1908–1935) bestowed fabulous fortunes on the dictator's family and henchmen, while his army was pampered with the best guns and planes that European munitions makers could provide.

The military's predatory role in Latin American politics was made possible by the fundamental weakness of civilian political institutions and by the consequently central role of coercion in the political process. By no means, however, was this simply a matter of military officers con-testing with civilian authorities for control over the state. Military institu-tional boundaries were severely fragmented as a reflection of the as-yet low state of military professionalism in the region. Often a military leader was also a landowner with familial ties to the Church. His political role thus could scarcely be differentiated from his other roles. Control over state resources was the objective of various social forces competing within the civilian sphere, and these frequently sought alliances with powerful leaders and groups within the armed forces. The military was just one of a number of interest groups taking an active part in the formation of political coalitions and countercoalitions. Military dictatorships were rarely established and maintained without the support of important sectors within the civil society. By modern Western standards the performance in office of military politicians was often corrupt and even baldly self-seeking; yet the historical evidence does not suggest that, as a class, the civilian politicians of the era were appreciably less corrupt or that their rule was necessarily more attuned to serving the general interests of society. There is little reason to conclude that civilian rule was viewed as either more or less legitimate by the peoples of Latin America. In fact there was very little consensus regarding the types of political institutions most appropriate for these societies, and no one particular means of mobilizing political power, or of constituting governments, or of determining choices among policy alternatives was consistently accorded greater legitimacy than others.[48] In the absence of consensus on the fundamental rules of the political game, the military managers of society's coercive resources could hardly remain aloof from so deadly and vital a game.

This pattern of politics became fundamentally unstable for most Latin American countries around the early years of the twentieth century. Indigenous economic development and the beginnings of industrialization, combined with widespread social mobilization that upset the traditional agrarian social structure and the urban–rural balance, made government relevant to the national economic system. A new urban bourgeoisie with an industrial base sought control over government in order to facilitate economic expansion, and the nucleus of a politically conscious working class began to seek recognition of its demands through trade unions and populist political movements. These developments served to enhance the status of consent as a political currency. Up to this time both the civil and military bureaucracies of most Latin American governments existed essentially to serve their own interests. Enriching themselves through raids on the public treasury, they gave little heed to the needs and interests of the societies they ostensibly served. Now, however, modernization generated new social forces powerful enough to threaten governments with political sanctions. These forces made it necessary for governing elites, both civilian and military, to recognize a higher moral purpose for their existence. In most of Latin America and the rest of the world, new levels of social complexity and interdependence rendered old-style predatory militarism anachronistic. (Thailand, because of the uniqueness of its history, was an exception to this trend.)

These changes were paralleled by the spread of professionalization within the armed forces themselves. Beginning in the 1880's, modernization touched many Latin American armies in the form of training
missions from Europe and in the introduction of advanced weaponry and
tactics.[49] Service academies and higher war colleges were established,
with curriculums designed to educate officers in advanced military science
and emphasizing the responsibility of the armed forces to serve national
rather than special interests (as in Peru). Corporateness and a growing sense
of social responsibility among officers led to the emergence of a more
sharply differentiated institutional interest for the military. While these
changes did not lead to the political neutralization of the armed forces,
increasingly they began to act in politics in service of corporate rather
than personalistic interests, and in response to growing demands for change
in their societies rather than to protect entrenched and reactionary social
classes.

Reformist Military Regimes

When the armed forces become the spearhead of a general
movement toward political reform, it is the outcome of important changes
that have occurred both within the military and in the structure of society.
The military officer as political reformer, rather than predatory ruler,
usually makes his appearance in systems undergoing transition from traditional or oligarchic rule to rule by the urban middle classes.[50] In the
services, military officers develop a more professional outlook and their
institutions become more differentiated from those of the rest of society.
In society, the urban middle classes become sufficiently powerful and
conscious of their own interests to challenge the traditional monarch or
the landed oligarchy for control over national policy. Both the new military and the rising middle classes seek national economic development,
and together they forge a coalition to reform the traditional political institutions that block their aspirations.

The rise of military professionalism in nineteenth-century
Europe resulted largely from changes that occurred first within the societies: technological advances and social, economic and political developments. In other regions, however, professionalization took place later and
as a direct consequence of the visibility and influence of the European
models. In Latin America officers were affected both by professional
studies abroad and by the military missions they had requested from
Germany, Italy, and France. In Asia and Africa, foreign military models
were more often implanted and nourished directly by the colonizing
powers. The results in both of these patterns were similar. Military institutions tended to lead their societies in structural differentiation and
functional specialization, rapidly becoming one of their most modernized

sectors. Officer corps developed professional expertise, a sense of responsibility to the nation, and a cohesive corporate identity, all of which worked to promote the autonomy of their institutions from other social forces and to encourage a new military perspective on national political affairs. In Thailand, for example, the rising generation of professional officers viewed the absolute monarchy as outmoded and were disgusted with the corruption and inefficiency of their government. Their alienation from the traditional monarchy led to its overthrow in 1932. Many officers elsewhere came to believe that both the fulfillment of the national destiny and the development of their own institutions required governments committed to the promotion of industrialization. These officers found a natural and increasingly powerful ally in the developing commercial and industrial bourgeoisie. For its part, the bourgeoisie recognized in the military a potent weapon against the entrenched forces of conservatism.

Of course, the reconstruction of armies along professional lines did not take place overnight, nor was the middle-class perspective adopted uniformly throughout the military rank structure. Victor Alba highlights the disparate psychological outlooks of major groups within the Latin American officer corps in his classification of barracks officers, school officers, and laboratory officers.[51] The "barracks officers" were most often those who were advanced in age and rank, preprofessional in institutional values, and conservative in political outlook. Having held center stage during the predatory era, they were gradually giving way to the emerging class of "school officers." The latter were those of middle age and rank who had received professional training, either abroad or in locally established service academies, and who had risen more on the basis of professional competence than political influence. The third group, the "laboratory officers," were younger still and the most junior in rank, yet the best educated and most professionally competent. Ashamed of the backwardness of their countries, naively idealistic in their views regarding political and social change, frustrated by slow promotions in services top-heavy with superannuated and superfluous generals, the school and laboratory officers gradually asserted dominance over their reactionary superiors. They identified their corporate interests with national development. In contrast with the barracks officers, their origins were generally in the middle and lower middle classes. Their participation in politics took the form of interventions opposing the status quo, more or less in direct support of the goals of the rising urban middle class (as in the case of the 1925 coup in Chile led by Carlos Ibañez del Campo).

By contrast with the earlier predatory era, reformist coups tended to result in governing juntas rather than the personalistic *caudillo*. Professionalization raised what Martin Needler has called the military's "threshhold of intervention."[52] The decision to intervene in politics became a collegial one, requiring the assent of numerous officers representing a cross-section of viewpoints and interests within the armed forces. The military's growing sense of corporateness and social responsibility made them more sensitive to the need for maintaining unity of action. Acceptance of this need both complicated the mechanics of intervention and broadened its objectives. Once in power, the reform-minded junta announced sweeping programs of social change. The "school officer" juntas that seized power in Chile and Brazil during the 1920's followed this pattern, as did the Kemalists in Turkey and the followers of Nasser in Egypt and Kassim in Iraq.

The programs of these reformers were at first highly idealistic and often rather simplistic. They reflected the military's faith in problem solving by command decision, and thus were poorly suited to transform the political and social realities of these societies. They also reflected the new class basis of the military's role in politics. The majors and colonels became the vanguard of the middle class in its struggle for political dominance. In Latin America these reform-oriented juntas acted prematurely and usually had to give way to countercoups led by the "barracks officers" and backed by the oligarchies. Nevertheless, the new pattern of military political action in support of middle-class aspirations had been set.

As social systems become more differentiated and specialized, both the seizure of power and the exercise of governmental authority become more difficult for the military politicians. With the expansion of political participation to encompass new groups of the middle and later the lower classes, there was a marked decline in the efficacy of naked coercion as a political currency. These new groups sought to reinforce their demands for access to political decision making by establishing consent (i.e., the electoral process) as the sole legitimate basis for determining who shall rule. Under these conditions of expanded participation in politics, the technique of coup d'etat involves greater risks. Ideally, a coup is quick, precise, and bloodless. A wave of civilian indignation, however, might lead to organized opposition to the military and perhaps even civil war. Popular resistance increases the likelihood that armies will have to use, rather than merely brandish, their weapons. Countrymen may be killed in large numbers, and the armed forces may even become divided against themselves. The prospect of fractricidal combat is one that most military men abhor deeply. The more real this risk appears, the more difficult it is for officer conspirators to achieve the internal consensus required to cross the "threshhold of intervention."

Modernization also affects the feasibility of military rule. The development of modernized economic systems and of the urbanized, literate societies necessary to support them produces new levels of complexity and interdependence in social life. The domain of government increases, both in terms of its capacity to penetrate and regulate the society and in the numbers of people affected by, and seeking to influence, its decisions. A point is reached beyond which the coordination of complex economic and administrative units by military fiat, backed only by the threat of force, becomes impossible. Unless key civilian sectors agree to cooperate with the military (preferably, to support it) the military will find its capacity to govern effectively simply evaporates. Civil disobedience and general noncooperation with military rule may lead to a breakdown of vital governmental functions and widespread disruption of the network of social and economic transactions on which modern societies depend.

The advance of modernization means that might can no longer be readily converted into the right to rule. Military politicians are increasingly forced to establish their authority in the eyes of the governed. Thus, military intervention that is primarily self-serving and predatory becomes harder to mount, and periods of military rule following predatory coups become shorter in direct proportion to the military's reliance on coercion as the basis of its authority to govern. Historically, the military reformers have legitimized their rule by proclaiming their nationalism. Military rule was justified, they argued, because traditional institutions had failed to promote national development. Their claim to the mantle of authority was their alignment with the general movement for reform, the same middle-class movement, ironically, that sought to establish popular consent as the dominant political currency. Because of this inherent contradiction, the legitimacy of reformist military rule has tended to be unstable and transitory. The civilian middle sectors acclaimed such legitimacy during periods when the military's coercive resources were instrumental in wresting power from the hands of conservative oligarchies and monarchs. But they denied it once that battle had been won and they had become secure enough to exercise power in their own right.

Reformist military regimes in Latin America and the Middle East, and more recently in Africa, have been concerned primarily with creating a national identity and promoting orderly economic development. They have viewed industrialization as the means to enhance national power and hence military power. Although in the context of their countries their impact is reformist, their social consciences and commitment to sweeping social changes should not be overestimated. The military reformer makes his appearance on the political stage when it is the urban middle classes, not the masses, who are actively seeking to have their demands implemented through state institutions. Neither he nor the urban middle classes are much concerned with promoting agrarian reform, for example, or with reducing economic and social inequalities. As in Nigeria, reformist military regimes tend to be interested in economic growth as a means to modernizing and expanding the military establishment. They remain basically indifferent or even hostile to social reform measures that are not directly functional to economic growth and industrialization.[53]

In general, armies of the reformist stripe make their appearance in politics when (1) professionalization is more or less firmly established (yet hardly complete), (2) the middle class is locked in struggle with traditional and conservative elements for control over national policy, and (3) there is little agreement among contending groups within the society on the forms of legitimate authority and on "rules of the game" to moderate group conflict. The reformist role is above all a creature of middle-class politics. As the process of social mobilization produces a politicized mass with demands for a more sweeping reallocation of government resources, the reformist military role becomes increasingly untenable. Four broad possibilities for future directions then become open:

> 1. *The urban middle classes accept responsibility for leading the rural masses into modernity, forging new political institutions with mass support (i.e., modern political parties) and gradually asserting civilian control over the military.[54] This is the pattern followed in Chile, Costa Rica, and India.*

> 2. *Instead of the urban bourgeoisie, intellectuals provide the leadership for the rural masses. This alliance leads to social revolution, the establishment of new centers of civilian authority and new standards of political legitimacy, and a new and politically subordinate military establishment. This pattern was generally followed in Russia, Mexico, and Cuba.*

> 3. *The armed forces forge a populist coalition with the masses, committing themselves to a more radical path of modernization and fundamentally redirecting the character of the military's political role. To a greater or lesser degree, this has been the pattern of events in Argentina (under Peron), in Nasser's Egypt, and in Peru under the military government of General Juan Velasco Alvarado.*

> 4. *The armed forces choose to preserve their alliance with the urban middle classes, employing their coercive resources to shield these sectors against mass pressures for the redistribution of wealth and in resistance to demands for broadened participation in political life. With variations, this pattern has prevailed in societies as diverse as Greece, Brazil, Pakistan, Ghana, and Bolivia.*

Outcomes (1) and (2) above lead to the establishment of civic polities and some form of civilian control over the military. Those described in (3) and (4) lead to different forms of military-based regimes, considered in the following sections as radical and guardian (respectively).

Radical Military Regimes

The most prominent characteristic of the radical military regime is the linkage of interest between military officers, who are essentially of the middle and lower middle classes, and the masses, who previously had been unintegrated into national political life. Effecting this linkage requires an unusual level of political consciousness and will on the part of the armed forces leadership. By necessity, it involves a degree of politicization for the armed forces that both contravenes the spirit of military professionalism and undermines its cohesiveness. This political role gives rise to serious divisive currents within the officer corps, and therefore it occurs most rarely and is the most difficult to maintain.

Members of reformist armies can occupy governmental roles and participate in the political process, even while decrying the disunity and corruption of politics. This contradiction, which Janowitz calls the "politics of wanting to be above politics," reflects the professional soldier's technocratic approach to problem solving.[55] The military mind is attracted to direct administrative solutions. It is repelled by the politician's arts of compromise, obliqueness, and temporization as ways of handling difficult political matters. In his own mind, the military reformer conceives himself to be participating not in politics but in government. Whereas he generally has only disgust for the former, the latter he sees through the eyes of the professional bureaucrat as a task-oriented enterprise. To his way of thinking, government is a noble undertaking that is subverted by politics, especially party politics. He perceives the national interest to be thrust aside by the helter-skelter conflict of narrow selfish interests. His intervention into civil affairs is frankly aimed at lifting government above politics. As he defines it, his role in the governing process is thus compatible with the values of the professional soldier.[56]

This is the essence of the fundamental contradiction between military values and radicalism: the military officer must be more than idealistic; he must be willing to pursue his goals by means that are wholly foreign to his professional background. This is the reason why the military officer rarely aligns himself wholeheartedly with the cause of social revolution. When he does assume the role of radical reformer, he does so briefly. Though military officers often seek broad reforms within their societies and are willing to take part in government to bring them about, they seldom show interest in *political* as distinct from administrative organization. The thought of actually mobilizing and organizing the masses as a political resource is antithetical to their ingrained contempt for politics and to their sense of mission as professionals.

Since World War II, military-based regimes of broadly radical impulse have appeared in Argentina, Peru, Egypt, and Iraq.[57] In each of these cases a junta seeking fundamental alterations of the status quo has come to power, found its designs thwarted by reactionary social forces and structural impediments, and sought to overwhelm its opponents by developing a broad power base among the rural and urban lower classes. Unlike their reformist brethren, the military radicals venture to develop an independent (all-new) political organization. Mobilization of mass support is accomplished through the instrumental use of a body of myths, usually a heady mixture of nationalism and locally refined socialism. With the radicals in control, the collegial decision-making principle characteristic of reformist juntas tends to give way to charismatic leadership. Leaders such as Nasser and Peron, by providing a unifying focus for mass identification, are able to personalize and thus make more effective the linkage between mass aspirations and the modernizing goals of the military. Professionalism, while not entirely abandoned, becomes subordinated along with a measure of the military's institutional autonomy to the demands of political expediency.

The dissonance between military values and radicalism eventually becomes acute and manifests itself in strong pressures within the military for a return, if not to the barracks, then at least to a renewed commitment to professional standards. The military radical may well accept the need for mobilization of the masses into politics, and he strives to create a broad-based political party; but his experiments in the field of political organization are influenced by his institutional perspective. The organization he creates is unlikely to be of the grass-roots variety, with careful attention given to organizing and channeling support at the local level. Instead, he exercises authority predominantly through the charismatic relationship between leader and follower, which characteristically denies the need for any intervening organization. Such was the character of the ties between Peron and Argentina's *descamisados* and Nasser and the Egyptian *fellahin*. Though both leaders began their political careers as military radicals, their personal relationships with the masses eventually drove a wedge between them and their officer colleagues. In each case the demands of leadership broadened the leader's perspectives and thus strained his former ties to the military. The leaders themselves became "civilianized," pursuing political interests that were increasingly divorced from those of their military constituencies. As a result, both Peron and Nasser gradually disengaged themselves from their military roles. Some military followers remained alongside them, opting for new careers as politicians and administrators. Others, preferring the disciplined life of the professional officer, withdrew to the barracks to rebuild the autonomy of the military institution.

In effect, these charismatic leaders became the linkages between the newly politicized masses and the armed forces. Legitimation through charisma alone tends to be unstable and transitory, yet in these instances it served the purpose of linking two otherwise incompatible social forces. The masses could be mobilized to provide the political energy necessary for attaining the military's original progressive goals, while the officer corps itself could escape the need to assume a central role in political organization and thus maintain its professional self-image of being above politics. In each of these examples, moreover, the armed forces regained sufficient autonomy to pose a threat to the leader. Nasser's extraordinary political skill enabled him to hold on to power until his death in September 1970, despite his army's unrest in the face of defeats at the hands of Israel.[58] Peron was overthrown by a military coup in September 1955, but retained a large popular following.[59]

Thus, for the armed forces at least, the radical role is usually shortlived. The tensions it creates eventually give rise to renewed professionalism and a redefined role vis-à-vis civilian authority. This new role may take the form of subjective civilian control, provided that—as in the case of Nasser—the charismatic leader is successful in raising the general level of political institutionalization and advancing the cause of modernization within his society. Conversely, it may gravitate toward some form of military guardianship, as in post-Peron Argentina.

Guardian Military Regimes

The great majority of recent military regimes in Africa, Asia, and Latin America have tended to be neither radical nor reformist in orientation. They have instead reflected the propensity of military officers in praetorian societies to establish themselves as the unique custodians of the "national interest." These armies consider themselves to be the repositories of national honor and prestige. Relying on the broadest possible interpretation of their role as defenders of the nation, they assume the responsibility to protect their societies against threats from any quarter, including those resulting from the perceived malfeasance, corruption, and incompetence of civilian politicians. The essence of military guardianship, present in all its various forms, is the overwhelming value placed by the armed forces on political stability and order or on their own corporate interest. This is not to say that the guardian role necessarily opposes all social change, but merely that the officers consider change to be of secondary importance and require that it take place through a gradual and orderly process. Military guardians are, above all, "law and order" men. Their loyalty is owed to the national interest as they themselves define it, and ideologically they are the quintessence of the "politics of wanting to be above politics."

Rule by military guardians is conservative in effect if not openly so in philosophy. As in the reformist pattern, the officers act in politics as the representatives of middle-class interests. The difference is that the middle classes are now established on the political scene and no longer opposed to the status quo. It is they, not the traditional conservatives, who enjoy the status and privileges of the dominant social class. It is they, therefore, who feel most threatened by lower-class pressures for a radical redistribution of wealth. "The more backward a society is," in Huntington's words, "the more progressive the role of its military; the more advanced a society becomes, the more conservative and reactionary becomes the role of its military."[60]

Guardian regimes vary, however, not only in the circumstances and rationales underlying their interventions in politics, but also in the duration and consequences of their rule. Military guardianship is primarily characteristic of armed forces with integral institutional boundaries. Guardian interventions are initiated by armies as independent political actors, though substantial boundary fragmentation may subsequently develop as the officers in governing roles prove unable to stand above the conflicts of the society. In Latin America, guardian interventions have frequently forestalled the demands of low-status groups seeking access to the political process. The Peruvian military, for example, has intervened repeatedly to prevent the reformist Aprista party from coming to power. Argentina's armed forces have adamantly opposed the political resurgence of Peronism in a similar way since 1955. Conversely, military guardians may intervene—as in some states of sub-Saharan Africa—simply to stem general deterioration in public order, or to remove from power a civilian regime that, through its own malfeasance, has lost its claim to legitimacy. A good example is the 1966 overthrow of Ghanaian President Kwame Nkrumah. The coup leaders did not seek to reform Ghanaian society, but rather to terminate a government that had clearly lost touch with the people and that had—perhaps even more significantly—threatened the military's institutional interests.[61] Guardian regimes may be relatively short in duration, with the military withdrawing to the barracks once civil affairs have been placed in order. On the other hand, military guardianship in certain societies appears to have become more or less institutionalized. Military rule in both Greece and Brazil may be assuming a quality of permanence, with officers becoming part of a broad civil–military managerial elite exercising prolonged authoritarian control over national decision making.

Two essential elements distinguish military-based guardian regimes. First, it is the weakness of civilian political institutions, not military political ambitions *per se*, that eventually draws the armed forces into overt participation in politics. Military guardianship develops in systems where public disorder and uncertainty are high, where both essential public services and the rules of political competition are breaking down, and where civil authorities appear to be incapable of coping with the situation. Often the factor that precipitates the coup d'etat is the resort by desperate civil officials to large-scale use of the army as police forces. This role is universally abhorrent to professional officers, often uniting them against the government in power.[62] Second, the military junta that takes charge after deposing the civilian president usually has no political or social program of its own. It seeks no fundamental reforms in the structures of society and advances no goals of social redistribution. Its objectives are limited to the restoration of order, the preservation of stability in the existing patterns of social and economic interaction, and the protection of the military's corporate institutional interests. Guardian coups are often greeted with widespread civilian support, if only because decisive action on the part of the military leadership may signal an end to escalating social conflict. The coup alleviates uncertainty by freezing the status quo.[63] Often the guardian junta will restore power to civilians by permitting new elections to be held once the stabilizing functions of the coup have been fulfilled. More recently, however, guardian regimes in parts of Africa and Latin America appear to be increasingly convinced that the national interest requires an indefinite period of stable rule under authoritarian political restraints.

Military-based guardian regimes may be classified according to (1) the degree and nature of overt participation by the armed forces in politics, and (2) the general attitude of the military leaders toward social change and the expansion of political participation to new groups within the society.[64] The major categories of military guardianship are four: direct, arbiter, factional, and postcolonial.

Direct Guardianship   Contemporary examples of this type would be the military regimes of Greece, Brazil, and Pakistan (prior to the 1971 civil war that resulted in independence for Bangladesh). In these countries, the armed forces are highly professionalized with relatively integral institutional boundaries. Their decisions to supplant predecessor civilian governments (in April 1967 for Greece, April 1964 for Brazil, and October 1958 for Pakistan) were made as independent political actors, not as the instruments of other social forces. In each case, the military leadership assumed direct responsibility for government by ruling for indefinite periods themselves. The Greek army acted out of distrust of the country's political party system and fear of growing influence on the part of the left. Brazil's military leaders, similarly, despised President Joao Goulart's populist domestic policies and viewed his foreign policies as perilously favorable to communist nations. General Ayub Khan headed a coalition of the army and the civil service determined to prevent Pakistan's first general elections, and to oust civilian politicians who the army felt had failed to provide adequately for national security.[65]

Direct guardianship requires a large military establishment capable of performing a differentiated set of political–administrative roles.

Some officers must see to the affairs of government while the bulk of the officer corps continues to attend to professional duties. Generally also the acquiescence and cooperation of the civil bureaucracy are necessary to sustain prolonged military rule. Military bureaucracies have neither the technical expertise nor the motivation required to fill all levels of the civil service with officers. Hence, direct guardianship tends to evolve into a technocracy joining both civilian and military experts, who together view the tasks of government in administrative terms.

This form of military guardianship is most characteristic of societies in which the urban middle class is established in politics, but is unable or unwilling to absorb the socially mobilized lower strata. The military acts politically, in effect, on behalf of the insecure and threatened middle classes to resist the pressures of social mobilization. A special case of direct guardianship may occur in relatively modern societies where the scope of political participation is high, and where military strength is also high and exceeds that of the civilian institutions. This format conforms closely to Harold D. Lasswell's hypothesis of the emergence of "garrison-states," which is evaluated as part of the concluding chapter of this book.[66]

Arbiter Guardianship   In this pattern the military may not desire to rule, and civilian institutions may be strong enough to maintain at least minimally acceptable levels of public order. However, military elites may from time to time exercise a veto over certain public policy alternatives, or may be sufficiently powerful to determine which civilian politicians shall occupy high positions in the government. The armed forces act indirectly as custodians of the national interest, supporting civilian elites they deem acceptable and setting limits to the policy choices open to government leaders. This situation prevailed, for example, under the Weimar Republic in Germany.[67]

In systems where civilian institutions are considerably weaker and public order threatens to break down, juntas of the arbiter guardian type may actually seize power directly. The rationale for intervention may thus be similar to that given for direct guardianship, but the difference is that arbiters lack the impulse to rule for prolonged periods themselves. They relinquish power to civilians and withdraw to the barracks once stability and order have been restored. This may be because civilian institutions are strong enough to deny legitimacy to military rule, or because a major foreign power exerts pressure for a return to constitutional forms, or simply because a relatively small military establishment (out of concern for its internal cohesion) is unwilling to provide the differentiated roles that military rule would require.

Factional Guardianship   This posture is similar to the arbiter guardianship format, but with the difference that the armed forces are

relatively weak and their institutional boundaries are fragmented. Historically common in Latin America and apparently emerging in some sub-
Saharan African countries, it is a pattern which often sees the armed forces
internally divided along the lines of the predominant cleavages of the
broader society. Factions of the military form coalitions with civilian
groups pursuing compatible interests, sometimes in open conflict with
countercoalitions of civilian and military groups.[68] Ruling coalitions,
mobilizing a preponderance of both the consent and coercion currencies,
are rare. Reigning coalitions prevail, with the result that governments are
denied sufficient power and authority to bring about fundamental changes
in the socioeconomic status quo. Political decay develops as civilian institutions are undermined, not infrequently by civilians themselves. In Peru,
for example, Fernando Belaunde Terry, a contender in the presidential
elections of 1962, publicly solicited military intervention to nullify the
election results when it became clear that he had lost. The armed forces
in such systems often pursue an ambivalent course, attempting on the
one hand to uphold their cohesiveness and corporate interests, but on
the other, torn by factionalism in sympathy with the goals and interests
of particular civilian groups.

In cases where political institutionalization and military political strength are both low compared to the extent and rate of expansion
of social mobilization, a situation of "political vacuum" may develop.[69]
This is the extreme form of political decay, when the social order breaks
down into anarchy analogous to the Hobbesian state of nature. Where
the armed forces are small or their effectiveness is subverted by internal
strife, their coercive resources may not be powerful enough to stem social
disintegration or reimpose more than temporary political stability. Examples might be Zaire between independence in 1960 and General
Mobutu's consolidation of power in 1965, or Nigeria during the period
from January 1966 through the final suppression of the Biafra secession-
ists.[70]

Postcolonial Guardianship   This pattern of military rule
has been characteristic of numerous sub-Saharan African states since 1965.
The urban middle classes in these new states are as yet only slightly
developed by Western standards, and the masses remain essentially unpoliticized. Both political institutionalization and participation are low.
Governmental functions are performed by civil and military bureaucracies trained and left by the European colonizing powers. As they achieved
independence in the late 1950's or early 1960's, many of these systems
attempted to confront the problems of integrating their ethnically fragmented societies and of underdevelopment through single-party mobilization regimes; these were often under charismatic leadership, along the
lines of Nkrumah's Convention People's Party in Ghana.[71] Subsequent
events demonstrated, however, that most of these regimes were poorly

equipped to cope with the pervasive backwardness and persistent primordial loyalties of their societies. Their inadequacy ultimately led to political decay and, in Nkrumah's case, ruinous economic policies and despotism. In 1966 the armed forces intervened to oust his corrupt regime.

Ghanaian officers did not act out of fear of the forces unleashed by the process of social mobilization in their country. Ghana's social structure is quite different from that of, for example, Peru. It is not burdened with an entrenched rural oligarchy, nor has the articulation of demands for change been great from either the urban or rural masses. Throughout sub-Saharan Africa, populist movements of the left have been largely stunted. Ghana's armed forces did not oppose the entry of the masses into the political arena, but neither did they topple Nkrumah in order to implement a program of fundamental structural reforms. The principal thrust of their coup was to restore orderly processes to a social order distorted by misgovernment. Moreover, partly as a result of their continued identification with British military traditions, they did not then perceive themselves as the proper vehicle for government, much less for bringing about fundamental social change.[72] In other words, the African variety of military guardianship appears to be oriented more to true guardianship rather than to preservation of the status quo, while the Latin American often seems the reverse. The net effect of guardian rule in Ghana may thus be progressive. By restoring stability and investor confidence, the military rulers serve the interests of economic development and stimulate the growth of the middle classes. It is perhaps to be anticipated that, with the passage of time, Africa's military politicians may gravitate toward other forms of guardianship or possibly even active reformism, roles that are more characteristic of systems where the middle classes are politically dominant and social mobilization has spread to the countryside.

As Luckham points out, the military in a particular country may be able to adopt a guardian posture similar to one or another of the above variations at one point in time, yet be unable to do so at some other juncture. The politics of military guardianship exacts its costs, both from the military and from society. For the military, intervention in politics generates fragmentation in its institutional boundaries and exacerbates internal cleavages. The initial entry into politics may take place under the loftiest of rationales, but too often the military's custodianship of government degenerates into factionalism, extravagant defense budgets and corporate featherbedding, and social irresponsibility. For the political system as a whole, military guardianship has a debilitating and corrosive effect. In many instances it stifles sorely needed change and reinforces social inequality and injustice. Military guardians may too easily employ their coercive power to seize control of government, but they always can evade bearing full responsibility for their rule—as civilians cannot—by withdrawing to the barracks, leaving matters no better off than before.

Having described the four principal types of military regimes in abstract terms, we turn now to the case studies of civil–military relations in Thailand, Nigeria, Egypt, Peru, and France.

References

1. The term "praetorian," as used here, refers not simply to the presence of a military-based regime, but rather to a system in which "private ambitions are rarely restrained by a sense of public authority or common purpose; the role of power (i.e., wealth and force) is maximized." This is the broad definition offered by David C. Rapoport, "A Comparative Theory of Military and Political Types," in Samuel P. Huntington (ed.), *Changing Patterns of Military Politics* (New York: Free Press, 1962), p. 72.
2. See, for example, A.R. Luckham, "A Comparative Typology of Civil–Military Relations," in *Government and Opposition,* Vol. VI, No. 1 (Winter 1971), pp. 8–9.
3. These four variables have been adapted, with some redefinition, from the analyses in Samuel P. Huntington, *Political Order in Changing Societies* (New Haven: Yale University Press, 1968), pp. 1–92, and from Luckham, "A Comparative Typology of Civil-Military Relations," pp. 5–35. For a discussion of summary variables and their applications, see David Easton, *A Systems Analysis of Political Life* (New York: John Wiley & Sons, 1965), pp. 25–27.
4. See John J. Johnson, *Political Change in Latin America: The Emergence of the Middle Sectors* (Stanford: Stanford University Press, 1958), pp. vii–ix; and Manfred Halpern, *The Politics of Social Change in the Middle East and North Africa* (Princeton: Princeton University Press, 1963), pp. 51–78.
5. J. Roland Pennock, "Political Development, Political Systems, and Political Goods," in *World Politics,* Vol. XVIII, No. 3 (April 1965), pp. 413–434.
6. The term "social mobilization" was introduced by Karl Deutsch, "Social Mobilization and Political Development," *American Political Science Review,* Vol. LV, No. 3 (September 1961), pp. 493–514.
7. Huntington, *Political Order in Changing Societies,* pp. 4, 12.
8. Ibid., p. 196.
9. See Morris Janowitz, *The Military in the Political Development of New Nations: An Essay in Comparative Analysis* (Chicago: University of Chicago Press, 1964), pp. 40–49; Harold D. Lasswell, "The Garrison-State Hypothesis Today," in Huntington (ed.), *Changing Patterns of Military Politics,* pp. 51–70; and Luckham, "A Comparative Typology of Civil-Military Relations," pp. 13–17.

10. Alfred C. Stepan III, *The Military in Politics: Changing Patterns in Brazil* (Princeton: Princeton University Press, 1971), pp. 253–266.

11. Samuel E. Finer, *The Man on Horseback: The Role of the Military in Politics* (New York: Praeger, 1962), pp. 80–83.

12. Arthur K. Smith, *The Peruvian Military Coup D'Etat of 1962: A Crisis in United States-Peruvian Relations,* Master's thesis, University of New Hampshire, 1966, pp. 63–115.

13. See Colonel A.A. Afrifa, *The Ghana Coup, 24th February, 1966* (New York: Humanities Press, 1966), pp. 31–42 and 93–105.

14. On the concepts of "system boundaries" and "interchanges" (transactions), see David Easton, *A Framework for Political Analysis* (Englewood Cliffs: Prentice-Hall, 1965), pp. 59–75.

15. Boundaries may also be analyzed under a third category, i.e., *permeated,* implying that there is no clear demarcation at all between a social organization or procedure and its environment. Luckham employs this category to account for certain quasi-military roles such as those found in premodern and primitive societies and perhaps in some contemporary revolutionary movements, such as Cuba's 26th of July Movement or the National Liberation Front in South Vietnam. See Luckham, "A Comparative Typology of Civil-Military Relations," pp. 25–26. Because our own study deals only with military forces organized as the coercive arm of the state, and not with other types of organizations which may employ coercive resources, we have omitted this category for lack of any contemporary empirical reference.

16. The terms "objective civilian control" and "subjective civilian control" have been adapted from Samuel P. Huntington, *The Soldier and the State: The Theory and Politics of Civil-Military Relations* (New York: Vintage Books, 1957), pp. 80–85.

17. On the relationship between national ideology and military professionalism in reinforcing objective civilian control, see Huntington, *The Soldier and the State,* pp. 85–94.

18. Colonel T.N. Dupuy and Colonel Wendell Blanchard, *The Almanac of World Military Power,* 2nd Ed. (New York: R.R. Bowker, 1972), pp. 216–217, 249–250, and 276–277.

19. Robert D. Tomasek, "Costa Rica," in Ben G. Burnett and Kenneth F. Johnson (eds.), *Political Forces in Latin America: Dimensions of the Quest for Stability,* 2nd Ed. (Belmont: Wadsworth, 1970), pp. 135–136.

20. See Richard E. Feinberg, *The Triumph of Allende: Chile's Legal Revolution* (New York: Mentor Books, 1972), pp. 163–165.

21. Stephen P. Cohen, *The Indian Army: Its Contribution to the Development of a Nation* (Berkeley: University of California Press, 1971).

22. Not all observers would agree that military role expansion in the United States has not overstepped the bounds of civilian control; see Adam Yarmolinsky, *The Military Establishment: Its Impacts on American Society* (New York: Harper & Row, 1971).

23. Edward Bernard Glick, *Soldiers, Scholars, and Society: The Social Impact of the*

American Military (Pacific Palisades: Goodyear, 1971), pp. 9–10.

24. Bengt Abrahamsson, "The Ideology of an Elite: Conservatism and National Insecurity," in Jacques van Doorn (ed.), *Armed Forces and Society: Sociological Essays* (The Hague: Mouton, 1968), pp. 71–83.

25. Morris Janowitz, *The Professional Soldier: A Social and Political Portrait* (Glencoe: The Free Press, 1960), pp. 417–430.

26. C.P. Fitzgerald, "Reflections on the Cultural Revolution in China," in *Pacific Affairs*, Vol. XLI, No. 1 (Spring 1968), pp. 51–59.

27. S. Encel, "The Study of Militarism in Australia," in van Doorn (ed.), *Armed Forces and Society*, pp. 127–147.

28. See William Kornhauser, *The Politics of Mass Society* (New York: The Free Press, 1959).

29. Roman Kolkowicz, "The Dynamics of Party–Military Relations," in *The Soviet Military and the Communist Party* (Princeton: Princeton University Press, 1967), pp. 11–35.

30. Irving Louis Horowitz, "The Political Sociology of Cuban Communism," in Carmelo Mesa-Lago (ed.), *Revolutionary Change in Cuba* (Pittsburgh: University of Pittsburgh Press, 1971), pp. 138–139.

31. On civil–military relations in modern Cuba, see Horowitz, "Political Sociology of Cuban Communism," pp. 127–141; and Andres Suarez, *Cuba: Castroism and Communism, 1959–1966* (Cambridge: The M.I.T. Press, 1967), pp. 196–197, 227–229.

32. The concept of the "Revolutionary Family" is given in Frank R. Brandenburg, *The Making of Modern Mexico* (Englewood Cliffs: Prentice-Hall, 1964), pp. 2–7; on the structure of Mexico's ruling elite, see Brandenburg, pp. 141–165, and also Arthur K. Smith, *Mexico and the Cuban Revolution: Foreign Policy-Making in Mexico Under President Adolfo López Mateos (1958-1964)*, Cornell University, Latin American Studies Program Dissertation Series, No. 17 (September 1970), pp. 20–43.

33. Robert F. Smith et al., *Mexico, 1968* (New York: North American Congress on Latin America, 1968).

34. On the relationship of civilian values and military professionalism, see Rapoport, "A Comparative Theory of Military and Political Types," pp. 77–98.

35. Amos Perlmutter, "The Israeli Army in Politics: The Persistence of the Civilian Over the Military," in *World Politics*, Vol. XX, No. 4 (July 1968), pp. 606–643.

36. See Dupuy and Blanchard, *The Almanac of World Military Power*, pp. 81–82.

37. See Donald N. Levine, "The Military in Ethiopian Politics: Capabilities and Constraints," in Henry Bienen (ed.), *The Military Intervenes: Case Studies in Political Development* (New York: Russell Sage Foundation, 1968), pp. 5–34.

38. Lucian W. Pye, "The Legitimacy Crisis," in Leonard Binder et al., *Crises and Sequences in Political Development* (Princeton: Princeton University Press, 1971), pp. 135–158.

39. On the general concept of political legitimacy, see Reinhard Bendix, *Max Weber: An Intellectual Portrait* (Garden City: Anchor Books, 1962), pp. 294–457.

40. See Warren F. Ilchman and Norman Thomas Uphoff, *The Political Economy of Change* (Berkeley: University of California Press, 1969), pp. 54–55.

41. This interrelationship of consent and coercion is based on the concept of "dual-currency" political regimes given in Eldon Kenworthy, "Coalitions in the Political Development of Latin America," in Sven Groennings et al., *The Study of Coalition Behavior* (New York: Holt, Rinehart and Winston, 1970), pp. 103–140.

42. Kenworthy, "Coalitions in the Political Development of Latin America," p. 129.

43. See Huntington, *Political Order in Changing Societies,* pp. 140–191; C.E. Black, *The Dynamics of Modernization: A Study in Comparative History* (New York: Harper & Row, 1966), pp. 56–94; and Barrington Moore, Jr., *Social Origins of Dictatorship and Democracy: Lord and Peasant in the Making of the Modern World* (Boston: Beacon Press, 1966), pp. 413–483.

44. Charles W. Anderson, *Politics and Economic Change in Latin America: The Governing of Restless Nations* (Princeton: Van Nostrand, 1967), pp. 3–45.

45. The concept of "legitimacy vacuum" is taken from Martin C. Needler, *Latin American Politics in Perspective* (Princeton: Van Nostrand, 1963), pp. 35–39.

46. Edwin Lieuwen, *Arms and Politics in Latin America* (New York: Praeger, 1960), pp. 17–35.

47. Ibid., pp. 102–103.

48. Anderson, *Politics and Economic Change in Latin America,* p. 90.

49. See Lieuwen, *Arms and Politics in Latin America,* pp. 31–35.

50. Huntington, *Political Order in Changing Societies,* pp. 198–208.

51. Victor Alba, *El militarismo: Ensayo sobre un fenómeno político-social iberoamericano* (México, D.F.: Instituto de Investigaciones Sociales, Universidad Nacional Autónoma de México, 1959), pp. 59–70.

52. Martin C. Needler, "Political Development and Military Intervention in Latin America," in *American Political Science Review,* Vol. LX, No. 3 (September 1966), pp. 621–624.

53. This conclusion is generally supported by the empirical findings in Eric A. Nordlinger, "Soldiers in Mufti: The Impact of Military Rule Upon Economic and Social Change in the Non-Western States," in *American Political Science Review,* Vol. LXIV, No. 4 (December 1970), pp. 1131–1148 (see also Part III of this book).

54. See Huntington, *Political Order in Changing Societies,* pp. 72–78.

55. Janowitz, *The Military in the Political Development of New Nations,* p. 65.

56. See Edward Feit, *The Armed Bureaucrats: Military-Administrative Regimes and Political Development* (Boston: Houghton Mifflin, 1973).

57. For accounts of civil–military relations in these countries, see: Jose Luis de Imaz, *Los que mandan* (Buenos Aires: Editorial Universitaria de Buenos Aires, 1964, pp. 45–84; James F. Petras and Robert LaPorte, Jr., *Cultivating Revolution: The United States and Agrarian Reform in Latin America* (New York: Random House, 1971), pp. 253–330 (and our chapter on Peru); R. Hrair Dekmejian, *Egypt Under Nasir: A Study in Political Dynamics*

(Albany: State University of New York Press, 1971); J.C. Hurewitz, *Middle East Politics: The Military Dimension* (New York: Praeger, 1969), pp. 123–162 and our chapter on Egypt.

58. See Dekmejian, *Egypt Under Nasir,* pp. 287–310.

59. See Peter G. Snow, *Political Forces in Argentina* (Boston: Allyn and Bacon, 1971).

60. Huntington, *Political Order in Changing Societies,* p. 221.

61. Jon Kraus, "Arms and Politics in Ghana," in Claude E. Welch, Jr., *Soldier and State in Africa: A Comparative Analysis of Military Intervention and Political Change* (Evanston: Northwestern University Press, 1970), pp. 154–221.

62. See, for example, William H. Brill's discussion of the Bolivian military's "operational code" in the events leading up to the coup d'etat of 1964: *Military Intervention in Bolivia: The Overthrow of Paz Estenssoro and the MNR* (Washington, D.C.: Institute for the Comparative Study of Political Systems, 1967), pp. 29–32.

63. See James Payne, "Peru: The Politics of Structured Violence," in *Journal of Politics,* Vol. XXVII, No. 2 (May 1965), pp. 362–374.

64. These variables combine the major elements of Luckham's and Huntington's approaches to military guardianship, respectively; see Luckham, "A Comparative Typology of Civil–Military Relations," pp. 27–29, and Huntington, *Political Order in Changing Societies,* pp. 219–237.

65. Discussions of civil–military relations in Pakistan, Brazil, and Greece may be found in Herbert Feldman, *Revolution in Pakistan: A Study of the Martial Law Administration* (London: Oxford University Press, 1967); Stepan, *The Military in Politics;* and Andreas Papandreou, *Democracy at Gunpoint: The Greek Front* (Garden City: Doubleday, 1970).

66. Lasswell, "The Garrison-State Hypothesis Today," pp. 51–69.

67. Kurt Lang, "The Military Putsch in a Developed Political Culture: Confrontations of Military and Civil Power in Germany and France," in van Doorn (ed.), *Armed Forces and Society,* pp. 202–228.

68. Luckham, "A Comparative Typology of Civil–Military Relations," pp. 30–33.

69. Ibid., pp. 33–35.

70. See the general treatments of civil–military relations in Africa in Aristide R. Zolberg, "The Structure of Political Conflict in the New States of Tropical Africa," in *American Political Science Review,* Vol. LXII, No. 1 (March 1968), pp. 70–87, and Cluade E. Welch, Jr., "The Roots and Implications of Military Intervention," in Welch, *Soldier and State in Africa,* pp. 1–59.

71. See David E. Apter, *The Politics of Modernization* (Chicago: University of Chicago Press, 1965), pp. 179–222 and 313–390.

72. Robert M. Price, "A Theoretical Approach to Military Rule in New States: Reference-Group Theory and the Ghanaian Case," in *World Politics,* Vol. XXIII, No. 3 (April 1971), pp. 426–427.

The Military in Politics: Five Case Studies

The second section of this book focuses on five states, each distinct in its historical background and political development, but all characterized by extensive military involvement in politics.

Case studies are central to comparative politics. General observations, propositions, typologies, and other academic paraphernalia of Part I can serve as useful means of analysis only if linked to the "real" world. Part II provides the empirical test to our overall formulations. In Part III, we shall use our knowledge of concrete events to reformulate these observations.

The countries we shall consider come from four continents and the Middle East. In terms of economic development, they range from per capita gross national products of $105 per year (Nigeria) to $2904 (France). Some are relatively homogeneous, with long histories of political independence; others experienced colonial rule within the past two centuries. Yet all have been governed by military regimes, which seized power as the result of some of the factors we examined in Part I.

We shall study Egypt, France, Nigeria, Peru, and Thailand as examples of the classifications we have just formulated. For an example of a predatory regime, we turn to Thailand; under continual military rule since

1932, save for a few brief interludes, Thailand seems an unlikely candidate for reduction of the armed forces' political dominance. As an example of a reform regime, we examine the Federal Military Government of Nigeria, in power since 1966. Two states illustrate radical regimes and the pressures that lead toward the emergence of subjective civilian control or of military guardianship: Egypt under Nasser achieved international repute for the dramatic socioeconomic alterations proposed, particularly for his attempts to mobilize peasants; however, the present Sadat government seems far more in the guardian mold. The post-1968 military government of Peru has proclaimed itself the leader of social revolution—a proclamation that has not, however, led the regime to encourage political mobilization. There is no military regime now in France, nor is military intervention of the 1958 style currently likely. On the other hand, French history, especially the 1958 coup, illustrates several ways of achieving civilian control over the armed forces. The guardian-type efforts of French military leaders during the Algerian war illustrate how industrialized states with a heritage of the military's political subordination may nonetheless fall victim to overt intervention.

4

Thailand: Predatory Military Rule
in a Bureaucratic Polity

The shadow of military intervention has long lingered over Thailand. Since the thirteenth century, members of the armed forces have never been far removed from political power. The coup d'etat of 1932 ratified officers as the supreme decision makers in Thai society, though they cloaked their dominance within the traditional authority of the monarch. This pattern remains unchanged in its basic outline to this day.

Despite occasional forays back to civilian rule, Thailand is a praetorian political system, in which military factions and personal rivalries constitute the crucial factors in governmental change. Intervention has resulted in predatory regimes. Although professionalism has increased within the officer corps, factionalism remains endemic. As for the populace, political participation is low, and the appeal of the monarchy is strong. Accordingly, various shortlived civilian governments have failed to change the political primacy of the armed forces. Government in Thailand is a combination of military power, self-serving bureaucracies, and traditional authority—which forms a distinctive pattern of predatory military rule.

On November 17, 1971, the Royal Thai Army ended Thailand's most recent experiment in parliamentary government by summarily abolishing the three-year-old constitution and replacing both the parliament and cabinet with a military-dominated junta.[1] The coup was executed with precision and without bloodshed. Fewer than fifty soldiers and four tanks surrounded the parliament building. Other troops and police occupied or posted sentries around the radio stations and key government buildings. The great bulk of the Thai populace responded with apathy to the announcement that the Revolutionary Party (*Khana Pathiwat*), a military-based clique organized by the late Field Marshal Sarit Thanarat, had made the country "again secure." A small minority of students and intellectuals struggled to organize opposition to the coup, but the junta quickly imposed martial law and prohibited political meetings of more than four persons. Businessmen and civil servants generally supported the military, apparently hoping that strong leadership would dispel the aura of uncertainty and drift that had characterized Thailand under the democratic institutions created by the 1968 constitution.

In effect the coup turned the Thai political clock back at least a decade and a half, returning to official power the same group of military officials who had controlled the country from 1957 through 1968. The new junta was headed by Field Marshal Thanom Kittikachorn, who had become prime minister in December 1963 and had retained the post even during the period of parliamentary rule. General Praphat Charusathien, commander in chief of the army and reputed to be the most powerful man in Thailand, continued in *de facto* control of the Ministries of Interior and Defense. The coup, one of many in the military's long history of involvement in Thai politics, merely struck down the facade of civilian parliamentary rule that had briefly masked the real power relationships of the country. King Bhumibol, Thailand's reigning monarch and chief of state, was informed of the impending coup only hours before the event. The king did not oppose the coup in any overt manner, but he did not bestow his official royal pardon for the conspirators and his relations with them remained correct but cool.

The coup developed from a complex of factors. The military's announced justification focused on the recent entry into the United Nations of the People's Republic of China, and on the possible effects China's re-emergence into world politics might have on Thailand's three million ethnic Chinese. Economically powerful but politically passive, this huge Chinese minority posed a potential domestic threat should China seek to restore her historic hegemony in Southeast Asia.[2] Moreover, Thai military leaders had been growing increasingly restive over their country's tightening alliance with the United States, and particularly over the expanding American presence in Thailand as a consequence of the Vietnam war. The Thai army was engaged in a prolonged campaign of its own against communist insurgents in the northeastern part of the country. The progressive American withdrawal from Vietnam, coupled with concern over the Nixon doctrine (to the effect that Asian wars should be fought by Asians) and President Nixon's approaching trip to Peking, had given rise to a debate in the parliament over the desirability of seeking an accommodation with China. Apart from these foreign policy and security concerns, however, the coup appeared to be directed primarily at reversing the disturbing—to the military, at least—trend toward civilian parliamentary rule.

The tension between the military leadership and reformist civilian politicians had become acute. The implementation of the 1968 constitution had given rise to a "one hundred flowers" period, marked by heightened expectations for civilian political participation and civil liberties.[3] Some parliament members who belonged to the governing United Thai People's Party (UTPP) had recently dared to threaten obstruction of a supplemental appropriation for the army unless the cabinet doubled the members' annual allowances for vote-winning public works projects in their home provinces. The parliament had also begun to threaten bureaucratic privileges heretofore sacrosanct in Thailand, giving rise to military charges that its members were intervening too much in the administrative process. The judiciary was showing signs of independence, and Bangkok's newspapers were venturing sharply critical editorial judgments of Prime Minister Thanom's domestic policies. Moreover, the democratic institutions were widely blamed for the country's rapidly rising crime rate. After three years the military had had enough of participatory politics and were determined to return Thailand to authoritarian rule.

The coup was fundamentally the result of Thailand's factional political system and the desire of the armed forces to protect their own power base from erosion by the nascent civilian political institutions.[4] The Royal Thai Army had been the dominant political force in the country since the overthrow of monarchic rule in 1932. Over the past four decades Thai politics had been developing in the context of a "bureaucratic polity," a system of governance by administrative officials essentially in their own behalf.[5] Both civil service and military officials were accustomed to making policy decisions on their own terms, with little regard for popular wishes and needs. Real decision-making power rested in the hands of top-ranking military leaders, who usually enjoyed the support of both the civil service and the king. One of the more remarkable elements of this arrangement has been the linkage of military rule with traditional monarchical authority. This unusual combination has meant that the military politicians share the awe, deference, and legitimacy of the Thai monarchy. Cloaked by this mantle of legitimization, a succession of military rulers has been able to govern Thailand since 1932 relatively free of extrabureaucratic constraints. Civilian political demands have remained poorly articulated and uncoordinated. In view of the extreme political weakness of civilian groups outside the government bureaucracy, Thailand's political development has taken place within the context of a closed bureaucratic framework that is particularly conducive to military domination.

Three great military coups have shaped Thai politics in the twentieth century, those of 1932, 1947, and 1957. Others, including that of November 1971, have been of lesser consequence and have served generally to consolidate the state of affairs established by one or another of these three major turning points.

The Thai Military in Historical Perspective

The nation of Thailand—known as Siam until 1939—has a military officer corps that began in the formative years of the Thai kingdom, the thirteenth century. These roots are identical with those of the civil service, for the emergence of differentiated roles marking a professionalized military is relatively recent. During the four centuries of the Thai Kingdom of Ayudhia, which preceded the founding of the present Chakri dynasty in 1782, all officials were also soldiers in times of military threat. No warrior class as such existed. However, prowess in the military arts was highly valued and officials who demonstrated their mastery were granted distinctive titles and honors. Military leaders were elevated to important political positions subordinate to the king. These traditions thus underlie the relatively professional, yet highly politicized officer corps of contemporary Thailand.[6]

Shortly after the first Chakri monarch had ascended the throne, Thailand came under severe pressure from European colonizers. To the west, Burma, a traditional rival and nearly constant foe in war, was gradually subjugated by the British. To the east the French began their conquest of present-day Vietnam, Laos, and Cambodia. The Chakri kings responded at first with isolationist policies, closing even the doors of trade against the merchant adventurers of Europe. Finally, however, they recognized the need to accommodate themselves to European imperialism. Thai independence was ultimately preserved, partly as a result of skillful Thai diplomacy but also because Britain and France came to recognize the country's usefulness as a buffer state between their respective colonies.

The closed-door policy followed by the first three Chakri sovereigns was reversed by the fourth, the far-sighted King Mongkut (1851–1868). Mongkut recognized and appreciated the technological superiority of the West and resolved to adapt to it rather than attempt to perpetuate his traditional society. The changes he introduced were designed to achieve "defensive modernization," i.e., preservation of Thai social structure and traditions alongside the modern reforms necessary to protect Thailand's independence.[7] He negotiated treaties formalizing relations with

Britain and France, opened the country to commerce with the West, and initiated reforms designed to enable his bureaucracy to adapt to modernizing change. However, it was under Mongkut's son and successor, King Chulalongkorn (1868–1910), that the most sweeping changes took place. The entire bureaucracy was overhauled, and the traditional feudalistic officialdom gave way to new organizations based on Western administrative principles. Foreign technicians were brought in to advise in the restructuring of the legal system, in the rationalization of government finances, and to a lesser extent in the modernization of the armed forces and police. The king's rule was extended into upcountry provinces where local chieftains had until then been virtually sovereign, and dynastic claims to the ethnically non-Thai border territories were yielded to the European empires. The Thai kingdom was thus consolidated, and power within it was tightly centralized. Unlike their less fortunate neighbors, the Thais were able to enter the modern era with their traditional authority symbols intact and without the traumas of colonial rule.[8]

Under Chulalongkorn a corps of professional officers was created and the military became an institution differentiated from the remainder of the royal bureaucracy. Both an army and a navy were formed with highly centralized organizational structures. The corporate identity of the officer corps was rooted in the country's military traditions as an imperial power. Its expertise was nurtured by an enlightened ruler determined to emulate Western military science, and its sense of social responsibility rested in its loyalty to the absolute monarch whose modernizing goals and pride in the Thai nation the officers shared. But although military professionalization made great strides forward under King Chulalongkorn, no tradition of an apolitical military developed along with it. A form of subjective civilian control existed: military institutional autonomy and potential for expanding its political role were limited by dynastic controls, and Chakri princes remained at the center of the reorganized and modernized armed forces. By royal law in 1905, the crown prince was made commander in chief of the army. The Thai kings made no attempt to establish separate spheres of authority for civil and military officials, and hence there were few areas of public policy in which military leaders could not assert influence if they wished. This blending of political and military roles was manifest in the creation in 1912 of the Council of National Defense, a body headed by King Wachirawut (1910–1925) whose deliberations drew no distinction between military and civil affairs.[9]

In the twentieth century the Royal Thai Army became the focus of national pride and the showcase of the country's modernization (as was the case in Egypt; see Chapter 7 on Egypt). Thailand joined the Allies in World War I, sending a token expeditionary force to France. The government was able to point to its participation in the war effort in the 1920's when it succeeded in negotiating revisions of its treaties with the major European powers.[10] Thus the foreign policy advantages of a strong military establishment made a lasting impression on Thai political leaders. The army successfully used its growing leverage to press for an ever-increasing share of the national budget, often at the expense of the king's plans for the development of Thailand's natural resources.[11]

Through the 1920's and early 1930's the armed forces continued to develop as a powerful pressure group. As their own institutional identity became more clearly defined, their conflicting loyalty to the institution of the monarchy became openly questioned. A gulf began to widen between the two, foreshadowed as early as 1915 by an abortive coup staged by high-ranking officers who were also commoners. The king and his princes successfully put down the revolt, but even within the royal family the competing institutional loyalties were evident. At one point Prince Bowaradet resigned as Defense Minister when the Council of National Defense refused to approve new budgetary appropriations for the army. Such events were outward symptoms of the officers' deeper frustrations; they were laying the foundation for the coup d'etat of 1932, which established the military as the dominant actor in Thai politics.

The breach between the Thai monarchy and the military is illustrative of the dilemma faced by traditional monarchs who seek both to preserve their authority and to modernize their countries.[12] Modernization involves the centralization of political power in order to advance needed social and economic reforms. To the extent that the monarch's efforts to centralize power are successful, however, the more difficult becomes the task of integrating the new groups created by his reforms into the traditional authority structure he seeks to preserve. In Thailand's case, the Chakri kings used their highly centralized power to promote the sweeping reforms they considered necessary for accommodation to the West. These reforms produced a Westernized and heavily Western-educated civil service and military officer corps, whose growing autonomy as social organizations gave them corporate identities and interests increasingly distinct from those of the monarchy. Many young Thais returned from university or technical training in the West infused with resentment of royal absolutism. They took up positions in the civil and military bureaucracies, but their frustrations grew as the king tried to maintain his personal authority and control by keeping princes in all the highest positions.[13] During the nineteenth century and the early decades of the twentieth, when the principal tasks of government were the safeguarding of Thai independence and the advancement of modernizing reforms, the political interests of the monarch and the bureaucracies had been compatible. Once the administrative reforms had been consolidated, however, and especially after continued independence seemed assured by the renegotiation of treaties in the aftermath of World War

I, bureaucratic pressures for expanded roles in political decision making began seriously to undermine royal authority.[14]

Despite the rumblings of bureaucratic discontent, King Prachatipok (1925–1934) insisted that the royal family's monopoly of senior positions be preserved. The Great Depression of the 1930's served to catalyze the broad antimonarchist resentments among civil and military officials. For economy, the king resorted to cutbacks in both personnel and salary levels of the civil service and the armed forces (often a precipitating element in military coups d'etat; note proposition 7, Chapter 2). This abrupt halt to the decades-long pattern of lavishing favors on the bureaucracies finally led to the coup of June 24, 1932, in which a small group of military and civilian conspirators succeeded in the bloodless termination of the absolute monarchy.

The "promoters" of the 1932 coup consisted of three elite factions whose subsequent internecine struggles and realignments were to shape Thai politics over the next four decades. One faction comprised senior military officers led by Colonel Phraya Phahon Phonphayuhasena, who later became prime minister of the new government organized by the promoters' so-called "People's Party." Colonel Phahon, a competent officer who had received military training in Germany, had risen to the highest level attainable by a commoner in the Royal Thai Army. Those above him were members of the royal family, who Phahon felt were much less expert than he in military science and who tended to slight his advice.[15] For Phahon and his colleagues, the Chakri dynasty had offended both their professional pride and their personal ambitions. This group of senior officers lent the prestige of the military institution to the coup effort, but their goals were much more limited and their outlook more conservative than those of their two allies.

The second group was made up of civilian officials led by Pridi Phanomyong, who had received the degree of Doctor of Law from the Sorbonne in Paris. Members of this group also felt professional frustrations under the royal family monopoly, but for them the coup had a certain ideological dimension as well. Mostly educated in France, they sought a system of state socialism and a virtual bureaucratization of Thai society. The coup had apparently been in the planning for years among Thai students in Paris, but these students evidently recognized no serious contradictions in their cooperating with the military to overthrow the monarchy. Though infatuated with Western political forms and ideas, their purpose was not to organize and lead Western-style political parties as the vehicle for Thai political development. Nor had they become committed to the principle of civilian supremacy in political matters. Despite their espousal of a limited monarchy and socialization of the economy, the civilian promoters of the coup constituted a small group with little support outside the civil service and among certain of

the younger military officers. In any event, the societal base to support
a political party system was lacking. Few autonomous interest groups
or organizations existed outside the government bureaucracy. The urban
middle classes were small and politically inconsequential, and the mobilization of Thailand's traditionally passive masses was out of the question.
It seems implausible, therefore, as Riggs observes, that this group really
sought to establish effective organs of parliamentary government. Their
subsequent actions lend support to Riggs' conclusion that their purposes did not extend beyond aggrandizement of their own bureaucratic
power base.[16]

The third group was composed of younger military officials who
shared to some extent the ideological convictions of their civilian allies,
but who also shared with their senior colleagues a deep concern for the
preservation and growth of the military as an institution. The most prominent among them was Phibun Songkhram, later both a field marshal of
the Royal Thai Army and prime minister. Phibun received his advanced
education in France, and was among the Paris group who were the ideological progenitors of the 1932 coup. These three groups, collectively
known as the "promoters," formed the elite that gradually overcame royalist opposition during the unstable post-coup months of 1932-1933. Despite frequent quarrels and factional reshufflings, and despite the later
divergence of interests between the civilian and military elements, real
political power remained in the hands of this small bureaucratic elite
and their political heirs through the late 1950's.

Although the promoters promulgated a manifesto denouncing
the monarchy in the most scathing terms, they did not really seek to
abolish it outright. They and King Prachatipok agreed to a constitution
organizing the Thai polity as a limited monarchy, under which the king
remained head of state. Legislative and executive authority both rested
in a parliamentary Assembly of People's Representatives. The People's
Party leaders appointed themselves as the members of the Assembly and
organized a Council of Ministers to carry out the Assembly's policies.
The first prime minister, however, was a civilian judge who had not been
a conspirator but who sympathized broadly with the coup's objectives.

The military did not clearly dominate the first government
following the 1932 coup. Civilians comprised 54 of the 70 members of
the Assembly, holding the premiership and controlling the Council of
Ministers. But the People's Party was not really a party in the strict sense.
It had been able to generate no organized support outside the government and was really no more than a faction of the combined military
and civil bureaucracies. Its members, individually and as a group, did
not seek to develop an extrabureaucratic power base capable of imposing control over the government. As bureaucrats, they conceived of
political power in terms of official positions.[17] Still, had they remain-

ed unified with the king as their ally, Dr. Pridi's civilian group might have become the dominant force in the new government. Almost immediately following the coup, however, their unity was sundered. The younger, more radical promoters chafed under the leadership of the older, more established civil servants who had been brought in to lend an aura of respectability to the regime.[18] With the publication of Pridi's controversial Economic Plan of 1933, a document calling for the nationalization of all land and industry, which immediately gave rise to cries of Bolshevism, the growing schism between the civilian radicals and Colonel Phahon's group of conservative senior military officers finally led to a crisis.[19]

The tumult that followed the release of Pridi's plan was seized upon by the civilian prime minister, who was no ally of Pridi, as a justification for dissolving the Assembly and ruling by decree. Communism was formally outlawed and Pridi was forced into exile. However, the prime minister's decisive actions were viewed as threatening the interests of the promoters as a group. The military commanders under Phahon engineered a consolidating coup and regained control over the government for the People's Party.[20] In effect the military assumed an arbiter guardianship role in this 1933 coup, opposing both Pridi's radical economic plans for the country and the highhanded methods used by the prime minister. These events signaled the new central role of the military in the People's Party coalition.

After June 1933 the combined military and civil service bureaucracies emerged in control of the government, but their rule was fundamentally amoral. No outside groups were powerful enough to impose sanctions against irresponsible and unresponsive governors, hence the bureaucracies were able to function mainly in service of their own selfish interests. The boundaries of the Thai political system thus coincided, for practical purposes, with those of the government and the bureaucracies. The passivity of the Thai people made irrelevant the political currency of popular consent. Within the tightly closed bureaucratic polity there was now no political force capable of countering the military's coercive resources. The new rules of the political game were simple: given the factional basis of intrabureaucratic politics, whichever clique commanded the alliance of the military would control the vital coercion currency and hence the government.

The Phahon government (1933–1938) depended on a delicate balance between the military and civilian promoter groups, since the officer corps remained politically fragmented. During this period, however, control over the military inexorably shifted from the hands of Phahon and his supporters to those of the younger and more radical military promoters, led by Colonel Phibun. Phibun had been an instrumental figure in the consolidating coup of 1933. He had distinguished himself once again in October of that same year in the suppression of an abortive monarchist rebellion.[21] On the basis of these accomplishments and through his own considerable skill in factional politics, Phibun became minister of defense under Phahon in 1934 and proceeded to launch a vigorous program of development for the armed forces. Military appropriations doubled during Phibun's tenure. Through a concerted public relations campaign he embellished the image of the armed forces, portraying them as the indispensable protectors of the nation and the chief symbol of national honor. While doing all this, Phibun carefully built a decisive personal constituency within the officer corps. By 1938 the influence of his *khana,* or clique, so surpassed that of his rivals that he was able without visible struggle to assume the premiership upon the voluntary retirement of General Phahon.[22]

Phibun's regime was characterized by an extreme and militaristic nationalism, patterned to some extent after the models of Germany, Italy, and Japan. His policies glorified the Thai nation, using as a whipping boy Thailand's Chinese minority and later directing nationalist feeling against the French in Indochina.[23] Phibun's principal problems, however, were in coping with Japanese ambitions for empire in Southeast Asia. On the eve of the Pearl Harbor attack, Thai relations with Japan were cordial (a friendship treaty between the two countries had been concluded in December 1940), but Thailand's strategic location made Phibun's diplomatic situation a difficult one. The Japanese coveted Thailand as an invasion route to Burma and Malaya. Precisely as Japanese planes were bombing Pearl Harbor, Japanese troops invaded Thailand by land and sea and presented an ultimatum: collaborate with Japan's imperial strategy, or fight.

Confronted by overwhelming odds, Phibun chose to follow the Chakri tradition of accommodation rather than resistance, in order to preserve as much Thai independence as possible. His government accepted Japanese occupation of Thailand and later declared war on the Allies. Despite the presence of Japanese troops, Phibun managed to preserve a wide latitude of control over domestic affairs. The wartime situation greatly expanded the role of the military in the government, especially because many civilians—including Dr. Pridi, who became the leader of the anti-Axis underground—resigned or were ousted from their official positions. The People's Party ultimately became a political casualty of the war. The balance between civilian and military influence in the government, upset by the consolidating coup of 1933, now became weighted in overwhelming favor of the armed forces.[24]

By 1944 it was clear that Japan would lose the war and that Thailand would soon be forced to placate a different set of foreign powers. Even among the officer corps, Phibun's continued leadership was recognized as a liability in Thailand's dealings with the victorious Allies. There was thus little overt army opposition when Dr. Pridi and others succeeded in engineering his overthrow. Phibun was replaced as prime minister by a respected but politically uncommitted civilian, Khuang Aphaiwong.

The war ended before the Allies were obliged to invade Thailand, and once more Thai independence was preserved by the diplomatic dexterity of her leaders. Dr. Pridi emerged in the forefront of the Free Thai movement. His war record of underground activities made him acceptable to the Allies, but still the British argued that Thailand, as an Axis collaborator, should be occupied and her armed forces dismantled. However, the United States suspected the British of postwar imperialist designs in Southeast Asia and refused to agree to an occupation. Thailand was obliged to return the territories won as Japan's ally in Indochina, Burma, and Malaya, and she had to accept an Allied order to make war reparations in rice.[25] The war left civilians in apparent political control, but stability hinged on an uneasy truce between the royalists and Pridi's more liberal supporters. Despite their tarnished public image, the armed forces were undiminished in strength and, even more significantly, the officer corps was left virtually intact.

With the old People's Party in ruins, postwar politics developed as a struggle for dominance among three principal groups: (1) the military, in which Field Marshal Phibun still exercised considerable personal influence; (2) a civilian faction initially under the leadership of Dr. Pridi, based primarily in the civil service and the rejuvenated parliament; and (3) a second civilian faction, less powerful but highly prestigious, composed largely of supporters of the monarchy and led by Khuang Aphaiwong.[26]

The political resurgence of Dr. Pridi and his civilian faction was brief. Thailand's postwar economic situation was precarious, domestic political maneuvering was intense, and corruption had become rampant. In January 1946, new parliamentary elections were held under a revised constitution, a provision of which prohibited permanent government officials (including military officers) from holding political office. This was an attempt to establish civilian political dominance over the armed forces by legal means. It was not backed, however, by adequate legal or political sanctions, and thus was quite ineffective (though it remained part of the three constitutions in force during 1946–1951).[27] The 1946 elections provided the Pridi faction a substantial majority in the new bicameral parliament, but his government never really got off the ground. In June the young King Ananda Mahidol was assassinated under mysterious circumstances that led to charges of regicide against Pridi. His resignation from the government left Thailand in a highly unstable political situation.

On November 8, 1947, army leaders made their move to regain control over the government. The coup was led by Field Marshal Phin, then commander in chief of the army, but the conspirators found it necessary to bring in Marshal Phibun at the last moment in order to ensure military unity behind the coup action. The weakened civilian regime was quickly toppled. However, perhaps in fear of adverse international reactions to the coup, its perpetrators stopped short of establishing outright a military regime. The royalist group of Khuang Aphaiwong agreed to form an interim government pending new elections.

The coup was justified by its leaders (Wilson lists the 36 leading figures as 33 army officers, 2 air force officers, and 1 police officer) as necessary to "exonerate the honor of the army which had been trampled under foot."[28] The officers deeply resented Pridi's efforts to assert civilian control over the military. Pridi's constitutional provisions to prevent renewed political participation by officers could be circumvented, but his efforts to dismantle the Phibun clique within the army constituted a fundamental threat to the military's internal autonomy.[29] Political influence was by this time considered a "right" of the armed forces. Civilian interference in army internal affairs, on the other hand, was viewed as intolerable.

Before the new government of Khuang Aphaiwong could establish itself, Phibun's followers organized a consolidating coup of their own on April 6, 1948, and Phibun himself returned to power as prime minister. The Thai military establishment remained politically fragmented, however. The dominant Phibun clique was opposed by a substantial minority of the army officer corps, and much of the navy and marines were also in opposition. In the eyes of many younger army officers, the Phibun group had been discredited by its wartime policies. Senior naval and marine officers were closely aligned with the civilian faction led by Dr. Pridi. These intra- and interservice rivalries prevented Phibun from consolidating his power within the armed forces, which in turn necessitated restraint in Phibun's handling of his civilian opponents. Parliament continued meeting and was controlled by a cautious but threatening majority of Khuang Aphaiwong's Democrat Party.

Phibun's inability to legitimize his new regime in the eyes of the armed forces themselves made for a three-year period of extraordinary political instability. In October 1948 several officers of the army general staff were arrested by Phibun's security forces and convicted of fomenting a rebellion. February 1949 saw an open revolt in Bangkok by marines, apparently in an attempt to restore Pridi to power.[30] In June 1951 a group of navy and marine conspirators actually succeeded in kidnapping Phibun, setting off three days of heavy interservice fighting (Phibun managed to escape and the army's superior forces finally suppressed the revolt).[31] Although he continued as prime minister through 1957, Phibun was never able to regain the power he had lost as a result of the war. He found himself increasingly dependent on two younger and emerging leaders, General Phao Siyanon and General Sarit Thanarat. Each had been a participant in the coup group of 1948. Phao was also the son-in-law of Field Marshal Phin, the army commander, and thus was linked to a group with substantial army support as well as power in the commercial and business sectors. Moreover, as commanders respectively of the police and of the Bangkok army garrison, Generals Phao and Sarit together controlled the forces most strategically vital to Phibun's hold on power.

With the support of Phao and Sarit, Phibun gradually managed to subdue overt opposition to his regime within the military establishment. By late 1951 his military support was sufficiently consolidated to permit him to move decisively against his civilian opposition in parliament. Under the revised constitution written by the royalists, which entered into force in January 1949, a bicameral legislative body was established whose composition was for the first time in Thai history free of direct control by the prime minister. The lower house was elected completely by universal adult suffrage (rather than appointed by the prime minister), while the new upper house was appointed by the king. The principal effect of this new arrangement was to make the Phibun government dependent on the parliament. The majority Democrat Party exercised caution in its relations with Phibun but still dared, for example, to vote down the government's budgetary legislation for 1950 and 1951. Phibun perceived the authority of parliament as an irritating constraint on his executive prerogatives. In November 1951, he employed his consolidated military support to announce the suspension of the revised constitution and the restoration of the constitution of 1932. Parliament was dissolved and a new unicameral House of People's Representatives was appointed with an overwhelming majority of military officers. From this point in time through the end of the Phibun regime in 1957, parliamentary democracy was a facade covering direct rule by the military.[32]

Phibun justified his move against parliament by asserting the need for stronger powers in the face of an alleged communist threat. In 1950 Phibun had adopted anticommunism as the keystone of his domestic and international policies. A military assistance pact was signed in that year with the United States, and Thailand agreed to send a contingent of troops to Korea. The civil wars then going on in Burma and Malaya, and especially the active roles of the Chinese minorities in those countries, contributed significantly to Phibun's anticommunist drive. Thailand's own Chinese minority was subjected to various restrictions, but Phibun used anticommunism as a cloak to cover his repression of all opposition to his regime. Internationally, Phibun's recognition of the Bao Dai government in Vietnam and of the semiautonomous governments in Cambodia and Laos marked the further movement of Thailand into the protective orbit of the United States.[33]

Between 1951 and 1957, Thai politics was dominated by the interaction of the three cliques headed by Phibun, Phao, and Sarit.[34]

As time passed Phibun found himself in the position of balancer between his two ambitious subordinates, playing one off against the other. General Phao, as director of police and leader of the government party's parliamentary organization, became the head of a complex political faction with important ties to the business community. Field Marshal Sarit, as commander in chief of the army after 1954, gradually built up his own personal following within the armed forces in competition with the Phao faction. Phibun's personal support among the military continued to decline, partly as a result of executive responsibilities that drew his attention away from the decisive arena of military internal politics. Phibun became increasingly dependent on United States diplomatic support to maintain his authority as part of this triumvirate. When Phibun, partly to improve his domestic political position, attempted to return to a more traditional "Siamese" policy of accommodation toward China in the wake of the Bandung Conference, his American support began to wane. Sarit ultimately took advantage of this and of the more generalized military dissatisfaction with Phibun's policies, especially in the wake of controversial parliamentary elections in February 1957 and widespread student protests against electoral fraud. Sarit's coup d'etat of September 17, 1957, succeeded in ousting both Phibun and Phao and heralded a return to a more benevolent but absolutist military rule.[35]

Sarit held new elections in December 1957 to legitimize his newly formed parliamentary faction, which comprised mostly military officers. However, poor health prevented Sarit himself from assuming the post of prime minister. His deputy commander of the army, General (later Field Marshal) Thanom Kittikachorn, took over the government as Sarit left the country for medical care abroad. The Thanom government proved ineffective as Thailand's economic situation worsened during the following year. With Sarit away, his coalition of military officers fell into factional disputes. Finally, in October 1958, Sarit returned to reassert his leadership. General Thanom stepped aside, the constitution was suspended, and Sarit assumed dictatorial powers.

Sarit appointed a new parliamentary assembly in January 1959 and charged it with drafting a new constitution (a task finally completed nearly ten years later, in June 1968). Primarily, however, he used the parliament as a device to legitimize his policies. As prime minister, Sarit enjoyed the broadest discretionary powers of any ruler since the end of absolute monarchy in 1932. Political opposition was severely repressed. Military officers dominated not only the parliament but also the middle and upper middle levels of the government bureaucracy. Sarit justified his extraordinary executive powers by pointing to the growing instability in neighboring Laos and Cambodia, and he reaffirmed Thailand's commitment to anticommunism. The following year, 1960, the government promulgated a broadly conceived plan for national economic development. Sarit claimed in a 1961 address to parliament that through a broadening of educational opportunities and the growth and diversification of the economy, his government would establish the necessary foundations for a future democratic system.[36] In fact, Sarit contributed substantially to Thai modernization in several areas. He overhauled the administrative structure of the government, pushed projects to develop Thailand's industrial infrastructure (hydroelectric dams, highways, port facilities, etc.), reduced the country's dependence on exports of rice and rubber, and cracked down on criminals, beggars, and prostitutes. He also reorganized the national educational system, extending compulsory education to seven years (previously four), and launched a slum clearance program in Bangkok.[37] Despite these advances, little progress was made toward the "future democratic system" Sarit had promised. Civilian political institutions remained backward, and the social and economic inequalities of Thai society actually increased.

Field Marshal Sarit died in 1963 and Thanom Kittikachorn succeeded to the post of prime minister. Control of the government remained firmly in the hands of the group of promoters of the 1957 coup, and the fundamental policy directions established by Sarit were maintained. Perhaps partly as a result of the growing United States military presence in Thailand with the expansion of the war in Vietnam, perhaps also in deference to the wishes of King Bhumibol (whose political influence had greatly increased under the Sarit regime), Thanom consented in 1968 to another of the periodic experiments with parliamentary democracy that have interspersed the more absolutist military regimes since 1932. A new constitution was promulgated in 1968 (Thailand's eighth since the overthrow of the absolute monarchy) calling for a bicameral legislature with a popularly elected lower house. In elections held in February 1969, the Thanom group's United Thai People's Party (UTPP) won 35 percent of the seats and another 33 percent was won by independents, many of whom sympathized with the UTPP. Thanom thus retained the premiership. His government awarded six lesser cabinet posts to civilians, following the established pattern of military co-optation of senior civil service officials, but the other six more important cabinet portfolios went to military and police officers. Apart from new parliamentary limitations on Thanom's former discretionary powers, little of substance was changed by the implementation of the 1968 constitution. The military leadership continued to run the country, and it was plain that Thailand's latest experiment in parliamentary government would survive only through their tolerance.

Sources of Military Political Strength

In 1966 the Thai military establishment was estimated to consist of some 95,000 officers and men, organized within the four services of army, navy, air force, and marines. The army is overwhelmingly dominant with some 85,000 of the total. Its forces are strategically distributed throughout the country, but by far the most important are those stationed in and around Bangkok. Although the national police force performs a political role in support of military rule, the Bangkok army garrison controls the great preponderance of coercive resources that can be quickly deployed for decisive political effect. Command of the Bangkok garrison is therefore a position of great political importance, and the commander in chief of the army usually ensures that the garrison remains politically reliable. It is partly for this reason that Thanom's deputy prime minister, General Praphat Charusathien, who was also commander in chief of the army, minister of the interior, and commander of the Communist Suppression Operations Command (CSOC), has been generally considered for the past decade to be the most powerful figure in Thai politics. Like other former army chiefs who ascended to the position of prime minister, Thanom forfeited a considerable measure of his own direct personal influence over the armed forces when his attentions became focused on national administrative and political matters.

The four services are organized for general administrative and logistical purposes under the Ministry of Defense, but each retains individual autonomy over internal matters. The Ministry of Defense is dominated by the army, which far overshadows the navy, air force, and marines in influence over the budgetary process. Neither constitutional provisions nor Thai political traditions proscribe military officers from holding nonmilitary positions within the government bureaucracy. Military influence is thus exerted directly through officer–bureaucrats in virtually every department of the civil service, in middle as well as top ranks. As a rule, an infiltration of the civil service on a similar scale has occurred in all military regimes of more than guardian status. However, despite its dominance over government decision making, the Thai military's share of the gross national product (GNP) is estimated at only 2.8 percent (compared to 3.1 percent for Peru and 11.6 percent for Egypt).[38] This figure may be somewhat misleading, since the Thai Ministry of Defense also operates the principal industrial enterprises that supply the armed forces, i.e., uniforms, canned foods, shoes, as well as the distribution systems for these and other products. The Ministry also participates as a shareholder in the Military Bank, which is considered a private commercial enterprise, and operates a majority of the commercial radio stations in Thailand.[39]

The present Thai defense establishment shows many of the characteristics of a true "military–industrial complex," a burgeoning conglomerate that appears responsible only to its own directives and inner logic. The Ministry of Defense is almost completely autonomous in its operations. Its budgetary allocations are given in gross figures without itemization. No independent agency exists to oversee its accounting procedures, and virtually all ministry officials are officers subject to military discipline.[40] Moreover, the military has interpenetrated the Thai business community to an extraordinary degree. The "promoter" groups identified with the great coups d'etat (1932, 1947, and 1957) have been heavily represented on the boards of directors of the principal business corporations of the country. The cross-representation of the various cliques (People's Party, Phibun, and Sarit groups in particular) on business boards is demonstrated empirically by Riggs, who concludes, however, that members of the Thai military elite use such memberships to increase their personal incomes, not to enhance their political power.[41] Given the structure of the bureaucratic polity, which is virtually closed to participants who are outside the government itself, political power flows from official positions and control of bureaucratic resources, especially military resources, rather than from the economic and organizational resources of the larger social system.

The military officer corps in Thailand is drawn overwhelmingly from the upper middle class and, to a lesser extent, from the middle class. The various armed services maintain academies for officer training, and while admission criteria generally reflect achievement rather than ascriptive norms, only the sons of the relatively wealthy and educated classes can compete successfully in the highly selective process. The armed forces enjoy great social prestige and thus there are many applicants for comparatively few openings. A military career has been a prominent avenue of social mobility for middle-class males, but access has been increasingly narrowed for this group in recent years. The military has never really opened its doors to citizens of Chinese background.

Service academy graduates are the elite of the officer corps and their career patterns carry them into the choicest billets. Other officers are recruited from civilian universities under Thailand's universal military training laws, but these are generally not accepted as career officers and are assigned to less glamorous and more routine administrative tasks. The military socialization process imbues academy graduates with a deep sense of professional esprit as members of a successful corporate entity. This process stresses three attitudes or orientations that relate closely to the participation of the officer corps in politics. First, the Thai officer is deeply nationalistic, proud of his country's record of independence, and certain that its international status and honor are owed to its military institutions. Second, the officer is infused with pride in the simple military virtues of duty, honor, country, and discipline. Finally, his training places great emphasis on leadership, on aggressive and decisive action. From these fundamental attitudes the officer corps tends to the position that "what is good for the army is good for the country." Government is viewed as an administrative task subject to command discipline, and politics is conceptualized in a limited and highly personalistic fashion.[42]

Thailand has had universal military conscription since 1905, and large numbers of recruits are readily available to fill the enlisted ranks for tours of active duty ranging from eighteen months to two years. Recruits are drawn largely from the rural villages and are minimally educated. The overall effect of this conscription procedure is the maintenance of a disciplined and politically docile enlisted force.[43] According to one study of Thai political culture, social organizations tend to be conceptualized primarily in hierarchical terms, with group coherence dependent on clearly demarcated situations of social stratification.[44] Interpersonal relationships in both family and village are governed by strict rules of behavior based on status inequality. Military organization is thus reinforced by the dominant values of Thai society, producing a general deference toward authority and respect for hierarchical procedures that operates throughout the rank structure. Discipline is further enforced by the juridical autonomy of the armed forces, which are solely responsible for the content and administration of military justice.[45]

The officer corps is deeply anticommunist and sensitive to domestic and foreign policy developments that relate to this preoccupation. Thailand's geographical location makes this concern understandable. The People's Republic of China is perceived as an ambitious great power with historic expansionist designs in Southeast Asia. Thailand's large Chinese minority is therefore a constant and unsettling presence. Moreover, the Vietnam war and the North Vietnamese presence in the border states of Laos and Cambodia have driven the Thai government to accept an extensive military alliance with the United States since 1965. This alliance has yielded seven American airbases on Thai soil from which much of the air war in Vietnam and the rest of Indochina has been waged. Thai troops have also been committed in limited numbers to the fighting, openly in South Vietnam and more clandestinely as "volunteers" in Laos. In Thailand's own troubled Northeast, a communist-led insurgency backed by the North Vietnamese has been expanding its capabilities and operations. As of late 1971, 37 of Thailand's 71 provinces had been declared "sensitive areas," meaning that the insurgents were organizing villages and attracting recruits with growing success. The total number of guerrillas under arms was estimated at only 1700 (compared to 1500 in 1970), but army security forces were enjoying little success in overcoming either the guerrillas or the local sources of discontent on which they thrive.[46] An even more severe insurgency has been underway in the northern region of the country among Meo tribesmen; and in the South, terrorists of the Malaysian Communist Party have been seeking to separate the four southernmost provinces of Thailand (which are predominantly populated by Muslims) for eventual annexation by Malaysia.[47] In view of all these threats, the Thai military considers itself under siege by an international communist conspiracy. The armed forces give overriding importance to the necessity of combatting these various menaces.

The Thai military's interest in modernization is ambivalent. Apart from a continuing interest in economic growth and diversification, the Thanom group and its predecessor ruling cliques have shown little evidence of pursuing any programmatic design for the overall modernization of the country. Fundamental social change through revolutionary education and land reform programs has not been a military goal. One explanation may be that the officer corps remains closely tied to the social and economic elites from which it is drawn. The various insurgencies within the country are seen as military rather than social problems, emanating from the activities of foreign *agents provocateurs* rather than from local conditions of social injustice or from the ineptness and exploitativeness of government administrators in the provinces. Rural unrest is conceived partly in military terms, but also as a problem to be alleviated in the long run by expanded rural public works programs. In short, there has been no real linkage of military institutional interests with the general movement—nascent at best—for reforms in the country (as there has been, for example, in Peru and Egypt; see the chapters on each nation).

As for the three dimensions of military professionalism defined by Samuel Huntington, the Thai military should rank relatively high among Third World countries in terms of its expertise, but lower in the development of its senses of corporate identity and social responsibility. Especially since the escalation of the Vietnam war in the mid-1960's, the armed forces have received a considerable quantity of modern weapons and weapons systems from the United States. Despite their undistinguished record to date in counterinsurgency operations—a formidable problem for even the most modern military forces—the armed forces of Thailand are well trained and effectively organized. However, the development of a true corporate identity among the officer corps has been retarded by the persistence of personalism and cliques within it. The army's hierarchical command structure has shown itself to be reasonably effective overall, but particularly in the upper ranks its institutional boundaries are severely fragmented by the factional character of the bureaucratic polity. The principal cliques cut across organizational boundaries, encompassing not only military officers but also civilian bureaucrats and some business leaders. Membership in a dominant clique is a culminating career goal. For example, Sarit's supporters received more rapid and sure promotion after the 1957 coup, as well as opportunities for personal enrichment through participation in a well-developed system of official corruption.[48] On the other hand, certain issues serve to bind the military together as a corporate entity, despite the prevailing pattern of factionalism. Anticommunism, most foreign policy issues, excessive parliamentary interference, and resistance to mass participation in politics are some of the key issues around which the Thai military will usually rally.

Cultural traditions of bureaucratic corruption and the absence of countervailing civilian political forces have together worked against the growth of a deep sense of social responsibility among the officer corps. While it is true that most officers are deeply nationalistic and take great pride in the military's role as protector of the nation, their self-conceptualization as public servants tends to be narrow and self-serving. Military needs take precedence over the needs of Thai society, and indeed the officers may well consider the two to be identical. Since 1932 the political role of the armed forces has been largely predatory. The military bureaucracy has functioned as its own clientele, and the same can be said of the civil service. Since for practical purposes these bureaucracies contain the Thai political system, the output of that system has been geared to satisfy hardly more than the self-defined needs of the bureaucracies themselves. This is the essence of Riggs's concept of "bureaucratic polity."[49]

Societal Factors Affecting Civil–Military Relations

The visitor to Thailand is struck by the many examples of traditional values and practices surviving among or adapted to modern needs, and the political system also fits this generalization. The Thai political system is characterized by the grafting of modern administrative organizations upon traditional social structures, including the monarchy as the traditional source of political legitimization. The great strength and endurance of Thailand's traditional institutions are responsible for the relative stability and continuity of the system of predatory bureaucratic rule that has prevailed since 1932, despite that system's unrepresentativeness, its unresponsiveness to local interests, and its manifest failures to fulfill the goals of democracy and modernization that were heralded by the "revolution" of 1932.

The principal actors of Thai politics are the military, the civil service, the monarchy, the parliament, and the business community. Apart from the commercial and business elites, whose influence in politics is expressed through corruption linkages to civil service and military bureaucrats, private organizations such as interest groups or political parties have only a minor role. In large part this is because the traditional political culture places great value on deference and obedience toward those who occupy official positions of authority. The political passivity of the vast majority of the Thai people is a remarkable phenomenon. The twentieth century has witnessed the dramatic fall of the absolute monarchy, a Japanese military occupation, and a series of momentous military coups and dictatorships; yet the Thais have been spectators rather than participants in these events. According to the several available studies of Thai political culture, the dominant world-view of the Thai people has three major components that underlie this passivity.[50] First is the pervasive acceptance of and deference to constituted authority, especially toward the king whose great prestige continues to bestow legitimacy on governmental actions. Second, Thai society and indeed the entire universe is conceptualized in terms of hierarchies of statuses, to which are ascribed moral qualities that stipulate unchallengeable rules of conduct in nearly every social situation. Finally, there is the view that a person's social position and power are determined by himself, in part through his deeds in the present life or in a previous incarnation, and in part through his good fortune. Thus, those who have power and wealth are deemed to deserve them; in effect, the possession of power serves to legitimize the exercise of power. This world-view, widespread among the ethnically homogeneous Thai nation, serves as the basis for the profound passivity with which Thais accept the actions of their political elite.

Reinforcing this world-view are several quirks of Thai history that have helped to prevent the emergence of dissident political forces outside the government. Unlike her neighboring states, Thailand did not suffer the humiliation of colonial rule that tends to undermine traditional authority symbols and to produce an alienated and militant indigenous educated class. Moreover, the country has not suffered defeat in the modern era in a major war. The elites have never had to employ the techniques of mass mobilization to arouse the peasantry in a nationalist struggle against a foreign enemy. Furthermore, an estimated 85 percent of the population resides in rural areas and is primarily engaged in small-scale agricultural activities. Thailand has no landholding aristocracy comparable to those formerly characterizing Peru and Egypt. Land tenure patterns are individualistic in character, and the life of the Thai peasant is basically secure. Because of these major factors, the gradual and controlled pace of social mobilization has not given rise to a serious gap between mass aspirations and their fulfillment. Economic development since World War II has been sufficiently extensive and sustained to absorb the great majority of the potentially frustrated. Buttressing these factors have been the firm government controls over the content and staffing of the educational system and, more indirectly but no less effectively, over the mass media. Those who do attempt to organize opposition to the government are repressed, often through bureaucratic harassment or withholding of favors, sometimes more harshly through exile or imprisonment. Potential dissidents generally have preferred to allow themselves to be co-opted into the government bureaucracy, or have entered academic life, or in some cases have accepted exile.[51]

Thus, Thai political culture and national political experience tend to reinforce the authoritarian character of the regime in preventing the development of mass politicization and organized political opposition (or organized support, since the regime has had no real need for this). Even in the commercial–industrial urban complex of Bangkok, neither the working class nor the bourgeoisie has provided an independent nucleus for party or pressure politics. The urban labor force of some two and a half million workers is divided ethnically (skilled workers are nearly all Chinese, unskilled are about half Chinese and half Thai) and is perhaps as politically fragmented as the more dispersed peasantry. The Chinese community as such is politically inactive. Labor unions have been proscribed by the government since 1958, and the few labor organizations that do exist are in the category of "protective interest associations" whose leadership has been co-opted by the regime.[52] The Thai business community has also lacked the motivation and organizational skills necessary to become an independent political force. An even stronger division along ethnic lines persists among businessmen than that among the labor force. Businessmen from the Chinese community have preferred to limit their activities to attempts to influence politicians and bureaucrats for narrow special-interest goals, contributing to the widespread official corruption, rather than becoming an interest group seeking to influence public policy relating to economic development.[53] The urban middle class per se, in the sense of a coherent social force seeking to displace the traditional groups of society, has simply not asserted an independent role in the political arena.

For these reasons, political competition in Thailand is restricted to a very narrow elite stratum, whose members share a substantial consensus regarding the political structures and values that uphold the status quo. Cleavages within this elite stratum tend to be based on struggles between personal cliques for power, wealth, and status, rather than on conflicting policy goals or differences in ideology.[54] Power is generated through control over government organizations, particularly the armed forces but also including civil service departments such as the National Police, the Ministry of National Development, and the Department of Local Administration.[55] The memberships of the major cliques cut across the lines of the military and civil bureaucracies and are represented in the parliament and business community. The cliques themselves are based on the patron–client relationship, the client supporting the patron in return for his protection and favors. The strength of the bond depends on the leader's continuing ability to deliver patronage, the main source of which is government employment, and on opportunities for financial gain through corruption.[56] This is why the "promoters" of the three great coups since 1932 have subsequently monopolized the highest positions of authority in the government, and also why the coup d'etat has become the fundamental means of transferring power within the Thai political system. Once a clique has established itself in power, it can be dislodged only through violence. The key to a successful coup depends on the prior shift in loyalty of the army, particularly the Bangkok garrison, from one personalistic clique leader to another.

The relationship between clique politics and bureaucratic corruption is described in a study by James C. Scott. A coup-group is organized into a conspiracy by the leader's promises of rewards of power, status, and wealth to those who are willing to support his grab for power. Once the coup is successful, the leader must continue to consolidate his power by attracting the support of other military leaders as well as of key civil service officials and businessmen. Support is purchased through the distribution of concessions, i.e., influence over government decisions regarding publicly owned enterprises and contracts. This process of clique solidification amounts to a "feudalization" of the government administration, with each important member of the clique being conceded a virtual free rein in directing the affairs of his particular sector of the bureaucracy. Each department head runs his sector more or less as a personal fiefdom, awarding favors to those who demonstrate personal loyalty to him, seeing that government contracts go to his particular allies in the business community, and accepting lucrative positions on the boards of directors of corporations seeking his favor.[57] Thus it is not simply the case that the role of the *military* in Thailand is predatory, but that this characterizes the competing civil–military cliques that make up the Thai political system. Corruption is inseparable from clique politics.

The clique currently in power was originally organized by Field Marshal Sarit. Since his death in 1963, no personality has arisen to assert a degree of control over the clique comparable to Sarit's. A rough balance currently exists between the Thanom and Praphat factions, with intense jockeying for position to influence the succession upon Thanom's anticipated retirement.[58] The clique's power now depends on the cooperation of several strategically placed officials, both military and civilian, whose self-interest in leaving a working profitable arrangement undisturbed is the cement that binds the clique together and guards against the rise of a challenging faction. The competition among cliques, and among the factions within them, has been moderated by the tacit acceptance by the leaders of certain rules. One is the principle that the monarchy must be preserved and its prestige maintained at a high level. There is a deep and symbiotic relationship between King Bhumibol and the military officers who dominate the Thanom–Praphat clique. The king endows the government with its only substantial claim to legitimacy. In return, his role as the symbol of Thai nationhood is emphasized by the government and he has been made secure in his social status, religious leadership position, and royal privileges. Second, the elites agree that the government itself is the only proper arena for political competition. An appeal for outside allies—for example, students, the labor movement, or peasants—would involve an unacceptable risk of expanding political participation and thus undermining the basis of the bureaucratic polity. A reaffirmation of agreement on this issue was at the heart of the

1971 coup.[59] Finally, it is recognized among the officer corps that it is the army which controls the decisive instruments of power. Therefore the military's self-interest demands its unity above all else. Although interservice rivalries have on occasion led to open violence, the army has remained remarkably steadfast in its loyalty to the officer who is its commander in chief at the time.

As Scott observes, there is a distinctively amoral character to the pattern of elite competition in Thailand. The government's civil and military bureaucracies exist essentially to serve their own interests, since no outside social forces are powerful enough to threaten the government with political sanctions and thereby force it to recognize a larger moral purpose for its existence.[60] The main potential for developing such an extrabureaucratic force lies in the parliament and in the nascent political party system. Because the democratic political institutions created by the 1968 constitution threatened to nourish this potential, Thailand's latest experiment in constitutionalism was doomed to fail. By 1971, after three years of coexistence with a parliamentary structure that had given rise to a growing volume of extrabureaucratic demands on the political system, the Thanom–Praphat clique resolved the rising tension by simply abolishing parliament as a competing political arena.

The causes of the November 1971 coup were, of course, more complex than the underlying dimension of a self-preservation reaction on the part of the managers of the bureaucratic polity. In addition to the resentment within the executive branch at legislative interference in policy making, the debate over the need for new flexibility in Thailand's foreign policy was an important factor. Among the cabinet ministers who lost their positions as a result of the coup was Foreign Minister Thanat Khoman, who had played a major part in forging the alliance with the United States. In the months preceding the coup, Thanat had been urging a closer relationship with China. The uncertainty resulting from the gradual but steady withdrawal of the United States from Southeast Asia, coupled with signs of impending detente between the United States and China, had apparently convinced Thanat and others that their government should move quickly to accommodate to the new situation. The majority of the ruling clique disagreed, however, and quickly followed the coup with assurances that the alliance with the United States would be continued. Nevertheless, signs of possible new initiatives in other directions persisted. Thailand signed the "Southeast Asia neutralization declaration" formulated by a regional gathering in Kuala Lumpur that same month. [61]

At bottom, however, the coup was probably caused primarily by growing tensions in the factional balance of Thai politics. The struggle for political succession was central to these tensions. In particular, there apparently was pressure from middle-ranking army officers on their commander in chief, General Praphat, to move decisively to protect the central political position of his own faction. Praphat found himself in an ambivalent situation. His own following included not only the army but also an increasingly influential civilian faction among the government party's (UTPP) majority in parliament. With the increasing exertion of parliamentary prerogatives after 1968, Praphat was pressured to choose between his two constituencies. The coup really represented a consolidation of power by Praphat's military-based faction, in preparation for the political succession to Thanom and for an even more monopolistic grip on the government by the military.[62]

The Outlook for the 1970's

The ascendance of General Praphat's faction was apparent in the reshuffling of responsibilities that took place following the coup. The new regime abolished both the parliament and the cabinet, and hence no ministerial portfolios as such were distributed. Instead, the military junta announced the formation of a "National Executive Council" comprised mainly of military officers. This body, dominated by Thanom, Praphat, Air Chief Marshal Thawee Chullasaphya, and Police Director General Prasert Ruchirawong, assumed supervisory responsibilities over the various government ministries.[63] The NEC represented the most extreme degree of military rule yet to appear in Thailand. Constitutional restraints on its power were abolished. Its executive powers were therefore virtually absolute, and its members wasted little time in consolidating the position of the Praphat faction. This task and preparations for the political succession to Thanom appeared to be the NEC's principal preoccupations during 1972.[64]

After some thirteen months of absolute military rule under the NEC, the dominant clique felt secure enough in its power to allow a return to constitutional forms. On December 15, 1972, the king promulgated Thailand's ninth constitution, an interim document preserving wide-ranging executive powers but establishing a 299-member National Assembly. The Assembly's appointed membership included 187 military officers (134 army men, 30 navy, and 23 air force), 13 police officers, and 99 civilians. The political significance of the new constitution and legislature rested in their importance as legitimizing devices. The facade of a limited constitutional monarchy once more covered the reality of entrenched military rule.[65]

With the possible exception of foreign affairs, where it is still too early to detect a pronounced shift in Thailand's orientation, the policies of the new government appear to follow the pattern established before the 1968 reintroduction of democratic institutions. The primary interests of the Thanom–Praphat clique lie in the preservation of its power, status, and wealth. Thailand's economic problems remain an area of concern as world prices have been steadily declining for the country's principal exports of tin, rubber, and rice, and as military aid from the United States appears to be falling off. However, there is little evidence to suggest that the military leaders are seriously concerned with finding solutions to Thailand's social problems, any more than they are motivated to expand political participation outside the government bureaucracies.

There is little question that the present regime is overwhelmingly military in its makeup and that it has the legitimacy—through its renewed symbolic relationship with the monarchy—to govern the country for the foreseeable future. The power of the dominant clique, based on its coercive resources, wealth, bureaucratic authority, and control over information, is vast. Among Third World countries, the Thai polity and its particular pattern of civil–military relations are in many ways highly anomalous. Economically and, to a lesser extent, socially the country has developed to the general level where the urban middle classes might be expected to assert a dominant role in national policy making. Yet the middle classes remain ethnically and politically fragmented, unable to exercise significant influence over the directions of government policy. On the other hand, decisive political power does not rest in the hands of an entrenched and reactionary landholding oligarchy, as has often been the case in political systems marked by low participation levels. Neither of these social forces is politically significant in Thailand, and the great mass of the population seems far too passive at present to offer real potential for mobilization. (The situation thus differs markedly from that of Nigeria, in which mobilization sharpened ethnic rivalries, and from that of Egypt, in which military leaders pressed for greatly expanded popular involvement in politics.)

Despite the presence of several unsettling insurgencies in rural areas, it would be an overstatement to assert that the Thai political system is caught up in a crisis of legitimacy. The prevailing Thai attitudes toward authority and the awe and deference that continue to surround the monarchy serve to endow the regime with great traditional legitimation in the Weberian sense. Authoritarian bureaucratic and military rule is deeply rooted in the culture and traditions of the country. At the same time, however, it appears that the *general* level of political institutionalization is low and that, within the urban and socially mobilized sectors, the legitimacy of military rule (if not of the monarchy itself) is being seriously challenged.[66] For these reasons, Thailand is most usefully classified as a praetorian polity with a relatively low level of political participation.

The political role of the Thai military establishment also seems anomalous in some respects. While its level of expertise in the management of coercive resources is relatively high, its professional development

in terms of corporate identity and social responsibility has been markedly uneven. Thailand's military politicians are not inconsiderate of institutional interests, but it seems clear that the interests of personalities and
cliques more often take precedence. Whereas the armed forces in other
countries at comparable levels of professionalization have developed
political roles primarily as institutions, the military in Thailand remains
caught up in a pattern of personalism and predatory behavior that seems
anachronistic in the final third of the twentieth century. The explanation
for this pattern appears to lie in the peculiar historical factors which gave
rise to the present bureaucratic polity. The military has not been called
upon to mediate among contending social forces in the civilian sector,
and therefore it has not been impelled to imbue its political role with
the larger moral purpose implicit in the various forms of military guardianship or in the active advancement of social change.

Thailand's present bureaucratic polity seems firmly entrenched,
but there is no reason to suppose that it will endure forever. Several
possible situations could arise that could aggravate pressures for fundamental change. One of these is the abdication of the king or the abolition
of the monarchy, which would undoubtedly produce a serious crisis of
legitimacy. Alternatively, the king could exert his own influence more
vigorously to press the military for reforms, or to mobilize the population. A second source of destabilization could be a prolonged period of
marked economic reversal, but given the country's basic rice surplus and
stable land tenure patterns, a full-scale revolution does not seem an impending threat.[67] A third factor could be a greatly intensified insurgency aided by North Vietnamese or Chinese forces, which could serve to
discredit the military regime and lead to greater civilian participation in
some form. Finally, the stability of the present system will probably be
threatened by the current expansion of higher education. This expansion
may well produce a socially frustrated mass of graduates too large to be
absorbed by the bureaucracies. When this occurs, Thailand may finally
develop a civilian opposition capable of challenging the predatory basis
of military rule.[68]

However, short of a major defeat in war or economic catas-
trophe, the military's dominant position in Thai politics is not likely to
be eliminated soon. At most, the situations mentioned above would give
rise to extrabureaucratic political forces that might induce the military
to adopt a guardianship or even reformist stance. The unity of the army
might be temporarily sundered in such situations, but it would probably
be reconstituted in time to rally around vital institutional interests.
The military's politicization and control over coercion would probably
ensure its reascendance in the political arena. As in Nigeria, to which
we now turn, the armed forces cannot be pushed off the political stage.

References

1. The analysis of the November 1971 coup d'etat draws heavily on the excellent discussions of events in David Morell, "Thailand: Military Checkmate," in *Asian Survey*, Vol. XII, No. 2 (February 1972), pp. 156–167, and Daniel Lee, "The Thai Coup," in *New Left Review*, No. 71 (January–February 1972), pp. 36–43.
2. See Victor Purcell, *The Chinese in Southeast Asia* (2nd Ed., London: Oxford University Press, 1965), pp. 124–165.
3. Morell, "Thailand: Military Checkmate," pp. 157–158.
4. Ibid., pp. 156–165.
5. This concept is developed in Fred W. Riggs, *Thailand: The Modernization of a Bureaucratic Polity* (Honolulu: East-West Center Press, 1966); see especially Chapter X, pp. 311–366.
6. David A. Wilson, "The Military in Thai Politics," in John J. Johnson (ed.), *The Role of the Military in Underdeveloped Countries* (Princeton: Princeton University Press, 1962), pp. 254–256.
7. The concept of "defensive modernization" is discussed in Robert E. Ward and Dankwart A. Rustow, *Political Modernization in Japan and Turkey* (Princeton: Princeton University Press, 1964).
8. On the historical background to the development of modern Thailand, see: W.D. Reeve, *Public Administration in Siam* (London: Royal Institute of International Affairs, 1951), pp. 12–19; James C. Ingram, *Economic Change in Thailand Since 1850* (Stanford: Stanford University Press, 1955); Walter F. Vella, *The Impact of the West on Government in Thailand* (Berkeley: University of California Press, Publications in Political Science, Vol. IV, No. 3, 1955); David K. Wyatt, *The Politics of Reform in Thailand: Education in the Reign of King Chulalongkorn* (New Haven: Yale University Press, 1969); and Riggs, *Thailand*, pp. 15–207.
9. Wilson, "The Military in Thai Politics," p. 255.
10. Ibid.
11. A.W. Graham, *Siam: A Handbook of Practical, Commercial, and Political Information* (3rd Ed., London: Alexander Moring, 1924), pp. 318–319.
12. See the discussion in Samuel P. Huntington, *Political Order in Changing Societies* (New Haven: Yale University Press, 1968), pp. 177–191.
13. Donald Hindley, "Thailand: The Politics of Passivity," in *Pacific Affairs*, Vol. XLI, No. 3 (Fall 1968), p. 356.
14. Wilson, "The Military in Thai Politics," p. 256.
15. David A. Wilson, *Politics in Thailand* (Ithaca: Cornell University Press, 1962), p. 12.
16. Riggs, *Thailand*, pp. 312–313.
17. Ibid., pp. 161–162.
18. Wilson, "The Military in Thai Politics," p. 259.
19. See Wilson, *Politics in Thailand*, pp. 16–17.

20. Wilson, *Politics in Thailand,* p. 17. For the concept of a "consolidating coup" see Huntington, *Political Order in Changing Societies,* pp. 204–205.

21. The uprising was led by Prince Boworadet, a former Minister of Defense. King Prachatipok denounced the rebellion as it was being crushed, but the suspicious leaders of the People's Party subsequently forced him to abdicate in favor of the 16-year-old Prince Ananda Mahidol, then in school in Switzerland. The episode marked the beginning of a decline in the prestige of the throne, which was not reversed until the late 1940's. See Wilson, *Politics in Thailand,* pp. 17–18.

22. Wilson, "The Military in Thai Politics," pp. 259–260.

23. Anti-Chinese measures were nothing new in Thailand at this point; see Kenneth P. Landon, *The Chinese in Thailand* (London, 1924), pp. 34–43, and Purcell, *The Chinese in Southeast Asia,* pp. 144–154.

24. See Wilson, *Politics in Thailand,* pp. 20–22.

25. Frank C. Darling, *Thailand and the United States* (Washington: Public Affairs Press, 1965), pp. 40–47.

26. Wilson, *Politics in Thailand,* p. 22.

27. Wilson, "The Military in Thai Politics," p. 261.

28. Ibid., p. 262.

29. Wilson, *Politics in Thailand,* pp. 24–25.

30. Ibid., pp. 25–26.

31. John Coast, *Some Aspects of Siamese Politics* (New York: Institute of Pacific Relations, 1953), pp. 52–58.

32. Wilson, *Politics in Thailand,* p. 27.

33. David A. Wilson, *The United States and the Future of Thailand* (New York: Frederick A. Praeger, 1970), p. 33.

34. See Darling, *Thailand and the United States,* pp. 113–130.

35. Wilson, *Politics in Thailand,* pp. 29–33, and Darling, *Thailand and the United States,* pp. 131–166.

36. Wilson, *Politics in Thailand,* p. 34.

37. See Darling, *Thailand and the United States,* pp. 193–194.

38. Colonel T.N. Dupuy and Colonel Wendell Blanchard, *The Almanac of World Military Power* (2nd Ed., New York: R.R. Bowker Company, 1972), pp. 60, 161, and 331.

39. Wilson, *Politics in Thailand,* p. 184. On the integration of the military into the Thai economic system, see also Moshe Lissak, "Modernization and Role-Expansion of the Military in Developing Countries: A Comparative Analysis," in *Comparative Studies in Society and History,* Vol. IX (1966), pp. 248–249.

40. Wilson, *Politics in Thailand,* p. 184.

41. Riggs, *Thailand,* p. 297. A contrary view is that corruption is the basis of power relations in factional politics; see James C. Scott, *Comparative Political Corruption* (Englewood Cliffs, N.J.: Prentice-Hall, 1972), pp. 57–75.

42. See Wilson, *Politics in Thailand,* pp. 186–188. These attitudes tend to character-

ize military officers in general; compare, for example, the discussion of officer education in Peru, Chapter 6.

43. Wilson, *Politics in Thailand,* pp. 188 and 190.

44. Lucien M. Hanks, Jr., and Herbert P. Phillips, "A Young Thai from the Country-side: A Psychosocial Analysis," in Bert Kaplan (ed.), *Studying Personality Crossculturally* (New York: Harper, 1961), pp. 637–656.

45. Wilson, *Politics in Thailand,* pp. 181–186.

46. Morell, "Thailand: Military Checkmate," pp. 158–160.

47. Lee, "The Thai Coup," pp. 41–43, and Clark D. Neher, "Thailand: Toward Fundamental Change," in *Asian Survey,* Vol. XI, No. 2 (February 1971), pp. 135–136.

48. See Scott, *Comparative Political Corruption,* pp. 57–75.

49. Riggs, *Thailand,* pp. 311–366.

50. See especially Hindley, "Thailand: The Politics of Passivity," pp. 355–371; Wilson, *Politics in Thailand,* pp. 72–84; and Herbert B. Phillips, *Thai Peasant Personality: The Patterning of Interpersonal Behavior in the Village of Bang Chan* (Berkeley: University of California Press, 1965).

51. Hindley, "Thailand: The Politics of Passivity," pp. 362–363.

52. See Daniel Wit, *Thailand: Another Vietnam?* (New York: Charles Scribner's Sons, 1968), pp. 93–98. The concept of "protective interest associations" is found in Lucian W. Pye, *Politics, Personality, and Nation-Building: Burma's Search for Identity* (New Haven: Yale University Press, 1962), pp. 26–27.

53. Wit, *Thailand,* pp. 98–100.

54. See David Morell, "Thailand," in *Asian Survey,* Vol. XIII, No. 2, (February 1973), pp. 166–170, for evidence that the role of ideology in Thai politics may be increasing.

55. See Wilson, *The United States and the Future of Thailand,* pp. 104–105.

56. Scott, *Comparative Political Corruption,* p. 64. It is interesting to compare Kenneth F. Johnson's discussion of "circles of intimacy" as the basis of factional politics in Mexico; see *Mexican Democracy: A Critical View* (Boston: Allyn and Bacon, 1971), pp. 59–84.

57. Scott, *Comparative Political Corruption,* p. 64.

58. Morell, "Thailand," pp. 162–163.

59. Morell, "Thailand: Military Checkmate," pp. 162–163.

60. Scott, *Comparative Political Corruption,* p. 59.

61. See Morell, "Thailand: Military Checkmate," pp. 165–166, and Neher, "Thailand: Toward Fundamental Change," pp. 136–137.

62. Morell, "Thailand: Military Checkmate," p. 163.

63. Lee, "The Thai Coup," pp. 36–37. Responsibilities on the National Executive Council were distributed as follows: Thanom, President of the Council and Ministry of Foreign Affairs; Praphat, Deputy President of the Council and Ministries of the Interior, Defense, and Justice; Thawee, Chief of Staff and Ministries of National Development, Agriculture, and Communi-

cations; Prasert, Chief of Police and Ministries of Education and Public Health; and Pote Sarasin (the lone civilian member of the NEC), Ministries of Finance, Economic Affairs, and Industry.

64. Morell, "Thailand," pp. 164–166.

65. Ibid., pp. 176–177.

66. Ibid., pp. 166–170, and Lee, "The Thai Coup," pp. 38–43.

67. For a more optimistic view of the possibility of social revolution in Thailand, see Lee, "The Thai Coup," pp. 41–43.

68. See the discussion of the problems of modernizing autocracies in David E. Apter, *The Politics of Modernization* (Chicago: University of Chicago Press, 1965), pp. 402–407.

5

Nigeria: Moderate Reform and the Problem of Withdrawal

Reform-minded military regimes emerge in states marked by "middle-class politics." The emergence begins when urbanization and economic development start to undermine the traditional sources of authority, and increased professionalization differentiates the armed forces from other institutions. On the whole, the effect of such changes is greater discontent with the political system. Officers and the new middle-class political leaders find common ground in reformist policies. In such a setting, a coup d'etat will install a government attuned to a modest rate of change, capable of innovations that would result in either of two possible roles for the military: (1) the military's withdrawal from direct political involvement, or (2) its increased prominence in national decision making. In Nigeria, the second possibility is the one that has finally been realized; but it required many years to emerge. Nigeria epitomizes the complex, and at times contradictory, directions reformist military regimes take.

The military seizure of control in Nigeria in January 1966 was not the first coup d'etat in tropical Africa, nor was the ensuing civil war a unique occurrence on the African continent. Because of the size of the nation, however, both events had major impacts. Nigeria ranks as the most populous state of Africa. Its military establishment, modestly endowed with just over 11,000 men in early 1966, ballooned to a quarter-million in four years. Its army-based government has attempted significant changes in the overall structure and functioning of the political system—and, in the process, it has created a foundation for continuing military involvement in politics.

By early 1973, a single group of army leaders had held political office, without elections of any sort, for six and a half years. They assumed control just after the coup of July 1966 and maintained it throughout the civil war (mid-1967 to early 1970) and into the present. Nigeria has thus experienced a continuity of military administration practically without parallel in tropical Africa—an area where intervention has been punctuating political history with increasing frequency. In the period 1960–1972, eighteen other African governments succumbed to military seizures of power.

A successful coup represents the first step in the creation of a military regime. For a full-fledged army-based government to emerge, further steps remain: alliances with appropriate civilian groups; possible restructuring of the government and its policies; shifts in the boundaries between military and political spheres of responsibility. The result may be, as in Nigeria, the emergence of a reformist, modernizing military regime. Since 1966, coalitions of civilians and officers have governed the twelve states into which the Federation of Nigeria is divided. The central government similarly mixes men in khaki and men in mufti in government offices. Leaders of the Supreme Military Council have emphasized their willingness to step aside from politics. They attach a crucial provision, however. Total military withdrawal from politics depends upon basic reforms. Until and unless these changes are implemented, the armed forces will not leave their self-appointed role as political watchdogs.

Nigeria illustrates the extraordinary difficulties that confront officers dedicated to political reform when they ponder disengagement from politics. Having intervened to cleanse and reform the political system, officers are reluctant to undertake a hasty withdrawal. They are mired in a classic dilemma: Should they remain, and face the continual assaults of popular resentment? Or should they depart, and risk returning power to incompetent replacements? Self-doubts of this sort lead to equivocation, uncertainty, and occasional paralysis.

Thus, the governing military officers of Nigeria are unwilling to give strong encouragement to civilian politicians; the Supreme Military Council vacillates between the contradictory objectives of speedy restoration of civilian rule or of basic political reform. A decision to return to the barracks—seemingly a quick, simple issue to resolve—actually involves a thorough resolution of the military's willingness and ability to define its political role. In Nigeria, leading officers have dedicated themselves to moderate reform and to healing the scars of civil war. As they have gained increased confidence in their ability to rule, moreover, their reluctance to preside over the installation of a popularly elected government has grown ever greater. Restoration of a totally civilian government figures as a long-range possibility, not an immediate priority.

What Led to Military Intervention?

On the night of January 14, 1966, the Nigerian armed forces shot their way into political prominence. The seizure of power was quick, bloody, and unexpected. The conspirators sought to immobilize the Nigerian government by removing its most prominent members. In this gruesome task, they largely succeeded. The premiers of two of the four regions into which the country was then divided were assassinated. Army leadership was similarly decimated: among those eliminated that night were the commander of one of the country's two brigades, the adjutant general, the chief of staff, and the quartermaster general. The shock of this brutal intervention spread through Nigeria in widening circles, reinforcing the impression among civilians and soldiers alike that political change occurred only through violence. The coup d'etat should not be seen as a unique event, however, but as an additional manifestation of violence in a political system already reeling from blows to its legitimacy.

Despite a facade of democracy, Nigeria had been lacking many of the requisites for civilian control of the armed forces. To a distant viewer, it seemed that Nigeria had achieved a remarkably open, democratic system after achieving independence. Other African states had installed single-party governments but Nigeria had retained strong competition among its three major parties: the Action Group, the NCNC (National Council of Nigerian Citizens), and the NPC (Northern Peoples Congress). Appearances were deceptive. The veneer of parliamentary procedure was masking increased use of force and rising levels of political distrust, into which the military was drawn. The armed forces had remained largely apart from partisan strife, but when their political neutrality was ruptured by the "majors' coup" of January 1966, the military's political involvement became all the more intense and extensive.

To trace the growing political activity of the Nigerian armed forces, a dual approach is necessary. The first approach examines the Nigerian military as an entity unto itself: its history, values, bases of cohesion, command structure, and links to the government. The 1966 coup was particularly shocking because the Nigerian armed forces had been under civilian control. By comparison with most armies of tropical Africa, the Nigerian army had seemed to exhibit professional qualities of responsibility, corporateness, and expertise. What strains led to the severe weakening of these qualities? To get at this, we utilize the second approach, considering the political environment as a whole. In the view of many younger officers, the Nigerian government drew upon the military to support a sordid, unpopular clique of self-serving politicians. Rather than abet such efforts, certain majors preferred to sweep away the top layer of the government.

The 1966 Coups: Military Institutional Factors

Until the eruption of the civil war, the Nigerian army ranked among the smallest in the world, in terms of the ratio between total population and men in the ranks. The roots of the arrangement lay in British colonial rule. It was British policy in Nigeria to maintain as a supplement to the police a small army, one that was capable of rapid expansion in case of major war. The military propped up colonial control, at a relatively low cost to Nigerians. British taxpayers in the 1950's shouldered most expenses of the five infantry battalions, each of which included about 750 men on active duty.

The Nigerian armed forces just prior to independence in 1960 were overwhelmingly Nigerian in the ranks, overwhelmingly British in the officer corps (including noncommissioned, warrant, and commissioned officers). Only 15 of the 250 commissioned officers in 1956 were Nigerian: the 336 white noncommissioned and warrant officers received more than four times the pay of the Nigerians at the same levels. All 6400 men in the ranks were Nigerian, receiving a daily wage of 35 to 50 cents.

The British sought two conflicting objectives. On the one hand, they espoused the recruitment of Nigerians into the officer corps, at least in principle! On the other hand, they sought to maintain "standards." As in many other social settings, preservation of standards essentially meant maintenance of the status quo. Norman Miners correctly asserts, "in the matter of Nigerianization of the armed forces the Army authorities placed far more emphasis on the need for maintaining standards accepted by the British Army all over the world than on the need to keep progress in the Nigerian Military Forces in line with progress in other government departments."[1] As a result, the pace of Africanization in the officer corps lagged considerably behind the pace set by the civil service, and became an area of Nigerian resentment.

British policy attempted to isolate the armed forces completely from political contact—indeed, from political awareness. Recruitment for the ranks favored illiterate individuals, for whom twenty years' service represented a choice career. Knowing little outside the military context, such persons would follow commands without distaste or doubt. A substantial portion of the ranks was filled by men from the so-called Middle Belt, a relatively poor section of Nigeria where educational opportunities were extremely limited.[2] Educated Nigerians scorned the armed forces, which were far less attractive than the civil service. An essentially British officer corps thus maintained "standards"; a well-disciplined, obedient rank and file carried out orders; neither group questioned British control. As a result, the Nigerian army was responsive to civilian control—even though the civilians were British, not Nigerian. As Miners has observed, "In theory an army should be a passive instrument in the hands of the government, an efficient agent to carry out the ends decreed by its political masters without sentiment or complaint. Few armies achieve this ideal completely, but the Nigerian Military Forces before 1958 came very near to it."[3]

The Nigerian army stood apart from the nationalist currents that led to independence in 1960. As we have seen, the factors largely responsible for this lack of involvement were: the deliberate political neutralization of the armed forces by means of "standards" for officer recruitment; the political isolation of the armed forces, achieved by recruitment of soldiers from politically inarticulate sectors of Nigerian society; and the inculcation of norms of political disengagement. The British government retained control over the military until the actual grant of independence in 1960. British officers served short tours in Nigeria; they had no desire to become embroiled in local politics. Even Nigerians who served in the military seem to have remained at low levels of political awareness.[4]

Given near-total disengagement from politics, what elements can we find in the internal functioning of the military to explain the 1966 intervention? It appears that the most significant elements were the strains on military cohesion and values which had resulted from rapid Africanization of the officer corps, as well as the increased use of the armed forces to quell domestic discontent.

Training Nigerians to fill the officer corps proceeded at what can best be called a tortoise-like pace during the 1950's. Despite rapid change in the political arena, the British command was far from precipitate in encouraging Nigerians to acquire commissions. The reluctance of the British to loosen their control was the main constraint upon the indigenization of the officer corps. The slowness also reflected economic and social factors. Until 1958, Nigerian officers received considerably less pay than Nigerian civil servants with identical educational qualifications. The civil service offered more rapid advancements and better allowances, including allowances for that important status symbol, an automobile. Service in the military apparently repelled many, owing to a pervasive historic animosity toward the armed forces which had existed since the time of British conquest. Soldiers had low prestige. Recruitment into the rank and file centered in "the poorest parts of the country where military service was a traditional form of employment."[5]

An extraordinary regional disproportion characterized officer commissioning in the late 1950's; it was attributable to the unrealistic educational requirements, low levels of pay, and historic antipathy to the military. The Eastern Region, which accounted for less than a quarter of the population, accounted for two-thirds of the commissioned officers when the Union Jack came fluttering down. Half the Easterners came from a single ethnic group, the Ibo,[6] whose prominence in the first 1966 coup will be explored subsequently. Only in 1961 did the Nigerian government attempt to regulate commissionings so as to make them reflect the distribution of population. Half the officers were then to come from the Northern Region, a quarter respectively from the Eastern and Western Regions. This shift in policy meant that the criterion of education, which had disproportionately favored the East, would be diminished in favor of the criterion of regional origin. In the long run, this was a necessary step; in the short run, it may have affected the cohesion of the officer corps and, indirectly, the political activities of the armed forces.

In Part I, several propositions were suggested, relating military organization to the likelihood of intervention. Among these was a two-edged proposition: armies with high internal cohesion have greater capacity for intervention than less cohesive armies; however, a lack of cohesion may result in fragmented and unstable political involvement by the military. In the case of Nigeria, the armed forces manifested a high degree of cohesion in the first few years after independence—challenged by rapid promotions and almost completely destroyed after the coups of 1966. Since cohesion forms part of the background to any military coup, let us briefly consider the sources of solidarity within military units.

A central source is history. Units of an army share traditions, customs, insignia. Institutional continuity is carefully inculcated into new members, both officers and recruits for the ranks. Socialization stresses unity of the armed forces, because each segment (be it as small as a platoon or as large as a division) must conduct itself in an orderly, coherent, disciplined fashion. Military virtues, such as "honor," receive continual emphasis. Peer groups become focuses of friendship and solidarity. The barracks, the mess, and the parade ground exhibit the distinctiveness of the armed forces. Institutional history, socialization, and centers for camaraderie thus interact to create, and to maintain, unity and esprit de corps.

Yet military unity may be buffeted in many ways. Discontinuities in socialization may exist—leading, for example, to markedly different perceptions by noncommissioned officers and commissioned officers. Conflict can spring from inequities (real or imagined) in promotion. Promotions on the basis of seniority may embitter the competent and ambitious; promotions on the basis of personal qualities, such as ethnicity, may exacerbate internal rivalries. A military riven with dissent may push its conflicts out into the political system as a whole, which can lead to fragmented and unstable political boundaries. Within the Nigerian armed forces, marked strains upon internal organization and values became fused with grievances arising from the total political system, resulting in the explosive intervention of January 1966 and a second coup in July of the same year.

The Nigerian army grew slightly larger in the five and a half years between independence and the first military coup, yet Africanization of the officer corps transformed it to an almost totally different institution. In early 1960, only 50 of the 278 officers were Nigerian. In two years, the figures had changed to 157 of a total of 313, increasing the Nigerian proportion of the officer corps from 18 percent to 50 percent. By 1964, Nigerians filled 89 percent of the officer corps; by the time of the first coup, no expatriates remained.[7] At last the armed forces reflected the independence of the state and were capable of undertaking a coup d'etat, which can be carried out only by an army freed from colonial constraints.[8]

This is not to argue that Africanization of the officer corps "caused" the coups of 1966. Far from it. However, the nature and pace of Africanization dramatically altered the "nonpolitical" stance that marked the Nigerian army prior to independence. Four aspects deserve mention:

1. The replacement of British officers meant the officer corps as a whole became more aware of, and potentially more responsive to, local political trends. Expatriate officers, serving on short-term contract, inevitably must confront divided loyalties: duty to their employers, or duty to their native country, to which they intend to return.[9] Local officers do not face this dilemma. Their lot lies with their own country, which they serve directly. They feel far more strongly about the "national interest," an ideal perhaps all too easy to confuse with personal or corporate advancement.

2. Little time was available during which professional norms could be inculcated. The number of Nigerian officers leaped tenfold in the first five years of independence, with a substantial portion being commissioned after short-term training courses (generally in Great Britain) rather than rising from the ranks. These men did not experience prolonged socialization into the patterns the British had favored. Perhaps more significant, the British patterns were questioned by some. Should the criteria employed by Great Britain prevail in a newly independent country? Although British norms profoundly influenced many officers, the hold of these norms was bound to weaken with time, with expansion of the officer corps, and with the understandable effort to create "Nigerian standards." Because central components of professional conduct, as pressed by

the British, were political impartiality and unquestioning obedience to the government, shifts in professional conduct could well weaken both components. Henry L. Bretton foresaw this possibility in his prophetic 1962 study:

> *The major weakness in the Nigerian armed forces may be that they are proportionately too small for the population of Nigeria and that expansion, which must be commensurate with the rapidly deteriorating situation on the continent in general, must of necessity be conducted without the benefit of strict and impartial British supervision. If carried out by politically oriented persons, in terms of local partisan politics, for instance, the achievements of the original British tutors may be watered down substantially. The new, enlarged army may then be less immune to the hazards of subversion than could be said of the British-trained cadre.* [10]

3. Rapid promotions may have introduced unrealistic notions concerning personal advancement. Luckham indicates two consequences:

> *First, the officers who have experienced the fastest promotion are* themselves *likely to develop unrealistic expectations, to be unable to discern the limits between the possible and the impossible. Secondly, the officers whose promotions have not been as rapid as those of their salient reference groups will probably experience feelings of frustration and relative deprivation.* [11]

Nigerian officers promoted to the rank of captain before 1957 waited almost seven years to attain the rank of major; those promoted to captain during 1961 waited less than two years. [12] The escalator moved upward at ever-increasing speed, at least for a few years.

4. The rapid advancement in the early 1960's contrasted with a stark, frustrating reality. Those promoted were young, capable of many years of active duty. Blocks to advancement would clearly exist in the not-too-distant future, unless the armed forces became much larger. The rates of promotion characteristic of the early 1960's could not be sustained. Blocked channels for advancement contributed to stress within the Nigerian armed forces; stress stemmed thus from unrealistic expectations of promotion, the changing professional image of the military, and increasing awareness among officers of political trends.

Tensions within the armed forces became fuel for intervention only after profound weakening of Nigeria's political institutions, however. The steps that culminated in the 1966 coups could be taken only as the government forfeited more and more of its basis of support.

The 1966 Coups: Environmental Factors

Independence ushered in high hopes for Nigeria. The country was large, blessed with energetic and able citizens and a host of natural resources. The colonial experience had awakened nationalist fervor; yet the parting of Nigeria and Great Britain came peacefully. A robustly competitive party system contrasted with the single-party systems common elsewhere in tropical Africa; this fact seemed to augur well for democratic development. Moderate, experienced political leaders appeared ready to preserve the delicate balance between competition and cooperation that marks a "mature" political culture, in Finer's terms. Although notable deficiencies existed in local government, a cadre of Nigerian administrators ran governmental affairs well.

Nigeria thus appeared to be a civic polity in the early 1960's. Boundaries between military and society were integral, not fragmented. Political participation was relatively high in the south, channeled primarily through political parties, but low in the North. Other channels included so-called "native authorities" that updated traditional forms of local government in the North, elected local government organs in the south, trade unions, improvement unions based on ethnic descent, and many others. The armed forces remained responsible to the state, as shown by their effective and largely bloodless quelling of some disturbances. What, then, went wrong? What environmental factors abetted intervention?

In analyzing the reasons for the coups, let us start with the diagnosis of the main plotter, Major Chukwuma K. Nzeogwu:

> *We wanted to get rid of rotten and corrupt ministers, political parties, trades unions and the whole clumsy apparatus of the Federal system. We wanted to gun down all the bigwigs on our way. This was the only way. We could not afford to let them live if this was to work.* [13]

Those words came from a graduate of the Royal Military Academy, Sandhurst, the most prestigious military school in the British Commonwealth!

Nzeogwu, it should be noted, said nothing about internal military conditions. Unlike many military conspirators, who seize power to avenge slights to army prerogatives, Nzeogwu wanted a totally clean sweep of "the system." He would not be satisfied by reform; he wanted, in effect, to mow down those at the top. His objective was nothing less than the destruction of the federal government by which Nigeria was ruled.

Almost unique among African states, Nigeria gained independence as a federal state. Federalism made eminent good sense. It recognized the size and diversity of Nigeria. In terms of population, each of the three regions was larger in 1960 than any country in all West Africa.

In terms of ethnic heterogeneity, each region was dominated by a single major group (in the East, the Ibo; in the North, the Hausa–Fulani; in the West, the Yoruba); these three groups accounted for more than 65 percent of the total population. Most important, however, the federal structure reflected—and also amplified—the regional bases of political parties. Each region spawned its own major political party; hence, no single party dominated the entire country when independence was achieved.

Two distinct strategies faced Nigerian political parties. First, they could protect their regional bases and form a loose "grand coalition" to govern the Federation as a whole. Alternatively, they could attempt to create "national" foundations by rallying minority and disaffected elements from other regions. The NPC and NCNC adopted the first strategy, by forming a coalition prior to independence. The Action Group favored the second strategy. Despite its lack of success, the Action Group's efforts at nationwide organizing, and the attempts at retribution made largely by the NPC, led more than any other factor to the first 1966 coup.

The years after independence witnessed growing distrust among the three main parties. The Action Group, as we have seen, was the odd man out. In the 1959 Federal election, party leader Obafemi Awolowo waged a vigorous campaign, sending his personal helicopter and sound vans to far-flung parts of the Federation in an attempt to glean support from minority ethnic groups. The campaign costs, by Nigerian standards, were colossal; the results, minimal. One offshoot was profound Northern suspicion of the Action Group, whose leader seemed to meddle in Northern affairs and thereby upset the status quo.

Awolowo's abortive attempt to create a national foundation for the Action Group also split the party. The majority of party members, led by Awolowo, favored a platform based on expanded appeals to the disaffected outside the Western Region. A minority of party members, led by S.L. Akintola and including many of the Action Group's well-to-do patrons, preferred both to concentrate on the Western Region and to soft-pedal the party's national aspirations, in order to enter a coalition with the NPC. The conflict between the two wings broke into the open in 1962 when Awolowo demanded that Akintola resign as prime minister of the Western Region. (Awolowo was then serving in the Federal capital as leader of the Opposition.) A new prime minister was appointed in the West. Before he could take effective control, however, supporters of Akintola rioted in the legislative chamber, twice forcing police to clear it with tear gas. The Federal government used these disturbances as grounds for declaring a state of emergency—a rebuff to Awolowo and his hopes for a national party.

A more serious blow to the Action Group came in 1963, when the Federal government accused Awolowo of conspiracy to commit

treason. Found guilty, Awolowo was sentenced to ten years in prison.
[14] Akintola formed his own party, the Nigerian National Democratic
Party (NNDP), allied with the NPC. Clearly a clash between Action Group
and NNDP was imminent. It came with the 1965 elections in the
Western Region, which touched off widespread violence. The Action
Group expected to triumph. Instead, through intimidation and fraud,
the NNDP (according to preliminary results) emerged with 71 seats,
the Action Group with 5. The flagrantly rigged results escalated violence
in the Western Region even further. To supporters of Awolowo, Akintola and his cronies possessed no right to rule. Violence spread beyond
the capacity of the police to control. And, on the eve of the first coup,
the summoning of the army to quell the Action Group appeared likely.

The growing polarization and violence in the Western Region
represented only one facet of growing southern discontent with Federal
policies. The NCNC increasingly distrusted its Federal coalition partner,
the NPC. Although the NCNC was the oldest of the three major parties,
its influence over Federal policy was steadily ebbing. The junior status
of the NCNC could be attributed to the distribution of population. Prior
to independence, Nigerian politicians agreed to divide seats in the Federal
parliament on the basis of the regions' estimated populations: one-half
to the North, one-quarter each to the East and West. It took little foresight to realize that the party that controlled the North potentially
controlled the Federation—that is, if a census showed the populace to be
split evenly between the Northern Region and the two southern regions.
The NPC never concealed its desire to suborn all opposition in the
North. In the 1961 regional elections, the NPC won nearly two-thirds
of the total vote and all but 10 of the 171 seats in the Northern legislature.[15] Opposition parties (especially among the Tiv) were intimi-
dated by the police and judicial power arrayed against them by the
NPC.[16]

The census of 1962 represented far more than a simple count,
since it was to forecast the relative strength of the major parties. Official results were never published. Preliminary results obviously displeased
the NPC: according to unofficial figures, 22 million of an estimated 45
million Nigerians lived in the North.[17] The Federal prime minister,
a member of the NPC, canceled the results and ordered a new count.
The 1963 census, not unsurprisingly, demonstrated Northerners' willingness to turn the census to their own political ends. Figures for southern
Nigeria showed an increase in population of about 66 percent from
1952; for Northern Nigeria the increase was an incredible 100 percent!
The estimated population leaped from 45 million to over 55 million,
with nearly eight million additional Nigerians being "found" in the North.
By "careful organization with overlapping areas and systematic double
counts"[18] Northern leaders subverted the census. NCNC leaders de-

nounced the results ("worse than useless" was perhaps the mildest epithet applied); however, the NCNC could do little more than protest and unsuccessfully attempt to have the results invalidated. The upshot of the census was considerable weakening of the NCNC. The Federal coalition was fragile; should it desire, the North could evict its southern partner.

The Federal elections of December 1964 were conducted according to the results of the 1963 census. Of the 312 seats to be contested, 167, or just over half, were Northern. New electoral coalitions emerged. The Action Group and the NCNC buried their long-standing dispute to form the United Progressive Grand Alliance, or the UPGA. Akintola's NNDP and the NPC joined forces in the Nigerian National Alliance, or the NNA. The campaign was violent and was stacked against the UPGA from the start. Belatedly realizing their weakness, UPGA leaders called on their supporters to boycott the election, in the hope the results would be nullified and new balloting held. The decision backfired. With the UPGA out of the running, NNA candidates swept the North and West. A constitutional crisis ensued, in which former NCNC leader Nnamdi Azikiwe (president of Nigeria) was forced to back down. Azikiwe apparently considered nullifying the elections—in effect, staging a constitutional Putsch—but retreated from this idea under the pressure of military and police commanders. Northern power had earlier humiliated Awolowo and the West; now it seemed that Northern power would subordinate the NCNC and the East. Although the NPC–NCNC coalition was renewed in 1965, it was far from a partnership of equals.

Succeeding months brought crises in several organizations, such as the Universities of Ibadan and Lagos, the Railway Corporation, and the National Electricity Board. A number of prominent Easterners lost their posts as a result. When combined with the census dispute, the unsuccessful boycott, and Azikiwe's failure to have the electoral results rejected, Easterners had good cause for uneasiness.

The picture of regional discomfort must be completed by examining the North. Despite southern assumptions about a "monolithic" North, the region illustrated many diversities. The foundation of the NPC was not sufficiently secure to calm the unrest of Northern leaders.

To understand politics in Northern Nigeria—and the importance of the reforms later undertaken by the Supreme Military Government—a brief historical review is necessary. The British conquest of Northern Nigeria brought under colonial control a vast impoverished area, in which a fairly strong indigenous administrative system existed among the Hausa–Fulani and Kanuri in particular. Given the viability of the traditional system, the limited economic resources, and the British desire to not tamper with the existing structure, a system of "indirect rule" evolved. British colonial officers would assist and advise the emirs (chiefs); basic control over local police, courts, and taxation would remain in the hands of the emirs, who would be constituted as "native authorities."

The NPC built its strength upon the Native Administration system. As the party of the powerful and the privileged, the NPC had a foundation to protect against those lower in the social hierarchy, and against those restive under the Native Administration system. Violence occasionally resulted. The potential for unrest was particularly marked in areas where Hausa–Fulani rule had been superimposed upon minority ethnic groups. B.J. Dudley commented, "The close relationship between the NPC and the traditional ruling groups in the North, the inordinate zeal of party activists and the intolerance of the Native Administration functionaries have together created deep-seated resentment which on several occasions has led to outbreaks of physical violence."[19] Was the NPC poised on the verge of a volcano that, in erupting, would destroy the system that had been built?

Violence among the Tiv of the Northern Region led in 1964 to the first major involvement of the Nigerian army in maintaining domestic order. The Tiv held little affection for the NPC. In the 1959 Federal election, a party allied to the Action Group captured 85 percent of the Tiv vote. Efforts to press the Tiv into line led to arson and disruption, not to compliance. In 1960, 30,000 houses were burned in an uncontrollable outbreak of protest. As one observer wrote,

> The scale of the burning was so great that at this stage the Police were able to do no more than arrest perhaps a tenth of the total number of burners involved and temporarily delay the burning of certain compounds. As soon as the police convoys had passed, the burners resumed their operations. . . . It was not the work of a few travelling groups of professional strong-arm men but rather the uprising of a whole people into a collective paroxysm of anger and the following of a strange purpose of arson. [20]

Far more serious than the hut-burning was the Tiv uprising of July 1964, again sparked by resentment against the NPC. The Federal prime minister ordered the Nigerian army into action. Fighting soon came to a halt—boosting the prestige of the army, but at the same time identifying the military (in the eyes of some) as an agent of the NPC. Army patrols subdued the violence, but could not eliminate the root causes of tension.

The true picture was thus far from rosy. Accelerating violence in the Western Region; unease in the Eastern Region about ebbing influence in the Federal government; continued pockets of discontent in the Northern Region; suspicion and hostility engendered by the census and electoral disputes—all these produced a climate of profound distrust.

To these concerns must be added one further factor: growing popular resentment of politicians. Politicians seemed increasingly to live for "dash," the ten percent bribe that usually accompanied political transactions in Nigeria. Cynicism about their motives and competence was widespread. Political loyalty, it seemed, could be bought and sold.

The noted Nigerian novelist Chinua Achebe saw, far more prophetically than his compatriots, the fate of politicians seeking "dash." His novel, *A Man of the People,* traced the career of flamboyant Chief Nanga, strongly devoted to power, pleasure, and self-enrichment. Chief Nanga typified the ills of the old system. Achebe concluded his novel with this situation: violence breaks out in the populace; the army seizes power, political parties are abolished, and long-suppressed criticism comes to the fore. In Achebe's words, written prior to the real-life coup but forecasting the reaction of Nigerian citizens,

> *What I found distasteful however was the sudden, unashamed change of front. . . . Overnight everyone began to shake their heads at the excesses of the last regime, at its graft, oppression and corrupt government: newspapers, the radio, the hitherto silent intellectuals and civil servants—everyone said what a terrible lot; and it became public opinion the next morning. And these were the same people that only the other day had owned a thousand names of adulation, whom praise-singers followed with song and talking-drum wherever they went.* [21]

The Nigerian public felt they had been bilked of the fruits of independence. In this vacuum of legitimacy, members of the armed forces could easily assume power. The civilian regime had squandered its support. Tensions provoked within the parties and governments afflicted all sectors of society. The coup was not long in coming.

From Coup to Coup to Coup: The Events of 1966

Saturday, January 15, 1966: a day of governmental and popular confusion in Nigeria. In the Western Region, crowds sacked the houses of Akintola supporters, as news spread of his death. In the capital of the Northern Region, the murder of the head of the NPC (who also served as prime minister of the North) surprisingly aroused no strong protest. Lagos, the Federal capital, witnessed troop maneuvers and counsels of desperation among confused civilian leaders. The political ascent of the Nigerian army had started; its implications were unknown.

Military intervention in Nigeria resulted in a host of paradoxes. Those who intervened did not gain control, but they made army takeover the only possible temporary solution. The resultant Federal Military Government attempted to stamp out "tribalism"; its policies may have enhanced this phenomenon. Officers eschewed alliances with civilian politicians; yet as civil war became imminent, military rulers had to buttress their claim to govern by gaining civilian support. Intervention unleashed new rounds of violence that fragmented the army, brought the cataclysm of civil war, and replaced the hitherto-limited responsibilities of the military with a wide-ranging set of political duties. The eighteen months between the elimination of leading politicians and the outbreak of civil war saw the Nigerian military move into political dominance.

There were three coups in 1966: the first involving the murder of leading politicians; the second a "coup within the coup," leading to a partial restoration of army discipline; the third in late July splintering the armed forces. Leadership of the first coup resided with a small, cohesive group of plotters. Ringleader was Major Nzeogwu—Sandhurst graduate, pious Catholic, and apparently highly puritanical individual. (One of his first acts after seizing the Northern Region was to decree the death penalty for a multitude of offenses, including embezzlement, homosexuality, and looting.) The other six conspirators included one captain and five majors; all but one were Ibos, a fact of later significance. What were to have been coordinated uprisings in the Federal and regional capitals failed. Assassinations were carried out, it is true: in Lagos, five leading officers, the Federal minister of finance and the Federal prime minister; in the West, Chief Akintola; in the North, the Northern prime minister. Fragmentary evidence suggests the conspirators were sick of politics and of politicians; they were highly idealistic nationalists, fed up with the corruption around them and prepared to resort to violence to remold Nigeria in their own image of the "ideal society."[22] They were young (average age of the chief conspirators was 29.3 years), well educated (three of the six university graduates in the entire Nigerian army were among the leading plotters), and on the radical rather than conservative end of the political spectrum. However, they lacked any clear set of priorities, apart from the simplistic extermination of politicians and senior officers.

The second 1966 coup, on the following day, completed the military seizure of control. It came from the top—specifically, from commanding officer General J.T. Aguiyi-Ironsi. Marked for assassination, Ironsi escaped and was able to rally troops. Civilians were in a dilemma. They could do little, as Miners observes, "except hand over to General Ironsi with the best grace that they could muster."[23] On January 16, by "unanimous and voluntary" cabinet agreement, Ironsi was invited to assume control. He was entrusted with restoring military discipline, gaining public confidence, and knitting together the distrustful segments of Nigeria. A Federal Military Government was established; politicians were thrust aside.

As a national leader, Ironsi was an unmitigated failure. His ill-advised policies undercut military unity. Though the populace had initially welcomed military rule, Ironsi squandered his support. His conceptions of what was politically appropriate were far off the mark. In Ironsi's defense, it should be noted that little in his personal experience and little in the British-style training Nigerian officers enjoyed had prepared him and the Nigerian army as a whole for governing. As a silent force outside politics, the Nigerian army had followed commands, not questioned them, nor had it commanded others.

To whom could the Federal Military Government have turned for advice and support? Most politicians were discredited and, more important, distrusted by the armed forces. Despite frequent urgings, Ironsi refused to release Chief Awolowo from prison. Young radicals and university students loudly proclaimed their advice, but were ignored. Yet the need for assistance was acute. The Nigerian army lacked the manpower to govern. The January coups led to the death of seven of the nineteen top officers; those who remained lacked administrative experience and were confronted with enormous tasks in restoring military discipline. General Ironsi necessarily depended almost entirely on civil servants. From its very inception, the Federal Military Government could draw only a few officers totally away from their military duties.

If one theme stands out in the six months of Ironsi's rule, it was opposition to "regionalism." Ironsi and his advisers were convinced that the root cause of disintegration had been the powers the regions enjoyed. The federalism and squabbling of the pre-coup government had differed markedly from the unity of the army. The military was a national institution, with ethnic mixing at all levels and a corporate solidarity transcending place of origin. Since the military was so satisfactory, Ironsi found it easy to idealize the extrapolation of military virtues to the political system as a whole.

Ironsi's policies of national unity proved disastrous. Two decrees, issued in May 1966, reduced rather than enhanced cohesion within the state as a whole—despite Ironsi's claim they would "remove the last vestiges of the intense regionalism of the recent past. . . ." Decree 33 abolished all political parties for three years; Decree 34 formally unified the Federal and regional civil services. The decrees testified to the profound political ignorance of the Federal Military Government, and hence deserve brief analysis.

Abolition of political parties is, of course, a standard ploy of military governments. Their "politics of wanting to be above politics" led the Ironsi government to proscribe 81 political parties and 26 tribal associations. By removing such groups, the Federal Military Government apparently thought a firm basis might be laid for national parties. The decree on the civil service was intended to remove the bureaucracies from the temptations of regionalism and, in a broader sense, to bring to the civil service the national outlook that purportedly characterized the armed forces. The decree replaced the four regions with 35 provinces. All executive and legislative power was to be vested in a National Military Government. Most important, the distinctions between Federal and regional civil services would be abolished, although unification would initially be confined to high-paying positions. This was, in Luckham's words, a "major political miscalculation."[24]

General Ironsi and his advisers were insulated from popular feeling. They did not realize how quickly their support could be destroyed. The North in particular resented the decrees.

Despite its size, the North feared the southern regions. Fear sprang largely from the limited educational and economic opportunities in the region. Preference for recruitment into the Northern civil service was given Northerners, even with lower educational qualifications. Abolition of such preferences would close the major avenue by which Northerners could advance themselves. Deprived of what they considered legitimate expectations, many Northerners, including noncommissioned officers and former NPC leaders, were willing to consider drastic political action. Solicitation of army support by social groups came on the heels of the two decrees.

The National Military Government was interpreted in the North as an imposition of Ibo rule. The Ibos clearly controlled the army after the January coups: 27 of the top 50 officers were Ibo; only five were Northern. Ironsi seemed to surround himself with Ibo advisers. As Miners comments,

> . . . a Northerner could be easily induced to believe that, in the next three years, the Military Government proposed to remove control of [civil service] appointments to Lagos and pack the public service in the North with Southerners, who had longer years of service; that a census would be held which would "discover" a Southern majority in the country; that this Southern majority would then ratify a new constitution in which the Northerner would be for ever a second-class citizen in a "backward" area of the country. [25]

The coup of July 29, 1966, should accordingly be viewed as an explosion of the North against an apparent seizure of control on behalf of a single ethnic group. The coup, in short, built upon tribal tensions.

Resentment of the Ibos rose from several factors, particularly their alleged clannishness and commercial dominance. The May decrees aroused previously latent anxieties and hostilities. Apparently with the connivance of former NPC politicians, crowds attacked Ibos. The police and army stood by as several hundred were murdered. The situation threatened to degenerate even further. The National Military Government had to retreat. After consulting Northern emirs, the government announced that Decree 34 "in no way affected the territorial divisions of the country."[26] The North had reawakened, and would lash out against those who seemed to subvert its interests. Still to come, however, was the upsurge of Northern officers.

The third coup testified to the fragmentation of boundaries between Northern civilians and members of the armed forces. Tensions grew within the Nigerian army itself. Dissent spread through the ranks—how else can one explain the government's unwillingness to issue ammunition to troops, or to call upon the army to suppress the anti-Ibo riots? General Ironsi and his advisers, despite their retreat on Decree 34, gave scant indication of acceding to other Northern demands. For example, no action was taken on the creation of a state in the Middle Belt area, the southern part of the North from which many soldiers were recruited. One informed scholar has singled out this failure as a "good candidate" for the most significant cause of Ironsi's overthrow.[27] Those who had led the January coup were imprisoned, but were not brought to trial, as Northerners demanded.

Belief in an Ibo conspiracy against the North, coupled with stresses internal to the military, precipitated revolt among the Northern ranks and noncommissioned officers. Pent-up tensions burst forth the night of July 28, when Northern soldiers succeeded in seizing all but one of the major garrisons. Northern noncommissioned officers appeared firm in their resolve to split Nigeria—unless Lt. Colonel Yakubu Gowon, the highest-ranking Northerner in the army, assumed control. Gowon agreed. Thus, he was propelled into power by troops who openly mutinied against the leaders of the armed forces (General Ironsi was one of 39 officers killed; 27 of them were Ibos). Gowon confronted an army rife with suspicion, prone to ethnic tensions, and restive under a government that had appeared to undercut the North. Restoration of military discipline was essential, if further bloodshed was to be avoided.

Three effects on civil–military relations in Nigeria resulted from the turmoil of 1966.

1. The armed forces were shattered as a national entity. The January coups had accentuated the role of Ibo officers; the July coup resulted in the resurgence of Northern officers. In a vicious cycle of distrust, regionalization of the army became the only expedient. In August 1966, Gowon permitted soldiers to return their regions of origin. Nigeria emerged from the coups not with a single military, but with four armies harboring varying degrees of hostility toward each other—North, East, West, and Mid-West (created in 1962). Secession was not long in coming. As Luckham has suggested,

The integration of the nation depended in the last resort upon the cohesion of the army: when the latter was lost the nation also was on the verge of disintegration. [28]

The Ironsi government—in a pattern quite common to army-based governments—had preferred the blunt to the politic; it lacked political savvy. Cloistered with a small group of advisers, Ironsi had lost touch with his troops. Trained manpower was too limited to undertake a full-fledged military regime; however, Ironsi had made no significant gestures toward withdrawal. He tried to play the political role without playing the politician's role. He assumed that issuance of a command would result in action and did not test out his ideas with individuals attuned to popular feeling.

2. Violence could not be controlled readily once segments of the army independently decided when and how force should be used. The first January coup weakened the chain of command and the July coup almost totally destroyed it. The Nigerian army could not be trusted to preserve public order. Its discipline and cohesion were severely tried. One shocking incident came in October, when Northern troops forcibly removed fleeing Ibos from an airplane in Kano and murdered them. In many parts of the Northern Region, Ibos were mutilated or killed, a slaughter that helped precipitate secession of the Eastern Region.

3. Military intervention scarcely affected national governmental affairs in Nigeria in 1966. This assertion may seem to fly in the face of the evidence just presented. It must be recalled, however, that soldiers' bullets were directed against politicians and officers, not against civil servants. The Federal Military Government gave bureaucrats considerably more discretion than had the NPC–NCNC coalition. The dearth of trained officers for civil positions enhanced the opportunity for rule by the technocracy.

The year 1966 was thus a disastrous year in a period during which the high hopes of independence were ground down. The ease with which Major Nzeogwu and his fellow conspirators removed leading officials manifested the regime's lack of legitimacy. General Ironsi was dangerously ignorant of the repercussions of the policies he was pressed into announcing. The July coup seemed to cast Nigeria into the classic praetorian mold. Decisions about the military's role were, in reality, decisions about politics. Still to come was a bloody civil war.

The Civil War and Its Aftermath

Military intervention not only signals the presence of conflict within a political system but probably increases it. Intervention introduces a new prize, control over the machinery of government, for which the armed forces can contend. Should officers identified with a particular region or sector of society seize control, political differences resulting from regional or class distinctions may enter and fragment the armed forces. The first coup d'etat touches off a crescendo of intervention that can be softened only with patience, luck, and care.

The coups of 1966 dragged the Nigerian army into supreme decision-making responsibilities. Nothing in their British-style backgrounds prepared individual officers for the tasks they assumed. Tensions spawned by intramilitary issues—promotion policy, Ironsi's selection of advisers, Gowon's good fortune in escaping murder the early morning of January 15, 1966—spilled over to afflict the entire country. The culmination of violence came with the civil war of the late 1960's.

It would be inaccurate to attribute sole responsibility for the war to the political blunders of army members. The heritage of distrust bequeathed by electoral falsification and regional tensions helped prepare the way. Yet, certain aspects of the Nigerian military's behavior in 1966 facilitated the trauma of internal war. The ingredients that went into the conflict included an army that had lost its national character, profound disagreement among military leaders as to appropriate forms of government (surely a breech of the boundary between military and civilian realms that marks civilian control!), a sense of shock in the Eastern Region that enhanced pressure for secession, and Eastern confidence that separate independence could be attained.

A partial dismantling of the Nigerian army resulted from the strains of the July coup. The anti-Ibo explosion made it unsafe for Easterners to remain in Northern garrisons, while soldiers of Northern origin were disarmed in the Eastern Region. The sole solution seemed to be repatriation of members of the armed forces to their regions of origin, which the Supreme Military Government and regional governors accepted early in August. With this act, which sprang partly from humanitarianism, partly from realism, and partly from pressure from Lt. Colonel Odumegwu Ojukwu (military governor of the East), the die was cast for war. The Eastern Region gained 93 combat officers; the Supreme Military Government counted 184 when conflict erupted.[29]

The disorders of 1966 made it clear that Nigeria could not be restored to the status quo that had existed before the first coup. Ironsi's failure ruled out a highly centralized form of government. The three realistic alternatives included: (1) a revised federal structure, (2) a confederal structure that moved most powers from the center to the regions, or (3) breakup of the nation. Gowon desired federation—on the understanding, however, that new regions would be created. On November 30, he broadcast a firm rejection of secession: "My long term aim is the preservation of one Nigerian Army and one country. . . . if circumstances compel me to preserve the integrity of Nigeria by force, I shall do my duty to my country."[30] Many Eastern leaders called for total breakup. Confederation became the common ground for advocates of revised federalism and advocates of secession as well. Following a two-day meeting in Ghana in January 1967, the Supreme Military Council reached an agreement remarkable for its ambiguity. The army would be reorganized, with the Supreme Military Council at the top, but with area commands corresponding to the regions. Any decision "affecting the whole country" was to be made by the Supreme Military Council. But who would make decisions affecting only part of the country? Was unanimity necessary within the Supreme Military Council? What would happen if one of the regional military governors boycotted the Supreme Military Council? What powers would the Federal government exercise? Could new regions be created? The vague formulations of the Ghana meeting, as a group of civil servants later commented, "makes the Federal Military Government subordinate to the regional Military Governments and this amounts to accepting Confederation."[31] It was an untenable position.

The third position, division of Nigeria, became the central objective of Eastern Region leaders. Lt. Colonel Ojukwu became its prime spokesman. His background was unusual, to say the least. Son of a millionaire businessman, he graduated from Oxford University, and entered the officer corps after serving in the Eastern Region civil service. He maintained close ties with the NCNC and Eastern Region intellectuals. With personal affluence and the prestige brought by a university degree, Ojukwu seemed scornful of other officers. Despite his friendship with Gowon, Ojukwu rejected Gowon's claim to head the Federal Military Government. Ojukwu's control over the Eastern Region could not be disputed. Did this pre-eminence give him, in effect, veto power in the East over Federal acts? Ojukwu consistently rejected any exercise of Federal power that did not carry his express approval, and thereby played into the hands of those who favored secession.

Ojukwu never attended another session of the Supreme Military Council after January 1967. The Eastern Region took de facto steps toward secession: expulsion of non-Easterners from the region; takeover of Federal agencies, such as the broadcasting, electricity, coal, and railway boards; halting all payments of revenues to the Federal government; and seizing aircraft of Nigerian Airways. On May 30, the Republic of Biafra was proclaimed.

It was only under the imminent threat of Eastern secession and civil war that Gowon broke the political logjam that had threatened Nigeria since its independence. Early pages in this chapter chronicled how the North gained political control prior to 1966. Dangers exist in any federal structure dominated by a single unit. Breakup of the North would be necessary to re-establish a climate of political trust—and

Gowon, himself a Northerner, was willing to take the step. Excellent intramilitary reasons favored the creation of new states. A significant portion of the Nigerian army (including Gowon) was drawn from the Middle Belt, a part of the Northern Region inhabited by non-Hausa–Fulani. Substantial pressure had built up within the military (especially among Tiv soldiers) for separation of the Middle Belt from the North. When Gowon assumed emergency powers in late May, he ordered the division of Nigeria into twelve states. The Northern Region was split into six states, the Eastern Region into three. Maintaining the unity of the Western Region was, of course, an obvious play for Yoruba support. The Mid-West Region also remained intact, and the Federal Territory of Lagos was made into a state. This decision, taken on the eve of civil war, stands as the military's major contribution to political development in Nigeria.

Gowon took a second step that represented a major break with the policies of his immediate predecessors. His increasing skill and experience in governance enabled him to move toward an open alliance with civilians. Politicians had been excluded by Ironsi from participating in Federal decisions; Gowon initially hesitated about inviting their direct participation. With conflict impending, however, civilian support was imperative. On June 3, 1967, Gowon invited Chief Awolowo to assume the vice-chairmanship of the Federal Executive Council—in effect, to become number-two man in the government. This astute move ensured Yoruba support for Gowon and his policies. No successful war could have been waged against Biafra had the Western Region carried out its threat to secede.

The invitation to Awolowo and eleven other prominent civilians did not constitute a plan for restoring civilian control, however. Gowon had pledged to maintain Nigerian unity by force if necessary; with the secession of Biafra, the occasion for force had come. For at least the duration of the war, civilians would occupy cabinet posts, but essential control would remain in military hands. A war had to be fought and won—and surely this was a task for the armed forces!

The outcome of the civil war belongs to history. Biafran forces scored spectacular successes in the early months of fighting, seizing the Mid-West Region and sweeping to within 90 miles of the Federal capital. Gradually, however, the superior resources of the Federal government tipped the balance. In the prolonged war of attrition, Federal victory came, as Biafra was compressed into a small area, isolated from sources of supply. In January 1970, Ojukwu fled into exile; Nigeria formally returned to peace, and to healing the wounds of war.

What role was the Nigerian army going to exercise, now that domestic unity had been restored? Would political leadership continue to stem from the armed forces, or might civilians resume power? Could the former secessionist area be fully and peacefully reintegrated?

The Armed Forces as Governors

As we have seen, nothing in their professional background prepared members of the Nigerian armed forces for wide-ranging political responsibilities. With a fair degree of success, the British inculcated the notion that "politics is not for soldiers." The ballooning of the army during the civil war did not bring immediate political repercussions; after all, there was a war to win. Combat ren_ained the prime duty. Successful prosecution of a war does not necessarily entail subsequent political order, however.

The most significant moves of the Federal Military Government since the start of the civil war are in three different areas: implementation of the twelve-state system; reintegration of the secessionist areas; and hesitant efforts to restore civilian rule.

Toward a New Federalism

No federal state can long survive if one region can overpower the others.

The Federation of Nigeria, as granted independence by Great Britain, was inherently unstable. The extraordinary disparities in size, patterns of colonial administration, and ways of life in the regions made integration an overwhelmingly difficult task.

The Northern Region was physically larger than the other regions combined; but irrespective of census manipulations, the North contained about half the Nigerian population. On the basis of these facts, control of that region would result in control of the entire country. More fundamentally, however, Nigeria was divided by contrasts that the early years of independence could not reduce. The precolonial differences between the Northern Region and the southern regions had been accentuated by British administration for close to a century. The North was open savannah but the south was largely forest; Islam was professed by most inhabitants of the far North, but not in the south; centralized power held by Northern emirs contrasted with the much more diffuse political responsibilities of southern chiefs. Southern Nigeria was gradually carved out in the mid-nineteenth century, as trade and missions followed the British flag and British-chartered companies. The Colony of Lagos, the Oil Rivers Protectorate, and the Niger Coast Protectorate were the constituent elements, acquired in fits and starts. Northern Nigeria, by contrast, was conquered in 1898–99, as British-officered troops subdued numerically superior Hausa–Fulani troops, who were not as well armed. The North witnessed "indirect rule," designed to retain and very gradually adapt the emirs to more effective local government. Experiments in the south with indirect rule proved abortive. Party politics waxed in southern cities, especially among the educated, as an attempt to hasten self-government; but party politics in the North, as practiced by the NPC, were designed to maintain and reinforce differences of status.

In reality, of course, the picture was far more complex. All the regions contained several minorities who were restive under the dominance of Hausa–Fulani, Ibo, or Yoruba. The Nigerian politician most attuned to the concerns of the minorities was Awolowo, whose unsuccessful electoral efforts among the minorities we have already considered. Shortly after World War II, while studying law in London, Awolowo published a prescient book, *Path to Nigerian Freedom.* He advocated dividing the regions, to give each major group a state of its own. The British government gave little attention to Awolowo's suggestions; Northern leaders, as noted previously, resented any effort to carve up their region. Only with the supreme challenges of secession and civil war could the deadlock be broken, and the political map of Nigeria redrawn.

The creation of twelve states will likely stand as the armed forces' major contribution to Nigerian politics. The step was dictated by political realism, literally on the eve of the Federation's demise. On May 27, 1967, Lt. Colonel Gowon proclaimed a state of emergency, assumed full powers as army commander in chief, and ordered the creation of the states. The once-overpowering North was to become six states; the East, three; the Federal Territory of Lagos was to be raised to state status, while the West and Mid-West would remain unchanged. Gowon took these steps to gain greater military and civilian support, for war was imminent. New states, notably in the Middle Belt, helped assure the loyalty of the armed forces; the Middle Belt, and the Tiv area in particular, furnished a substantial portion of the rank and file. Creation of new states helped win the support of Awolowo, who had threatened a few weeks earlier that the West might follow the East out of Nigeria. Seeing his ideas of 1947 implemented twenty years later, Awolowo (who had been freed from prison on Gowon's command) turned his political acumen to the Federal Military Government, and in July he was named vice-chairman of the Federal Executive Committee.

The creation of additional states held further advantages. First, the new states could help draw away from Biafra the Eastern minorities disaffected with the Ibos. The division of the regions enhanced the controlling power of the Federal Military Government, which in turn allocated shares of import and export revenues to the states. Nearly three-quarters of the revenue of some state governments came from the center, whose power was thereby enhanced. Secondly, the division of the North and the East focused political attention on the new states, giving the Federal Military Government greater latitude in shaping national policy. The establishment of state governments involved several steps: dividing regional assets and liabilities; staffing the civil service (and in the process, creating a not inconsiderable number of new jobs); clarifying relationships among the several layers of government. The occasion was seized for a striking alteration of local government in the North. The influential journal *West Africa* spoke of a "quiet revolution" that substantially reduced the power of the former Native Authorities—which had served, it should be recalled, as the foundation for the NPC. The seemingly monolithic North was no more.

The Reintegration of Biafra

Knitting together the fabric of a society torn by civil war poses unparalleled challenges. Civil war may arouse desires for revenge on the secessionist territory. It is not sufficient merely to block such desires; rather, successful reintegration requires conciliation rather than retribution.

The Gowon government has pursued conciliatory policies toward the former "Republic of Biafra." Take, for example, the fate of Biafran officers. At the conclusion of the war, a Military Board of Inquiry examined the conduct of 159 Nigerian officers who served in the Biafran army during the conflict. Of these, 65 were reabsorbed into the Nigerian army, 64 dismissed, and 30 kept in "protective custody"; none were executed.[32] The Federal Military Government did proclaim a general amnesty at the end of the war; however, conspirators and ringleaders of secession were excluded. In August 1970, the Federal Government stated it would dismiss or retire all public officials who had supported Biafra, or who had committed "hostile acts" against the Federal or state governments. Men who had served in the Biafran rank and file, Gowon stated a few weeks after Biafra's surrender, would not be absorbed into the Nigerian army. (Apparently some officers could be redeemed, but the ranks could not!)

Relief efforts were quickly mounted after the war, coordinated by the Nigerian Red Cross and Federal Government. In May 1970, ten civilian commissioners were appointed to the government of the East-Central State, and an Ibo doctor was named to the Federal Executive Council. The long, difficult reintegration had started, with remarkable lack of rancor.

Restoration of Civilian Rule?

No significant steps were taken by the Gowon government, in its first six years, to restore full civilian rule. What evolved instead was a coalition between civilians, the "outs" of the 1962–66 period, and members of the armed forces.

Prior to the outbreak of the civil war, the Supreme Military Council spoke of restoring civilian rule by early 1969. In April 1967, for example, the Supreme Military Council set forth a detailed timetable: Within eight months, a special commission on new states would be established, civilians would be named to the Federal Executive Committee, and a constitution-drafting committee would be created. In 1968, a Constituent Assembly would draft a new constitution, which would be promulgated by the Supreme Military Council; also, a transitional government would be installed and party activities would be resumed. In early 1969, so the timetable concluded, elections would be held for Federal and state governments, and formal handover to civilians would occur. These pronouncements suggested that the army saw itself playing a guardian/status quo role, restoring public order and correcting political abuses, then returning quickly to the barracks.

But even the most prudent plans of the military in this situation are often not workable. The tumult of the civil war made the Supreme Military Council increasingly hesitant about withdrawing from power. In his 1967 Christmas message, for example, Gowon listed the goals for which the Federal Government was fighting. Conspicuously absent was any mention of civilian rule. Earlier in the same month, Gowon warned that military rule might continue longer than had been expected, since the Supreme Military Council "would have to be sure that the situation in the country was such that power could be handed over without prejudice to the country as a whole."[33] The military alone, in other words, would decide when, and whether, it would withdraw from politics. Gowon reiterated this view in February 1970: Nigeria would not be "returned to civilian rule in chaotic conditions."[34] Once embarked upon reform and the full exercise of power in alliance with civilians, the military seemed less and less likely to undertake total withdrawal from politics.

On October 1, 1970, the tenth anniversary of independence, Gowon suggested that the armed forces might return to the barracks by 1976. Gone, then, was the expectation of a quick military retreat from political life. Before withdrawing, the Supreme Military Council was first intending to preside over a nine-point program [35] of mind-boggling complexity:

1. Reorganization of the armed forces.
2. Implementation of a national development plan and repair of war-related damage and neglect.
3. Eradication of corruption in national life.
4. Settlement of the question of the number of states (in Gowon's words, ". . . the twelve-State structure has, in fact, produced a basis for political stability. . . . the instability and

the difficulties involved in embarking on an exercise of creating more States will not be worthwhile in the present circumstances"). [36]
5. Preparation and adoption of a new constitution.
6. Introduction of a new formula for allocating federal tax revenues among the states.
7. Holding a national population census (presumably free from the double counts and falsifications of the 1962 and 1963 censuses).
8. Organization of "genuinely national political parties."
9. Organization of elections and installation of elected Federal and state governments.

The year following Gowon's statement brought only one significant step, the announcement of a national census in November 1973. On the question of civilian political activity, Gowon upheld the ban upon political parties initially imposed by the Ironsi government. He expressed his reasons in these words:

> *It is only in the context of such commonly accepted [national] objectives and goals that the development of political parties can be a positive factor in nation-building. If we were to return to partisan politics before the country consolidates its unity and national purpose we would be going back to the old days of permanent crisis and mutual blackmail. . . . When the time comes, brand-new parties founded on the widest possible national basis will arise.* [37]

When and how might these "brand-new parties" arise? Can the Supreme Military Council accurately assess whether national goals have been "commonly accepted"? Might members of the armed forces be tempted to doff their uniforms and themselves start to campaign? No clear answers have been forthcoming. Perhaps closest to the truth was a cryptic remark by Colonel Obasanjo in March 1970: the armed forces should form "the bedrock of the political stability and effectiveness of any future civilian government." [38]

Stamping out corruption figures prominently among the nine points. Gowon's exhortations have not been matched by performance. The record of the Federal Military Government suggests that "dash" remains as prominent a feature of Nigerian politics as prior to 1966. The installation of a military-based government in no way guarantees less corruption, despite rhetoric to the contrary. [39] The financial attractions of political office may account, in part, for the apparent hesitation about returning to the barracks. In October 1971, fifteen officers were arrested in connection with alleged embezzlement; the ever-active rumor mills of Lagos continue to spread stories of widespread and increasing corruption within the armed forces.

But the most complex issues arise internal to the armed forces themselves. It should be noted that military reorganization stood first in Gowon's list of necessary steps. The expansion brought by the civil war introduced profound strains within the military as a whole. It is notoriously difficult to maintain professional standards and unity in times of rapid growth. By the end of the war, the Nigerian army may have counted as many as a quarter-million men—no one knew for sure! The absence of precise information about the size and costs of the Nigerian military continued to embarrass the Supreme Military Council. In the first nine months of fiscal 1971–72, the armed forces spent more than double its appropriation for the entire year. The conquest of Biafra did not bring rapid demobilization; indeed, the Nigerian chief of staff said the armed forces would be maintained at their existing strength (whatever that might have been), to reduce potential social disruption. A postwar upsurge of violence and armed robbery, together with continued high urban unemployment, have been used to justify the retention policy. A large military establishment represents a costly form of public works, however. Although the Nigerian economy has been buoyed by soaring exports of oil (15 percent of the state's foreign exchange earnings in 1964, 55 percent in 1971), the armed forces seem far too large and far too costly for the economy to support. What factors explain the apparent paralysis in reducing the size of the armed forces? Perhaps the Supreme Military Council recalls the 1963 murder of Sylvanus Olympio, then president of Togo, who refused to take demobilized soldiers back into the armed forces. By 1967, Olympio's assassin had become president of that small West African state. Mass discharges could unleash strong pressures against the government—and fiscal hemorrhage by itself cannot justify such steps against military self-interest. Rare indeed is the military regime that reduces its own army.

What lessons can be drawn from seven years of military rule in Nigeria?

Intervention sprang from generalized discontent with the Nigerian political system, crystallized by the audacious acts of Major Nzeogwu and his cohorts. The conspirators lacked specific prescriptions for the state. By lopping off corrupt leaders, and by instituting military virtues, they apparently believed they would receive political hosannahs. General Ironsi likewise lacked a clear set of political objectives. He tossed aside much of the support he had initially garnered, within the army and in large parts of the Federation. His ultimately fatal step on Decree No. 34 hinted that Ironsi wanted sweeping political changes, against the wishes of a restive, divided military. Lt. Colonel Gowon was thrust into political prominence as a result of Northern reactions against Ironsi. Gowon's dedicated efforts to keep the army from total fission, then his successful prosecution of the civil war, left him little opportunity for pondering the most important lesson to be drawn from Nigeria—that establishment of an army-based government considerably exacerbates strains and tensions within the armed forces, leading to frequent and unstabilizing intervention by aggrieved sectors. Nigeria teaches this lesson with a vengeance.

Nigeria bears out two propositions suggested in Part I. The armed forces did not enter Nigerian politics because of specific policy grievances, but because of generalized political discontent. As a result, no clear policies could be implemented which would lead to speedy withdrawal. The more diffuse the grievances, the more likely intervention will result in long-term military rule. Secondly, fission within the officer corps complicated and prolonged the armed forces' stay in politics. Lack of cohesion results in fragmented political involvement. Officers are caught in a quandary—uncertain whether withdrawal, reform, or renewed intervention will clear away the generalized discontent they feel.

Gowon and his fellow members of the Supreme Military Council have taken on awesome responsibilities. In setting the terms for their withdrawal, they have proclaimed themselves the official arbiters of Nigerian politics. Pandora's box may have sprung open. Reform of the total Nigerian political system, explicit in Gowon's nine conditions of 1970, represents a far more complex task than winning a civil war. Although the Federal Military Government regularly underscores its willingness to return to the barracks, these may be more rhetorical flourishes than substantive policy.

The Nigerian military will withdraw from its current political primacy only if two conditions are fulfilled. First, there must come into existence a strong, widely supported civilian group that represents a political alternative to the existing Federal Military Government. Second, and more important, the Supreme Military Council must decide that its own ends will best be served by a return to the barracks. Withdrawal will come about when the armed forces set the date.

But is it realistic to suppose that the Nigerian armed forces will significantly reduce their current political involvement? The broad-gauged tasks the military has set itself do not admit of easy solutions. And it will be easy to retain control, on the grounds that unresolved problems remain on the agenda. In addition, a substantial number of civilians have been co-opted; Awolowo, who resigned in mid-1971, represents the only major defection. (Awolowo charged that military government "constitutes at best a benevolent and at worst a malevolent oligarchy."[40] He declined, however, to characterize the intentions of the Nigerian high command.) Many civilian leaders—politicians and civil servants alike—

seem content to let the Supreme Military Council take the rap for what-ever goes wrong. If army leaders find no groups to whom they willingly will turn over control, prospects for withdrawal seem slight. The tasks ahead, though too difficult for the armed forces to resolve, will make nec-essary the continued rationalization of military involvement. It may be that change will come only through another round of military interven-tion. Nigeria has yet to find a political formula that produces a civic polity.

References

1. N.J. Miners, *The Nigerian Army 1956-1966* (London: Methuen, 1971), p. 20.
2. Ibid., p. 26. It should be noted, however, that the Middle Belt enjoyed con-siderably more educational opportunities than the northernmost section of Nigeria, where as late as 1972 less than one child in ten attended primary school.
3. Ibid., p. 100.
4. G.O. Olusanya, "The Role of Ex-Servicemen in Nigerian Politics," *Journal of Modern African Studies*, VI, 2, 221-32.
5. Miners, *The Nigerian Army*, p. 32.
6. Ibid., p. 52.
7. Robin Luckham, *The Nigerian Military: A Sociological Analysis of Authority and Revolt 1960-67* (Cambridge: Cambridge University Press, 1971), p. 163.
8. Edward Luttwak, *Coup d'Etat: A Practical Handbook* (Greenwich: Fawcett, 1969).
9. General H.T. Alexander, *African Tightrope: My Two Years as Nkrumah's Chief of Staff* (New York: Praeger, 1966).
10. Henry L. Bretton, *Power and Stability in Nigeria: The Politics of Decoloniza-tion* (New York: Praeger, 1962), p. 98.
11. Luckham, *The Nigerian Military*, p. 173.
12. Ibid., p. 172.
13. Quoted in Ibid, pp. 32-3.
14. Richard L. Sklar, "Nigerian Politics: The Ordeal of Chief Awolowo, 1960-65," in Gwendolen M. Carter, ed., *Politics in Africa* (New York: Harcourt, Brace & World, 1966), pp. 119-66.
15. B.J. Dudley, *Parties and Politics in Northern Nigeria* (London: Cass, 1968), pp. 139-40.
16. Ibid., p. 186.
17. Luckham, *The Nigerian Military*, p. 213.

18. John P. Mackintosh, *Nigerian Government and Politics* (London: George Allen and Unwin, 1966), p. 554.

19. Dudley, *Parties and Politics in Northern Nigeria,* p. 189.

20. J.M. Dent, "A Minority Party—The United Middle Belt Congress," in Mackintosh, *Nigerian Government and Politics,* pp. 496, 498.

21. Chinua Achebe, *A Man of the People* (London: Heinemann, 1966), p. 166.

22. John N. Colas, "The Social and Career Correlates of Military Intervention in Nigeria: A Background Study of the January 15th Coup Group" (Paper delivered at the meeting of the Inter-University Seminar on Armed Forces and Society, Chicago, 1969), p. 5.

23. Miners, *The Nigerian Army,* p. 165.

24. Luckham, *The Nigerian Military,* p. 265.

25. Miners, *The Nigerian Army,* p. 200.

26. Quoted in Ibid., p. 206.

27. Ibid., p. 212.

28. Luckham, *The Nigerian Military,* p. 298.

29. Ibid., p. 92.

30. Quoted in Ibid., p. 316.

31. Ibid., p. 355.

32. It should be noted, however, that only one major and 23 captains were reabsorbed; one colonel, 12 lieutenant colonels, and 9 majors were dismissed. For a full list, see *West Africa,* November 26, 1971, p. 1402.

33. *Africa Research Bulletin,* IV, 12 (December 1967), Col. 934A.

34. Ibid., VII, 2 (February 1970), Col. 1674A.

35. Ibid., 10 (October 1970), Col. 1898B.

36. Ibid., Col. 1898C–1899A.

37. Ibid.

38. Ibid., 3 (March 1970), Col. 1700B.

39. Take, for example, Gowon's remarks at an army sports festival: he regretted "the absence of ideals and the preponderance of materialistic and selfish tendencies" in Nigerian society, and pledged, "We are determined to strive at the noblest of ideals and to maintain the highest standard of morality in our public life." *West Africa* (December 17, 1971), p. 1497.

40. *West Africa* (November 26, 1971), p. 1401.

6

Peru: Soldier=Politicians as " Revolutionaries"

Members of the armed forces have figured prominently in Peruvian politics since independence was wrested from Spain in 1821. The first fifty years of Peruvian history witnessed a series of oligarchical, predatory military regimes. Even as the middle classes and political parties developed, the military remained politically active, playing a direct role in the initiation of several governments. The facade of civilian rule could not disguise the political centrality of officers. With growing social mobilization and with greater professional awareness within the armed forces, however, the most recent intervention of the Peruvian armed forces manifested a new brand of political involvement. As self-proclaimed "revolutionaries," the governing officers have moved toward a radical model of political change.

On October 3, 1968, Peru's military leaders deposed President Fernando Belaunde Terry, a constitutionally elected and reformist civilian politician. Ironically, Belaunde's rise to power some five years before had been actively supported by many of the same officers who now brusquely pushed him aside. In itself this military usurpation of power was hardly an unusual event in Peruvian history. In the century and a half that followed the winning of independence, Peru had seen many military *caudillos* ("strongmen") and juntas occupying the Pizarro Palace in Lima. Most of the country's nineteenth-century presidents had come from the ranks of the military. More recently, military regimes had governed Peru during more than half the years since 1930.

In several important respects, however, the coup of October 1968 marked a significant turning point in the established pattern of Peruvian civil–military relations. It had long been accepted as axiomatic that the armed forces were tools of the so-called "forty families," the country's conservative landholding oligarchy. Yet the new junta, headed by General Juan Velasco Alvarado, launched a series of reforms that constituted a radical departure from the military's traditional stance. The Velasco regime, instead of upholding the status quo and hence the interests of the oligarchy, proclaimed itself the vanguard of social revolution. In Latin America, where the military's role in politics is crucial, the Peruvian junta's commitment to this radical course provoked both anxiety and jubilation.

For students of civil–military relations, recent political events in Peru have raised questions of particular significance. Why has a military establishment with a long tradition of social conservatism committed itself to promoting fundamental social change? Does its commitment to modernization include a willingness to permit the participation of Peru's Indian masses (who comprise roughly forty-five percent of the population) in political decisions? What are the military's prospects of success in its effort to modernize the country? What kinds of political structures and processes will emerge in the long run? What, finally, are the repercussions likely to be for the military institutions themselves? We shall examine these and other questions by first reviewing the historical role of the Peruvian armed forces and then turning to the causes and consequences of the 1968 coup.

The Peruvian Military in Historical Perspective

The authoritarianism, personalism, and pervasive instability of nineteenth-century Latin American politics were described in Part I in the typology of political systems. In Peru as in most of these countries, the military leaders of the independence movement became the foremost political leaders of the young republic. The traditional social structure of the colonial era remained unchanged by independence. Democratic institutions imported from abroad were peripheral and practically irrelevant to the country's social system. For nearly the remainder of the century a virtually unbroken string of autocrats, the great majority of them military men, governed Peru in highly personalistic and often predatory style. The only significant political forces of the period were the landholding oligarchy, the Church, and the military; and these seldom found their interests conflicting.[1] The great bulk of Peru's population was made up of Indians unassimilated by Hispanic culture. This great social cleavage, persisting even to the present, has been of central importance in the development of the military's political role.[2]

Professionalism did not gain a firm foothold in the Peruvian armed forces until the early part of the twentieth century, and as a result the military as a corporate interest group did not develop a prominent political role until that time. Political leaders of the nineteenth century, whether military or civilian, were caudillos—personalistic strongmen who represented only limited factions or cliques. In the words of Victor Villanueva, a prolific scholar of the Peruvian military, it was "true armed parties and not the army itself" that established caudillos in power and then toppled them.[3] Military dictators governed Peru from 1821 until 1872. Among them only General Ramón Castilla, who served two terms during 1845–1851 and 1858–1862, managed to give Peru a semblance of effective government. One historian characterizes Castilla as the "second liberator" of his country, which before him had been "covered with misery and pain, accustomed to living in perpetual anarchy." [4] Most of his fellow military politicians, however, preyed shamelessly on the public treasury. By the 1870's their excesses finally brought on a civilian revolt against military rule.

In the second half of the nineteenth century the growth of a modern sector oriented toward the export economy generated an urban middle class whose economic interests and political ambitions were incompatible with the existing political system. The civilian revolt that brought Manuel Pardo to power in 1872 was partly an outgrowth of these new socioeconomic currents. Civilians remained far too weak and politically disorganized to assert control over the armed forces, but the growing strength of their demands impressed on the military an enduring lesson: the strongest military caudillo no longer could claim an exclusive right to the presidency. New civilian political forces competing for that office must now be reckoned with.[5] Pardo's supporters formed Peru's first political party, the Partido Civilista, which committed itself to promoting economic progress and ending the military's accustomed dominance of political life. It was Pardo who made the first concerted attempts to professionalize the Peruvian armed forces, by establishing service academies for the army and navy. His reforms failed to insulate the military from politics, but the Civilista revolt succeeded in establishing a new pattern of civil-military relations. After 1872, the military tended to participate in politics through the channel of the nascent political party system, reflecting that the armed forces acknowledged its new need for civilian allies. So effective became the military at this game that the Civilistas nominated a general as their candidate in the elections of 1876, thereby exposing as premature the civilian revolt four years before.[6]

The military role in Peruvian politics was even more severely shaken by a disastrous performance in the War of the Pacific (1879–1883). The army's humiliation at the hands of Chilean forces stimulated a new wave of antimilitarism, centered on a new civilian party (Partido Democrata) and its leader, Nicolás de Piérola. The army responded with a campaign to improve its public image and formed a political party of its own (Partido Constitucional). One of the very few Peruvian heroes of the war, Colonel Andrés Avelino Caceres, won the presidency in 1886 at the head of this army-based party. His campaign justified renewed military rule on the grounds that a strong defense-oriented government was necessary if Peru was to avenge her war losses. When Caceres ultimately proved unable to recover lost territories from Chile, however, a new civilian revolt led by Piérola succeeded in toppling him, thus ushering in Peru's first era of civilian dominance over the military.

In a sense, Piérola's civilian coup d'etat of 1895 represents Peru's only successful popular insurrection. The coup was supported by the great majority of the politically active civilian sectors and succeeded in binding together temporarily the oligarchy-based Civilista and Democrata parties. It was also a tumultuous and bloody event; Villanueva estimates that some ten thousand lives were lost.[7] Most notably, however, the coup heralded the beginning of nearly two decades of constitutional government under seven civilian presidents. But despite the surface appearances of representative government and party competition, Peru's political institutions were weak and narrowly based. Personalism remained the basic element of political life, and the oligarchy remained secure in its privileges, status, and wealth.[8]

The two decades of civilian rule from 1895 to 1914 had important consequences for the military. Piérola assumed the task of professionalizing the officer corps, hoping, as did President Pardo some years before, to transform the military into an apolitical institution. At the same time he expanded and modernized the army to bolster Peru's defenses against the expansionist Chileans to the south. Piérola arranged for a French military mission to supervise the reorganization and training of the Peruvian armed forces (the Chileans had accepted a mission from Germany). He established the Escuela Militar in Chorrillos as a professional staff college for officers. Promotions and pay increases were largely taken out of the hands of individual generals and based on merit. These reforms, together with a compulsory military service law, moved the Peruvian army a giant step forward in professionalization.[9] By no means, however, was the army apolitical during this era, nor was the traditional alliance between the military and the oligarchy broken. Of the seven civilian administrations from 1895 to 1914, four were coalitions which included Caceres's militaristic Partido Constitucional. Whereas before 1895 the military caudillos governed with the support of the oligarchy, afterward the civilian caudillos governed with the support of the military. Despite the civilians' public rhetoric of antimilitarism, there was no real consensus among the various factions that the military should be barred from politics. The civilian parties continued to seek allies from among factions within the armed forces. Civilians themselves were thus responsible for maintaining a high level of military politicization and for undermining the norm of civilian supremacy.[10]

The period of constitutional government begun by Piérola in 1895 came to an abrupt end in 1914 when Democrata President Guillermo Billinghurst was overthrown by a coup. With respect to both its causes and its consequences, this coup marked another significant turning point in Peruvian civil–military relations. Its leader, Colonel Oscar Benavides, was backed by powerful segments of the oligarchy. The coup occurred in the context of increasingly strident labor demands for an eight-hour day and other reforms. Billinghurst appeared to be on the verge of acceding to these demands, and moreover he had threatened to reduce the military's budget.[11] In part, then, the coup could be explained by the military's budgetary concerns, but 1914 also represented the first time that the military had intervened in direct support of the interests of the oligarchy against pressures from lower social strata. According to Villanueva, Benavides inaugurated a "new variety of militarism, no longer in direct benefit of uniformed caudillos backed by the oligarchy but, on the contrary, in benefit of the ruling class which the armed forces back, defend, and support with the sole condition that the military budget must remain intact."[12] Faced with the growing restiveness of Peru's lower strata, the landed and commercial elites closed ranks behind Benavides. This upper-class solidarity was manifested in 1915 when the two oligarchic parties and the military agreed on the presidential candidacy of José Pardo, son of the Civilista reformer of 1872–1876.

The half century before 1914 had witnessed important changes in Peru's economic structure, with concomitant implications for the country's politics. Economic modernization received its first major impetus in the 1840's with the discovery that guano, deposited in vast quantities over centuries by sea birds on offshore islands, was rich in nitrogen and hence commercially valuable. Operated as a government monopoly, the guano trade with Europe produced immense profits for the national treasury through the end of the century. Concurrently the government issued licenses to foreign concessionaires for the development of sodium nitrate deposits in the arid Atacama desert, and still other foreigners were engaged to construct a modern railway system. By 1914 the guano deposits had long been exhausted and the Atacama had been lost to Chile as a price of Peru's defeat in war, but the Peruvian economy was booming again through the export of copper and cotton. World War I lent further impetus to this prosperity. However, the war's aftermath exposed Peru's economic vulnerability and her extreme dependence on the health of the international economic system. Demand for copper and cotton fell disastrously in 1919, in conjunction with plummeting world prices and mounting labor strife at home. Strong leadership was needed, and the armed forces cooperated with civilian elites to elevate a true civilian caudillo, Augusto B. Leguía, to the presidency.[13]

Leguía ruled Peru for the next eleven years (1919–1930). His regime was severely autocratic but, more than any other civilian president before or since, Leguía was able to dominate the military. By various maneuvers he succeeded in dividing the officer corps against itself, but in doing so he rolled back many of the gains of recent decades toward professionalism. With extravagant favors to a particular clique of officers (known scornfully as *cautreros,* "horse thieves"), Leguía bought the loyalty of the highest ranking officers and dealt harshly with any who opposed him. An even more blatant affront to the military corporate interests was Leguía's organization of the Guardia Civil, a uniformed militia with officer perquisites similar to those of the army and with obvious potential as a counterweight to the military's political influence. At the same time Leguía de-emphasized the army's importance and stimulated interservice rivalries by bolstering naval appropriations and creating an air force.[14] Despite these obvious threats to the army's vital institutional interests, Leguía's favoritism and expert divisive tactics rendered the officer corps incapable of unified action in its own defense.[15] By his ruthlessness and political skill, Leguía succeeded temporarily in establishing a form of subjective civilian control.

Although Leguía was finally ousted by a military revolt in 1930, his downfall was primarily a result of the Great Depression and Peru's continued dependence on international economic events. During his eleven years in office Leguía had opened the doors wide to foreign investors, chiefly American, offering them substantial concessions. The national debt increased tenfold under his administration. The Depression finally brought to a grinding halt both the economic boom and Leguía's patronage machine. The coup against him was led by another colorful caudillo, Colonel Luis M. Sánchez Cerro, and at first there was considerable doubt whether it would succeed. Two major factions within the army opposed Sánchez Cerro, one made up of Leguía's cuatreros and the other of senior officers apparently resentful of Sánchez Cerro's relatively junior rank. A fratricidal civil war threatened until naval officers managed to mediate the dispute, and agreement on a provisional government was reached. As a result of a later vote taken among all army officers, Sánchez Cerro was designated the army's candidate in carefully controlled elections held in 1931. Thus, with the lessons of the Leguía era making officers acutely sensitive to threats against their institutional solidarity, the Peruvian army reasserted its "right" to manage the country's affairs.

The elections of 1931 became another important political landmark. A new civilian political party had been taking form during the 1920's, the Alianza Popular Revolucionaria Americana (American Popular Revolutionary Alliance, or APRA). The APRA party and the military were shortly to develop a profound mutual enmity that remains the most significant element in Peruvian civil–military relations through the present day. The true nature of APRA, the role of its magnetic leader Victor Raul Haya de la Torre, and the deep-rooted military distrust of both the man and the party have all been sources of controversy, and therefore merit particular attention.

APRA originated in a radical student movement at Lima's San Marcos University during the period 1918–1923. Haya de la Torre and other students took part in a series of strikes to demonstrate solidarity with the emerging labor movement, and in 1921 the students undertook the organization of "popular universities" to educate and politicize workers. These activities irritated the dictator Leguía. When in 1923 Leguía sought to ingratiate himself with the Church by dedicating Peru to the Sacred Heart of Jesus, Haya de la Torre led an anticlerical protest that resulted in his jailing and subsequent exile. Haya de la Torre founded APRA in Mexico in 1924 as an inter-American socialist movement, ideologically tailored to the circumstances and needs of Latin America. The core of the Aprista program prescribed five major points of emphasis: (1) opposition to "Yanqui" imperialism; (2) political unity for Latin America (which Haya de la Torre called "Indo-America"); (3) nationalization of land and industry; (4) solidarity of workers and oppressed classes; and (5) the inter-Americanization of the Panama Canal.[16]

APRA had little success as an inter-American movement, but in Peru it quickly became a magnet for intellectuals, middle-class professionals, students, and the more advanced labor elements. APRA also stirred support among Peru's impoverished and disenfranchised Indian masses. By 1931 the movement clearly had become the country's largest and best organized political party. Its populist strength was recognized as a formidable threat by the more established actors in Peruvian politics. Opposition to APRA united the landholding and commercial segments of the oligarchy. Both Washington and the American business community were repelled by Haya de la Torre's views on foreign investment and the Panama Canal. For their part, the Peruvian armed forces concluded that APRA represented a menace to their institutions. In the events surrounding the elections of 1931, a deep and lasting hatred of APRA became rooted within the military.

The APRA program called not only for the removal of the military from politics. It sought the virtual abolition of the armed forces and the rechanneling of military appropriations into education and other social reforms. The armed forces branded the APRA programs as Bolshevist. They feared that the Apristas would organize a revolutionary militia and plunge the country into civil war. By most accounts these fears of APRA radicalism had become baseless by 1940, when participation in the struggle for power had considerably moderated APRA demands.[17] At the time of the 1931 elections, however, the military's fears seemed very real indeed. The officers were also alarmed by the Aprista tactic, continued through the 1930's and 1940's, of infiltrating the enlisted and lower officer ranks in the hope of subverting and using the army for its own purposes.[18] More even than APRA's extremism, this provocative tactic solidified the military's opposition. The mutual hostility was exacerbated by the army's blatant imposition of Colonel Sánchez Cerro as president in a fraudulent election in 1931. The Aprista response was to seek redress through violent means. In a few months, Sánchez Cerro outlawed the APRA party and ordered the arrest of Haya de la Torre; Apristas in northern Peru, the party stronghold, erupted in outrage and successfully overran the army barracks in the city of Trujillo. Infuriated by this affront and particularly by the APRA execution of all captured officers and many of the soldiers (200 men in all), the army retook the barracks in a bloody action and in reprisal massacred some 2000 Apristas.[19] Army officers circled the date of the Trujillo massacre for solemn annual observation. APRA was forced to go underground.

These events established what has been for forty-five years the dominant theme of civil–military relations in Peru. The fundamental mutual hostility between these two powerful political actors, one controlling a preponderance of organized coercion and the other mobilizing broad popular consent, has critically impeded the growth of political institutions in the Peruvian system. Both APRA and the military were and remain essentially middle-class organizations, yet cooperation between them has proved impossible. As a result, "APRA's influence on the military [has been] largely negative. . . . [Moreover] this alienation of the military from APRA, the only significant antioligarchic political organization, made it possible to maintain discipline and standards in the army while it was used as an instrument for maintaining the power of the upper classes."[20]

Sánchez Cerro was assassinated by an Aprista in 1933. His successor, General (and former President) Oscar Benavides, was duly installed by the military with the approval of the conservative congress. Benavides governed the country through 1939, when carefully controlled elections returned the presidency to the hands of the civilian oligarchy in the person of Manuel Prado y Ugarteche. World War II prosperity and border conflicts with Ecuador stimulated a sharp rise in military appropriations under Prado. His government was authoritarian in practice, but prosperity and the absence of serious domestic strife brought a gradual relaxation of persecution of the Apristas. Despite rumblings of opposition from the officer corps, Prado issued a decree legalizing APRA in time for the party to organize for the presidential elections of 1945.[21]

Having by this time grown realistic about oligarchic and military resistance, Haya de la Torre and the other APRA leaders did not offer an official candidate for the presidency in 1945. Instead they chose a strategy of trading support for a less controversial candidate in return for promised roles for Apristas in the new government. With the APRA vote giving him a two-to-one margin, Dr. José Luis Bustamante y Rivero, a highly respected but politically inexperienced lawyer, was elected and allowed to assume office. Bustamante indeed appointed Apristas to numerous posts in his government, and APRA succeeded also in dominating a coalition of parties with a majority in both houses of congress. The portents of these events alarmed both the military and the oligarchy. Senators and deputies opposing APRA seized upon the tactic of boycotting congress in order to forestall a quorum. President Bustamante was obliged to govern by decree, and his desperate measures shortly engendered a split with his erstwhile APRA allies. With the period of prosperity terminated by postwar economic dislocations and with civil disorders on the rise, Bustamante, fearful of a military coup, denounced APRA support in February 1948 and formed a new cabinet composed mostly of military officers.

At this impasse, both the oligarchy and the Apristas fell to conspiring with factions of the armed forces. The oligarchy entreated the generals to intervene to restore order, and Apristas worked to foment a revolt of noncommissioned officers.[22] General Manuel Odría, Bustamante's new minister of the interior and a hero of recent border skirmishes with Ecuador, demanded that APRA again be outlawed. When Bustamante refused to go this far, Odría resigned from the cabinet, taking several other officers with him. The explosive situation was brought to a head in October 1948 with an APRA-instigated mutiny of petty officers and seamen at the Callao naval forts. The Apristas had won the support of enlisted factions in all three branches of the armed forces as well as a segment of the Guardia Civil. General Odría, however, countered with a revolt of his own at the head of the key garrison in the southern city of Arequipa. Odría and the main elements of the army prevailed, Bustamante was overthrown, and Odría assumed dictatorial powers.

General Odría justified his coup by asserting that President Bustamante had reacted with insufficient vigor against APRA excesses, and that he had lost the capacity to maintain public order. Moreover, Bustamante was accused of inaction in the face of the country's deteriorating economic conditions and, more pointedly, of attempting to weaken the military by undermining its unity and prestige. According to Bustamante's memoirs, this final charge had some validity from the military's point of view. The postwar recession had forced Bustamante to refuse military demands for new budgetary increases.[23] The matter tends to bear out Villanueva's observation (see page 147 and reference 12) that Peru's armed forces have consistently refused to sacrifice their own share of the national budget even in times of economic difficulty for the country.

APRA was again outlawed—one of Odría's first actions. The new dictator proceeded to cloak himself with a semblance of legitimacy by holding presidential elections in 1950, in which he was the sole candidate. His government coincided with a period of economic boom stimulated by the Korean war. Odría sought with some success to co-opt APRA labor support through extensive public works projects and social reforms. These actions indeed earned Odría some support among urban workers, but by and large his regime favored the interests of the landowning and commercial oligarchies. Especially favored were the armed forces. Odría concluded a mutual security pact with the United States that included extensive military aid. He also purchased a quantity of high-performance aircraft from Britain, and instituted a number of new perquisites for career officers. But despite his political acumen and the largesse of his regime, by the mid-1950's Odría was confronted by demands from both oligarchic and military factions that he step down in favor of a constitutionally elected government.

These pressures for a return to civilian rule were rooted in changes under way within the oligarchy, the armed forces, and the APRA party. The longstanding and mutually beneficial relationship between the oligarchy and the military was beginning to show signs of strain. An important segment of the upper-class elite was voicing antimilitarist sentiments, partly as a result of Odría's strongarm methods (from which the oligarchy had not been entirely exempted), and partly as an outgrowth of Peru's continuing economic development and social mobilization. The divergence of economic interests between the commercial and landholding oligarchies had become more pointed after World War II. The commercial sector had come to favor gradual and controlled social reforms to serve the needs of industrialization. The landowners remained committed to maintenance of the status quo, but even for this group the violent social revolution of 1952 in neighboring Bolivia had served notice that an Indian population similar to Peru's could revolt against the established order. The more progressive elements of the oligarchy were therefore disposed to accommodate some of the demands of the rising lower classes, and were ready to enter into collaboration with the APRA party as the most logical vehicle for reform. The APRA–oligarchy rapprochement was consummated in a pact with former President Manuel Prado, in which the Aprista chiefs traded electoral and later congressional support for Prado in return for legalization of APRA and Prado's promise of support for the APRA candidate in the 1962 elections.[24]

As the oligarchy's views had begun to change, so had those of important groups within the military. Young officers in particular had come to resent Odría for the poor public image his regime had brought them. Even some high-ranking officers, perceiving the decline in public support for military institutions, were demanding an end to the Odría dictatorship and promising respect for the outcome of the 1956 elections. [25] A second significant current of change, however, was the perception of a growing circle of officers that they should no longer permit their institutions to be used by the conservative oligarchy to buttress the status quo. This circle, whose focus was the Centro de Altos Estudios Militares (Center for Advanced Military Studies, CAEM), had recognized the need for fundamental changes in Peru's antiquated social structures and underdeveloped economy.[26] Moreover, as Richard Patch observes, deepening military resentment toward the oligarchy also emanated from "the essentially mestizo [racially mixed] background of the military men and career officers, and from their growing belief that while it is their police actions which maintain the social and business elites in power, they themselves participate little in the benefits."[27]

The growing discontent with Odría's rule persuaded him to step down and permit free elections in 1956. With heavy Aprista support, Manuel Prado was overwhelmingly elected and the military, despite some misgivings about Prado's prompt legalization of the despised APRA movement, returned to the barracks. Significantly, the APRA leadership's new moderation and pragmatism—or cynicism, as some charged—and its alliance with the oligarchy meant that Peru was now deprived of an anti-oligarchic mass party on the left. Dissident Apristas who could not accept the machinations of the party chieftains were increasingly attracted, as were other radicals, to the Acción Popular (Popular Action) movement led by Professor Fernando Belaunde Terry. As Prado's six-year term proceeded, the 1962 elections shaped up as a three-way contest between Belaunde, APRA's Haya de la Torre, and the former dictator Odría, who had formed a personalist party called the National Odriist Union (UNO).

The 1962 elections posed an acute dilemma for the armed forces. The Cuban Revolution of Fidel Castro had lent some credence to those officers who argued that the military should align itself with the modernization process. Timely social reforms, according to this view, would serve to defuse Peru's seemingly explosive rural unrest. Moreover, the spectacle of several hundred Cuban officers being led to the execution wall by Castro's supporters produced an even stronger argument that violent social revolution in Peru must be averted. The prospect of an APRA government wreaking similar vengeance on Peruvian officers seemed an unacceptable risk. The chasm of hatred and mistrust between APRA and the army remained deep. Yet the officers were also concerned about their public image and wanted to avoid an intervention that could not be credibly justified. During the election campaign the military's suspicions of the Prado government's arrangement with APRA were made manifest in public warnings against electoral fraud by the three ministers of the armed forces. Peru's National Elections Court responded by tightening the voter registration and verification procedures for the June elections. The ministers and generals were not reassured, however. When the election produced a three-way division of votes in which no candidate obtained the one-third plurality required under the constitution for election (there were four minor-party candidates in the race as well), Peru faced a severe political crisis.

The military leaders clearly favored the candidacy of Fernando Belaunde Terry. Abhorrent of the prospect of Haya de la Torre in the presidency and unwilling to return to the "old politics" represented by Manuel Odría, the army released its own tabulation of the voting which showed Belaunde the winner with just over one-third of the total vote. However, the official count showed Haya de la Torre (557,047 votes, or 32.98 percent) with a small plurality; Belaunde (544,589) in second place, and Odría (480,798) in third, with no clear victor. Peruvian law provides that in such circumstances the new president be elected by majority vote in a joint session of the newly elected congress. However, no party had won a clear majority in that body either. Ironically and somewhat astonishingly, the jockeying for a majority coalition in congress produced an agreement between the two old enemies, Haya de la Torre and Odría, in which the Apristas would support Odría for the presidency in return for cabinet posts in his government. In a move significantly revealing of the nature of civil–military relations in Peru, Belaunde denounced the APRA–UNO pact and called for a military coup d'etat to prevent its fulfillment.[28] No less dismayed, the armed forces united in opposition to the grotesque agreement and prepared once more to block APRA's access to power.

The coup itself was bloodless and precise. Minutes past the hour of three in the early morning darkness of July 18, some 200 commandos of the Peruvian army, supported by twenty U.S.-made Sherman tanks, were deployed before the gates of the Pizarro Palace. After a token resistance, President Prado was placed under arrest and quickly spirited out of the country. Other troops seized radio stations and strategic locations. When Peruvians awakened in the morning they learned that the armed forces had deposed President Prado to "preserve democracy," that congress was dissolved and all constitutional guarantees suspended. A four-man military junta was sworn in to serve as a collegial executive, with General Ricardo Pérez Godoy as *primus inter pares*, the recognized leader. The day following the coup was marked by a few relatively minor disorders, but for the most part the news was received calmly throughout Peru. Observers even noted a general air of relief after the tense and uncertain days of the election campaign.[29]

The junta's announced justification for intervention focused on allegations of electoral fraud (not unfounded but almost certainly exaggerated) and on the theme of anticommunism. The latter element was curious, since the Apristas and the Peruvian Communists were bitter rivals and Belaunde, the military's favorite, had been the only candidate receiving substantial Communist support. The most likely explanation was the junta's concern about international reactions to the coup. United States President John F. Kennedy sternly opposed military intervention in Latin America on the grounds that it contravened the democratic spirit of the Alliance for Progress. When the coup occurred despite clear warnings from Washington, Kennedy angrily ordered the suspension of both military and economic aid and demanded that the junta arrange prompt and free elections to return the government to civilian control.[30]

The junta very shortly did announce that elections would be held within a year, but Washington's influence in this decision was probably slight.[31] As shown by their opposition to Odria, the military leaders continued to be deeply conscious of their public image. From the outset the junta projected a caretaker quality and a determination to return the country to civilian government, albeit a civilian government acceptable to the military. The junta clearly manifested the growing professionalization of the armed forces. For the first time in Peruvian history, a coup had produced a military government that was institutionalist rather than personalist in nature. This conclusion was borne out when the junta announced that the armed forces would not run a candidate in the 1963 elections, and even more clearly some months later when the junta summarily ousted General Perez from its ranks. Apparently the general had given indications of personal ambition to wear the presidential sash, despite earlier promises to the contrary.[32]

True to its word, the junta held elections in June 1963 and did not proscribe APRA participation. With a revision of the electoral law making it virtually impossible for minor parties to get on the ballot, only the three major parties from the previous year offered candidates. The balloting was orderly and the issues were essentially the same as in 1962. Fernando Belaunde Terry won some 40 percent of the vote to register a clear victory over Haya de la Torre and Odria, and constitutional government was restored on July 28, 1963.[33]

At this point there seemed to be substantial basis for optimism, both for the future of civilian government in Peru and for the country's prospects for modernizing reforms. President Belaunde appeared committed to fundamental social and economic change, and he enjoyed the support of the armed forces as well as business elites. Peru's economy, while admittedly heavily dependent on foreign investment and trade, still ranked among the most diversified in Latin America and the *sol* was solidly backed by hard currency reserves. The armed forces stood ready to implement their commitment to national development by taking part in civic action programs, including the building of new roads, airfields, and schools. Yet by 1968 the economy had tumbled into recession and Belaunde found himself ousted by another military coup, this one followed by a military regime that made no attempt to hide its contempt for civilian politicians nor any pretense of considering itself a caretaker regime. General Pedro Velasco Alvarado not only asserted the military's right to rule on an indefinite basis, but embarked on a sweeping and—for a Latin American military regime—unprecedentedly radical program of reforms in open defiance of Peruvian conservatives and American corporations. These developments can be understood only in the context of institutional changes under way since the 1950's within the military establishment, changes that in 1968 produced a major watershed for civil–military relations and an apparent shift in the military's political role from guardianship to radical leadership of the modernization process.

Military Institutional Factors

By the mid-1960's the Peruvian military establishment consisted of some 44,000 officers and men, organized within the three services of army, navy, and air force. Of this total the army counted approximately 33,000, including as many as 3500 officers on active duty. These forces, well trained and equipped by Latin American standards, were divided administratively into five regional commands responsible for personnel recruitment and training and for providing logistical support for the army's tactical units, consisting of six light infantry divisions and one armored division.[34] This politically optimal dispersion of its forces, combined with its near monopoly over those coercive resources capable of being deployed for political effect, gives the Peruvian army a nearly incontestable basis for decisive participation in political affairs.

Although the three services are not organized within a unified defense structure, there exists a board (Comando Conjunto) comprised of the commanders in chief of the three services and a permanent staff charged with joint planning. Primary command authority, however, is effectively vested in the ministers of the separate services. Each of the services exercises individual autonomy over internal matters. Despite constitutional stipulations to the contrary, the ministers are always officers on active duty rather than civilians, and the service commanders function as their deputies.[35] The hierarchical solidarity and effectiveness of this command structure is confirmed by the fact that military coups in Peru overwhelmingly have been led by the service ministers and commanders, rather than by the middle-rank majors and colonels. [36]

The officer corps takes great pride in its character as a national institution, and on the evidence this pride seems well deserved. Line commissions are earned through graduation from the Escuela Militar— admission to which is determined by a combination of class ranking in public high school or military preparatory school, competitive examinations, and geographical quotas.[37] Peruvian officers are drawn primarily from the lower middle class. An occupational preference survey conducted in the early 1960's suggests that male students in public and private secondary schools rank a military career second in attraction only to engineering.[38] Great stress is placed on merit, not only at the Escuela Militar but throughout the career patterns of officers. All air force and naval officers and over 90 percent of army officers are graduates of their respective service academies, and figures for the army show that over 80 percent of those promoted to divisional generals between 1940 and 1965 had graduated in the top quarter of their classes at the Escuela Militar. [39]

This emphasis on merit (which departs significantly from prevailing societal norms) is further reflected by the central role of advanced education in promotional considerations. Graduation with distinction from the two-year course of instruction at the CAEM is now virtually a prerequisite for higher rank. Its importance is underscored by the fact that the military cabinet established following the 1968 coup contained 13 CAEM graduates out of 19 members, including the prime minister and the chief of the Council of Presidential Advisers. The CAEM is an important key to understanding the postwar shift in the political role of the military. Its courses include analyses of comparative political, social, and economic systems, with emphasis given to the study of a wide range of social problems and to contributions the military might make to their solution. The dominant themes instilled by the CAEM include: (a) the perception that Peru is enmeshed in a fundamental and protracted social crisis brought on by persistent inequalities in the distribution of wealth and status in the country, and by Peru's situation of dependency vis-à-vis the industrialized countries of the world; (b) the realization that this crisis threatens their institutions as well as the emerging capitalist system in Peru, which they, as members of the middle class, support; (c) the conclusion that the state must take an activist role in overcoming this crisis; and (d) that, as a consequence of the manifest failure of civilian politicians, it is both proper and necessary that the military should accept a primary political role in the modernization process.[40]

Contempt for civilian *políticos* is a manifestation of the integral institutional boundaries and internal cohesion of the Peruvian military. The armed forces institutions have gained a high degree of autonomy as a result of the fundamental weakness and division of the Peruvian middle classes and the consequent weakness of civilian political institutions.[41]

Despite its self-identification with the middle classes, the officer corps has traditionally set itself apart from civilian values and norms. The officers' feelings toward the oligarchy are predominantly those of frustration, generated by oligarchic exclusiveness and a pervasive sense of social inferiority among officers, and of resentment, rooted in the military's perceptions that the oligarchy is responsible both for past military defeats and for Peru's underdeveloped status. Studies of membership in elite social clubs and on boards of directors of corporations suggest that in fact there is "almost a complete lack of contact between the military and the social and financial elite of Peru."[42] Since the early 1950's the desire to demonstrate independence from the oligarchy has been an important element in the military's psychology. However, rejection of civilian values has not meant that the officers reject close cooperation with like-minded civilians. When we later examine the context of post–1968 military rule, we shall see that there are increasingly important linkages between the politically activist officer corps and a growing technocratic civilian elite.[43]

The self-image of the Peruvian officer is that of the professional who sacrifices himself through dedication to an arduous career distinguished by self-discipline and efficiency. Pride in military discipline is contrasted sharply with the self-indulgence and corruption attributed to civilians. One result is that political compromise is viewed with disdain. Moreover, officers who allow themselves to become too closely identified with civilian politicians run a serious risk of "contamination," of compromising their discipline in the eyes of fellow officers and thus debasing their military virtue.[44] The officers see themselves as professionals, not only in the management of violence but in organization and problem solving. Their advanced technical skills are seen as central to the tasks of modernizing their country. They see their institutions as the true repository of patriotism and themselves as the custodians of the national interest and honor.

The Peruvian armed forces rank high in expertise, social responsibility, and corporateness, the three dimensions of professionalism described by Samuel P. Huntington. Since World War II the three services have received a considerable quantity of advanced United States and European weapons, together with the technological training necessary to employ them effectively. This effectiveness was demonstrated in the antiguerrilla campaigns of 1965–1966, when army units succeeded in eradicating several Castroite insurgent groups operating in the southern Andes. The officers' sense of social responsibility is seen in the curriculum of the CAEM and in the policies of the government headed by General Velasco. The corporateness of the military is high relative to most other Latin American countries. Intra- and interservice cleavages are not absent but, as McAlister observes, "they are based increasingly on military issues and personalities rather than on the intromission of factional and party politics into the military system."[45] However, during the 1960's significant cleavages developed over the desirability and rate of reforms in Peruvian social structure and over the part the armed forces should play in the development process. Another source of tension is related to attitudes toward the United States. There is still considerable sentiment for regarding the United States as Peru's most important friend and anticommunist ally, but this is increasingly countered by arguments that there are many areas in which the national interests of the two countries are not compatible. The dependence of the Peruvian economy on American corporations is one such area, and the intricate question of fishing rights and the extent of Peru's territorial sea is another. Both of these became sharp issues of contention between Washington and Lima after the 1968 coup.

In Peru's case, military professionalization has obviously not led to institutional depoliticization. The norm of civilian political supremacy has never really flourished in Peru, nor have civilian politicians proved effective in establishing a claim to legitimacy based on performance. By the mid–1960's the armed forces were commanded by a group of officers committed on grounds of institutional preservation to seeing that their country had a government capable of sustaining a comprehensive development program. The caretaker junta of 1962–1963 laid some of the groundwork for this program by drafting a progressive agrarian reform law and establishing a National Planning Institute. All three services responded to President Belaunde later in 1963 when he announced Cooperación Popular, a Peruvian "war on poverty" that included a central civic action role for the military. The army in particular accepted a major part in civic action projects between 1963 and 1968, which reportedly had an observable effect in ameliorating the military's public image. Yet there was in the military's support of Belaunde a strong element of fatalistic sufferance, as though the generals were giving civilian government "one last chance" to succeed.[46] Should the civilians not prove themselves equal to the task of supervising stable and orderly development, the officers were prepared to assume that responsibility themselves.

Environmental Factors

The political history of Peru through the mid-1960's suggests the inconclusive nature of the political process under weak and narrowly based political institutions. With the possible exception of President Leguia's regime from 1919 to 1930, Peruvian governments have reigned rather than ruled. By the end of the nineteenth century the cooperation between the military and the oligarchy had become an affair of convenience. Together these two political actors could determine who should preside over the government, but their relationship did not include agreement on a longrange program of social and economic change. The oligarchy was satisfied with this arrangement because the policies of caretaker military governments seldom challenged its base of power. The military benefitted institutionally from the freedom they were given to develop as a virtual "state within a state," unchecked by superior civil authority.[47] Military guardianship over the status quo finally became unstable, however, when armed forces leaders recognized that their institutional interests had become interdependent with the developmental needs of the larger society.

The Peruvian political system is characterized by a phenomenon Martin Needler has called a "legitimacy vacuum."[48] No agreement exists among the dominant political actors on a single standard of legitimacy, either for determining who should govern or for prescribing which policies should be adopted. Although the armed forces have clearly mobilized a preponderance of coercion resources, no single actor has proved able to marshal the consent of a working majority coalition of Peru's civilian political forces. The APRA party has come closest to achieving this objective, but the apparently unbridgeable abyss of hatred between APRA and the military seemed to mean that no ruling coalition—i.e., one mobilizing a preponderance of *both* the consent and coercion currencies—was feasible. APRA could not rule without military support. The armed forces could reign but were denied the power to rule as long as they were unable to link their claim to some accepted principle of legitimacy.

Two additional aspects of Peruvian politics bear elaboration here—the first relating to the great potential power of the presidency; and the second, to the fragmentation of the country's middle class. In part because of the authoritarian structure of Spanish colonial rule, in part because of the dominance of statist ideologies in Latin America, the Peruvian executive plays the central role in the political process. Interest groups tend to look directly to the president for action on their demands and redress of their grievances. No other prize bestowed through politics compares with the presidency, and hence the struggle for control over that office is extreme and unremitting. One author perceives this struggle in terms of a "politics of structured violence," in which opposition forces are inclined to use any extreme means to unseat an incumbent president, including assassination, riots, and insurgency.[49] To continue in office the president must be both ruthless in his use of repression and adept where necessary in his concessions to those groups threatening to employ violence. Both the incumbent and his opposition are aware that the armed forces will tolerate only a certain level of public disorder before they will step in to oust the president and stabilize the situation. Because of this, politically structured violence can be a tactical instrument employed effectively by numerous groups outside the military. Military coups have at times been openly solicited by civilians opposing the government, as in the case of Belaunde's taking to the barricades in Arequipa in 1962 and calling for the overthrow of President Prado. In this context the 1962 coup, as well as those of 1914, 1919, 1930, and 1948 may be seen as manifestations of arbiter military guardianship. The armed forces acted at least in part to restore order and moderate the struggle for the presidency, playing a mediator role among civilian factions and itself governing for varying periods on a caretaker basis.

The political debility of the middle classes is another key to understanding the military's place in Peruvian politics. The role of the middle classes has differed sharply from that of similar social strata in the Anglo-European countries. There the middle classes have served as a principal vehicle of national integration, performing the central functions of interest articulation and aggregation through political party systems. In Peru as in much of Latin America, however, the middle classes have remained politically fragmented and unable to perform these functions with the same degree of effectiveness. This situation has evolved from a number of interrelated causes—the more important being rooted in the relatively late emergence of the middle classes onto the political stage, the dependence of their countries on the international economic system, and their own dependence on the oligarchies for their cultural values and economic opportunities.[50] The overriding element has been dependence, which has led to deep insecurity, a lack of cohesion, and retarded growth of identity and autonomy as a political force. In place of broadly based aggregative parties led by an independent middle class, Latin America has produced a panoply of populist movements characterized by an unstable alliance between sectors of the dependent bourgeoisie, the intellectuals, and the oppressed lower strata.[51] As with APRA in Peru, these movements have generally failed to perform a stabilizing and integrative role. With the postwar rise of the "revolution of rising expectations" and particularly since the Cuban Revolution, APRA's influence and ideological force declined rapidly and the legitimacy of bourgeois political leadership in general was challenged. The inadequacy of the middle classes has been paralleled by the even more abject failure of popular revolutionary movements patterned on the Cuban model.[52]

These developments have given rise to an interesting phenomenon: the growing autonomy and political assertiveness of two institutional bureaucracies, the military and the managerial technocracy. These two groups share a strong interest in the gradual and orderly modernization of Peru. Of the two the military is clearly the more effectively organized and in control of the more decisive political resources. Given the fundamental fragmentation of power and the vacuum of political legitimacy in the country, an alliance between these two bureaucracies had become by the mid-1960's a real possibility.[53]

The immediate causes of the 1968 coup lay in the weakness of the Belaunde government and in political events whose portents for the 1969 presidential elections were viewed with much apprehension by the military. In his "first 100 days" Belaunde initiated a series of reforms designed to confront the country's economic and social problems. The majority APRA–UNO coalition in congress emasculated his agrarian reform proposals, however, and slashed appropriations for the Cooperacion Popular program.[54] Employing the censure power of congress, the APRA–UNO opposition succeeded in keeping the Belaunde administration on the defensive. Belaunde was forced into making a total of ninety-four cabinet changes through 1968.[55] Despite his reputation as a mercurial and charismatic leader, Belaunde refused to employ his presidential authority to mobilize mass support for his programs. His popular support gradually dwindled as his regime failed to deliver on his promises of reform.

Belaunde's image as a weak president was exacerbated by the International Petroleum Company (IPC) affair. A simmering dispute with IPC involved Peruvian allegations that IPC's titles to the La Brea and Pariñas oil fields were illegal. Belaunde had promised in the 1963 campaign to resolve the issue within three months, committing his personal prestige on a matter that had become a highly emotional symbol of Peruvian national honor. However, Belaunde encountered adamant IPC negotiators who were strongly backed by Washington. Peru was threatened with a cutoff of American aid should IPC holdings be nationalized without satisfactory provision for prompt and adequate compensation to the company. The Johnson administration applied economic pressure by withholding credits from Peru while the negotiations dragged on, forcing Belaunde to seek financing from other international sources at much less favorable terms.[56] The imbroglio persisted throughout Belaunde's term, contributing to an economic decline that reached serious proportions by 1968. The government tried to maintain both fiscal integrity and public favor through a combination of increased public spending and very liberal policies toward foreign investment. A devaluation of the sol (from 27 to over 40 to the dollar), compounded by an inflation rate in excess of 20 percent, led to widespread public dissatisfaction with Belaunde. The military joined in the criticism, later citing the need to restore economic health to the country as a prime justification for the 1968 coup. Characteristically, however, the generals contributed directly to deepening the economic crisis in May 1968 when they forced Belaunde to buy supersonic jets from France at a cost of some $20 million.[57]

The guerrilla insurgencies of 1965 also hastened the decline of Belaunde in the estimation of the armed forces. Although the rebels were competently contained by the army's counterinsurgency units, the experience apparently had the effect of confirming both the CAEM analysis of Peru's social crisis and the military's judgment that civilians were incapable of engineering the solutions necessary to overcome it.[58] Moreover, several years of experience in intensive civic action had convinced many officers that the military was best equipped to provide the technical expertise and, above all, the disciplined leadership required.

There was also an anti-APRA dimension to the 1968 coup. With defections from his AP (Acción Popular) coalition on the rise, Belaunde apparently encouraged the conservative wing of his party, representing principally that sector of the urban bourgeoisie connected with foreign investments, to enter into agreements with APRA.[59] These negotiations produced a coalition cabinet of AP and APRA ministers, which became the impetus for a fundamental restructuring of the principal political coalitions in existence since 1962. The reformist wing of AP deserted, claiming that the rapprochement with APRA constituted a betrayal of principle. The Odria forces largely broke away from APRA, but then split into quarreling factions. The military denounced the new AP–APRA arrangement and effectively withdrew its support of Belaunde. Out of this fragmentation and realignment, the coalition between APRA and the urban middle-class sector of AP emerged as a potent political force. The prospect was that 1969 would bring a presidential victory at last to the Aprista candidate, who would probably be Haya de la Torre.[60]

With both APRA and the urban bourgeoisie supporting him, Belaunde apparently concluded that Peru's economic recovery hinged on an amicable resolution of the IPC wrangle, which presumably would bring new loans and investments from the United States. Suddenly, after five years of stalemated negotiations, the Peruvian government and IPC announced an agreement whereby IPC would transfer the disputed oil fields to Peru in exchange for a waiver of Peruvian claims to some $690 million in excess profits alleged to have been extracted over the years by the company. IPC would retain ownership of its refinery and would receive the oil rights to a huge tract of land in the Peruvian jungle. In substance this agreement closely resembled Belaunde's original proposal to the company in 1963. The mood of the country had changed, however, in the intervening years. The agreement's generosity to IPC now offended Peruvian nationalists, who demanded the outright expropriation of IPC's holdings with no compensation whatsoever. The country was plunged into turmoil when the manager of the government petroleum enterprise PETROPERU denounced the alleged absence of a page of the agreement on which oil sale prices between IPC and the government were listed. The public outcry forced the resignation of Belaunde's cabinet amidst charges that the national honor had been betrayed.[61]

Thus, by October 1968, the military had both the disposition and the opportunity to intervene. The coup of October 3 was executed with typical precision and was received with approval by an apparent majority of Peruvians. The armed forces leaders accused Belaunde of "sacrificing the national dignity" and then announced the expropriation of all IPC holdings. This move stimulated an outpouring of nationalist rejoicing. It was to become the symbol of legitimation for the new military regime. Under the leadership of General Velasco the new government defied Yankee imperialism and moved vigorously to implement a series of reforms that substantially pre-empted the programs advocated for years by the radical left.

The New Military Populism

For the first time in its history the Peruvian military was able to form a government with the power to rule rather than merely reign. The country's civilian political forces were in complete disarray. Their claim to legitimacy was largely discredited by corruption and failure to carry out agrarian reform and other needed changes. General Velasco's government began with a strong potential for legitimation: its anti-imperialist mantle was the result of the expropriation and expulsion of IPC and of co-optation of the leadership role in the drive for modernization. Velasco quickly capitalized on these advantages. Proclaiming the "revolutionary government of the armed forces," he roundly denounced elements of the Peruvian bourgeoisie for collaborating with foreign imperialists and thereby deepening Peru's economic dependence. He asserted the urgent need for sweeping structural changes to transform Peruvian society, particularly in agrarian reform and education. Finally, Velasco announced that the military intended to maintain control over the government at least through 1975, in order to establish and implement a twenty-year plan for national development (1968–1988).[62]

As soldiers, Velasco and his advisers were experienced planners and this was not their first attempt at planning on a national scale. The principle of developmental planning was adopted under the second Prado government, although the first national plan announced in 1961 was nearly a total failure, owing to inadequate statistical data and an even less adequate commitment of national resources. The 1962–1963 military junta devised the second plan, which was more solidly conceived but was unrealistic in counting on foreign investment to provide the main impetus for economic growth. Three additional plans were promulgated by the Belaunde administration, but these focused largely on short-term goals and suffered from the same inadequacies of data and organizational support. Peru's sixth national plan, announced by the Velasco government to cover the five-year period 1971–1975, appeared to overcome many of these defects. Strongly flavored with Marxist rhetoric, the plan called for completion of a thoroughgoing land reform by 1975 and established as a principal goal an annual GNP growth rate of 7.5 percent. [63] Taken as a whole, the plan represented a serious blueprint for construction of a modern industrial capitalist system in Peru, with realistic targets for public and private investments and projections for fundamental alterations of the systems of land tenure and economic dependence. [64]

      Other actions demonstrated that the military meant business. Besides the virtual confiscation of IPC, Velasco moved to expropriate the huge coastal sugar plantations of W.R. Grace & Company and converted them into cooperatives, owned in part by the workers themselves. Two opposition newspapers were seized and similarly converted into cooperatives. When a dispute broke out between Peruvian copper workers and the Cerro de Pasco Company, Velasco sided with the workers. The government also expropriated Cerro de Pasco's agricultural holdings of some 260,000 hectares (one hectare = 2.471 acres), the largest in the country. Velasco moved vigorously to stem the outflow of hard currency reserves by "nationalizing" the Central Reserve Bank (the private banking sector had previously controlled its management), and "Peruvianizing" the private banks themselves (through restrictions on their holdings of foreign capital). A new law required banks to reserve a certain percentage of investment capital for the financing of development projects organized by the national government. As further proof of its independence from Washington, the Velasco regime seized a number of American fishing trawlers who had flouted Peru's claim of a 200-mile territorial sea. When the United States Congress threatened to suspend both military aid and imports of fishing products from Peru, the Peruvian government promptly expelled the United States military mission and declared that the scheduled Rockefeller Mission visit to Peru was "unnecessary." [65] To show that Peru was not to be bullied into submitting to the will of the United States, Velasco followed Castro's example and established diplomatic and trade relations with the Soviet Union.

      The promised structural reforms were also not long in coming. The government bureaucracy was reorganized, with elimination of some departments and the creation of four new ones designed to facilitate implementation of the state's new activist role in development. Key positions in most ministries were filled by military officers, although a substantial number of civilian technicians and administrators were retained. Velasco established the Corps of Officer Advisers to the Presidency

staffed largely with CAEM colonels and charged with putting into opera-
tion the military's program of reforms. The new agrarian reform law,
prepared largely by these planners, was no less than a frontal assault on
the power base of the landholding oligarchy. It was national in scope,
establishing 150 hectares as the maximum limit for agricultural holdings and 1500 hectares as the maximum for grazing lands. A minimum
of 3 hectares was set for individual farms. Large estates were to be taken
over and converted into peasant cooperatives, and their former owners
compensated primarily through nontransferable government bonds
maturing in twenty to thirty years. The law emphasized the strengthening of peasant community ties and recognized the inviolability of
communal lands. Even Victor Raul Haya de la Torre applauded the
rhetoric and substance of the law. Unlike earlier agrarian reform laws,
which had been progressive in the drafting but evaded in practice,
this one was quickly and vigorously implemented by the government.
[66]
     In the field of education policy, the Velasco regime began
less auspiciously but quickly demonstrated a degree of pragmatism
unprecedented among Peruvian military politicians. Military planners
in the Ministry of Education moved to revise the authority structure
of the universities, radically diminishing student participation in university governance and providing for expulsion of students and faculty
who engaged in partisan political activity. A second decree upheld the
principle that secondary education costs should be borne largely by
the student, a position that ran counter to public expectations that social
mobility through education would be facilitated. Both actions inflamed
student opinion and at least one major outbreak of violence followed.
However, General Velasco responded with persuasion rather than repression, appearing in person to open a dialogue with the students and
eventually giving ground by modifying both measures. Velasco and
other prominent military leaders spoke warmly of their conviction that
both students and the armed forces sought an identical goal in pressing
for social change, appealing successfully for student cooperation with
the regime in the name of progress and national unity.[67]
     Despite the prevailing military view that political compro-
mise is inherently corrupt and demeaning, a willingness to negotiate
rather than coerce became characteristic of the Velasco regime. The military had become highly sensitive to its need for legitimacy. Officers sought
to build a populist coalition of the lower-middle and lower classes led
by a technocratic elite of officers and civilian professionals. Nevertheless, their emphasis was clearly on "revolution from above." The actual
participation of the lower strata in the reform process was not part of
the military's design. The symbolic output of the regime—celebration
of the anniversary of the IPC expropriation as a "Day of National Dig-

nity," and liberal use of the rhetoric of revolutionary anti-imperialism—has been heavy, but Velasco has shown little inclination to organize mass participation in the form of a political party. Military intentions aside, however, its quest for legitimation through identification with revolutionary symbols has obviously created an atmosphere that may be conducive to mass politicization. The proliferation of grass-roots "Committees for the Defense of the Revolution" in emulation of Castro's Cuba has taken place outside the aegis of the government. These CDR's have been organized by the radical left and may in the long run threaten the gradualism and stability of the military's "revolution from above."

The overall impression generated by the policies and rhetoric of the Velasco regime has been a mixture of nationalism, modernization, and radicalism. Yet there is a certain ambivalence to the military's posture in each of these dimensions. It is certain that the Peruvian armed forces are committed to building an industrial system under national control with a concomitant eradication of dysfunctional and antiquated social structures.[68] In Latin America this much is a radical departure in itself. But, on closer inspection, it is clear that the military seeks not socialism but a capitalist economic system with heavy state participation; not outright rejection of foreign investment but a modification of Peru's dependence on the industrialized countries; and not an egalitarian society achieved through class struggle but a more modern multiclass society, based on a partial redistribution of income and the growth of a national market for locally produced consumer goods. In sum, the social system envisioned by the military as a goal conforms closely to the traditional Iberian concepts of corporatism and of society as an ordered organic whole.[69]

Even as the army was engaged in occupying the IPC oil fields and as General Velasco was publicly committing himself to refusing any compensation to the company, he insisted repeatedly that these actions were totally sui generis and did not establish a pattern for his government's relations with foreign investors. Indeed, the properties of several other foreign oil companies were not threatened and, after an initial hesitancy, these companies responded to a series of new inducements on the part of the government by actually increasing their investments and extending their contractual arrangements with Peru. The pattern established during Velasco's first several years in office suggests that the military's primary aim in this regard was to renegotiate the country's relationship with the international economic system. The decades of concessions to foreign investors under previous governments had led to a situation in which Peruvians had lost the capacity to direct their own national economy. The economic well-being of the country had become dependent on the policies of a few multinational corporations, whose decisions were not responsive to the economic policies established by their host government. The military sought to re-establish national control through "Peruvianization" of the decision-making boards of the subsidiary companies and restrictions on the repatriation of company profits. This redefined relationship between Peru and the foreign companies was to take place gradually and, where possible, through negotiation rather than outright expropriation. At the same time, Velasco sought with considerable success to recreate a favorable climate for foreign investments that would be less offensive to nationalist sensibilities and more functional in terms of the military's national development plan.[70]

On closer inspection, one sees too that the military's agrarian reform law also tends to belie the surface image of radicalism. Despite its drastic nature and its far-reaching impact on the traditional land tenure system, its object is clearly to "convert agrarian capitalists into industrial capitalists."[71] Former landowners holding long-term government bonds in payment for their lands are permitted under the law to obtain immediately up to fifty percent of their value if the funds are invested in government-approved industrial enterprises, provided the other fifty percent is deposited for investment use by the state.[72] Thus the dispossessed oligarchy is encouraged to preserve its economic power by shifting its capital from land to industry, contributing to the development of a strong private sector of the economy under government regulation. Moreover, the law does not distinguish between native and foreign landowners, both of whom are enticed to invest in the industrial sector.

Even the agrarian cooperatives established under the reform law are considerably less radical than their name implies. Relying on the same technocratic approach it employs in general problem solving, the military has considered that the transition from huge estates to peasant cooperatives should be made under the management of state-appointed professionals. In other words, government interventors replace the *patron* and his overseers, with little change taking place in the actual role of peasants in decision making. In effect, the military planners are engaged in the distribution of land to peasants while at the same time inhibiting the peasants' social mobilization.[73] In a perceptive essay Julio Cotler observes that the agrarian reform law really constitutes, for the military, an "omnibus" law:

> . . . *it seeks to pacify the peasant masses and eliminate the possible operational basis for another guerrilla attempt; likewise it attempts to undermine the Aprista bases and the rural political mobilization of that party generally; it provokes a state of confusion among the fragmented Left; it eliminates the rural sector of the bourgeoisie, which had been the most important*

obstacle for the development of the country and for social homogeneity. [74]

The definitive element of a radical military regime is its alliance with the lower strata of society. The Velasco government, more than any of its predecessors, appears to enjoy considerable legitimacy among the masses. To date, however, that legitimacy seems to derive more from the government's symbolic acts than from its actual performance in ameliorating the conditions of life of Peruvian peasants and workers. The nearly universal support given Velasco in the IPC expropriation and in subsequent disputes with the United States over fishing rights and compensation for expropriated property has probably been the central element in the legitimation of military rule. Support for Velasco's foreign policy has been bolstered by admiration at its successes. The Nixon administration apparently concluded that little was to be gained by forcing Peru to follow the path of Cuba. In the IPC affair, Washington drew back from invoking the aid cutoffs required under the Hickenlooper Amendment. Furthermore, steps were taken to annul the Pelly Amendment (which provided for suspension of military aid); negotiations were opened on Peru's claim of a 200-mile territorial sea; and Mrs. Nixon was sent on a goodwill mission to Lima in the wake of disastrous Andean earthquakes. Certainly the agrarian reform law has also been instrumental in generating support for the regime, and in this area a number of rural wage-earners have begun to see improvement in their standards of living. On the other hand, in national terms their number remains small and confined largely to laborers on the great commercial farms of the coastal region. Many others have probably encountered a decline in their conditions and will migrate to the already-overcrowded cities, where urban labor has been the group least favored by the regime and bears much of the costs (through suppressed wages) of the military's industrialization program. Nevertheless, though not advancing economically, urban labor has largely closed ranks behind the regime as a result of the military's emphasis on "democratic capitalism." A recurring theme is working class participation—as yet mostly symbolic—in both the profits and the management of industrial enterprises.[75]

Those who have benefitted most from the policies of the Velasco government, apart from the armed forces themselves, have been the civilian professionals who form Peru's emerging technocratic elite and the middle-class entrepreneurs who have been favored under the industrialization plan. Among these groups there has been some restlessness at the populist overtones of Velasco's rule, but generally this has been submerged by cautious support for the military's modernization policies and by eagerness to take advantage of proffered economic incentives.[76] The landowners have been most disaffected, but many have responded to the regime's investment opportunities rather than suffer having their capital tied up in long-term government bonds at low interest rates. Though they felt threatened by the agrarian reform, the landowners have begun to recognize that they were also being given the opportunity of becoming a central element in the country's new economic growth.[77]

Despite its radical appearance, the present Peruvian military regime remains committed to supporting the interests of the middle classes. Its perception of those interests, however, is the key to understanding its current stance. The military believes that the realization of those interests can only be assured through progress toward resolution of Peru's social crisis. This means steady growth toward the development of a nationalist and capitalist industrial economy, which should involve the lower strata symbolically in the short run and integrate them in the long run as the economy expands. Whether this plan will prove successful, and what changes its success or failure may bring for the current military–civilian technocracy, are of course problematical.

Military Populism and Modernization

We have seen how the political role of the Peruvian armed forces has evolved through a number of distinct phases in the 150 years since independence. After the initial era of highly personalistic and usually predatory military politicians (1821–1914), the armed forces assumed the role of arbiter guardianship favoring first the oligarchy (1914–1956) and later the middle class (1956–1968). Since the coup of October 1968, the military's role could be classified as reformist in view of its fundamentally middle-class nature and goals. Yet that classification is less than satisfactory, since the Velasco regime has projected a populist image unusual among military regimes. In any event, 1968 clearly marked a momentous shift in the political role of the armed forces. The officers have become policy makers and promoters of change. In both rhetoric and actions, they have brushed aside all pretense of commitment to the principle of civilian political supremacy. Their rule is based on the military as an institution, is virtually open-ended, and is remarkably autonomous. Finally, the Velasco government appears to enjoy a degree of legitimacy unparalleled by any predecessor, civilian or military, in the long history of Peru.

The present structure of governance, we repeat, is not purely military. It is more accurately perceived as a civil–military technocracy in which the military clearly dominates.[78] Unlike previous civil–military coalitions, the military actor is not subordinate to the interest of another social group. The military's ideology appears to be guided by a restrained nationalism defined within the present domestic and international economic orders; yet at the same time it appears to be committed to class reconciliation and national integration. The new institutional autonomy of the military permits it to play the role of social intermediary with considerable effectiveness. The policies of the Velasco government have been designed in part to promote modernization through national unity and to prevent the resurgence of partisan politics. Perhaps the most noteworthy elements of the current situation are the attempted leadership of a populist movement by the military *as an institution,* and the development of its legitimation through populism without a political party or a charismatic leader.

In the view of Carlos Delgado, a civilian sociologist who is an adviser to the Velasco government, the traditional political distinction between civilian and military is no longer viable in Peru. Delgado perceives the only important dichotomy existing now as between those who support the military's efforts to promote "revolutionary" modernization and those who oppose them. Therefore, he argues, those who seek a consolidation of civilian forces against the military are in fact counterrevolutionaries.[79] Although support for constitutionalism and liberal democracy has scarcely disappeared, organized civilian resistance to military rule—even among the Apristas—has visibly eroded. The professionalism and autonomy of the Peruvian military have produced a tremendous growth in its institutional capacity over the past two decades, and this is presently reflected in its central political role. Yet in spite of this growth, the current political framework probably cannot be maintained without serious implications for the military as an institution.

With their long experience in politics the Peruvian armed forces are not unaware of the dangers to themselves in their new political role. Even the far less activist caretaker governments of the earlier era of military guardianship exacted their costs in accentuating divisions within the armed forces. The present role of the military as national policy maker, extended over time, will almost certainly aggravate the deep differences of opinion that persist over such questions as which structural transformations should be advanced and at what rates. This threat to institutional cohesiveness is real. The current Revolutionary Government has taken certain precautions to safeguard the unity of the armed forces, notably a statute stipulating that the ministers who command all three services must agree unanimously in choosing who is to be president. Moreover, all three must add their signatures to show their approval before any government decree takes effect. The military's reorganization of public administration showed a sensitivity to the need for keeping the military institution as aloof as possible from day-to-day politics. In effect the Velasco government represents the creation of a new set of differentiated roles, in that the president's advisers devote themselves full time to their new tasks. These arrangements provide for overall military responsibility for national policy while insulating the military institution from the daily pressures of policy execution.[80]

Despite these and other precautions, it seems likely that the fundamental tension between the military's role as policy maker and social intermediary, on the one hand, and its need to preserve the discipline of its profession, on the other, will undermine the present structure of military rule. General Velasco was elevated to presidency largely on the basis of his military virtues, yet his success in that office ultimately depends on his political skills. To the extent that he proves successful as a politician, the psychological gulf between him and his officer colleagues is likely to widen. To the extent that he is successful in leading the struggle for national development, he will almost surely cease in any practical sense to be a military officer.

The development problems faced by Peru are immense. So intractable are they that one frequently encounters the assertion that Peru is simply unmanageable. The reformist approach currently being pursued by the military may well be doomed by its own gradualism and self-imposed limitations. Though the Velasco regime unquestionably enjoys significant legitimacy, its support among the Peruvian masses is shallow and based primarily on transitory symbolic accomplishments. Sustained legitimacy will require much firmer emotional and organizational bonds, such as those generated by charismatic leadership, an external enemy, or a political party with a mobilizing ideology. The officers themselves have a profound suspicion of charismatic leaders, especially from within their own ranks. Thus far the actions of the Nixon administration have denied Peru the opportunity to use the United States as an external enemy, as Fidel Castro succeeded in doing in the 1960's (although Peru's traditional enmity toward Chile may yet fill this function should the Chilean Communists undertake any attempt to export revolution to Peru). The armed forces have shown no inclination whatsoever to employ mass mobilization techniques, apparently on the suspicion that once unleashed such forces might prove unmanageable. The Peruvian model of radical change thus differs significantly from the Egyptian example, analyzed in the following case study. The radical regime of Egypt, under Nasser's leadership, cultivated charisma, militant opposition to Israel, an ideology of Arab Socialism, and the facade of widespread political participation. As self-styled revolutionaries, Velasco and his colleagues could have taken notes from their Egyptian counterparts.

The principal concern of the Peruvian armed forces continues to be the preservation of their own institutions and their autonomy to develop them as they wish. Their concern for institutional preservation led to the abandonment of a guardianship posture in favor of the present strategy of "survival through leadership of change." Yet the armed forces contain a considerable degree of internal political diversity that is likely in the long run to inhibit their leadership of the modernization process. The degree of structural complexity attained by the military bureaucracy has so far permitted that diversity to be overcome, but complexity also functions as a self-regulating mechanism that protects the institution against threats to its cohesion.[81] If the present policies prove less than adequate in promoting social change—as seems likely—and there follows a serious deterioration of the legitimacy of this regime, the officers will probably return once more to the barracks and permit the civilian politicians to become the targets of renewed social unrest.

References

1. See Hubert Herring, *A History of Latin America,* 2nd ed. (New York: Alfred A. Knopf, 1966), pp. 539–543.

2. Egil Fossum, "Factors Influencing the Occurrence of Military Coups d'Etat in Latin America," *Journal of Peace Research,* Vol. IV (1967), pp. 228–251.

3. Victor Villanueva, *El militarismo en el Perú* (Lima: Empresa Gráfica T. Scheuch, 1962), p. 18.

4. Luis Humberto Delgado, *El militarismo en el Perú, 1821–1930* (Lima: American Express, 1930), pp. 12–13.

5. See Stephen L. Rozman, "The Evolution of the Political Role of the Peruvian Military," *Journal of Inter-American Studies and World Affairs,* Vol. XII, No. 4 (October 1970), pp. 543–544.

6. Arnold Payne, *The Peruvian Coup d'Etat of 1962: The Overthrow of Manuel Prado* (Washington: Institute for the Comparative Study of Political Systems, Political Studies Series No. 5, 1968), p. 4.

7. Villanueva, *El militarismo en el Perú,* p. 33.

8. See Marvin Alisky, "Peru," in Ben G. Burnett and Kenneth F. Johnson, eds., *Political Forces in Latin America: Dimensions of the Quest for Stability,* 2nd ed. (Belmont: Wadsworth, 1970), p. 378.

9. See Delgado, *El militarismo en el Perú,* p. 16, and Lyle N. McAlister et al., *The Military in Latin American Sociopolitical Evolution: Four Case Studies* (Washington: Center for Research in Social Systems, January 1970), pp. 24–25.

10. Payne, *The Peruvian Coup d'Etat of 1962,* p. 6, and Delgado, *El militarismo en el Perú,* pp. 38–40.

11. Villanueva, *El militarismo en el Perú,* p. 39.

12. Ibid., pp. 34–36. Villanueva argues further that every military coup after 1914 had as a major dimension the element of a president threatening to reduce military appropriations, and that each coup resulted in a significant increase in same; see pp. 297–300.

13. Payne, *The Peruvian Coup d'Etat of 1962*, pp. 8–9.
14. Villanueva, *El militarismo en el Perú*, p. 54.
15. Rozman, "The Evolution of the Political Role of the Peruvian Military," p. 549.
16. See Harry Kantor, *The Ideology and Program of the Peruvian Aprista Party* (Los Angeles: University of California Press, 1953), pp. 24–29.
17. Thomas Davies, "The Indigenismo of the APRA Party: A Reinterpretation," (Paper presented at the Rocky Mountain Social Science Conference, Colorado Springs, Colorado, May 1970) pp. 9–12; cited by Rozman, "The Evolution of the Political Role of the Peruvian Military," p. 551.
18. According to Arnold Payne, APRA perpetrated ten unsuccessful revolts against the Peruvian government in the 1930's and 1940's, securing the support of some military elements in seven of them; see *The Peruvian Coup d'Etat of 1962*, p. 12.
19. Villanueva, *El militarismo en el Perú*, pp. 75–77.
20. Liisa North, *Civil–Military Relations in Argentina, Chile, and Peru* (Berkeley: Institute of International Studies, University of California at Berkeley, 1966), pp. 48–49.
21. Robert J. Alexander, *Prophets of the Revolution* (New York: Macmillan, 1962), p. 98.
22. Edwin Lieuwen, *Arms and Politics in Latin America* (New York: Praeger, 1961), pp. 80–82.
23. See Jose Luis Bustamante y Rivero, *Tres años de lucha por la democracia en el Perú* (Buenos Aires: Bartolome Chiesino, 1949), pp. 262–280.
24. In these connections, see Villanueva, *El militarismo en el Perú*, p. 133; Richard W. Patch, *A Note on Peru and Bolivia*, American Universities Field Staff Reports, West Coast South America Series, Vol. VI (July 1959), p. 17; and Rosendo A. Gómez, "Peru: The Politics of Military Guardianship," in Martin C. Needler, ed., *Political Systems of Latin America* (Princeton: Van Nostrand, 1964), p. 298.
25. Payne, *The Peruvian Coup d'Etat of 1962*, pp. 19–20.
26. On the CAEM, see Villanueva, *El militarismo en el Perú*, pp. 174–187; Luigi R. Einaudi and Alfred C. Stepan III, *Latin American Institutional Development: Changing Military Perspectives in Peru and Brazil* (Santa Monica: Rand Corporation, R-586-DOS, April 1971), pp. 21–29; and Richard W. Patch, *The Peruvian Elections of 1963*, American Universities Field Staff Reports, West Coast South America Series, Vol. X (July 1963), pp. 5–6.
27. Richard W. Patch, *The Peruvian Elections of 1962 and their Annulment*, American Universities Field Staff Reports, West Coast South America Series, Vol. IX (September 1962), p. 6.
28. *The New York Times*, July 13 and 14, 1962, pp. 7 and 4 respectively.
29. *The New York Times*, July 19, 1962, p. 1; also, Martin C. Needler, "Peru Since the Coup d'Etat," in *The World Today*, Vol. XIX (February 1963), p. 80.
30. In this case the Kennedy administration had itself intervened in various ways in Peru's electoral process in favor of Haya de la Torre, considering the

APRA party the best vehicle for implementing the reformist goals of the Alliance for Progress; for an analysis of the international aspects of the coup, see Arthur K. Smith, Jr., *The Peruvian Military Coup d'Etat of 1962: A Crisis in United States–Peruvian Relations,* M.A. Thesis, University of New Hampshire, June 1966.

31. Interestingly, this case demonstrated the divergence of interests between the United States government and the American corporate community in Peru. The latter, including representatives of the First National City Bank of New York, the International Petroleum Company, the Cerro de Pasco Company, and W.R. Grace & Company, solidly supported the military junta; see Smith, *The Peruvian Military Coup d'Etat of 1962,* pp. 92–93.

32. At least this was the official reason given for his ouster. According to Martin C. Needler, Pérez Godoy was removed because he had shown himself willing to accept the APRA–UNO agreement as a basis for the 1963 elections; see *Political Development in Latin America: Instability, Violence and Evolutionary Change* (New York: Random House, 1968), p. 72.

33. The 1963 elections demonstrated the essential fairness of those held the previous year, suggesting the shallowness of the military's allegations of fraud. APRA and UNO totals remained basically the same, while Belaunde profited when the four minor parties, unable to run candidates of their own, threw their support to him. See Patch, *The Peruvian Elections of 1963,* pp. 7–14.

34. McAlister et al., *The Military in Latin American Sociopolitical Evolution,* pp. 26–27.

35. Ibid., p. 28.

36. Einaudi and Stepan, *Latin American Institutional Development,* p. 59.

37. McAlister et al., *The Military in Latin American Sociopolitical Evolution,* p. 31.

38. William F. Whyte and Graciela Flores, *La mano de obra de alto nivel en el Perú,* (Lima, 1964), pp. 52–56; cited in McAlister et al., *The Military in Latin American Sociopolitical Evolution,* p. 32.

39. Einaudi and Stepan, *Latin American Institutional Development,* p. 23.

40. For more on the education of Peruvian officers, see Einaudi and Stepan, *Latin American Institutional Development,* pp. 21–29; McAlister et al., *The Military in Latin American Sociopolitical Evolution,* pp. 35–38; and James F. Petras and Robert LaPorte, Jr., *Cultivating Revolution: The United States and Agrarian Reform in Latin America* (New York: Random House, 1971), pp. 259–260.

41. Aníbal Quijano, "Nationalism and Capitalism in Peru: A Study in Neo-Imperialism," in *Monthly Review,* Vol. XXIII, No. 3 (July–August 1971), p. 10.

42. Einaudi and Stepan, *Latin American Institutional Development,* pp. 41–45 and 55–57.

43. It is significant that 16 members of the CAEM class of 43 in 1971 were civilians, attesting to the growth of a civil–military technocratic elite; see Einaudi and Stepan, *Latin American Institutional Development*, p. 25.

44. Einaudi and Stepan, *Latin American Institutional Development*, pp. 11–14.

45. McAlister et al., *The Military in Latin American Sociopolitical Evolution*, p. 45.

46. Rozman, "The Evolution of the Political Role of the Peruvian Military," pp. 560–561.

47. See McAlister et al., *The Military in Latin American Sociopolitical Evolution*, pp. 38–44, for a discussion of the "Estado Militar" (military state) in its legal and budgetary aspects in Peru.

48. Martin C. Needler, *Latin American Politics in Perspective* (Princeton: Van Nostrand, 1963), pp. 37–39.

49. James Payne, "Peru: The Politics of Structured Violence," in *Journal of Politics,* Vol. XXVII (May 1965), pp. 365–366.

50. In these connections, see Claudio Véliz, "Introduction," in Véliz, ed., *Obstacles to Change in Latin America* (New York: Oxford University Press, 1965), pp. 1–8; François Bourricaud, "Structure and Function of the Peruvian Oligarchy," *Studies in Comparative International Development,* Vol. II (1966), pp. 26–27; and Merle Kling, "Toward a Theory of Power and Political Instability in Latin America," *Western Political Quarterly,* Vol. IX, No. 7 (March 1956), pp. 21–35.

51. See Torcuato di Tella, "Populism and Reform in Latin America," in Véliz, ed., *Obstacles to Change in Latin America,* pp. 47–74.

52. For a perceptive summary of the state of such movements, see Eldon G. Kenworthy, "Latin American Revolutionary Theory: Is It Back to the Paris Commune?" *Journal of International Affairs,* Vol. XXV, No. 1 (1971), pp. 164–170.

53. Quijano, "Nationalism and Capitalism in Peru," p. 8.

54. Julio Cotler, "Political Crisis and Military Populism in Peru," *Studies in Comparative International Development,* Vol. VI (1970), p. 99. On the problems of Belaunde's agrarian reform efforts, see Petras and LaPorte, *Cultivating Revolution,* pp. 33–115.

55. Rozman, "The Evolution of the Political Role of the Peruvian Military," p. 560.

56. On the IPC dispute and its domestic and international ramifications, see Richard Goodwin, "Letter from Peru," in *The New Yorker* (May 17, 1969), and Cotler, "Political Crisis and Military Populism in Peru," pp. 102–104.

57. See Victor Villanueva, *Golpe en el Perú* (Montevideo: Editorial Sandino, 1969), pp. 40–48.

58. Einaudi and Stepan, *Latin American Institutional Development*, pp. 25–27.

59. Cotler, "Political Crisis and Military Populism in Peru," pp. 100–101.

60. Ibid.

61. See Goodwin, "Letter from Peru."

62. See Petras and LaPorte, *Cultivating Revolution,* pp. 253–255 and 261–269.

63. Robert E. Klitgaard, "Observations on the Peruvian National Plan for Development, 1971–1975," *Inter-American Economic Affairs,* Vol. XXV, No. 3 (Winter 1971), pp. 4–6, 12–16.

64. James F. Petras and Nelson Rimensnyder, "What is Happening in Peru?" *Monthly Review,* Vol. XXI (February 1970), p. 15.

65. Cotler, "Political Crisis and Military Populism in Peru," pp. 103–105.

66. Ibid., pp. 106–108.

67. Ibid., p. 106.

68. Petras and LaPorte, *Cultivating Revolution,* pp. 280–285.

69. On corporatism and the Peruvian military, see Petras and LaPorte, *Cultivating Revolution,* pp. 287–292; and Howard J. Wiarda, "Toward a Framework for the Study of Political Change in the Iberic-Latin Tradition: The Corporative Model," *World Politics,* Vol. XXV, No. 2 (January 1973), pp. 206–235.

70. Quijano, "Nationalism and Capitalism in Peru," pp. 47–48.

71. Ibid., pp. 16–17.

72. Cotler, "Political Crisis and Military Populism in Peru," p. 107.

73. Petras and LaPorte, *Cultivating Revolution,* pp. 292–299.

74. Cotler, "Political Crisis and Military Populism in Peru," p. 108.

75. Quijano, "Nationalism and Capitalism in Peru," pp. 59–60.

76. Ibid., pp. 55–58.

77. See Petras and LaPorte, *Cultivating Revolution,* pp. 300–306, on the military's industrial policy and its effects.

78. Ibid., pp. 306–309.

79. Carlos Delgado, "Militares y civiles en el Perú de hoy," *Oiga,* Vol. IX, No. 413 (March 5, 1971); cited in Einaudi and Stepan, *Latin American Institutional Development,* p. 62.

80. Einaudi and Stepan, *Latin American Institutional Development,* p. 60.

81. Ibid., p. 61.

7

Egypt: Radical Modernization and the Dilemmas of Leadership

No military coup of the twentieth century has had greater international impact than the 1952 coup of the Free Officers of Egypt. Intervention in Nigeria, Peru, and Thailand spread few ripples beyond the frontiers of the individual states. Intervention in Egypt affected the entire Arab world. Through foreign policy success, the personal charisma of Gamal Abdel Nasser, and significant domestic transformations, the military-based government of Egypt exercised influence far beyond the Nile Valley. This influence was mostly attributable to the extraordinary alterations proclaimed, if not necessarily fully achieved, by the Nasser government.

Radical military regimes, as we saw in Part I, manifest a fundamental ambiguity about popular mobilization. Officers may seek major changes, yet they tend to favor administrative rather than political organization. The Velasco government in Peru eschewed mobilization. The Nasser government in Egypt, by contrast, moved increasingly toward legitimating its claim to rule on the bases of charisma and party politics. This dramatic departure from the traditional roles of Middle Eastern armies resulted in significant strains. As we shall see in the conclusion of this chapter, the radical regime of Nasser has given birth to the guardian regime of Sadat, illustrating the fundamental contradiction between military values and radicalism.

178

The Free Officers ousted King Farouk July 23, 1952. For more than 20 years, members of the original eleven Free Officers have presided over the state. The regime now headed by Anwar Sadat enjoys the longest continuous history of any army-based government examined in this book. Top officers have never been far removed from the corridors of power. In the long run, however, military attempts to build a broadly based political party and to carry through domestic reforms may ease the way for military disengagement from politics.

As have many other military regimes in their inception, the Free Officers showed initial reluctance to take the reins of power. Their early unwillingness to govern directly was superseded in a few months by the emergence of the Revolutionary Command Council (RCC) and Nasser. In 1956, when the RCC proclaimed the official end of martial rule, the Free Officers shed their uniforms. However, as J.C. Hurewitz states, " The switch to mufti and even the formal surrender of commissions do not necessarily herald the civilianization of a military political system."[1] The nature and extent of civilianization remain unresolved questions in contemporary Egypt.

Why did the RCC jettison its early promises of a return to civilian rule? The answer includes many elements: the attractions of power; the absence of strong internal challenges to the RCC's rule, or perhaps the existence of challenges sufficient to make the regime uneasy about loosening its grip; the growing prestige of Nasser. But possibly the most important reason lies in the decision, early in the history of the RCC, to undertake major alterations in the political, economic, and social systems. The development of an ideology of radical modernization distinguishes the Egyptian military regime from other military regimes considered in this book, with the possible exception of post-1968 Peru. In Egypt, we find experiments with mass-based parties and the gradual emergence of a pan-Arab philosophy that enhanced the grip on the government of leading officers.

The impact of Arab Socialism was not confined to Egypt. Nasser's pan-Arab interests touched a sympathetic chord. Nasser became the chief spokesman for much of the Arab world. He epitomized Arab longing for world recognition of dignity and importance; he crystallized their hopes after centuries of political suppression. His quest for union in the Middle East, symbolized by the United Arab Republic of Egypt, Syria, and Yemen formed in 1958, seems to have aroused widespread support. Paradoxically, the international impact of the Egyptian military regime was initially greater than its domestic impact. But after rebuffs to their proposals for pan-Arab unity, the Egyptian government turned more to domestic affairs and party organization. "Arab Socialism" emerged as the key ideology.

The ideology of Arab Socialism entailed significant domestic economic transformations. Landholding regulations were thoroughly revised, if not necessarily effectively enforced. As will be shown later, Nasser and his colleagues derived from rural backgrounds. They spoke often of the need to raise the standard of living of the *fellahin* (peasants). Nasser wished to rally active, enthusiastic support from the fellahin, recognizing that no political group (with the possible exception of the Muslim Brethren) had tapped such support. Post-coup Egyptian history is studded with efforts to achieve popular support: the Liberation Rally of 1953, the National Union of 1957, and the Arab Socialist Union of 1962 were all intended to build a foundation for political legitimacy. The land distribution, widespread economic nationalization, and efforts to incorporate farmers and workers into the political mainstream signaled the RCC's interest in creating a populist basis for their rule.

These internal alterations occurred against a background of war, ongoing or imminent. The Egyptian army is among the largest in the Third World. With 391,000 troops and military expenditures in 1968 of $666 million, Egypt devotes more than one-ninth her gross national product to war-related costs.[2] The rationalization for such heavy expenditures is, of course, Israel. The intervention of the Free Officers was sparked in part by Egypt's 1948 defeat at the hands of Israel. The Suez crisis of 1956, in which Israeli forces decisively defeated Egyptian forces, was the occasion for redoubled efforts for Arab unity. The Six-Day War of 1967, Egypt's third setback by Israel, severely tested the legitimacy of the Nasser government.

Domestic and international aspects thus interweave in the complex, fascinating history of Egypt since 1952. The military regime has evolved through four phases. The first phase, 1952–54, saw initial experimentation with civilian leadership jettisoned in favor of direct RCC rule, notably by Nasser. The second phase, 1954–58, witnessed a series of foreign policy triumphs that buttressed Nasser's claim to speak on behalf of the Arab world. The 1958–61 period stands as the apex of Arab unity. But with the collapse of the United Arab Republic, the foreign policy magic Nasser had exercised turned to setbacks. Although he was the dominant political figure of the Arab world, he could not dominate it. The fourth phase, as a result, has been characterized by a turning inward. Increased stress has been placed on domestic transformation, with Nasser leading a "revolution from above." Tensions with Israel remain high. It is in this context of half-war / half-peace that Nasser and his successor Sadat have attempted to create a strong political party. Should this effort succeed, the leaders of the army will have built an institution that could limit future political ambitions of the armed forces. The fate of the Arab Socialist Union thus has significance for the entire Arab world.

The Political Role of the Military in the Middle East

In the Middle East, the military and politics have been practically inseparable for hundreds of years. One major reason for this situation is that Islam, by far the predominant religion of the area, exalts martial skills.

Theorists of civil–military relations, drawing largely on European and North American examples, have distinguished between the realms of the army and of the government. Such differentiation is based on the "civic" polities analyzed in Chapter 3. However, the integral boundaries characteristic of such systems have been essentially confined to Western settings.[3] In the Middle East, boundaries are fragmented. "There has never been a tradition in the Middle East of separating military from civilian authority," Manfred Halpern has written.[4] In a similar vein, P.J. Vatikiotis has suggested that the concept of the army outside politics is "quite alien to the Islamic tradition and state."[5]

The early expansion of Islam helps explain the longstanding political prominence of the military. Within 150 years of Mohammed's death in A.D. 632, men inspired by his teachings had swept from the Arabian peninsula through the Middle East and North Africa, reaching the Pyrenees and India. The "commander of the faithful" exercised a combination of military, political and religious power. "Islam . . . is in its origins the most martial of major world religions."[6] The result:

> Islam's attitude toward political and military power is not one of negation, dissociation or suspicion, but of complete affirmation. A religious value is attached to power, success and victory as such. Islam endows the army with the prestige and authority of an institution meriting divine blessing, and its heritage paves the way for military intervention which is to be regarded as most fitting and proper in the eyes of God and man. [7]

Lines of political succession were never clarified for Islamic political regimes as, for example, they were in European nations which authorized the automatic succession of the eldest son. Palace cliques sought armed support for their favored candidates, leading to what Hurewitz calls "military politics." "Military intrusion was thus built into the succession process . . . . the struggles for succession were mostly settled by civil war and by coup d'etat."[8] The tradition of Islam was thus one of martial glorification and bloody internal political conflict, marked by a prominent role for the armed forces.

As a bridge between continents, the Middle East has been fought over for thousands of years, almost without interruption. The continual threat of conflict kept Middle Eastern nations well aware of the importance of their armed forces. And, in defending against invasion, Middle Eastern armed forces often found themselves the chief purveyors of new techniques. As the Industrial Revolution unlocked the door for significant

European expansion, the armies of the Arab world saw that updating their techniques and equipment was necessary for survival. Napoleon's invasion of Egypt in 1798, the French conquest of Algeria after 1830, and the various wars of independence in the Balkans against the Ottoman Empire, emphasized the need for modernization. Officers concerned with military preparedness found themselves drawn toward change in the entire society; the armed forces "could not be reformed in isolation from the rest of the body politic."[9]

Scholars have argued at length about the contribution officers make to political modernization. A rare unanimity exists about the historical role of Arab officers, however. For example, Halpern notes that the armed forces of the Arab world "have supplied an education in modern technology when industry was scant to provide it, a disciplined organization without peer, and a unity in the face of the corrupt and unprincipled competition of domestic interests and the threat of foreign imperialism." [10] In the same vein, Vatikiotis comments,

> *In their attempt to build modern armies, the Arab countries in the Middle East introduced Western technology. But Western technology was not simultaneously extended to other social institutions. Consequently, the army not only became the technologically most advanced institution in the Arab world, but also acquired a special role in the political evolution of these countries. Army officers became conscious of their access to physical force, and of their importance, as a highly organized and stable group, in spearheading national movements.* [11]

In essence, Vatikiotis argues that the capabilities and awareness of officers, as members of an organized group, outstripped the strengths of potentially countervailing groups, such as political parties. The prominence of Middle Eastern armies in politics can thus be explained in terms of the weaknesses of civilian political institutions. Without countervailing institutions, the armed forces can readily arrogate the leading political roles. Thus, the central role of the armed forces in Islamic history and the innovative role of the military must be linked to the shortcomings of political institutions. Their most fundamental shortcoming may be lack of legitimacy.

Before turning specifically to Egypt, let us briefly review five factors—Islam, Arab solidarity, nationalism, popular mobilization, and charisma—that might be used as bases for legitimacy.

1. Islam is more than a religion. It is a way of life, embracing social conduct, the law, familial ties, and the so-called Five Pillars of personal conduct. As with any complex, longstanding system of belief,

Islam admits of many interpretations. At the risk of oversimplification, three politically relevant aspects should be emphasized. The first aspect, political passivity, enables Muslims to accept the edicts of the men at the top with little protest. Individuals should accept Allah's will, following those with greater knowledge. Second, the Koran upholds the notion of an Islamic community embracing all believers: "The believers are naught else but brothers." This injunction underlies the quest for Arab and Islamic unity with which Nasser became identified. And, third, Islam (literally, surrender or submission to the will of God) represents a total way of life. The combination of belief and practice, of religious leadership and political acquiescence, makes Islamic communities particularly difficult to change. A change in one element might weaken the entire structure. Resistance to alteration has always been marked. As Richard Pfaff notes, "The tightly interwoven social fabric [of Islam] could submit to no breach in its seams. Thus, the main feature of Islamic traditionalism became the general support given to the status quo (an'anat, or tradition) in the face of any proposed change."[12] The notion of "political" legitimacy outside the community of the faithful could not readily be squared with Islamic beliefs. Islam thus simultaneously challenged and affirmed the foundation on which a political community might be built.

2.   A classic foundation for political community comes through a shared language, way of life, and set of beliefs—in short, through a common culture. The Arab world shares an underlying cultural unity of potentially great political significance. The tenets of Islam, the common script of Arabic, shared historical experiences, and a geographic setting in which most state frontiers date from the end of World War I, result in marked homogeneity. An appeal to Arab solidarity can touch deeply held beliefs. One stunning result of Nasser's energies was a further crystallization of pan-Arabism—a set of beliefs and aspirations that (like Islam) concurrently enhanced and undercut a nationalist foundation for political legitimacy.

3.   Nationalism based on the states into which the Middle East is divided confronts both the wider appeals of pan-Arabism and the historical fact of great power rivalries. Following the defeat of the Ottoman Empire in World War I, France and Great Britain divided the Arabic-speaking areas—France taking political supervision of Lebanon and Syria, Great Britain, of Iraq and Palestine. The "community of the faithful" cut across the boundaries drawn through post-World War I jockeying. The presence of British and French troops affected the growth of nationalist movements. For the armed forces, the imperial presence limited their political involvement, leading one scholar to suggest, " . . . a military seizure of power by indigenous officers will not occur during foreign occupation. . . . The Middle Eastern evidence would seem to suggest that it takes four to five

years after *de facto* independence for civilian institutions to be sufficient-ly discredited and the army officers to be sufficiently self-confident to set the stage for the first coup."[13] It has been difficult to awaken a strong sense of nationalism in the various states carved out of the Arab world. Resentment of aliens and a sense of Islamic community are in-sufficient to create a sense of nationalist legitimacy.

4.   The quest for political legitimacy was complicated by the hesitant, incomplete nature of popular mobilization. Political parties with broadly based constituencies did not emerge for much of the twentieth century. Middle Eastern politics seemed to pay little heed to the fellahin; participation instead remained confined to urbanized elites, intellectuals, businessmen, and especially landowners. Unlike Peru and other Latin American states, no triumvirate of Church, army, and landowners emerged in the Middle East. The Middle East in the twentieth century appears sub-stantially to have avoided the predatory phase that characterized nine-teenth-century Latin American politics. The reason military regimes in the Arab world are often deemed reform is the alliance, or at least similarity of views, between officers and members of what Halpern calls the "new middle class." In his enthusiastic analysis, Halpern comments, "army coups have ceased to mirror merely the ambitions of individuals. . . . The army has become the instrument of the new middle class."[14] As an "instrument," the army lacks institutional autonomy; its boundaries are fragmented; the political process as a whole is still influenced more by coercion than by consent. Nonetheless, the partial extent of political mo-bilization meant that parties were weak. Legitimacy based on identification with widely supported political parties has not existed in the Arab world.

5.   A very significant potential basis for political legitimacy lies in charisma. In Part I, we noted that radical modernizing regimes have often rallied mass support by reliance on personal appeals, that is to say, the unique prominence of the charismatic hero. Charisma depends on emotional ties, and on the trust of the populace in their leader. As a foundation for legitimacy, charisma combines intensity with brevity. It serves short-term ends. As Max Weber recognized, charisma must be-come institutionalized, or "routinized," if it is to survive the passing of the leader. Emotional intensity by itself creates the illusion, not the sub-stance, of legitimacy; charisma must be succeeded by the establishment of institutions. A military leader such as Nasser may gain overwhelming popular support—but his charisma by no means precluded the involvement of the armed forces in direct political action.

Egypt cannot escape her history or, more significantly, the for-mative elements of her history, which are still influential in her present-day functioning. As in other parts of the Middle East, great scope for military intervention exists. The traditions of Islam, the longstanding prominence of the armed forces in encouraging social change, and the ill-defined and often conflicting bases for political legitimacy all cause inherent weakness in civilian political institutions, whose shortcomings invite coups d'etat. Let us turn specifically to Egypt and the conditions that prompted a radical modernizing regime.

The 1952 Coup: Military Institutional Factors

Until a few years before the coup, Egypt lacked the sine qua non for military intervention: an army under national control, alienated from the government. Only when indigenous officers gained key positions in the armed forces, without tight control from the British or the court, was seizure of control possible.

Except for the period during which the British government exercised direct control over the country (1882–1936), members of the armed forces have played leading roles in Egyptian politics since 1800. At the beginning of the nineteenth century, the Napoleonic invasions left Egypt torn among competing adventurers, over whom Mohammed Ali soon gained dominance. He took the first major steps toward launching Egypt into the modern world, as "the founder of modern Egypt."[15]

At first consideration, Mohammed Ali might seem an unlikely person for a role of leadership. Born in a remote part of present-day Albania, he took up trade as a tobacco salesman, then drifted into the military. As an officer in an Albanian regiment, Mohammed Ali profited from the unsettled conditions after Napoleon's withdrawal from the Nile Valley. He eliminated rivals by skillful maneuvering. His de facto control was legitimized in 1805, when he was named governor (pasha) of Egypt. Mohammed Ali recognized that his power ultimately depended on a combination of reform and effective coercion. He professionalized his troops— by eliminating the ill-trained Albanians he once headed, by sending officers abroad for training, and by importing French and Italian instructors. (It must be noted, however, that native-born Egyptians were essentially barred from the officer corps.[16] Mohammed Ali and his successors preferred to rely on other Ottomans—Greeks, Albanians, Kurds, or Turks—and later on Circassian Mamelukes—hereditary warriors and rulers who were descended from white slaves that had seized power in Egypt in the thirteenth century.) Egypt was thus ruled by a largely foreign elite who, until 1936, prevented indigenous Egyptians from rising very high in the armed forces.

Mohammed Ali did not confine his attention to the military, but turned it also to commercial agriculture. With the cultivation of long-staple cotton came irrigation canals, port improvement, land taxes—and, of course, the enrichment of Mohammed Ali, who administered the country "as though it were a state farm."[17] Major economic investments were channeled through the government, with the court playing a major role. No longer did the fellahin produce for their own subsistence; they fed the mills of England and France. Thus, as in other Middle East states, the transformation of the armed forces was coupled with broader efforts at economic and social modernization. We can see that the energetic government role in the Egyptian economy under Nasser had abundant precedent.

The second noteworthy military figure of the nineteenth century lived in the latter half of it: Colonel Ahmed Arabi was, like Nasser, a full-blooded Egyptian. Arabi's father was a village headman; his son was required by decree to enter military preparatory school when he was 13. Arabi found that the armed forces suited his talents. By the age of 19, he achieved the rank of colonel—but, owing to preferential promotions for non-Egyptians, he could rise no further. His quick rise to prominence in 1881–82 bears some parallels to the 1952 coup, for both were directed against a monarchy overly concerned with self-enrichment and contemptuous of Egyptians in the armed forces.

Arabi's rise resulted from financial retrenchment undertaken by Ismail, grandson of Mohammed Ali. The government's indebtedness spiraled from £3 million in 1863 to £100 million in 1879.[18] European creditors demanded repayment. The army was an obvious target for reduction: it was cut from 45,000 to 18,000, with 2500 Egyptian officers being dismissed in 1879. The fired officers demonstrated, and helped hasten Ismail's departure from office. One scholar has deemed this demonstration "the first serious attempt by army officers in Egypt to influence policy and exert political authority."[19] Further military reorganization followed, under external pressure, with a decree in mid-1880 that seemingly further reduced the opportunities for indigenous Egyptians to become officers. Colonel Arabi and two fellow officers protested; their reward was a court-martial, which was followed by a spontaneous uprising of the rank and file. Lines of opposition were thus drawn between the court and the military. The officers initially demanded perquisites, such as higher salaries and nondiscriminatory promotion policies; however, the demands escalated, and they resulted in the court's permitting elections for a legislative assembly and drafting a constitution. The challenge originating in the armed forces affected the entire political structure of Egypt. "Local Turks in Egypt were now in danger of losing their landed wealth and privileged political position."[20] But the intervention of British troops in September 1882 aborted this effort at change through the officer corps.

The British occupation was not an isolated instance of European pressure. In 1841–42, Mohammed Ali had run afoul of European interests when he attempted to invade Turkey. He was defeated by a European–Ottoman alliance and stripped of territories he had conquered in the Arabian peninsula and Middle East; in addition, he was forced to cut his armed forces by over 90 percent, scrap his navy, and end his monopoly over trade. The 1882 occupation came after several years during which creditor states controlled Egyptian finances and, by their cost-cutting efforts, "compounded the resentment of Egyptian officers and higher civil servants who were already chafing under the preferential treatment of Europeans employed by the government and of Ottomans and Circassians who constituted the bureaucratic and military elite."[21] British officers filled command positions after 1882 and relaxed their control over the Egyptian army at a pace best described as tortoise-like. When Great Britain withdrew its protectorate in 1922 and recognized Egypt as an "independent sovereign state," it nonetheless "absolutely reserved" security of communications and "the defence of Egypt against all foreign aggression or interference, direct or indirect."[22] A treaty revision in 1936 required Egypt, independent in other respects, to obtain all military supplies and officer training from England. Even further, British troops remained in the Suez Canal zone, to defend this vital link to India. Their presence was doubtless a galling factor to young Egyptian officers. And, thirdly, both World Wars substantially affected Egypt. In World War I, as many as 200,000 troops were stationed in Egypt to fend off Ottoman attacks; heavy-handed tactics were used to requisition laborers and animals; prices soared; normal political activities were suspended; the British grip grew tighter. British–Egyptian contact became more distant and formal.[23] In World War II, German troops advanced to within 70 miles of Alexandria. Under great pressure, King Farouk gave his reluctant support to the British cause, against the wishes of some officers who favored joining forces with the Germans to end, once and for all, the British control over Egypt. One of the major plotters was Anwar Sadat, president of Egypt, who later wrote, "We made contact with the German Headquarters in Libya and we acted in complete harmony with them. . . . We had suffered insult and provocation, and now we prepared to fight side by side with the Axis to hasten England's defeat."[24] The grievances that surfaced in the coup of the Free Officers clearly bore upon the British influence over commerce and the court, and upon their control over the Suez Canal.

Precisely how did the Free Officers come into existence? The roots of the group lie in the nationalist awakening of 1936, when the constitution was restored after five years of royal dictatorship and the Wafd party swept into office despite palace opposition. British influence remained strong, however. Although a treaty between Egypt and Great Britain in 1936 recognized the Suez Canal "as an integral part of Egypt," Great Britain could station forces near the canal until the two states agreed "that the Egyptian Army is in a position to ensure by its own resources the liberty and entire security of navigation of the Canal."[25]

There was widespread resentment over the treaty—a resentment that spilled over into the Egyptian military academy.

Students of military sociology give close attention to the experiences that link members of peer groups. Just as Sandhurst provided a common background for several of the Nigerian conspirators, and the Center for Advanced Military Studies (CAEM) bound together Peruvian officers, the Egyptian military academy linked the Free Officers. Eight of the 11 founding members of the group entered the academy in 1936, the three others immediately thereafter. Most of them, Vatikiotis notes, were of "humble origin . . . their fathers and grandfathers were peasant farmers, small landowners, or minor officials. . . . "[26] Many of them had been politically active. Nasser, for example, had been wounded by a British bullet when he participated in a demonstration a year before entering the academy.[27] There seems to be no convincing evidence that those who formed the Free Officers did so prior to 1948–49, although Sadat dated the "real revolutionary conspiracy" as springing up in February 1942— naturally enough, with himself at the center.[28]

The real impetus for the formation of the Free Officers came with the Palestine war of 1948. The striking victory of Israeli armies came as an unexpected shock to Egyptian leaders. Many officers were shocked by later revelations of apparent royal complicity in shady arms deals. One result of disgruntlement born of defeat was increased political activity among officers. Conditions in the country prompted conspiracy, and boundaries between civil and military spheres became fragmented. For example, many officers openly sympathised with the Muslim Brethren, a right-wing movement wishing to "purify" Egypt by following Islamic principles and destroying secular forces.

It must be quickly noted, however, that the Free Officers shied away from direct contacts with civilian groups. They remained underground, although they did circulate some anonymous pamphlets. For two years, late 1949 to late 1951, King Farouk and his civilian ministers took no steps against the Free Officers, who were generally men of low to middle rank, apparently believing that the loyalty of top officers guaranteed the support of the armed forces. The court did not intervene until a seemingly trivial incident—elections in the Officers' Club—showed the great strength of the Free Officers; when the court stepped in, it helped precipitate its own downfall.

Following his usual practice, King Farouk openly supported a candidate to head the Officers' Club. The particular individual may have pleased the court, but he infuriated the officers, who scorned him because he had been cashiered from the army for corruption, then named chief of staff only through royal intrigue.[29] The Free Officers favored the election of General Mohammed Naguib. A few moments before the officers were to ballot, the election was canceled; nonetheless, they decided to move ahead, and a few days later about 500 officers elected

Naguib and at least five known members of the Free Officers to preside over the Officers' Club. By December 1951, the lines of opposition between the Free Officers and the court had been clearly drawn. By July 1952, conflict came into the open. Farouk dissolved the Executive Committee of the Officers' Club, ordered its members posted to rural garrisons, and formed a new cabinet in which his brother-in-law, a man totally lacking military experience, was to be minister of war. On the afternoon of July 22, 1952, a small group of Free Officers decided to strike. In scarcely twelve hours, they had succeeded with an ease and speed they had not imagined. [30]

We have seen that the precipitating factor in military intervention was direct royal meddling in military affairs. However, the preconditions for intervention lay further back, in the limited legitimacy of the government, the alienation of the officer corps, and the withdrawal of British control over the Egyptian army.

Five of the propositions suggested in Part I seem applicable to the coup carried out by the Free Officers. Class and ethnic differences separated them from the court. The Free Officers derived from middle- and lower middle-class backgrounds, not from well-to-do, landowning Turkish backgrounds. Farouk persisted, like his forebear Mohammed Ali, in regarding army and country as practically his personal property. Nasser and his coconspirators, like Colonel Arabi, emphasized their Egyptian backgrounds and interests. Second, a series of shared experiences, starting with the 1936 entry to the military academy, gave leading Free Officers a number of personal links employed later for conspiracy. United in their disgust by the defeat in Palestine, they could extend their friendship into plotting. Third, the royal steps against the Free Officers, manifested in the Officers' Club election, had abruptly reduced the military's sphere of decision making. Such a shift precipitated military intervention. Fourth, the coup was planned and carried out by middle-grade officers, with General Naguib being brought in at the last moment. Finally, the Free Officers assumed political control with specific grievances about royal interference with the armed forces, but with only general attitudes about political affairs. Such vaguely expressed discontent, as we have seen, leads to the establishment of military regimes. So much, then, for the internal factors that helped precipitate intervention. Before turning to the political initiatives of the Free Officers, we must examine the environmental factors that lay behind their coup d'etat.

The 1952 Coup: Environmental Factors

The social, economic, and political setting provided the external impetus for the Free Officers to assume and exercise control. Intramilitary grievances, as we have seen, fueled the Free Officers' discontent.

However, their seizure of control was eased by the citizens' failure to support the regime in power. The lack of legitimacy should be viewed in the context of intensifying population pressures, widespread distrust of the central government despite apparent acceptance of its edicts, and a lack of opportunities for the urbanized middle class to become politically active.

Population pressures were growing prior to the 1952 coup. Cultivable land in Egypt is limited to areas flooded or irrigated by the Nile. With the construction of dams in the nineteenth and twentieth centuries, flooding was controlled. The continuous irrigation fostered both agricultural commercialization and population increases. In 1800, Egypt counted 2.5 million inhabitants; by 1897, the figure had risen to 9.7 million; in 1948, there were nearly 19 million Egyptians, and over 30 million in 1966. The area under cultivation remained nearly constant, although irrigation did make double cropping possible. By 1970, seventy percent of all families owned less than one acre—although maintaining a minimal standard of living required three to five acres.

By 1952, land ownership had become concentrated in the hands of a few. The result was a propertied class linked to the court, adamantly opposed to policies that might threaten their holdings. In the year of the coup, 11,000 landowners held a third of all cultivable land in Egypt. Rents consumed about three-quarters of what the fellahin could earn, leaving a precariously thin margin for survival. The only solution seemed to be trust in Allah's providence.

That Egypt remained quiet during these two centuries of intensifying squeeze may be attributed to Islam. As we have seen, Islam was a total way of life that encouraged subordination to the government: "Obedience to a political structure sanctioned by God"[31] was inculcated for centuries. Villages remained essentially self-governing; individuals considered themselves exploited rather than assisted by the central government. The fellahin accepted the situation, but they did not assess it as desirable. The result was "mutual and widespread distrust" among the fellahin, due to "fear of getting involved with an uncontrollable and unpredictable government."[32] This distrust carried two political consequences. First, changes of regime in Cairo might pass scarcely unnoticed in the villages. Second, mobilization of the rural populace was nearly impossible; the only issues that could possibly break through the apathy of the fellahin might be land reform and defense of Islamic values. As Nasser was to learn, villagers often preferred to live their own lives, not become involved in abstruse matters of national politics.

The slow rhythm of change in the countryside contrasted with growing urbanization. Migration to cities provided some vent for rural discontent. One-quarter of Egypt's population crowded into cities of more than 20,000 in 1937; about one-third, by the time of the coup; and over two-fifths, by 1966. Many belonged to the "new" middle class, identified earlier in this study as a major agent of change in the contemporary Middle East. However, this new class lacked a political voice. The Wafd party, which had basked in undoubted popular acclaim between the World Wars, had enjoyed little opportunity to govern; and when it later gained control, it quickly became corrupt. The "new" middle class could not turn to traditionalistic groups, such as the Muslim Brethren.

Egypt on the eve of the 1952 coup lacked a deep-rooted, legitimate government. The acquiescence encouraged by Islam did not constitute strong support, merely acceptance in a sullen manner. Demographic pressures were leading toward a crisis in the countryside. In the cities, the venal policies of the civilian government and the monarchy enjoyed little support. The defeat at the hands of Israel made the armed forces feel they had been betrayed. British troops remained stationed along the Suez Canal, their presence exacerbating nationalist tensions. Most important, perhaps, public order could not be maintained. In January 1952, much of Cairo was deliberately burned. The ineffectiveness of the government in the face of this crisis illustrated its inadequacies. That military seizure of power occurred should not have been surprising. The only surprise element may have been those who moved into control, for the Free Officers did not, like officers elsewhere in the Arab world, "represent the class which was the direct successor of colonial rule in the Arab countries: the large landlords and their intellectual hangers-on." [33]

The Armed Forces as Governors: A Radical Regime in Action

Colonel Nasser and the other Free Officers embarked on their political careers with little experience. Their aims were diffuse, their criticisms of the vanquished former regime were general. Distaste for court extravagance and interference in military matters was not readily translatable into concrete policies. The Free Officers found themselves groping for an appropriate formula. Not until they had first toyed with a facade of civilian rule, and then eliminated opposing groups, did they emerge as a full-fledged, army-based regime.

Like many other coup makers, the Free Officers did not leap immediately into the political forefront. They deposed Farouk but named a regent to govern for Farouk's infant son. They replaced the discredited government with civilians unsullied by corruption. But these efforts lasted barely a year. The civilian prime minister was pushed aside two months after the coup, when he proved unenthusiastic about agrarian reform. The Free Officers titled themselves the Revolutionary Command Council (RCC), and embarked on the elimination of organized political groups and possible opponents within the military. General Naguib became "Chief of the Revolution," as well as president and prime minister; Nasser, the real power behind the coup, became deputy prime minister. He dismissed about 400 officers, a tenth of the officer corps, including all but one of the brigadiers and more than half the colonels. [34] In August 1952, trade unions were cowed by the bloody breaking of a strike. In January 1953, political parties were dissolved, their assets were confiscated, and a three-year period of military dictatorship was announced; the monarchy was formally abolished in June, with RCC members taking cabinet positions for the first time; in October 1954, the powerful Muslim Brethren was outlawed following their unsuccessful assassination attempt against Nasser.

These steps proved the Free Officers' independence from civilian groups. They had not consulted civilians in the ouster of Farouk and refused to be beholden to potential competitors. The Free Officers seemed initially to distrust those who curried public favor; thus, they held little in common with most Egyptian politicians. Proud of their acts, impatient about the need for change, Nasser and his colleagues viewed the RCC as the inspiration and undisputed leader of Egypt. They increasingly saw themselves, in the words of Naguib, as the "vertebral column" of the "revolution." "The whole movement was initiated by you; the nation looks to you for leadership," he told officers as they swore allegiance to the new, army-dominated republic in June 1953.[35]

Central to the RCC's self-image was its emphasis on "revolution." To them, July 23rd was not a coup d'etat pure and simple; it was the start of profound transformation. But what precise steps should be taken? For close to a decade, the RCC struggled to define the key steps. They improvised. "From the outset," Dekmejian writes, "the officers' behavior as rulers testified to their total lack of a program for concrete political action."[36] Not that there was any lack of targets. Eliminating land shortages, reducing the power of large landowners, industrialization, revenge against Israel—these were among the many possible objectives. The first question to be settled, however, was who controlled the country. It was in the solution to this question that the RCC showed itself bent on the creation of a military regime.

The RCC prevented the crystallization of opposition to its rule. "Its determination to become the ruling elite in the country precluded any long-range alliance with rival groups . . . the Free Officers Executive became the nucleus of a new ruling class. . . ."[37] To view the RCC as "agents" of a class is inaccurate. The officers were not solicited by others; instead, they co-opted into their regime those individuals (particularly technicians) who would further the cause of the "revolution."

Dekmejian has statistically documented the political supremacy officers have held in Egypt since 1952. When officers took over cabinet positions in June 1953, the result was a "massive infusion of officers into key bureaucratic positions for purposes of control and supervision." [38] The portion of leadership posts held by officers increased in a few months from 26.3 percent to 40.9 percent, and reached 52.1 percent in September 1954. After the disastrous Six-Day War of 1967, the figure leaped to 65.4 percent, then later returned to 39.4 percent.[39] Similar statistics are provided by Be'eri. As of early 1967, there were 65 individuals in the governing group, of whom 27 were officers. However, of the ten men at the apex, all were officers, almost all born between 1917 and 1920.[40] Be'eri further asserts that about 1000 officers have doffed their uniforms and "entrenched themselves" in crucial economic and administrative positions. "These 1,000 officers provide the majority of the ministers, provincial governors, ambassadors, directors of companies and enterprises, newspaper editors and molders of public opinion in the New Egypt."[41] Partnership with new economic and technical elites, coupled with a dramatic expansion of government control, have enabled members of the armed forces to retain policy control. The officer class—for the word class seems apt in the Egyptian context—has benefitted from a substantial reorientation of the entire government apparatus.

Extension of the government's economic control, like extension of political control, came hesitantly. "The first four years of the revolution, although politically they constitute a turning point in Egyptian history, from the point of view of the economic system may be regarded as a continuation of the economic system of the post-war years."[42] The officers espoused a mixed capitalist–socialist system. Their one main act, the Agrarian Reform Law of September 1952, affected only six percent of the cultivated land. This act limited an individual's holdings to 200 acres, but its effects could be readily circumvented. The law did break the political grip of large landholders. It did not, however, markedly improve the lot of the landless, for the purchase of land required capital they lacked.

Starting in 1956, and especially during 1961, the government switched course toward a more socialized economy. The Misr bank was nationalized; commerce was placed under government auspices; the maximum size of landholdings was cut to 100 acres and the interest rate for land purchase was halved. An extraordinary series of economic decrees in 1961 ended what Dekmejian calls a "slow process marked by groping, indecisiveness, and experimentation."[43] Between 1962 and 1965, the payroll for government employees doubled.

The effects of increased official involvement in the economy were three-fold. First, potential opponents of the regime were undercut. Entrenched commercial interests had been linked to the Wafd, and tended to be disproportionately controlled by foreign minorities (Greeks, Maltese) or by Copts, an Egyptian Christian sect. Nationalization had a

second and more important effect: it helped carry through the ideology
of Arab Socialism. Nasser saw political and economic change as linked.
For example, in his brief book *Egypt's Liberation,* he spoke of the
necessity for a nation to experience two revolutions, "a political revolution by which it wrests the right to govern itself from the hand of
tyranny, or from the army stationed upon its soil against its will; and a
social revolution, involving the conflict of classes. . . ."[44] Class conflict cannot be reduced without economic redistribution—and economic
redistribution was central to Arab Socialism, as we shall see shortly.
And, third, nationalization further cemented the officers' control, making
them more clearly into a ruling class. Their alliance with "technocrats"
may have strengthened their position. As Be'eri stated,

> *The bonds connecting the technocrats and the officers are*
> *strong and numerous. . . . They are dependent on one anoth-*
> *er and each can be secure in his own position only if the other*
> *is also firmly entrenched. . . . When the state is the principal*
> *capitalist and the owner of the leading economic develop-*
> *ment enterprises, the ruling class is that which exercises con-*
> *trol over the administrative establishment—the officials—and*
> *over the forces of coercion—the police and the army.* [45]

If economic nationalization represented one strategy of building
support, a second strategy lay in land distribution. Both the legislation
and the official statistics tell an impressive story—that is, if they are accurate. Holdings are now limited to a maximum of 100 acres. Nearly one
million acres were acquired by the government for redistribution; this
represented 15 percent of Egypt's arable land, and benefitted more than
a quarter-million families. Large landowners have disappeared as politically
significant factors—and, not unexpectedly, small landowners have given
their support to the government. Fragmentation of small holdings seems
to have been reversed, with an increase of 20 percent in their average size.
But who, precisely, has gained from distribution? The landless seem to
have gained little ground, as it were, since they lack the resources for purchase, even on favorable terms. Be'eri notes that, in the twelve years
after the military's assumption of power, the number of landowners grew
12 to 13 percent, while the total population grew 25 percent. "The medium
land-owners [10–100 acres] . . . succeeded in preserving their position
and prosperity. . . . The village wealthy had preserved their position and
riches during the period of the republic, and have even enhanced them.
Nor is it surprising, for the officers now in power are bound closely to
them."[46]

In point of fact, land distribution has scarcely changed the basic
conditions of rural life. Fellahin remain locked in a vicious circle of overpopulation, apathy about change, and a lack of capital and knowledge.

Economic dilemmas stemming from the high birth rate seem practically insoluble. The modernizing values espoused by Nasser have yet fully to penetrate and transform the rural areas. As one recent observer noted,

> *The crucial problem facing rural Egypt is the fact that new values are being introduced, but only a part of the citizenry is accepting them. . . . In many of the institutions being introduced, traditional attitudes, values and behavioral norms, rather than being neutralized or weakened, are in fact being strengthened. . . . the bulk of the citizenry is denied meaningful participation and thus lacks one of the most effective means of generating the acceptance and feelings of legitimacy necessary to institutionalize the new processes of decision making and political control.* [47]

Twenty years of military rule have thus brought some structural alterations in the economy, especially through nationalization and significant efforts at land reform; but there has been no revolutionary change in either the attitudes or the position of the landless. Most fellahin remain apart from the political process.

The third means the military regime used to bolster support was the charisma of Nasser. Few modern men have gained as great popular attention as Gamal Abdel Nasser. The phenomenal success he enjoyed in foreign policy made him an Arab leader without rival. For example, Nasser frustrated American-led efforts to create a collective security pact in the Middle East; he spoke forthrightly at the Bandung conference, at which the Third World first found its collective voice; he turned to the Communist bloc for arms; and he nationalized the Suez Canal. These steps, interpreted as hostile by the West, gave Nasser impeccable anti-imperialist credentials. Nasser became a hero. He inspired a trust no Egyptian leader in recent history had ever enjoyed.

In the classic formulation of Max Weber, charisma arises at times of profound social stress, as norms of legitimacy are challenged. Charisma is a notoriously short-lived phenomenon. Individuals place their confidence in a strong leader, identifying completely with him. However, because of the instability of charisma, it must be "routinized." It requires an ideology, an organization, that can survive the death or debunking of the charismatic leader. When Nasser's major diplomatic triumph, the creation of the United Arab Republic, turned sour, a new base for charisma was necessary. In the words of Dekmejian, "The externally stalled revolutionary dynamic had to be switched to internal revolutionary action to justify and consolidate the leadership's power."[48] The crisis induced by Syrian secession prompted the creation of the Arab Socialist Union, the regime's most serious attempt at building political foundations.

Political parties serve varied functions. They channel demands and supports. They furnish candidates, platforms, rationales. In linking government and populace, parties can abet a sense of political community. And, in the Egyptian context, they could rally support to the regime.

When the Free Officers assumed control, Nasser apparently expected quick, easy mobilization of popular sentiment behind his efforts. This expectation was rebuffed. His sense of chagrin and disappointment clearly emerged in his 1954 book:

> *Before July 23rd, I had imagined that the whole nation was ready and prepared, waiting for nothing but a vanguard to lead the charge against the battlements, whereupon it would fall in behind in serried ranks, ready for the sacred advance towards the great objective. And I had imagined that our role was to be this commando vanguard. . . . Then suddenly came reality after July 23rd. The vanguard performed its task and charged the battlements of tyranny. It threw out Farouk and then paused. . . . For a long time it waited. Crowds did eventually come, and then came in endless droves—but how different is the reality from the dream! The masses that came were disunited, divided groups of stragglers. . . . At this moment I felt, with sorrow and bitterness, that the task of the vanguard, far from being completed, had only begun. We needed order, but we found nothing behind us but chaos. We needed unity, but we found nothing behind us but dissension. We needed work, but we found behind us only indolence and sloth.* [49]

The neutralization of opposition was accomplished in the first thirty months of military rule. In January 1953, shortly after political parties had been banned, the RCC created the so-called Liberation Rally, intended (in Nasser's words again) not as a "political party . . . [but as] a means to organize popular strength for the reconstruction of society on a sound new basis."[50] But the Liberation Rally failed to grow roots. Its creation represented a defensive move, to forestall agitation from banned groups. Membership seems to have been based on personal opportunism. Scarcely a year after its founding, Nasser openly criticized the Rally's shortcomings. Those who became members, he stated, "only support us in order to obtain favors or to be excused for their past mistakes." Then, added Nasser, "We neither can nor will allow the capitalists and moneyed classes to regain power. If we gave them a chance to be elected now, it would be as if the Revolution had never happened."[51]

To build stronger support, rather than simply neutralize the lingering influence of the once-powerful, the regime turned in mid-1957 to the so-called National Union, through which "the people would realize the aims of the Revolution."[52] It failed in this objective. The National Union served as a screening device, whereby members of the RCC (disbanded in mid-1956, but whose former members still controlled political power) approved candidates for the National Assembly. Some 2500 candidates wished to run; nearly half were rejected by the ruling junta. Nearly two-thirds of the 350 seats were won by lawyers, businessmen, exofficers, and high civil servants. The National Union could not attract farmers or workers as candidates for office. No wonder: the required £50 deposit for candidates constituted two years' income for most farmers.[53]

Nasser's disappointment with the National Union echoed his earlier disappointment with the Liberation Rally. The serried ranks could not keep in step. Perhaps they could not even hear the command to march! The 1958 effort to implement Arab unity through federation with Syria backfired. The union, hastily entered into, suffered from nearly irreconcilable differences in political style. Following a coup, Syria withdrew from the United Arab Republic in September 1961; the Kingdom of Yemen, which also had joined the UAR, was ousted three months later. Faced with checks to his aims of unity, and faced with manifest shortcomings in the National Union, Nasser initiated a series of major moves, in the spirit of "the Revolution." The key change came with the inauguration of yet another party, the Arab Socialist Union.

Shortly after Syria's secession, Nasser noted that the National Union must be changed "into a revolutionary organ in the hands of the national people." The party was dissolved in November 1961, and a 250-member "Preparatory Committee for a National Congress of Popular Powers" set to work. This body helped open the way for a far-reaching consultation. Some 1500 representatives, of whom farmers constituted 25 percent and workers 20 percent, approved the "National Charter," a 30,000-word document prepared under Nasser's personal supervision.[54]

In *Egypt's Liberation*, Nasser wrote of a role in the Arab world, "wandering aimlessly in search of a hero."[55] By 1961, Nasser had emerged as the hero, whose search for an ideology might well have seemed to be aimless wandering. The National Charter stands as his testimony to the paths Egypt should follow. A few quotations will illustrate its general themes:

> *Revolution is the only way to overcome under-development, forced on the Arab Nation through suppression and exploitation. . . . the peaceful resolution of class struggle cannot be achieved unless the power of reaction is first and foremost deprived of all its weapons. . . .*

*1.   The popular and political organizations based on free and
direct election must truly and fairly represent the powers forming the majority of the population. . . .*

. . .

*3.   There is a dire need to create a new political organization,
within the framework of the Arab Socialist Union, recruiting
the elements fit for leadership, organizing their efforts, clarifying the revolutionary motives of the masses, sounding their
needs and endeavouring to satisfy them. . . .*

. . .

*Efficient socialist planning is the sole method which guarantees
the use of all national resources, be they material, natural or
human in a practical, scientific and humane way aimed at
realising the common good of the masses, and ensuring a life
of prosperity for them.* [56]

Central to Nasser's objectives was creation of the Arab Socialist
Union (ASU). The tasks of the ASU were set forth boldly. It would become a "positive motive force of revolutionary action"; protect the
Revolution's principles; liquidate remaining influences of capitalism and
feudalism; and prevent deviations such as reactionism, opportunism,
negativism, deviation, and "improvisation"—that is, operating in ad hoc
or pragmatic ways without adequate national planning. The document
thus illustrated a basic distrust of spontaneity, of group conflict, and of
events potentially outside the view and control of the center. The ASU
itself would spread through the country in pyramidal fashion. Individuals
in the "basic units" (for example, a factory, city ward, or village) would
form a "conference," which would in turn elect a "committee." The
"committees" were to be chosen in the twenty-five provinces (governor-
ates) into which Egypt is divided. Thus, party and administrative structures
were deliberately made parallel, to serve as checks on each other. Pro-
ceeding up the pyramid, we successively find the National Congress of
the ASU, which names the Central Committee; this, in turn, names the
Supreme Executive Committee. Nasser, not unsurprisingly, became the
first president of the ASU.

Detailed analysis of the ASU would require space beyond the
confines of this volume. The party has attempted to spread participation widely. In 1966, nearly seven million people had joined, of whom
an estimated three-quarters were active members. In the mid-1968 elections for the 7584 basic units, over 180,000 candidates presented themselves for the 76,000 positions. According to official statements, more
than half the 1648 individuals chosen for the National Congress were
workers or peasants. Officially, the ASU represented the "supreme popular authority which assumed the leadership role in the people's name"; it
would exercise "popular political control on the government organism."

[57] Few social scientists have probed the ASU's effectiveness. In the judgment of one, however, the party has yet to effect basic transformations in village life. "Party membership in the rural areas tends, unfortunately for the ASU, to ensure that a former traditional leader will be able to maintain his position of power and authority in the village or rural community."[58] The tendency of local party leaders and government administrators to band together for mutual protection "breeds inefficiency, encourages traditional leadership and patterns, and prevents the information necessary for efficient national planning from ever reaching those in positions responsible for that planning."[59]

The Free Officers thus changed course dramatically in twenty years of control. Initial political hesitancy gave way to increasingly bold steps in political and economic organization. The foreign policy successes and charisma of Nasser gave Egypt a pan-Arab reputation it had never previously enjoyed. The old, propertied upper class was substantially supplanted. But, even a score of years after the seizure of power, the regime found it difficult to infuse sufficient enthusiasm, order, unity, and work into the masses. Its members still stood in the vanguard, their tasks far from complete. As radical modernizing rulers, the Free Officers–RCC–ASU leaders have found the creation of a new political order incredibly complex and difficult.

Toward a Party Structure for Egypt?

The RCC officially disbanded itself in 1956, the period of martial law at an end. Although its members continued to control decision making, they did so in conjunction with technocratic elites, increasingly relying on a party structure.

Nasser realized that profound change in Egypt would require long-term efforts. He feared dilution of his vision by unsympathetic groups, notably drawn from the power groups of the old regime. But he apparently felt that his vision of a better life would kindle widespread support. The RCC's failure to rally the populace led Nasser to realize the limits of military rule. Commands "work" in any army, for its members form a cohesive, disciplined body, usually with a fixed set of responsibilities. Commands do not necessarily work in a civilian political system, for its members pursue a number of different, conflicting goals. Either a ruler must move toward a coordination that might involve totalitarian measures, or he must give relatively free play to diverse forces. If the nation is to march in serried ranks like the military, then strong steps toward uniformity will be needed. If the nation is to exhibit a varied, participatory political life, then citizens must enjoy—both want and have—

the opportunity to share in shaping their own destiny. In Egypt, this means the participation of the fellahin.

"The ability of the military to develop stable political institutions," Huntington asserts, "depends first upon their ability to identify their rule with the masses of the peasantry and to mobilize the peasantry into politics on their side."[60] The twenty years of military-based rule in Egypt have witnessed extraordinary rhetoric about reaching the fellahin. The rhetoric masks what is, at best, an uneven performance. Dekmejian cautiously asserts it is "possible" that the fellahin are starting to identify themselves with the political system and the nation as a whole.[61] James Mayfield states that the new structures, institutions, and organizations set up by the regime "have generally failed to generate a strong commitment or sense of loyalty among the rural peasants."[62] Why do these difficulties exist? Islamic fatalism, the sense of accepting Allah's will, remains. Basic schooling has yet to reach a majority of the Egyptian population; most studies of political participation have concluded that literacy is both determinant and measure of feelings of political efficacy. But the most fundamental reason may lie in the incompleteness of Nasser's and other officers' views of the place of political conflict.

Officers inevitably will be influenced by their perceptions of the armed forces as "models" for the society as a whole. Recall Naguib's assertion, quoted earlier in this chapter, about the military as the "vertebral column" of the revolution. Officers see Egypt passing through political and social revolutions, in which traditional rural attitudes must be remolded. Convinced of the rightness of their course, and equally convinced that history will applaud their efforts, members of the military regime in Egypt have viewed political conflict as detracting from their goals. They cannot sanction what they perceive as retrograde, parochial, village-centered interests. The image that officers hold of their society is one of smooth coordination, of subordination of narrow or personal interests to the imperatives of national reconstruction. As Nasser wrote in *Egypt's Liberation,* "To be successful, the political revolution must unite all elements of the nation, build them solidly together and instill in them the spirit of self-sacrifice for the sake of the whole country."[63] Individual Egyptians thereby would come to share the same visions, move toward the same goals. They would be organized, at long last, into the serried ranks Nasser had envisaged. Politics, conflict, or pursuit of self-interest did not enter into this view. It is, as Heaphey perceptively suggests, a "nonpolitical" model.[64]

The officers' view of society is one of modernized coordination. Class struggle would be replaced by class harmony. Enlightened national interest would prevail over narrow self-interest. Political movements would be directed from the top down to instill the appropriate view of the future. Huntington aptly expresses this view: "Their goal is community without politics, consensus by command."[65] As a result, local government organs remain essentially powerless; they are closely controlled from the provincial capitals or from Cairo. These village institutions of government lack the resources and responsibility to resolve many local issues—and, as a result, they cannot gain legitimacy. The "old" way of life in the villages thus continues. Paradoxically, the centralization of power, carried out to foster rapid change, may further widen the gap between city and countryside, between urban elites and the peasantry the regime wishes to woo. One scarcely sympathetic Egyptian critic of Nasser noted, "Between the impoverished workers in town and village, on the one hand, and the rest of the classes, on the other, the abyss ten years after the military coup remains as deep as it was in the past."[66]

The Egyptian officers did overturn a decaying regime. They altered the internal balance of power among social groups and classes by destroying the court and many large landowners. Once the RCC decided to entrench themselves in power, they sought backing from certain strata—officers, technocrats, middle-level farmers, village wealthy, and skilled workers—who gained considerable benefits from the "Revolution."[67] The involvement and support of the peasantry—especially with the passing of Nasser and his charisma—remain uncertain. The step of organizing a responsive political party, able to articulate and support the interests of the fellahin, has not yet fully succeeded. The ASU was built from the top down, not from the bottom up. The fellahin have not yet fully awakened from the acquiescence and torpor that have characterized them for centuries.

It seems unlikely that the ASU will actively mobilize the rural population in ways the modernizing men at the top might disapprove. The ASU can mobilize individuals only in directions suggested from above. The dilemma thus turns on the dichotomy between guided mobilization toward goals that may not be widely supported and mobilization toward goals of more intense local interest. Were the military regime of Egypt to accept the latter form, it would have to come to terms with politics as conflict, not as coordination. The regime has now substantially departed from its self-appointed radical modernizing role.

The possible disengagement of the armed forces from political roles and rule depends on the performance of the Arab Socialist Union. It could, on the model of the PRI of Mexico, become a countervailing institution to the armed forces, able to achieve the military's subordination. It must be recalled, however, that Mexico reduced the size of its army during the 1930's, and that the armed forces became one of four "sectors" of the party—nominally on a par with agrarian, bureaucratic, and labor interests. The Egyptian military has continued to swell, with extensive Soviet aid and the perpetual talk of war with Israel. The ASU has not encouraged the emergence of organized groups in society, unlike the PRI. If we follow the reasoning of Huntington, the PRI–ASU contrast emerges most clearly by examining the nature of "revolution" in both societies:

> *Strong one-party systems are always the product of nationalist or revolutionary movements from below which had to fight for power. In contrast, efforts to establish one-party systems from above, as in the case of Nasser, lead nowhere: mobilization and organization are processes for acquiring or building power. Authoritarian leaders in power normally lack the need to do either.* [68]

Let us close with a brief summary. The officers' view of coordination saps the strength of possible mobilization among fellahin, for Egyptian society as a whole must be pressed toward modernization. Individual officers have continued to play key roles in the regime. The ASU and the government are run from the top down; groups within Egyptian society remain atomized, lest they challenge the system. As long as the vision of "serried ranks" remains, the Egyptian government will manifest the predominance of officers, employing a rhetoric of radical modernization, but in actuality preferring programs of reform guided from above. The most appropriate model now may be that of military guardianship. The simmering war with Israel rationalizes heavy military expenditures and, with them, increased stress upon professionalism. The boundaries between military and government, clearly fragmented by Farouk's meddling and Nasser's dual roles in leadership, may become less fragmented. The regime in Egypt increasingly seems a civil–military coalition, one based on the middle-class technocracy, skilled workers, medium landholders, and (of course) officers. In the meanwhile, the fellahin scratch out their living, occasionally wondering what is going on in Cairo, but rarely involved in matters outside their own village circles.

References

1. J.C. Hurewitz, *Middle East Politics: The Military Dimension* (New York: Praeger, 1969), p. 123.
2. For further details, see the Appendix.
3. David Rapoport, for example, cites several examples of what he deems a "civilian-military polity," all drawn from the West, with the exception of Japan. David C. Rapoport, "A Comparative Theory of Military and Political Types," in Samuel P. Huntington, ed., *Changing Patterns of Military Politics* (New York: Free Press, 1962), pp. 74–75.
4. Manfred Halpern, *The Politics of Social Change in the Middle East and North Africa* (Princeton: Princeton University Press, 1963), p. 251.

5. P.J. Vatikiotis, "Dilemmas of Political Leadership in the Arab Middle East: The Case of the U.A.R.," *Journal of International Affairs*, XXXVII, 1 (April 1961), p. 199.

6. Robert E. Ward and Dankwart Rustow, eds., *Political Modernization in Japan and Turkey* (Princeton: Princeton University Press, 1964), p. 352.

7. Eliezer Be'eri, *Army Officers in Arab Politics and Society* (New York: Praeger, 1970), p. 281.

8. Hurewitz, *Middle East Politics*, pp. 18, 20.

9. Ward and Rustow, *Political Modernization*, p. 353.

10. Halpern, *The Politics of Social Change*, pp. 253, 259.

11. P.J. Vatikiotis, *The Egyptian Army in Politics: Pattern for New Nations?* (Bloomington: Indiana University Press, 1961), p. xii.

12. Richard H. Pfaff, "Disengagement from Traditionalism in Turkey and Iran," *Western Political Quarterly*, XVI, 1 (March 1963), pp. 80–81.

13. Sydney Nettleton Fisher, ed., *The Military in the Middle East* (Columbus: Ohio State University Press, 1963), p. 10. See the critique of this assertion in Be'eri, *Army Officers*, pp. 245–52.

14. Halpern, *The Politics of Social Change*, p. 253.

15. Christina Phelps Harris, *Nationalism and Revolution in Egypt: The Role of the Muslim Brotherhood* (The Hague: Mouton for the Hoover Institution on War, Revolution and Peace, 1964), p. 18.

16. Hurewitz, *Middle East Politics*, p. 34.

17. Harris, *Nationalism and Revolution*, p. 20; Hurewitz, *Middle East Politics*, pp. 31–2. Egyptian history since the Pharaonic period, it should be noted, has always been marked by heavy state involvement in the economy.

18. Hurewitz, *Middle East Politics*, p. 34.

19. Vatikiotis, *The Egyptian Army*, p. 12.

20. Ibid., p. 18.

21. Hurewitz, *Middle East Politics*, p. 34.

22. Harris, *Nationalism and Revolution*, p. 96.

23. Ibid., pp. 83–87.

24. Anwar el Sadat, *Revolt on the Nile* (New York: John Day, 1957), pp. 38, 48.

25. Hurewitz, *Middle East Politics*, p. 58.

26. Vatikiotis, *The Egyptian Army*, p. 46.

27. Be'eri, *Army Officers*, p. 77.

28. Sadat, *Revolt on the Nile*, p. 42.

29. For details, see Mohammed Neguib, *Egypt's Destiny* (London: Victor Gollancz, 1955), pp. 91–96.

30. Be'eri, *Army Officers*, p. 99.

31. James B. Mayfield, *Rural Politics in Nasser's Egypt: A Quest for Legitimacy* (Austin: University of Texas Press, 1971), p. 19.

32. Ibid., p. 37.

33. Be'eri, *Army Officers*, p. 465.

34. Ibid., p. 429.

35. Vatikiotis, *The Egyptian Army*, p. 85.
36. R. Hrair Dekmejian, *Egypt Under Nasir: A Study in Political Dynamics* (Albany: State University of New York Press, 1971), p. 23.
37. Vatikiotis, *The Egyptian Army*, p. 96.
38. Dekmejian, *Egypt Under Nasir*, p. 170.
39. Ibid., pp. 174–178.
40. Be'eri, *Army Officers*, p. 426.
41. Ibid., p. 429.
42. Galal Amin, "The Egyptian Economy and the Revolution," in P.J. Vatikiotis, ed., *Egypt Since the Revolution* (New York: Praeger, 1968), p. 40.
43. Dekmejian, *Egypt Under Nasir*, p. 122.
44. Gamal Abdul Nasser, *Egypt's Liberation: The Philosophy of the Revolution* (Washington: Public Affairs Press, 1955), pp. 39–40.
45. Be'eri, *Army Officers*, p. 432.
46. Ibid., pp. 435–436.
47. Mayfield, *Rural Politics*, pp. 254, 257.
48. Dekmejian, *Egypt Under Nasir*, p. 61.
49. Nasser, *Egypt's Liberation*, pp. 32–34.
50. Vatikiotis, *The Egyptian Army*, p. 83.
51. Jean and Simonne Lacouture, *Egypt in Transition* (New York: Criterion, 1958), p. 459.
52. Vatikiotis, *The Egyptian Army*, p. 99.
53. Ibid., pp. 105–106.
54. Dekmejian, *Egypt Under Nasir*, p. 62.
55. Nasser, *Egypt's Liberation*, p. 87.
56. Reprinted in Benjamin Rivlin and Joseph S. Szyliowicz, eds., *The Contemporary Middle East: Tradition and Innovation* (New York: Random House, 1965), pp. 433–439.
57. Dekmejian, *Egypt Under Nasir*, p. 284.
58. Mayfield, *Rural Politics*, pp. 118–119.
59. Ibid., p. 150.
60. Samuel P. Huntington, *Political Order in Changing Societies* (New Haven: Yale University Press, 1968), p. 241.
61. Dekmejian, *Egypt Under Nasir*, p. 294.
62. Mayfield, *Rural Politics*, p. 254.
63. Nasser, *Egypt's Liberation*, p. 40.
64. James Heaphey, "The Organization of Egypt: Inadequacies of a Nonpolitical Model for Nation-Building," *World Politics*, XVIII, 2 (January 1966), pp. 177–193.
65. Huntington, *Political Order*, p. 244.
66. Hassan Riad, quoted in Be'eri, *Army Officers*, pp. 441–442.
67. Ibid., pp. 431–439.
68. Huntington, *Political Order*, p. 418.

8

France: The Frustrations of Colonial War

France stands apart from the four other states discussed in this book. It is an affluent, industrialized country, with a gross national product in 1968 of $126.6 billion, roughly thirty times that of Peru. France can support a large military establishment without undue strain on its economy. Defense expenditures in 1968 totalled over $6 billion, or about $12,000 per soldier—more than 13 times the amount expended per soldier in Thailand.[1] The borders of France have remained stable for several hundred years; and within them, the French language is spoken almost without exception. A strong, centralized government rules over a country with few regional and ethnic differences, marked contrast indeed to the polyglot setting of Nigeria. Political parties and interest groups have operated within parliamentary and bureaucratic contexts for decades. By almost any measure, in short, France is a country of "developed" or "mature" political culture, in which the armed forces have pursued their goals more often by influence than by overt interference.

For the student of civil–military relations, France represents one of the most interesting case studies. French history can furnish data for almost any proposition about the political involvement—or the political neutralization—of the armed forces. Army leaders such as Boulanger, Macmahon, or de Gaulle have found themselves near the pinnacle of political success. Coups d'etat have punctuated French history on several occasions. Both Napoleon Bonaparte and his nephew Napoleon III seized power with army assistance; the First, Second, and Fourth Republics fell as a result of intervention; the Third Republic and the Second Empire were replaced after military defeat. But to perceive French history as a series of praetorian acts would certainly be inaccurate. For most of the nineteenth and twentieth centuries, the French armed forces were marked by political neutralization and subordination. Their obedience to political superiors was encapsulated in the phrase *la grande muette*— that is, the great unspeaking force. Civil–military relations based upon civilian control have characterized France far more than endemic praetorianism.

Maintenance of harmonious civil–military relations imposes duties on both the government and the armed forces. In the classic model of civilian control, the armed forces furnish information on which politicians can base their decisions. The military, like other parts of the government, functions in effect as a pressure group, exerting influence through appropriate channels. Political leaders, in turn, furnish overall guidance to the armed forces. By means of continuous consultation and maintenance of recognized spheres of responsibility, civil–military harmony is maintained—hopefully. Influence can be transformed into intervention, however, especially where governmental legitimacy is reduced. When consultation breaks down, when areas of responsibility shift suddenly, or when extraordinary tensions arise, discord can emerge. Civilian control was challenged in France when politicians faltered in providing direction to the military. As members of the armed forces gained their own perspectives on the "national interest" of France, their willingness to control the government themselves, rather than accept civilian control, was enhanced.

That officers may hold conceptions of the "national interest" differing from those held by politicians should come as no surprise. Preceding chapters have illustrated the range of issues over which the civilian and military spheres might conflict. In France, the crucial issue was whether the government should continue an unpopular and difficult war in Algeria. Convinced they understood the needs of France better than the parliamentary leaders of the Fourth Republic, some officers wished to press ahead with the conflict. The discredited political institutions of the Fourth Republic lacked the legitimacy and prestige to quell an army-supported uprising in Algeria in May 1958. The death of the Fourth Republic, and the birth of the Fifth, can be attributed to the French army.

The first section of this chapter examines two French concepts of civil-military relations: (1) the theory of the "nation in arms," derived from the French Revolution and usually associated with political parties of the Left; and (2) the conservative/professional theory of a small, hierarchical army, a concept usually associated with political parties of the Right. The second section of the chapter deals with the fall of the Fourth Republic, in particular the ways in which the Algerian war weakened the government's legitimacy in the eyes of the armed forces and the French populace as a whole. The concluding section examines the conditions under which civilian control was re-established in the Fifth Republic, and the implications of the process for other states.

Conflicting Visions of Civil–Military Relations

Two broad tendencies—egalitarianism and stratification—have clashed in French civil–military relations. Each gave rise to a distinctive view of effective military organization. And, since each was linked to a wing of the French political spectrum, the conflict between them sharpens at times of national stress.

The "Nation in Arms" Concept

The vision of the "nation in arms" traces its ancestry to 1789. The patriotic fervor and military imperatives of the French Revolution gave birth to mass mobilization. Only by arming the citizenry could the new republic spread liberty to adjacent territories, or defend this liberty against invading armies. The popular mobilization represented a sharp departure from the prerevolutionary pattern of civil–military relations. The armed forces had served the monarch, not the elected representatives of the people; aristocrats dominated the officer corps; the ranks were filled with volunteers for long-term service. Though its numbers were small, the French army accounted for more than half the annual expenditure of the government prior to the Revolution. Individual citizens had little contact with the armed forces, who defended the *ancien régime*. The military exigencies of the Revolution broke this pattern—based, of course, on the concept of egalitarianism.

The rhetoric of the French Revolution extolled participation, equality, the responsibilities of "citizens." It was the duty of the citizen to serve "his" republic. No longer should the armed forces reflect social stratification; each person, irrespective of his station in life, should serve the country, whether by making bandages or "preaching the hatred of kings." The Revolution carried with it a profound distrust of the military as a corporate entity. Only if the armed forces were drawn directly from the populace could they most effectively serve the nation. As Lazare Carnot commented in 1793, "In free countries it is absolutely necessary that each citizen be a soldier or that none be."[2]

Although the French infused the vigor of the Revolution into the "nation in arms" concept the basic ideas were soon obscured. Revolutionary fervor could not be maintained. Weary of war after Napoleon's downfall, leaders of the French Left did not complain when universal military service was abolished. Only a faint echo remained by 1834, for example, when a national lottery was established to select candidates for military training—candidates who could, by the way, purchase substitutes. The idea of the "nation in arms" resurfaced as a result of military defeat in the Franco-Prussian War of 1870, and gained further impetus as World War I neared.

Perhaps the most significant political statement about mass mobilization came from Jean Jaurès, noted French socialist leader. In 1911, Jaurès published L'Armée nouvelle (The New Army), a strong, lengthy fusion of military needs and the political concerns of the French Left. "It is necessary," he wrote, "in the interest of the army, the country, and civilization, that there be a democratic fusion of all social elements in the military institution, in the crucible of equality and under the fire of popular passion."[3] Civilian control would be ensured by the incorporation of all classes into the military. Jaurès proposed that citizens in frontier areas be formed into defensive units, armed with appropriate equipment and (more to the point) infused with a marked sense of enthusiasm. For men who demand full political and social liberty, Jaurès asserted, the "old forms" of obedience, discipline, and even patriotism cannot be imposed.[4] His proposals were rejected, and Jaurès himself was assassinated when World War I erupted.

Ironically, it was only in the shadow of World War I that the theory of the "nation in arms" was translated into practice. One out of 28 French citizens was killed on the battlefront; the French population suffered more casualties in the first two months than did the armies of the United States in all World War II. The unparalleled slaughter made universal military training a necessity. The professional army was transformed into an enormous enterprise, through which all adult males passed.[5] By that time, the passion that had fueled the Revolution and the writings of Jaurès had largely waned. Military necessity, not the quest for political equality, would determine the manpower policies of the French army.

The Conservative/Professional Vision

The "nation in arms" concept emphasized short-term service on the part of large numbers. The conservative/professional vision, by contrast, emphasized long-term service, continuity, and expertise. The theory of mass mobilization did not distinguish between populace and army, between society and its military. The theory of professional autonomy, by contrast, recognized a dual perspective. Officers would concern themselves with military issues, politicians with political issues; the twain would meet in defense of the state and its institutions. The motivating ideals differed markedly. Those on the Left saw in the "nation in arms" the equality of the Revolution; in General de Gaulle's words, "the general passion for levelling."[6] Those on the Right saw in the professional army the preservation of values of hierarchy, tradition, and obedience.

The conservative/professional vision sprang from the longstanding prominence of noble families in the officer corps. Even after the upheavals of the Revolution and the Napoleonic era, aristocrats contributed a substantial portion of manpower to the military establishment. Officer recruitment in the nineteenth century, Giradet comments, "remained dominated by representatives of the 'enlightened classes,' the old aristocracy, the upper and middle bourgeoisie of officials and members of liberal professions. . . ."[7] The military represented a refuge for former nobles, a "safeguard they could not abandon under penalty of ultimate forfeiture [of prestige]."[8]

This state of affairs could be perpetuated because the armed forces were isolated from French society through most of the nineteenth century. The conquest of Algeria after 1830, and the expansion of the colonial empire, offered an outlet for the militarily ambitious. The Concert of Europe, a peace unbroken by major conflict for close to a century, meant that the armed forces did not readily impinge on civilian life. Despite the presence of aristocrats in the officer corps, more than half the officers rose from the ranks.[9] But, most crucial to the civil–military harmony that marked this period, the French army deliberately espoused policies of subordination. This low profile in the nineteenth century contrasted with the efforts of Mohammed Ali and Ahmed Arabi in Egypt, or with the juntas of Peru after independence was won.

Central to the conservative/professional vision was the autonomy of the military within its specialized areas. As David Ralston has noted of French officers, "their primary desire was for independence in their own special sphere. This did not necessarily preclude governmental intervention in, or surveillance over, military affairs."[10] The self-imposed isolation and political neutrality enabled the French military to preserve many longstanding practices. For example, the promotions system "constituted practically a closed system of cooptation, almost completely escaping the action of public authorities."[11] While the National Assembly debated ways of reducing Catholic influence in schools, the portion of officers drawn from Church-sponsored schools increased.[12]

Military regulations enforced strict obedience. To quote the 1833 rules, "The right to protest is permitted to a subordinate only after he has obeyed."[13] Even the most noteworthy incursion of the French military into politics—the coup d'etat of December 1851, by which President Louis Napoleon eliminated the parliament and declared himself

emperor—did not stray from the principles of *la grande muette,* for
the president officially commanded the armed forces. As Giradet points
out, the military took neither the initiative nor the responsibility for
this coup; the Second Empire was "in no way" a government by the military; during the nineteenth century, "The military never deliberately . . .
sought to impose upon the country their own chosen laws, government,
or regime."[14] Even defeat in the Franco-Prussian War did not undermine the ethic of subordination. What Giradet calls a "cult of the army"
emerged, with attributes of a "quasi-mystical cult of discipline, the
imperative of absolute obedience, of submission in principle to the established government and to 'legal' authority."[15]

Even *la grande muette* cannot avoid clashes between civilian
and military realms. The aristocratic, Catholic character of the officer
corps came into conflict with the egalitarian tendencies of the Third Republic in the notorious Dreyfus case. Dreyfus was a Jewish officer convicted of treason by a court-martial—on the basis of evidence forged by
another officer. The armed forces adamantly resisted public inquiry into
Dreyfus' conviction, on grounds the trial represented an internal matter.
His conviction was reversed only after lengthy public discussion that
severely tested the political system as a whole, including antisemitic attitudes. A period of civil–military distrust ensued, broken by the cataclysm
of World War I. Thus, by the end of the nineteenth century, the French
army had discovered it could not exercise total control over "internal"
matters, in instances where its conduct contravened basic values of the society. Even unswerving obedience to the government could not guarantee
the military could act, in effect, as an island unto itself.

Under the professional/conservative vision, accordingly, civilian
control was ensured by two interrelated factors: (1) the armed forces'
ethic of subordination; and (2) the willingness of the government to allow
wide-ranging internal autonomy.

La grande muette meant soldiers must be carefully isolated
from any political currents. They should not be involved in decision making; they should not be privy to partisan disputes; in fact, they should
not even exercise the basic right of the vote! In 1872, the National Assembly concurred with the army's recommendation that its members be
deprived of the franchise. In the words of the minister of war, "the soldier
under arms can only be the soldier of the law; he must remain a stranger
to all parties and to all political strife. . . ." According to an army spokesman, "The vote is an element of discord and disunion which we do not
need," for it "would endanger the moral authority that the chiefs must
have over their subordinates. . . ."[16]

In effect, the French armed forces led an existence largely
removed from the populace as a whole. To be certain, when Jacques went
marching off for compulsory service, his family was aware of the military's

existence; annual budget debates reminded legislators of the costs of maintaining the army. But the army (save for the explosive controversy of the Dreyfus case) remained quiet and unobtrusive, posted in distant colonies or border garrisons. These conditions made unswerving obedience somewhat easier.

The French government reciprocated and reinforced apolitical tendencies by steering clear of intramilitary issues. Officer recruitment, as noted above, kept the armed forces a conservative, Catholic bastion. With the exception of the inquiry into Dreyfus, and an attempt to use loyalty to the Third Republic as a prime criterion of promotion, civilians left the military alone. The government thereby eschewed the central principle of the "nation in arms," namely that civilian control could be ensured only by making army and nation synonymous. A mutually agreeable bargain was struck between military and civil powers—resulting in political subordination, strong support within the military for the principle of strict obedience, and the isolation of the armed forces from most controversies.

The conservative/professional vision depended on integral boundaries, while the "nation in arms" required an absence of boundaries. Denial of the franchise to soldiers stands as perhaps the most striking example of separation between society and military; the principle of universal, compulsory service is perhaps the most striking example of combination. But even the Third Republic did not find it simple to define boundaries. Integral boundaries can be maintained only with general acceptance of what constitutes "political " and what constitutes "military" matters. *La grande muette* concept, with its acceptance of subordination, depended on basic similarity of views concerning the role the armed forces should play. The war in Algeria, to which we shall turn shortly, showed that the government and army might differ on the boundaries between "political" and "military."

The concept of *la grande muette* also required that the armed forces accept the choices made by civilian leaders. Are there conditions under which officers might appropriately refuse to follow the directives of their political superiors? The conservative/professional vision suggests absolute, total subordination. However, theorists of civil–military relations have maintained that professional officers can disobey, under certain conditions. According to Huntington, "the existence of professional standards justifies military disobedience" when a politician "enters military affairs" as in, for example, giving direct commands to troops.[17] Huntington also comments upon possible conflicts between military obedience and legality, and between military obedience and basic morality. If two governments of the same state both claim the legal right to rule, officers must make a political choice between them—a choice that French officers painfully made in 1940. The "right to make ultimate moral judgments"

cannot be surrendered by an individual soldier—yet Huntington adds,
"Only rarely will the military man be justified in following the dictates of
private conscience against the dual demand of military obedience and
state welfare."[18]

The disobedience of the French army in May 1958 did not
result from politicians involving themselves in military affairs. Quite the
contrary: the government had left almost all responsibilities to the armed
forces. Ultimate moral judgments were not involved—unless one regards
maintaining French control over Algeria as a moral issue. Rather, the
actions of the French army in May 1958 sprang from the military's
developing its own sense of what the "national interest" of France demanded, in the face of a government both unwilling and unable to define
boundaries between "political" and "military" issues. The strains of
the war in Algeria brought the temporary abandonment of the heritage
of political neutrality and subordination.

The Collapse of Political Neutrality

Times of national stress affect all parts of a political system.
Warfare particularly strains the patterns of civil–military relations established in times of peace. Should the war lack popular support, the armed
forces may find themselves out of step with public opinion. Should the
war prove unsuccessful, factionalism may divide the armed forces,
or deepen its alienation from the body politic. And, under conditions of
stress, the government may find it difficult to provide clear guidance to the
military, enabling it by default to substitute its own version of the national
interest for government policy.

Between 1940 and 1961, the French army experienced two sets
of instances in which its members cast aside the precepts of *la grande
muette*. The speedy defeat of France in 1940 led to a split within the military, the majority obeying the order to lay down arms, a minority following Colonel Charles de Gaulle into what became the Free French movement. World War II thus saw the French army divided against itself, with
a resulting deep embitterment. The second set of instances occurred between 1958 and 1961, as a consequence of the protracted Algerian war.
Many officers believed they had gained a military and political triumph,
which politicians in Paris threatened to snatch from them. Cultural–military boundaries became fragmented: French soldiers and civilian supporters of a "French" Algeria held common cause; the realms of military
and political action seemed to all parties to overlap dangerously. Under
such conditions, *la grande muette* seemed no longer a reliable guide as
to how the army should conduct itself.

The two sets of cases thus challenged the longstanding French assumptions of military discipline and subordination to civilian authority. Yet France did not gain military regimes on the model of Egypt, Peru, or Thailand. The political role the armed forces could play was limited by widespread belief the military should remain obedient. Military intervention could provide the *coup de grâce* to a faltering civilian government, but could not bring a military regime. The Fourth Republic—like its immediate predecessor—collapsed as a result of military conflict; however, the replacements for both ultimately were civilian governments dedicated to re-establishing control over the armed forces. The death tremors of both republics indicate that a government failing to provide policy guidance to its military risks possible intervention.

In 1940, the French army was admirably prepared to fight World War I: the lessons of 1914–18 had been heeded, too well. Strong defense lines and deep entrenchments honeycombed the border with Germany. Officers were prepared to mobilize the entire society for conflict, which was bound to be of long duration. How mistaken these assumptions were, as de Gaulle forecast in a lengthy memo as early as 1933![19] The German armies easily bypassed the admirable defensive positions; in six weeks, they were poised on the edge of Paris, from which the government had already decamped. Only three choices remained: immediate surrender, continuation of the struggle within France with probable total German conquest, or continuation of the struggle from positions outside France. The selection of the first alternative led to a split within the French forces.

Under the classic tenets of *la grande muette,* the officers' duty would be to provide information on the military aspects of policy, leaving the final decisions to civilians. Advice can be given in many ways, however. In the judgment of Philip C.F. Bankwitz, it is apparent that the French commander, General Maxime Weygand, overstepped the appropriate limits of his responsibilities. Weygand "first calmly requested and then emotionally demanded an armistice. . . . For the partisans of the armistice, this clear-cut statement of disobedience signified the Army was formally on their side."[20] That Weygand drew upon his own conception of the national interest became clear, as Bankwitz illustrates:

> *During the last hectic days of the collapse, Weygand became the guardian of the military institution and hence of the French people; and he drew upon two fundamental assertions in the army-nation concept. First, he contemptuously dismissed the regime as the real representative of the country. . . . Second, he maintained that the "army was nothing less than the Nation," as he wrote at the time in a remarkable passage which in effect declares that the civilian ministers had ceased to represent the "volonté populaire" [public opinion] because they opposed the armistice.*

That is, Weygand entered politics to "save the country" from the unworthy regime. At the same time, he was convinced that he was saving the Army from mutiny and the state from ruin. [21]

As Bankwitz also comments, Weygand's insubordination "illustrates the enormous difficulties which a democratic government may have in avoiding a major political upheaval resulting from an attempt to impose its strategical-political decisions upon a commander determined, rather, to carry out those of his own choosing."[22]

Charles de Gaulle did not hold a position on the front lines when Weygand was counseling armistice; he was serving as undersecretary of the army. He managed to flee to London, where he appealed for support. Barely a handful of French troops joined him; to be precise, 7000 rallied to his cause within a month of the armistice.[23] The overwhelming majority followed the new Vichy republic, initially permitted by the German conquerors to maintain an army of 100,000 men. When the tides of war turned, those who had remained obedient to orders—that is, those who had followed Weygand's command—found themselves liable to reprisals. A special court was established after the war, which purged 3000–4000 officers; nearly 13,000 officers were pensioned off. [24] Those suspected of collaboration with the Germans were in many cases (estimates vary from 20,000 to 40,000) murdered; a total of 160,000 treason trials were opened, with the conviction of 88,000 individuals.[25] Further stresses affected the officer corps with the postwar attempt, largely unsuccessful it turned out, to incorporate leaders of the resistance movement into the standing army.[26] The brand-new Fourth Republic started its life with an army wracked by dissension, the result of following what had once been the prized ideal of obedience. As Robert Paxton puts it,

The Fourth Republic, with its purges of the army and its lack of sympathy for traditional military values, had begun badly for [professional officers]. The Third Republic's military and colonial policies had seemed to threaten the military profession; the Fourth Republic's military and colonial policies actually brought death and permanent loss of territory. Clearly the challenge to accepted standards of discipline had been raised to a new order of magnitude, in face of which the old formulas of silent acquiescence seemed irrelevant if not treasonable. [27]

In the future, accordingly, an officer might well hesitate, "think it over," before according his obedience to a political superior.

The questioning of *la grande muette* combined with three

other factors to transform civil–military relations in France after World War II. The loss of colonial territories was galling to the armed forces, particularly because thousands of French soldiers had died in Vietnam and Algeria: Vietnam was lost in 1954; the war in Algeria started that same year and ended with Algerian independence from France in 1962. The emergence of a theory of "revolutionary war" rationalized the military's increased involvement in politics. And, with the weakening of the legitimacy of the Fourth Republic, the occasion arose on which the armed forces could join with other disgruntled groups to effect a change of regime.

Much of what came to be called "Overseas France" had been won by direct military action in the last half of the nineteenth century. Many officers gained experience and personal glory in the Sahara or Mekong valley. But the French Empire steadily shrank after World War II—because of a lack of political resolve, according to some officers. Bruised by the internal conflicts resulting from World War II, the French army sought to recoup its unity and serve the nation by defending colonial territories—only to find a lack of civilian support for their bloody efforts. John Steward Ambler correctly notes, "Had there been no lengthy and frustrating colonial wars after 1945, civilian control could have been restored over a disciplined military establishment."[28]

The wars were frustrating since French troops encountered a new type of military opponent, the guerrilla. For the most part, the struggles in Vietnam and Algeria were fought without a readily visible enemy. The heritage of the French army came from conflict in Europe where opposing forces, distinguished from civilians by uniforms, drew up in clear formations. Such was not the case in guerrilla warfare. Individual guerrillas were lightly armed, dependent on civilians for support, engaged in a longrange war of attrition in which sapping the opponent's will to resist was more important than destroying his armies. The struggle was to be carried out largely in the political realm. The teachings of Mao Tse-tung became required reading: "Weapons are an important factor in war, but not the decisive factor; it is people, not things, that are decisive";[29] "The revolutionary war is a war of the masses; it can be waged only by mobilizing the masses and relying on them";[30] "Our principle is that the Party commands the gun, and the gun must never be allowed to command the Party."[31]

The detailed history of the military campaigns in Vietnam and Algeria need not detain us unduly. French will to resist in Vietnam collapsed in May 1954, with the surrender of the garrison at Dienbienphu; Vietnam itself was provisionally divided, and independence was granted to it and to the kingdoms of Cambodia and Laos. What is most significant for the ouster of the Fourth Republic were the three lessons French officers learned from the debacle in Indochina. First, they passed the blame of defeat to the politicians, for failing to clarify the goals for which members of the armed forces risked their lives. Second, they developed new theories of warfare, taking to heart and to mind the political exigencies of guerrilla conflict. Third, they saw in guerrilla conflict an international effort to dislodge France and other Western states. The combined result was an army frustrated in accomplishing its goals, and subsequently developing political interests well outside the usual field.

General Henri de Navarre, whose plans at Dienbienphu failed so ignominiously, had no difficulty in pinning the defeat on the men in Paris. "This uncertainty over political goals is the real reason why we were *prevented* [sic] from a continuous and coherent military strategy in Indochina."[32] Or, in another ex post facto analysis, Eugene Carrias could speak of the "weakness" of the executive and the "sterile intrigues" of the legislature as leading to rebellion in the army.[33] There certainly existed many slights to the military's sense of self-esteem in Indochina. No draftees were sent there, for example; a cabinet that had dared do so might have found itself turned out of office. Blood given to the Office of Social Hygiene, it was announced in 1951, could not be given to wounded soldiers on the front.[34] Whether the blame officers attached to civilians is historically justified does not matter; the significance lies in the belief of many officers that the politicians deliberately downgraded the army during this nasty, bloody war.

The embittering experience in Indochina led to the formulation of a strategy of "revolutionary war." The French army held clear technological superiority in Vietnam, but failed to gain the support of the peasants. Henceforward, the argument ran, war must be fought with an eye to its psychological components. Political mobilization must become a central duty of officers—a belief soon to bear fruit in Algeria.

"Revolutionary war" taught a further lesson, in the eyes of French military theorists. They saw in Indochina, then in Algeria, an insidious, voracious, communist attempt to gain world dominance. Each territory must be protected lest it fall victim to communist expansion. The French, not less than the Americans, have been entranced by the domino theory. Let us quote General Allard, commander of the French army in Algeria, in November 1957:

> *The Soviet Union thereby has concealed from many the fact that her main effort is not directed toward the East–West axis, but rather towards a vast curve enveloping China, the Far East, Southeast Asia, the Middle East, Egypt, and North Africa, thereby encircling Europe. This is now almost a reality; the one step remaining is to wrest Algeria from France. . . . there is one obstacle to the realization of this plan which is less perfect than it appears. This obstacle is the determination of*

France not to be ousted from Algeria. . . . France had already attempted to stem the expansion of Communism in [Vietnam]. . . . The free world did not understand the importance of these attempts and they failed. Our last line of defense is Algeria. [35]

The main tenets of "revolutionary war" justified extensive military involvement in politics, first to win popular support for the French cause, second to preclude communist expansion. In a sense, warfare in Algeria became total warfare: a psychological struggle within the territory directed particularly toward the Muslim population; an international struggle pitting the major power blocs, or so many officers thought; and a war of colonial pacification rolled into one.

The conflict in Algeria broke out November 1, 1954, with a series of raids on military armories. The initial strength of the Algerian nationalists (later organized into the FLN, the National Liberation Front) numbered no more than 500 men, equipped with 50 obsolete rifles. [36] Only by arousing popular enthusiasm—by appealing to a spirit of Algerian nationalism, by carrying out land distribution, by emphasizing their Islamic heritage—could the Algerians hope to succeed. Popular mobilization would be necessary, to wear down the French will to remain. Guerrilla warfare was thus a strategic necessity.

To counter the success of the FLN in peasant mobilization, the French army turned increasingly to psychological action, as mandated by the new theory of "revolutionary war." On the whole, the French were ill-prepared. The academy at Saint-Cyr had not taught senior officers how to appeal to Algerian peasants. Interest in "revolutionary war" tended to be confined to junior officers, commissioned after World War II. Relations between the two factions of officers were none too cordial, as may be deduced from the following quotation, drawn from a military journal:

The military must fully understand the techniques of the war imposed upon it; it must realize that these techniques are not at all like those employed in '40 or '45 nor are they the ones learned at military school. . . . Traditional warfare is not the only possible answer. The disciples of Lenin are masters in two other types of conflict. These are psychological war and revolutionary war; the latter is being launched right now. [37]

With such ideas, the French army moved even further from its earlier precept of obedience. Raoul Giradet comments, "the intensity of these doctrinal, ideological preoccupations has led the military further and further away from the elementary and simply defined precepts on which was founded its traditional position of nonintervention in politics."[38] Such tendencies were in fact encouraged by successive cabinets. Finding themselves perplexed by the conflict, a series of Fourth Republic governments bestowed sweeping powers upon commissioners in Algeria, who in turn gave major responsibilities to the armed forces. A special administrative section was created, so that individual officers could carry out mobilization necessary to wage "revolutionary war." An individual captain might exercise responsibilities ranging from economic development and education to health and political guidance. "This one man was mayor, teacher, and engineer."[39] By steps such as these, the French army came to feel itself uniquely responsible for Algeria. Many officers sought a French-inspired revolution from below, to stave off an indigenous, nationalist revolution; they felt morally responsible for Muslims who supported France; they were convinced that full application of the techniques of "revolutionary war" would assure harmonious Franco-Algerian cooperation. These attitudes meant that disengagement from Algeria became, for many, a psychological impossibility.

Those who would lose most by a nationalist triumph were the more than one million French citizens who lived in Algeria. Many political differences existed among them, yet they united behind the slogan of *Algérie française.* By a quirk of colonial history, Algeria had been incorporated into metropolitan France, unlike the neighboring protectorates of Morocco and Tunisia, both of which were granted independence in 1956. The French in Algeria [40] strongly opposed any hint of self-determination to the Muslim majority.

Fraternization between French troops and the French citizens in Algeria was inevitable, and its effects predictable. Boundary fragmentation resulted. The elite paratroopers, who assumed a key role in the 1957 battle of Algiers, became particularly sympathetic to the notion of *Algérie française.* In other words, the French government could not expect its troops to act directly contrary to what the French citizens of Algeria desired; an order to move against European interests would have resulted in mutiny.

Confusion surrounded the goals France sought in the increasingly bloody and costly war. Were officers to help conduct an economic and social revolution on behalf of the Muslims, while maintaining French political supremacy? Was the war being fought to resist the spread of communist-inspired nationalism? Should the French army concentrate on protecting French citizens and investments? Was not the conflict in fact intended to preserve at least a remnant of the rapidly disappearing French Empire? No clear answers came from Paris. Civilian leaders vacillated. Given this vacuum of leadership, the role of the military was bound to expand, in keeping with its ideas of "revolutionary war." The vagaries of cabinets in Paris should not prevent the military from successful completion of its duties, officers came to feel.

Possibly the most galling area of friction between the government and the armed forces came in the conduct of the war itself. By professional standards, if you will, the French military gained a stunning victory by early 1958. The forces of the ALN (the national liberation army) were isolated in various strongholds, cut off from Algerian forces in Morocco and Tunisia. The city of Algiers seemed clear of nationalist influence. The resettlement of 1.8 million Algerians into fortified villages seemed to have gone well. Many officers believed that deep, genuine rapport existed between Muslims and the French army. Under these conditions, with the sweet taste of triumph in their mouths, a substantial portion of the officer corps believed they best understood what the national interest of France demanded in Algeria. A vicious circle existed. Lack of civilian direction had encouraged the armed forces to invent its own rationalizations for the war. The heady success of "revolutionary war," the ties with the French citizens of Algeria, and the belief that most Muslims truly desired continued French rule, made the military supremely confident in its chosen course of action. By early 1958, reversal of these trends had become impossible. Once the French army had been encouraged "to step into a civilian power vacuum in Algeria, once military honor, prestige, and self-esteem had been heavily invested in the defense of French Algeria, it was probably too late for any government of the Fourth Republic, no matter how vigorous, to abandon French Algeria without serious obstruction from the army. By the last years of the Fourth Republic, . . . the French Army in Algeria clearly preferred to be left a free hand in Algeria by a weak government in Paris, rather than to receive firm but unacceptable directives from a more vigorous government."[41]

Ultimately, however, the intramilitary grievances just noted— the questioning of *la grande muette* as a result of World War II experiences, the frustrations of colonial warfare, and the involvement of the military in broad administrative tasks and in the political mobilization of "revolutionary war"—were translated into political action because the Fourth Republic had lost its prestige, legitimacy, and ability to control the army as a whole. Obviously, French citizens in Algeria had little but hatred for governments that seemed ready to destroy their style of life. But the malaise of the Fourth Republic marked metropolitan France as well. The government seemed endlessly tied in parliamentary knots, unable to develop clear policies. A symptom of weakness was the short lease on life a Cabinet enjoyed in the Fourth Republic. In its twelve years, the Fourth Republic was headed by no less than 17 premiers and 20 cabinets. The premier with the longest term in office, Guy Mollet, enjoyed little more than 15 months in office.[42] Party coalitions shifted often and unpredictably. Immobility and an absence of vigorous policy making marked the Fourth Republic. Few of its cabinets were ready to "bite the bullet," in a sense, by issuing strong, clear directives to the armed forces. Such default, as already noted, enabled the French army to become ever more deeply enmeshed in Algerian affairs. Any solution concocted in Paris to resolve the war had to face the ineluctable fact that the military felt it alone could come up with a solution.

The collapse of the Fourth Republic can be attributed to the corrosive effects of the Algerian war. Premier-designate Pierre Pflimlin encountered strong opposition in May 1958 from French citizens in Algeria, since he purportedly favored a cease-fire. In classic French fashion, with ringing references to the Revolution, French citizens occupied the main government buildings in Algiers on May 13 and formed a Committee of Public Safety under General Jacques Massu. Barricades were hastily thrown up all over the city. The armed forces indicated their support and (through General Raoul Salan) indicated they would prefer to see de Gaulle assume power. A tense waiting game ensued between the government in Paris and supporters of de Gaulle, with the French army expectantly waiting. When French troops occupied Corsica on May 24, 1958 (eleven days after the initial tumult in Algiers) and called for de Gaulle's installation, the real possibility of military action in metropolitan France itself prompted action. Recognizing that the army could not be relied on, and further recognizing the widespread desire for an end to cabinet wrangling and instability, the leaders of the Fourth Republic took the only course out. Pflimlin resigned May 28. De Gaulle was invested as premier and was granted full authority for six months, during which the institutions of the Fifth Republic would be prepared.

Military intervention thus gave the *coup de grâce* to the Fourth Republic. However, intervention did not take the form of a guardian regime, on the model of Peru or Thailand. Few members of the armed forces desired to assume open political leadership. De Gaulle's catapulting to the top owed more to his reputation as a strong-willed leader and to his lack of identification with the Fourth Republic [43] than to his background as a leader of the armed forces, from which he had retired a dozen years earlier.

The armed forces thus effected political change by refusing to obey the old regime. Even though the French military had developed a set of assumptions about the national interest of France, insofar as Algeria was concerned, it did not attempt to impose these ideas directly when the Fourth Republic abdicated. It may have been, to be certain, that the armed forces were outmaneuvered. But the more plausible explanation seems to be that officers wanted autonomy in fighting in Algeria, and that they found themselves so psychologically involved in the defense of the territory they could not oppose the barricade builders of Algiers. The armed forces did not initiate *le treize mai*—the insurrection of the French citizens on May 13—though their support for the French presence made possible the success of the barricades.

The events of May 1958 substantiate several of the propositions about the causes of military intervention which we considered in Part I. Underlying the army's restiveness was its wide-ranging role in Algeria, which resulted in a sense of mission and conception of the national interest increasingly at variance with both French public opinion and the policies of the government.

Warfare in Algeria involved the prestige and self-concept of the French army. Its involvement was not in pure and simple military terms; "revolutionary war" forced officers to consider the economic, social, and political ramifications of their acts. They were to foster change that would short-circuit the appeals of nationalism. Little they had learned could assist this effort. *La grande muette* provided no guidance in a context where civilian authorities found themselves either unwilling or unable to set consistent, clear policy.

The autonomy the armed forces enjoyed was considerably augmented by sweeping grants of further power. It was easy for individual officers to see their roles as serving the "true" France—*le pays réel*—more than did the ambivalent, shifting Fourth Republic. The mission the French army developed, as much a result of civilian default as of officers' design, differentiated between the long-term interests of France as a whole and the pettifoggery of politicians. To put the matter succinctly, many officers denied the right of the Fourth Republic to interpret the will of the people—as had General Weygand in the dying days of the Third Republic. "Revolutionary war" gave the army a mission that distinguished between service to the government and service to the nation. Indeed, Edgar Furniss suggests that some officers in fact desired "the militarized state: the state made to serve military objectives." "The French army did not accept, let alone respect, civilian leadership because it was civilian and had been legalized by election and by constitutional referendum; instead the army was merely prepared to grant power to those authorities who were ready to make militarily approved decisions."[44]

The frustrations of Indochina and Algeria resulted in profound strains within the military. The fact that conscripts were not deployed in Vietnam resulted in tensions. Other cleavages resulted from the theory of "revolutionary war." Enthusiasm for the theory ran far higher among captains than among generals—themselves perhaps "too lethargic and unimaginative to understand changing modes of warfare."[45] But perhaps the greatest strain came between the elite "paras" (paratroopers) and regular members of the armed forces. The "paras" were prominent on the barricades in 1958; more striking, in the unsuccessful 1961 coup (to be discussed in the next section), 34 of the 51 convicted officers came from this group. The "paras" shared strong attachment to the idea of maintaining Algeria as an integral part of France, and they maintained the closest ties with the French citizens of the cities. The key role of the "paras" testified to boundary fragmentation.

Political awareness was escalated in the French army as a consequence of "revolutionary war." As Ambler suggests, "by finally forcing the transformation of French officers into policemen, propagandists, civil administrators, political organizers, and ideologists, France's revolutionary–guerrilla adversaries of sixteen years seriously undermined the power of that old and usually respected adage that 'l'officier ne fait pas de politique' [an officer does not participate in politics] ."[46] But it must be noted that intervention stemmed on the part of the military from a desire for continued autonomy in Algeria. The grievances were specific, not generalized, and were directed against the personnel of the Fourth Republic. This fact also eased post-1958 military disengagement from politics.

Pflimlin's purported support for a cease-fire seriously threatened the policy autonomy the French army wanted to defend. The vacuum of civilian authority that had marked the Fourth Republic could not be reversed without serious discontent. A perceived change in government goals, and hence in the areas of policy making, can readily undermine military loyalty. Again to quote Ambler, the army's response to a sudden shift in political direction may be "wrathful charges of defeatism, abandonment, and betrayal. When a large segment of the army believes the original goals to be vital to the preservation of the nation as they conceive of it, wrath may turn to disobedience and to revolt, as in France."[47] The proposition that military intervention becomes more likely when areas of military decision making are abruptly reduced without prior agreement thus appears to hold in the French instance.

The most important environmental factor in Algeria was the presence of the vocal French minority, who looked to the military for protection of their style of life. Officers' contacts with this group doubtless grew into direct solicitation of support. The fragmented boundaries mentioned above meant that discontent among the French citizens of Algeria was quickly felt, and probably amplified, within the armed forces. Strong antagonism against any "capitulation" to Algerian nationalists led to solicitation.

Why did France escape a military regime? The Fourth Republic found few defenders as its days ended. Its shortcomings, however, did not entail corresponding support for a form of government determined by the armed forces. It was the civilian supporters of de Gaulle—and, of course, the General himself—who determined upon a civilian government. The French military distrusted the personnel and policies on Algeria of the Fourth Republic. The armed forces, as the events of *le treize mai* unfolded, had no strongly held desire to build an entirely new government, in which the military would play the paramount role. The Fourth Republic collapsed because few wished to see it continue. Widespread agreement on the need for alteration meant the Fifth Republic started its life with high popular support. It was the task of de Gaulle to convert his popular support into a further taming of the armed forces, to restore a new balance in civil–military relations.

Intervention and Usurpation

The government of the Fourth Republic lacked the strength to command the army successfully. Conversely, however, the army was incapable of taking total control of the state. The result was a rare phenomenon: a coup that established stronger government control over the military. *Le treize mai* showed the military agreeing with the French citizens of Algeria and a significant portion of the populace in France that the system must change. This desire to remove the old did not entail full military involvement in the politics of the new. Giradet has drawn apt conclusions:

> The army's intervention on the political scene was in no way a traditional pronunciamento. The army had no intention of assuming complete power. Aside from a few officers who were ardently committed, almost no one considered installing a military junta to assume and exercise governmental authority. Nor was there any idea of supporting a party or particular political group by force of arms. . . . In fact, the army's action might justifiably be compared to that of a pressure group (a pressure group endowed, however, with a particular power). It did not attempt to impose precise governmental formulas, but essentially endeavored to influence the formation of a policy. [48]

Missing from *le treize mai*, therefore, was the set of attitudes necessary for the creation of a military regime. Why?

Officers disliked certain policies of the Fourth Republic; they did not reject the political system in its entirety, nor did they favor a total restructuring. The armed forces wanted, and needed, strong civilian guidance. The Fourth Republic lacked decisiveness, preferring to delegate responsibilities to the military rather than buck parliamentary immobility. Had the military's protest against the Pflimlin government not been linked with two other elements—the fears of the French citizens of Algeria and widespread distrust of the Fourth Republic in the home country—the government conceivably might have weathered the crisis. Even the barricades erected in May 1958 might have had only nuisance value had the malaise of the Fourth Republic not affected French public opinion as a whole. The common cause of the army, the French residents of Algeria, and public opinion spelled the end of the Fourth Republic. Unless all three elements coalesced, however, a change of constitution under military pressure would have been unlikely.

High among the priority issues for the Fifth Republic was assuring the armed forces' loyalty. Were the events of *le treize mai* an aberration, or a portent of deepening military involvement? Algeria had to be defused as an issue; it was necessary to provide other avenues for military interests and ambitions; military obedience had to be re-emphasized; it was essential to remove from positions of influence those who were wedded to an unaltered French role in Algeria. President de Gaulle chose his words and actions carefully while he decided on the appropriate steps. Only as civilian control became firmed up did the outlines of policy emerge from his misty rhetoric.

De Gaulle became the political heart of the new Fifth Republic. By means of referenda, he achieved sweeping popular mandates for many policies—including what turned out to be disengagement from Algeria. On September 16, 1959, he noted three possible paths for Algeria: outright independence, "Francization," or self-determination in association with France. Two months later, he called for negotiations with Algerian nationalist leaders. Early in January 1960, French citizens trooped to the polls to vote on a single proposal that asked: do you support President de Gaulle concerning self-determination for the Algerian populations? An overwhelming portion supported de Gaulle, better than three to one in the home country, more than two to one in Algeria. After the vote, rumors flew among the French citizens of Algeria. They noted the recall of General Jacques Massu, the victor of the battle of Algiers and a strong partisan of a "French" solution,[49] and the resignation of General André Zeller (army chief of staff) as a result of de Gaulle's speech in September. Once again, the barricades rose in French sectors of Algiers. The uprising left de Gaulle unruffled, however, for the armed forces stood aside from the partisans of *Algérie française*—the result of "agonized fear of precipitously dividing the army against itself," in the words of one scholar.[50] The "week of the barricades" collapsed. French citizens of Algeria were a small minority who could change French policy only with both military support and the acquiescence of the French populace as a whole. By the massive support in the referendum, French citizens had manifested their trust in de Gaulle.

Just as the "week of the barricades" proved the partisans of *Algérie française* an isolated, essentially powerless group, so did the unsuccessful coup effort of April 1961 illustrate the isolation of French military leaders. Four leading French generals joined in the coup effort:

Maurice Challe (chief commander in Algeria 1958–1960 and former supreme commander of Allied forces in central Europe); Edmund Jouhaud (an air force general, born in Algeria); Raoul Salan (supreme commander in Algeria during *le treize mai,* and transferred out of the territory by de Gaulle because of his support for continued French rule[51]); and André Zeller (first army chief of staff in the Fifth Republic, who tendered his resignation because of disagreement with de Gaulle). The court-martial transcript reflected an extraordinarily naive view of the realities of French politics, for the unsuccessful generals believed their troops, and the French people as a whole, would rally to their cause of maintaining the French presence. In the words of Zeller, intervention "proceeded purely and simply from the desire to keep Algeria under French sovereignty."[52] Challe felt he could impose what he called a simple and realizable plan: take control of the army, launch a general offensive against the "terrorists," and rally the Muslim population of Algeria by assuring them of a political future with France. "That was, in sum, a psychological offensive; to make pacification succeed in a few weeks, and to turn back to France saying, 'We have made peace and we are sending back your sons.' "[53] Despite their rank, the generals could not command support for this nebulous plan. It was obvious to most observers, though not to the four plotters, that "*le pays réel* was desperately tired of the war, its cost, confusion, and personal tragedy. . . ."[54] No massive public support greeted the generals. After all, did not de Gaulle have a plan for ending the war? But the real check came within the French army. As Challe and his fellow conspirators realized in a matter of hours, other officers would not follow them. The pervasive attitude was one of wait-and-see.[55] Not wishing to commit themselves to rebellion, they condemned the Challe Putsch to failure. And, even had a significant number of French officers joined the attempt, it is by no means clear whether the rank and file would have obeyed. Whether with foresight or good luck, the French government had issued transistor radios to individual soldiers. Those radios became an important weapon in the hands of de Gaulle, who broadcast, "If they [French officers in Algeria] have ceased being faithful to the Government and to France, they have by the same token ceased to be your leaders. In that event follow the orders of the most senior of your officers who have remained loyal."[56] The rising ended not with the bang of victory, but with the ignominy of surrender.

Re-establishment of *la grande muette* represented an impossible task as long as the French army remained trapped in Algeria. To the extent that the military gained awareness of extramilitary constraints on its policy, it moved further from the simplistic ideal of unswerving, blind obedience. *La grande muette* could not readily be sustained where individual soldiers could maintain close ties to politicized civilians. Clearly, then, a new formula for obedience was necessary. De Gaulle recognized that individual members of the military would be "lost soldiers," unless they had clearly defined national tasks to carry out.

The Fourth Republic had handed the professional army the "nasty war" of Indochina without clear instructions, then left the military to devise its own actions in Algeria. Both colonial wars were not "politics by other means," but war in default of political means. A high sense of military frustration was built up as the French army grappled with its new-style enemy, all the while fearing the results of their sanguinary efforts would be undone by unsympathetic politicians. Indochina and Algeria thus resulted in the substitution of a militarily defined national interest for a governmentally defined national interest, coupled with strong distaste for civilian efforts to regain control. Hence, de Gaulle appeared initially to support a continued army role in Algeria, while he built his own political foundation; then, as head of state, he could appeal over the heads of the senior officers when the Challe Putsch erupted. The legitimacy of the president helped bring the transition from untrammeled military autonomy to subordination to the government.

A coup attempt occurs when the armed forces see themselves as the appropriate formulators of national policy. When the Fifth Republic was established, many officers saw it as a means for fulfilling their self-appointed tasks. Take, for example, General Order Number 1, issued by Chief of Staff Zeller in 1958: the army, as the "best guide of the nation," must consecrate itself to "the grand task of renovating France, which has fallen to it."[57] Of such ambitions, coup attempts are born.

The success of a coup attempt ultimately rests with public opinion. The greater the popular support of a government, the less likely it will be unseated by military intervention. The case studies earlier in this volume have documented the ease with which the armed forces can achieve total political dominance in the absence of countervailing institutions. In Egypt, Nigeria, Peru, and Thailand, few barriers inhibited members of the armed forces from seizing the reins of power. In each of these nations, political leaders could readily be displaced because the political system as a whole enjoyed weak legitimacy. This possibility did not exist in France. Although French history has been frequently punctuated by the use of force, the armed forces have not pressed themselves to the top. The Second Empire and the Fifth Republic, though both created as a result of intervention, cannot be said to be military regimes. The armed forces in 1958 wanted free hand to pursue their Algerian policy, not total involvement in governing. They had a policy for Algeria, not necessarily a policy for France. The obstacles to total military takeover of the government were too great, for the French public would not have condoned a cabinet drawn from the troops in Algeria. As David Rapoport has commented, "the ability to seize power must never be confused with the strength to use it."[58] The resignation of the Fourth

Republic and the grant of extraordinary powers to de Gaulle satisfied public opinion; as Challe and his colleagues learned two and a half years later, an incumbent government enjoying a high degree of support can exert strength transcending the usual hierarchy of the armed forces.

What we are suggesting is that a government marked by a high degree of legitimacy is not necessarily immune to military intervention, but that it has reservoirs of support that lead perceptive officers to curb their own political aspirations. Only when there is serious disjuncture between the policies of the government and the policies of the military, and only when this is coupled with absence of public support for the existing institutions, is intervention a real possibility.

Kurt Lang, in considering an unsuccessful Putsch attempt against Hitler as well as the 1958–61 insubordinations of the French army, has pointed out that military intervention in developed countries becomes possible only under extraordinary conditions. He suggests four causes that, in combination, bring a common political orientation in the officer corps sufficient to challenge the government. Disruption of the channels by which the military usually exerts its political influence stands as the first cause. Officers with access to decision makers will rarely involve themselves in attempted coups—an explanation, by the way, of the prominence of middle-grade officers in intervention. Second, a history of political conspiracy within the armed forces facilitates intervention. Although French military history is studded with examples of factions and intramilitary cliques,[59] no consistent group of officers involved themselves in plots against the government. The emergence of single-mindedness within the armed forces serves as a third danger signal. Homogeneity of the officer corps in the face of rapid social and political change may give officers a misleading reading of existing conditions, as manifestly marked Challe and his cohorts. Finally, boundaries must be fragmented, with contacts with antigovernment groups providing political support and legitimation.[60] To all these, there are countervailing factors that diminish the possibility of a common political orientation emerging among officers. As Lang notes, "The officer corps of modern armed forces is usually of too heterogeneous an origin, the division of labor too complex, the number of functions performed by military men too diverse, and technocratic and careerist orientations too prevalent for the development of a unified point of view on the basis of either expertise or tradition without the development of a common political viewpoint."[61] This statement suggests that profound cleavages *within the society as a whole* are most likely to result in the politicization of the military; in other words, environmental rather than internal variables stand as the chief precipitators of coups. And, should deep rifts exist within the political system as a whole, is it not fair to conclude that its legitimacy may be limited?

In the collapse of the Fourth Republic, the armed forces represented but one of many contending groups. The desire for a free hand led officers to oppose the government. Frustration compounded by more than a decade of corrosive colonial war could be linked with the disquiet felt in other groups, notably among the French citizens of Algeria and the metropolitan supporters of de Gaulle. The existence of these groups, when coupled with the longstanding French presumption that officers did not indulge in politics, imposed limits on the extent to which the military could act as an autonomous entity.

France should thus be viewed as a state in which forms of government have been altered by military intervention, but in which the armed forces have generally remained loyal to the head of the government. *La grande muette* was not an accident of history, but a painstakingly constructed way of combining military effectiveness, professional autonomy, and national ideology. Civilian control, though it broke down in 1958, has generally characterized modern French history.

Civilian control requires governmental awareness of the military's needs: economic, professional, political, and even psychological. Civilian control must be regular, not episodic. (Obviously, 20 different cabinets in 12 years made consistent policy almost unattainable.) A government that abdicates guidance and awareness cannot claim to have exerted civilian control. Criticism must be offered, in a way that reduces rather than compounds professional frustration. Morris Janowitz has phrased the necessities as follows:

> *In a pluralistic society, the future of the military profession is not a military responsibility exclusively, but rests on the vitality of civilian political leadership. . . . the following requirements must be met by authorities: one, to limit military goals to feasible and attainable objectives; two, to assist in the formulation of military doctrine, so that it becomes a more unified expression of national political objectives; three, to maintain a sense of professional self-esteem in the military; and four, to develop new devices for the exercise of democratic political control.* [62]

The Fourth Republic failed on these counts.

A second requisite may be multiple goals for the armed forces. A military totally engrossed in a single activity, as was the bulk of the French army during the Algerian war, may develop a form of policy myopia. Too much zeal, too great involvement in a set of responsibilities, will preclude a detached view. Any abridgement of the military's powers might be interpreted as a direct blow to its self-esteem. As Ambler comments, "French military indiscipline and revolt in Algeria are understandable, not so much in terms of a 'breakdown of professionalism,' as in terms of the impassioned defense of military power, status, and self-esteem."[63] De Gaulle assuaged the pangs of disengagement from Algeria by emphasis on an independent nuclear retaliatory force and wider responsibilities, in Furniss's observation, "a smokescreen of sorts to cover the narrowing of French horizons to the continental hexagon."[64] Multiple goals may give the military a greater sense of investment in the political health of the nation; more important, they may diminish the singularity of view that may lead to intervention.

A strong sense of military professionalism represents a third necessity. Professionalism depends on corporate identity, a sense of responsibility, and expertise, as discussed in Chapter 2. For the French army, the price of professionalism, as it were, was adherence to *la grande muette*. But professionalism may not suffice.[65] Added to it must be an affirmation of civilian control. To quote Ambler, the armed forces in a liberal democracy must be motivated by more than professionalism; "since professional military values may clash with dominant civilian values, the officer must also have a positive commitment to civil supremacy."[66] This positive commitment stands as the fourth requirement.

The fifth and final requisite comes in that area often discussed in this book, political legitimacy. From his excellent study of the French army, Ambler concludes, "military intervention in politics is closely related to the degree of *legitimacy* of existing civilian political institutions, i.e. the strength and breadth of the national political consensus which supports them."[67] The Fourth Republic could not be sustained against the treble challenge of the armed forces, the French citizens of Algeria, and the Gaullists. For the Fifth Republic, however, the balance sheet looked quite different. De Gaulle enjoyed an enormous personal mandate; his legitimacy as head of state and the strength of the Fifth Republic could not be disentangled. As Challe and his coconspirators learned to their professional disgrace, the head of state possessed the powerful resource of public opinion. Their effort looked like usurpation, and was correspondingly resisted.

In conclusion, civilian control in France may in fact have rested on grounds quite distinct from the "nation in arms" and the professional/conservative vision delineated at the start of this chapter. A government that enjoys citizen support cannot be readily dislodged by the armed forces. There is no need to make army and nation synonymous, if the government is legitimate. As long as the armed forces can exercise influence through accepted channels, and as long as civilians offer direct policy guidance, civilian supremacy will be an accomplished fact. *Le treize mai* conveyed these messages in unambiguous terms.

References

1. *World Military Expenditures 1968* (Washington: Arms Control and Disarmament Agency, 1971), pp. 10–13.
2. Quoted in Jean Jaurès, *L'Armée nouvelle* (Paris: Humanité, 1915), p. 157. The work was originally published in 1911.
3. Jaurès, *L'Armée nouvelle,* p. 231.
4. Ibid., p. 7.
5. Richard D. Challener, *The French Theory of the Nation in Arms, 1866–1939* (New York: Columbia University Press, 1955).
6. Ibid., p. 248.
7. Raoul Giradet, *La Société militaire dans la France contemporaine* (Paris: Plon, 1953), p. 171.
8. Ibid., p. 198.
9. David B. Ralston, *The Army of the Republic: The Place of the Military in the Political Evolution of France, 1871–1914* (Cambridge: M.I.T. Press, 1967), p. 10.
10. Ibid., p. 3.
11. Giradet, *Société militaire,* p. 197.
12. Ibid., p. 195. Giradet notes that, in 1847, 2 of the 306 students entering the academy at Saint-Cyr came from religious schools. By 1869, the figures were 90 of 269; by 1886, 140 of 410.
13. Ralston, *The Army of the Republic,* p. 14.
14. Giradet, *Société militaire,* p. 252.
15. Ibid., p. 252.
16. David B. Ralston, *Soldiers and States: Civil–Military Relations in Modern Europe* (Boston: D.C. Heath, 1966), p. 124.
17. Samuel P. Huntington, *The Soldier and the State: The Theory and Politics of Civil–Military Relations* (New York: Vintage, 1964; originally published in 1957), p. 77.
18. Ibid., p. 78.
19. Charles de Gaulle, *The Army of the Future* (Philadelphia: Lippincott, 1941). De Gaulle wrote the book in 1934 while teaching at Saint-Cyr.
20. Philip C.F. Bankwitz, *Maxime Weygand and Civil–Military Relations in Modern France* (Cambridge: Harvard University Press, 1967), pp. 309–10.
21. Ibid., p. 318.
22. Ibid., p. 314. The most noteworthy American parallel comes, of course, with the dismissal of General MacArthur in 1952.
23. Robert O. Paxton, *Parades and Politics at Vichy: The French Officer Corps Under Marshal Pétain* (Princeton: Princeton University Press, 1966), p. 37.
24. The figure of 3000 comes from Paul-Marie de la Gorce, *The French Army: A Military-Political History,* translated by Kenneth Douglas (New York: Braziller, 1963), p. 350; the figure of 4000 from National Assembly debates, cited in John Steward Ambler, *Soldiers Against the State: The French Army in Politics* (New York: Doubleday, 1966), p. 84.

25. George Armstrong Kelly, *Lost Soldiers: The French Army and Empire in Crisis 1947–1962* (Cambridge: M.I.T. Press, 1965), p. 4 n. 1.

26. Paxton, for example, speaks of one group of 970 resistance leaders commissioned into the regular French army in 1945. Only 187 were given regular commissions, and of this number, a mere 22 were above the rank of lieutenant. Almost all officers drawn from the resistance were demobilized in 1946. Paxton, *Parades and Politics,* p. 413.

27. Ibid., p. 426.

28. John Steward Ambler, *Soldiers Against the State: The French Army in Politics* (New York: Doubleday, 1966), p. 84.

29. Mao Tse-tung, "On Protracted War," *Selected Works,* Vol. II (Peking: Foreign Languages Press), pp. 143–144.

30. Ibid., "Be Concerned with the Well-Being of the Masses, Pay Attention to Methods of Work," *Selected Works,* Vol. I, p. 147.

31. Ibid., "Problems of War and Strategy," *Selected Works,* Vol. II, p. 224.

32. Quoted in Kelly, *Lost Soldiers,* p. 55.

33. Eugene Carrias, *La Pensée militaire française* (Paris: Presses Universitaires de France, n.d.), p. 340.

34. Ambler, *Soldiers Against the State,* pp. 108–109.

35. Raoul Giradet, "Civil and Military Power in the Fourth Republic," in Samuel P. Huntington, ed., *Changing Patterns of Military Politics* (New York: Free Press of Glencoe, 1962), pp. 131–132.

36. Arslan Humbaraci, *Algeria: A Revolution That Failed* (New York: Praeger, 1966), pp. 33–34, quoted in Eric R. Wolf, *Peasant Wars of the Twentieth Century* (New York: Harper & Row, 1969), pp. 236–237.

37. Giradet, "Civil and Military Power," p. 132.

38. Ibid., p. 133.

39. Ibid., p. 136.

40. It should not be assumed that the "French" of Algeria were identical with their compatriots across the Mediterranean. In fact, half the French citizens of Algeria came from Malta, Spain, Corsica, or other Mediterranean territories of limited economic development, finding in Algeria a standard of living not attainable in their former homes.

41. Ambler, *Soldiers Against the State,* p. 245.

42. Ironically, it was the Mollet government that carried out the most delegation of power to the armed forces in Algeria. As Ambler notes, "the delegation of propaganda responsibilities to the army in 1956–57 was to prove an exceedingly dangerous act." Ibid., p. 232.

43. De Gaulle served as provisional president from the liberation of Paris until his resignation early in 1946, a result of the rejection by the Constituent Assembly of an executive president for the new Fourth Republic. His preference was for the primacy of the executive, not the legislature— a belief put into effect only with the drafting of the constitution of the Fifth Republic.

44. Edgar S. Furniss, Jr., *De Gaulle and the French Army: A Crisis in Civil–Military Relations* (New York: Twentieth Century Fund, 1964), pp. 289–290.

45. Ambler, *Soldiers Against the State,* p. 373.

46. Ibid., pp. 206–207.

47. Ibid., p. 207.

48. Giradet, "Civil and Military Power," pp. 141–142.

49. As indicative of Massu's attitude, this comment of December 1957 should suffice:
> It is evident that in Paris an attempt is being made to discredit the
> army in order more easily to reach an agreement with the F.L.N.; it
> is an old tactic which I have known since Indochina. Now it must be
> known that the army will no longer permit the intriguers to betray
> France. Algeria will remain French, I assure you.

Quoted in Ambler, *Soldiers Against the State,* p. 116.

50. Kelly, *Lost Soldiers,* p. 268.

51. Salan's views can be quickly deduced from a message he sent May 9, 1958, to
French President René Coty:
> The French Army, in a unanimous fashion, would feel the abandon-
> ment of this national patrimony to be an outrage. One could not
> predict its reaction of despair.
>
> I ask you please to call the attention of the President of the Repub-
> lic to our anguish, which can only be erased by a government firmly
> determined to maintain our flag in Algeria.

One could not ask for a clearer indication of impending military disloyalty;
Salan intimated that only a government whose policies accorded with the
desires of the armed forces would be permitted to take office. (The quote
is found in Ambler, *Soldiers Against the State,* p. 260.)

52. *Le procès des généraux Challe et Zeller* (Paris: Nouvelles Editions Latines, 1961),
pp. 49–50.

53. Ibid., p. 40.

54. Kelly, *Lost Soldiers,* p. 321.

55. *Procès des généraux,* p. 43. Challe adduced two other reasons: (1) the development of "communist cells" among the troops; (2) the General's desire
to avoid any spilling of blood.

56. Quoted in Furniss, *De Gaulle and the French Army,* p. 113.

57. Kelly, *Lost Soldiers,* p. 231.

58. David C. Rapoport, "The Political Dimensions of Military Usurpation," *Political
Science Quarterly,* LXXXIII, 4 (December 1968), p. 571.

59. In the mid-1930's, a few secret groups emerged within the officer corps, some
opposed to Fascism, others to Communism. De la Gorce suggests that the
"political universe" of the Vichy Republic "slowly crystallized around
the Army's anti-Communist networks." De la Gorce, *The French Army,*
p. 250. More research is necessary in this area, however.

60. Kurt Lang, "The Military Putsch in a Developed Political Culture: Confrontations of Military and Civil Power in Germany and France," in Jacques
van Doorn, ed., *Armed Forces and Society* (The Hague: Mouton, 1968),
p. 228.

61. Ibid.

62. Morris Janowitz, *The Professional Soldier: A Social and Political Portrait* (New York: Free Press of Glencoe, 1960), p. 435.

63. Ambler, *Soldiers Against the State,* p. 403.

64. Furniss, *De Gaulle and the French Army,* p. 297.

65. We part company here with Janowitz, who states:

> Professional democracies assume that officers can be effectively motivated by professional ethics alone. The officer fights because of his career commitment. The strain on democratic forms under prolonged international tension raises the possibility of the garrison state under which the military, in coalition with demogogic civilian leaders, wield an unprecedented amount of political and administrative power. In the garrison state the officer fights for national survival and glory.

(Janowitz, *The Professional Soldier,* p. 440.) Part III of our text examines the "garrison state" possibility.

66. Ambler, *Soldiers Against the State,* p. 402.

67. Ibid., p. 398.

Comparative Civil-Military Relations: The Balance Sheet

Melding the abstract and the particular constitutes the prime objective of Part III.

The first section of *Military Role and Rule* set forth a theoretical framework for studying civil–military relations. In contrasting civic and praetorian political systems, we attempted to show how four "summary" variables—the nature and extent of political participation, the strength of civil institutions, military strength, and the nature of military institutional boundaries—interacted to define the military's role in politics; and we noted that this role ranges from influence by means of recognized channels to total displacement of governments.

Praetorian political systems are susceptible to coups d'etat. Intervention follows certain patterns, which we examined first in terms of factors affecting the likelihood of coups; next, in terms of varieties of military regimes; in Part II, we looked at these patterns in case studies. What broad issues are raised by these studies? We must now unite the historical analysis of Part II to the theoretical concerns of Part I.

The foregoing chapters illustrate the diversity of military regimes in the contemporary world. In Thailand the military has been a predatory force in politics. Its dominance has remained unchallenged by countervailing civilian institutions, and its rulership has scarcely been moderated by the larger moral purpose that might stem from a more professionalized military's sense of social responsibility. Nigeria's armed forces have adopted a reformist stance. They have set conditions for their withdrawal from power that envisage sweeping changes in Nigerian society and establish the military as the fulcrum of the country's political affairs. In Egypt the military rulers employ revolutionary rhetoric but seek gradual and limited social reforms, which they reserve the right to direct. They have created a single-party government but eschew the organization and mobilization techniques that could broaden their political base among the fellahin. Peru's ruling junta also employs the rhetoric of the extreme left, but has avoided even the pretense of interest in organizing a mass party. Its leaders have preferred to promote a program of gradual reforms administered by a civil–military technocracy rather than be subject to the unpredictable consequences of allowing mass participation in politics. In France the army has in certain times of crisis pressed its own policy preferences in defiance of constituted civil authority. However, while its actions as guardian of the national interest were instrumental in bringing down the Fourth Republic, there was no significant threat by would-be military rulers to supplant the civilian government.

In each of these five political systems the military has carved for itself a prominent role in politics. In each the armed forces have intervened in domestic political matters at least once in the past twenty years; and in four, military governments hold power as of this writing. In these four countries, representing the four major regions of the Third World, the norm of civilian political supremacy is scarcely operative. External pressures and the impact of modernizing change have undermined the strength and legitimacy of civilian institutions, creating conditions of political uncertainty and instability that have drawn the military into the vortex of politics. The armed forces are established contenders for power in these polities. They possess the most effective organizational base, command the power resources that—for the present at least—are decisive, and have mobilized these resources to make themselves the policy makers in place of civilians. In France, the single industrialized country represented here, the military does not compete directly for power. Rather, it exerts influence within the government bureaucracy. The French civil authorities have been able for the most part to exercise control over their armed forces, but historically their control has sometimes hinged more on the military's acceptance of the principle of civilian supremacy than on the legitimacy, and hence the countervailing power, of civilian institutions. Under the Fifth Republic, however, it is primarily the strength of Gaullist institutions that has constrained the military from expanding its limited guardianship role.

These five case studies provide preliminary data that tend to support the twenty propositions regarding factors affecting civilian control and military intervention. These propositions related factors internal to the armed forces (their mission, recruitment and socialization patterns, organizational complexity and autonomy, and political awareness) and other factors making up the societal environment of the military institutions (class and ethnic cleavages, the state of the national economy, the political framework), to the propensity of the military to intervene in politics. In view of the small number of cases analyzed here, we do not pretend to have adequately tested these twenty propositions as scientific hypotheses. The state of knowledge about civil–military relations remains too underdeveloped, and the major variables involved still too imprecisely defined, for us to claim that more than a rudimentary beginning has been made in the building of theory in this field. The reflections in this concluding chapter should therefore be taken as illustrative and suggestive, pointing the way for future study, rather than as statements of conclusive evidence.

Military Internal Factors as the Wellspring of Intervention

The experiences of both Nigeria and Peru suggest the validity of propositions 1 and 2—that the likelihood of military intervention rises as the military's functions become those of a domestic police force, and especially as the armed forces are directed to employ coercive measures contrary to the advice of military leaders against domestic opponents of the government. The resentment of Nigerian officers when they were ordered to quell uprisings in the Western Region was a factor that accentuated their disposition to intervene in 1966. Likewise in Peru the military leadership deposed the civilian president in 1948 when he proved unable to maintain public order without their assistance. Under President Belaunde in the mid-1960's the officers chafed at the tarnishing of their public image when they were directed to crush land invasions by peasant groups. In these instances, the use of regular army troops as instruments of political repression on behalf of civilian politicians was held to be in direct contravention of the self-image of the professional military officer. Such usage belies his high moral purpose as defender, not oppressor, of the nation. It threatens his institutions by undermining service pride and morale in the ranks, by weakening public esteem for the military profession, and by exacerbating political dissension within the officer corps.

In any country the decision to use professional soldiers against domestic political opponents is fraught with danger for civil authorities. The officers may see themselves as unwilling tools in the service of some politician's selfish political interests. This threat to their own interests as a corporate entity may lead them to disobey or even to overthrow the offending chief executive. More broadly, the deployment of regular troops for domestic political purposes inevitably obscures the distinction between the military and the civilian spheres of authority, and ultimately it subverts the moral basis of civilian control. If prolonged, its result tends to be a sharp increase in the politicization of the military. The civilian imposition of domestic police functions on regular troops may thus be a useful indicator of impending political role expansion by the armed forces.

The converse of this relationship is stated by proposition 3— that the likelihood of intervention diminishes with the presence of a clear-cut external focus for national defense. The literature on the Latin American military abounds with the assertion that armies of the post-independence era turned to politics because of the implausibility of external defense as their raison d'être. In the Soviet Union and other communist countries, continual emphasis on the theme of capitalist military encirclement has helped party leaders to maintain subjective control over their armed forces. The supporting premise here is that where armies are preoccupied with measuring themselves against a foreign foe whose forces constitute a clear and present threat to national security, they are less likely to use domestic politics as an outlet for their energies and ambitions.

A similar case is often made for proposition 4, that civic action programs can provide a sense of purpose to armies who lack a credible foreign enemy and thereby can diminish the likelihood of intervention. [1] The rationale for the Alliance for Progress depended in part on this assumption. The evidence, however, is ambiguous. The American military, it has sometimes been argued, found a useful outlet for its energies in opening the West for settlement during an extended period in the nineteenth century when external threats to the United States were minimal. But whether the absence of this outlet would have caused frustrated army officers to desert the principle of civilian supremacy is questionable. In a more contemporary vein, civic action is often seen as an important adjunct to counterinsurgency efforts in the less developed countries. To the extent that combat troops can be successful in the building of roads, dams, and schools, and to the extent that these efforts actually increase public support for the government in power, then civic action may indeed diminish the likelihood of overt military intervention in politics. On the other hand, the Peruvian military's experience in civic action had the dual effects of enhancing the prestige of the armed forces as it sharpened their awareness of the depths of discontent among the rural masses. Both of these factors contributed to the military's decision to overthrow the Belaunde government in 1968. It may well be that civic action (as it applies to combat infantry troops rather than to, say, engineer battalions) stimulates politicization of the military in a way similar to that where armies are assigned domestic police functions. Perhaps *any* function that directs military energies into purposes within the national borders is fundamentally threatening to civilian control. Civic action may well increase the military's contribution to modernization, but there is little evidence to support the assertion that it enhances civilian supremacy. The most that can be said for civic action in this context is that its political effects depend on factors and events that are outside the military institution.

The central importance of proposition 5—that a mission differentiating between service to constituted civil authority and service to "the national interest" encourages members of the armed forces to move directly into politics—is clearly borne out by all five of the case studies. A distinction of this kind in the minds of young Thai army officers served to justify their conspiracy to overthrow the absolute monarchy in 1932. In Nigeria, military officers have taken the position that theirs is the responsibility to set and enforce conditions under which civilians may participate in political life. They have justified these measures by asserting the need to safeguard the strength and viability of the nation as a whole. Military leaders in both Egypt and Peru have defined their primary loyalties in terms of promoting their respective national "revolutions." This concept of mission has led them to push aside civilian leadership and assume direct control over policy making. In France the army's disagreements with leaders of the Fourth Republic over the war in Algeria were so profound as to lead it to place its own definitions of the national interest above those of the civilian government. The differentiation of mission between service to the government and service to some higher and abstract standard is the direct antithesis of the principle of civilian supremacy. Where it exists, the likelihood of military intervention and rule is sharply increased. But the military's sense of mission by itself does not lead automatically to these outcomes. Mission affects merely the military's *disposition* to intervene, a necessary but not sufficient condition for military intervention in politics.

The importance of internal cohesion (proposition 6) in determining the military's *capacity* to intervene is also demonstrated repeatedly in the case studies. It is rare that an officer corps is willing to risk its own disintegration and the possibility of a fratricidal civil war by acting in politics without first assuring a consensus within itself. High internal cohesion is a fundamental military value, a vital factor in the performance of the primary functions of armed forces. The more cohesive a military

establishment, the more likely it will be effective, whether in its role as
a coercive arm of the state or as an independent political actor. As with
mission, however, internal cohesion by itself is only an indirect determinant of intervention. Some highly cohesive armies have never intervened,
others with low cohesion have done so repeatedly. Internal cohesion
is less an indicator of the presence or absence of interventionist tendencies
than a predictor of the character of the military regime that would result from intervention. The second part of proposition 6 suggests that low
levels of cohesion will result in fragmented and unstable military involvement in politics. The presence of sharp cleavages within the officer corps
may not prevent intervention, but would probably mean that the result of intervention would be nonactivist or impotent caretaker regimes
of relatively short tenure.

Cohesion depends on a number of elements: the social origins
of the officer corps (with respect both to homogeneity and vis-a-vis
the civilian governing elite); the military socialization process (the symbols, rituals, and discipline of military life); the nature of the organizational boundaries separating the military institution from its societal
environment (integral boundaries promote greater cohesion); and the
degree of autonomy exercised by the military leadership over internal
matters. The record of Peru's armed forces provides an excellent illustra-
tion of the relationship between internal cohesion and intervention.
Coups in Peru are nearly always instigated and led by the generals, i.e.,
from the top, not by the colonels and majors who in many other countries seem to form the nucleus of antigovernment conspiracies. The 1968
coup was precisely executed and bloodless, and it hardly disrupted the
day-to-day activities of government and business. The new regime headed
by General Velasco has remained solidly entrenched in power, extraordinarily activist in reorienting government policy, and stable in its
leadership. By contrast, the 1947 coup in Thailand and that of 1966 in
Nigeria are examples of intervention undertaken by armies with much
lower levels of internal cohesion. In each of these cases the nucleus of
conspiracy was small and involved primarily middle-grade officers. Support
for the coup effort was uncertain within the officer corps as a whole. The
initial seizure of power in both cases was followed by a series of countercoup attempts, and military rule remained unstable and ineffective for
an extended period of time. Both officer corps were rent by fratricidal
struggles. Many officers who opposed the dominant groups were forcibly
retired, a few were executed.

Even in cases of successful intervention, the responsibilities
of governing may generate destructive pressures that threaten the maintenance of military cohesion. Once they have taken over the government,
the armed forces can hardly preserve their cherished illusion that they

stand above politics. Their policies will inevitably be seen as favoring this or that social group, as according primacy to this or that social philosophy. Despite the frequently encountered allusions to the "military mind," no officer corps is uniformly cut of the same philosophical cloth. Political decisions taken in the name of the military nearly always have internally divisive effects. All armies are acutely sensitive to threats to their cohesion. This sensitivity does not fade when armies venture into the business of governing. In Egypt and Peru this constant concern is central to the relatively gradualist and reformist policies of the military rulers, despite their rhetorical pretensions to radicalism and revolution.

Proposition 7 suggests that attempts by political leaders to alter the armed forces' spheres of decision making against their advice will produce strains in civil–military relations, and may precipitate intervention. Where military participation in politics is institutionalized, as in Thailand or Peru, the hands of civilian leaders may well be bound by the military's sensitivity to threats against its perquisites and organizational autonomy. The 1971 coup in Thailand demonstrated that the army has no intention of permitting any contraction of its role, by parliament or other authority. In Peru, any attempt by the president to reduce military appropriations is virtually a sure formula for a hasty end to his administration. Another example may be found in Egypt where the 1952 coup, although related to more fundamental strains in Egyptian society, was directly precipitated by King Farouk's interference in the internal affairs of the Officers' Club. Wherever military participation in politics is pronounced, high-ranking officers are particularly sensitive to any efforts on the part of civilians to counter military influence, especially where this involves threats to organize and arm an independent militia. Constricting the areas and the scope of military decisional autonomy is unquestionably part of any strategy for asserting civilian control, but just as surely its success hinges on prior attention to building a countervailing power base of public support. Without such a base, civilian leaders cannot expect the military to agree to its own political decline.

Civilian "meddling" in the military's internal matters tends to inflame and may ultimately unite officer opinion against the government or against a particular political movement. During the 1920's in Peru the dictator Leguia undertook tactics that seriously divided the officer corps. In the short run these tactics reduced the capacity of the military to oppose Leguia, but afterward memory of them sharply increased the sensitivity of Peruvian officers to threats of this sort. A good deal of the longstanding enmity these officers feel toward the APRA party has been based on Aprista attempts to divide the armed forces by winning over the enlisted ranks. More broadly, the stern anticommunism that is found almost universally among Western and Third World militaries is fundamentally a reflection of their concern for their own institutional self-preservation. Successful communist revolutions have invariably dismantled the armed forces of the prerevolutionary government, often with the summary execution of the officers.

The significance of officer recruitment patterns is suggested by proposition 8, that the likelihood of military intervention diminishes if officers are drawn from the same social strata as the governing elite, and increases when there are marked dissimilarities between the class or ethnic backgrounds of these two groups. Tribal imbalances in elite recruitment and advancement were an obvious factor in the Nigerian coups of 1966 and in the subsequent civil war. Class differences have frequently been cited in explanations of the political activism of both Egyptian and Peruvian military officers, whose middle-class origins set them apart from the aristocratic oligarchies of their countries. On the other hand, common social origins shared by the military and the civil service have not appreciably reduced the propensity of Thai army officers to move against civilians; nor have similar social backgrounds prevented French officers from contesting civilian supremacy at times. We might hypothesize from these few cases that the integration of military and civilian governing elites may be a necessary (but not sufficient) condition for the institutionalization of civilian control, but that it is a relatively minor factor in promoting the political neutralization of the armed forces. However, the social origins of officers do seem to be of some significance in determining the policy orientations of military regimes. We have argued that the middle-class backgrounds of Egyptian and Peruvian military politicians are of central importance in understanding their activist roles in the modernization process. Moreover, as we shall argue further below, political alliances of military officers and civilian technocrats, both with origins in the middle strata, may well be becoming the dominant pattern of civil–military relations in non-Western countries.

There is a certain temptation to give undue weight to social origins of officers in explicating military roles in politics. A number of social scientists, working with assumptions drawn from Western historical experiences, have concluded rather hopefully that the military would be the vanguard of middle-class progressivism and democracy in the Third World. These facile predictions overlooked the possibility that the middle strata themselves may, as in some countries of Latin America, be a conservative force in politics.[2] In these countries where the middle class is politically insecure and threatened by rising mass pressures for the redistribution of wealth, status, and power, the armed forces may be more inclined to guardianship and even social reaction than to progressivism. Moreover, these predictions neglected the further possibility that the military socialization process may be of significantly greater importance than social origins in explaining the military's political actions.[3] A persistent theme in our own case studies has been that the armed forces, irrespective of the sociopolitical contexts of their countries, are primarily concerned with the preservation of their own institutional well-being.

Proposition 9 suggests that the likelihood of military intervention is reduced by greater structural differentiation and functional specialization within the armed forces. The thrust of this argument is that more modern military establishments (such as that of France), with their great diversity of internal functions, individual technical specialties, and division of labor, are less likely to be readily unified and mobilized for intervention in politics. The greater the size and complexity of the armed forces, the more formidable the tasks of officer conspirators seeking to rally a workable coalition of their comrades against the government. Secrecy and coordination, both vital to success, become more difficult to achieve, especially by disgruntled middle-grade officers on the pattern of the Free Officers group of Egypt. As proposition 11 suggests, it is these middle-grade officers—the majors and colonels in direct tactical command of troops—whose career frustrations make them the most likely planners and executors of coups.

Although the logic of proposition 9 seems persuasive, the fact remains that large modern military establishments—e.g., those of France, Greece, Turkey—do intervene in politics, just as do some African armies of only a few infantry battalions. Great organizational complexity clearly does not preclude intervention altogether. However, as a corollary to both propositions 9 and 11, the evidence indicates that where large modern armies do intervene, it is the generals at the uppermost echelons of command rather than middle-grade officers who are the likely leaders.

Proposition 10 advances an argument often made by opponents of foreign military aid programs, i.e., that such programs tend to increase the likelihood of military intervention in recipient countries. The evidence for this assertion is not clear. Although both Peru and Thailand received large amounts of United States military aid prior to the most recent coups in these countries, the aid itself does not appear to have influenced directly either the decisions of these armies to intervene or the outcomes of intervention. The armed forces in both countries had intervened actively in political affairs long before the advent of military aid programs. Some observers (e.g., Samuel Huntington) argue that military aid and training are politically sterile; they neither increase nor diminish the propensity of officers in recipient countries to overstep the bounds of civilian control.[4] Certainly the reverse of proposition 10—that training missions and aid actually may reduce interventionism by inculcating through example a deeper respect for the principle of civilian supremacy—is unfounded, as some chagrined former proponents of United States arms aid to Latin America now acknowledge. On the other hand, Huntington's argument that military aid is politically neutral has been overstated. One effect of such aid is to increase the domestic and international political autonomy of the armed forces who receive it, by reducing their budgetary dependence on local civilian elites. Further study of this relationship is needed, but it seems reasonable that any increase in the political autonomy of the military will render more difficult the task of civilian authorities seeking to establish or maintain control over their armed forces.

Our case studies do not lend persuasive support to proposition 12, which states that officers with close ties to individuals or groups opposed to government policies form the nucleus of conspiracies leading to military intervention. The most recent coups in Egypt and Peru were planned and executed by officers whose links to the principal civilian political oppositions in their countries were negligible. In each of these cases the officer conspirators sought civilian allies and support after, not before, the act of overthrowing the government. But our purpose here is not to suggest that such linkages, where they are present in other systems, are politically irrelevant. They are indeed important, as studies such as William Brill's of the 1964 coup in Bolivia clearly demonstrate. [5] In praetorian polities where military institutional boundaries are extensively fragmented, military intervention is frequently solicited by out-of-power civilian elites. Coup attempts are commonly the work of civilian and military coalitions. What we are challenging, however, is the implication of proposition 12 that militaries with fragmented institutional boundaries are more prone to intervene then those whose boundaries are more nearly integral. This is another way of restating the controversy in the civil–military relations literature over whether military professionalism reinforces civilian control (Huntington) or may actually undermine it under certain circumstances (Finer). Our own case studies tend to support Finer's view that professionalization is not appreciably related to the political neutralization of armed forces. Intervention in politics is a game that both highly professional and less professional officers seem to play with equal readiness.

Proposition 13 proposes that defeat in war, particularly if accompanied by the belief on the part of the armed forces that the government failed to give them sufficient support, often increases the likelihood of military intervention. The Peruvian army attempted to use its defeat in the War of the Pacific in rationalizing the asserted need for strong defense-oriented governments dominated by the military. Judging from this and the more recent experiences of the Egyptian army in the 1948 war with Israel, or those of the French in the wars in Indochina and Algeria, defeat in war is indeed a potent agent of politicization. These armies held civilian politicians directly responsible for military failures; the Egyptian officers charged King Farouk with having given them inadequate support, the French blamed the Fourth Republic leaders for forcing them to conform to ill-advised strategies and tactics in countering guerrilla warfare.

Focusing on the nature rather than the degree of the military's politicization, proposition 14 states that intervention resulting from the armed forces' distrust of the total political system leads to the establishment of military-based regimes of extended duration, whereas intervention resulting from specific policy grievances on the part of the military usually leads to prompt restoration of civilian rule. The politicization of the French army under the Fourth Republic was based on highly specific policy differences, the resolution of which under de Gaulle brought a quick return to the barracks. The Peruvian military intervention in 1962 was aimed primarily at preventing the APRA party from gaining power. Once this goal was assured the generals promptly arranged for new elections the following year and respected their outcome. By contrast, the Peruvian coup of 1968 sprang from grievances that were far more diffuse. As in the cases of Egypt and Nigeria, these diffuse grievances centered on the military's fundamental dissatisfaction with the political system as a whole, and have led to a protracted period of activist military rule.

Proposition 15 suggests that the likelihood of military intervention rises as the content of officer education is expanded to encompass political issues customarily resolved by civilians. The most obvious empirical reference here is to Peru, where officers educated at the Centro de Altos Estudios Militares (CAEM) were in the forefront of the conspiracy that led to the overthrow of President Belaunde in 1968. The implication is that officers, who tend professionally to be contemptuous of civilian politicians, are more likely to supplant them when their own educational system leads to the conclusion that the armed forces are better equipped to resolve issues of public policy. Although this appears to have been the case in Peru, the validity of proposition 15 is still open to question. Broadened officer education in public policy issues may conceivably have an opposite effect, increasing the military's awareness of the intractability of many social issues and awakening them to the limitations of administrative solutions to civilian problems. Further study of the relationship between military education and intervention in politics is clearly needed.

These fifteen propositions aggregate some of the most commonly accepted hypotheses relating internal characteristics of armed forces to the phenomenon of military intervention in politics. Subjected to closer examination, several seem indeed to state significant relationships, others seem fallacious or at least ambiguous. As a group, they clearly do not provide a satisfactory basis for the development of a "theory" of military intervention. Searching among the internal characteristics of armed forces for the root causes of intervention leads the student to a recurring pattern of perplexing problems. As we have seen, armies with widely varying concepts of mission intervene in politics. Some armies with high cohesion may intervene while others do not. Some armies with low cohesion refrain from intervention, others blunder ahead despite the consequences. Officers with social origins in the middle class may lead coups, but then so may officers with upper-class origins. (However, practically no coups are of lower-class origin, the "Sergeants' Revolt" led by Cuba's Fulgencio Batista being an exceptional case.) Officers of both upper and middle classes have been known to overthrow civilian elites whose social backgrounds they share. Armies of great size and complexity intervene, as do those with only a few lightly armed battalions. Some armies who receive huge amounts of foreign military aid have subsequently overthrown civilian governments, others support civilian rule with exemplary loyalty. For some countries the evidence seems to support propositions we have examined, for others the evidence is contradictory. But while their bearing on the causes of military intervention in politics is inconclusive, the internal characteristics of armed forces nevertheless provide a fruitful focus for research. Their usefulness is found in the indications they afford of the kind of military regime that is likely to result from intervention: the structure and stability of the military-based government, its relationships to civilian groups, the policies it is likely to advance, its duration in power. Internal factors are not the most important causes of military intervention in politics. For these, we must examine the social, economic, and political structures of the society as a whole rather than the internal characteristics of the armed forces. We turn now to a review of propositions 16 through 20, which focus on these environmental variables.

Environmental Factors as Root Causes of Military Intervention

Proposition 16 states that the likelihood of military intervention increases as the intensification of domestic conflicts arising from ethnic or class cleavages threatens the status and power of the dominant group or class. Social cleavages are a primary characteristic of praetorian polities, where existing political institutions are ineffective in moderating social conflict and channeling the energies of contending groups toward common goals. As cleavages reinforce one another, the government becomes identified with the selfish interests of a particular group, region, or class. Those civilian factions who perceive themselves as not receiving their fair share of the available status, wealth, or political power may become alienated and actively work to overthrow the established order. In doing so, they may create the conditions of public disorder and government ineffectiveness that draw the armed forces into politics.

These circumstances seemed to prevail in three of our case studies—Nigeria, Egypt, and Peru—and were a factor behind the most recent coup in a fourth, Thailand. In Nigeria the dominant cleavages were ethnic, but tribal differences had come to coincide in many areas with distinctions of social class and wealth. The primordial loyalties of tribe ran deep, obstructing the creation of an integrated national society. Ethnic suspicions and jealousies were reflected in the army officer corps, which divided into warring political factions as ethnic conflicts intensified after the January coup in 1966. Egyptian society before the 1952 coup was rent by pronounced class cleavages generated by a grossly unequal distribution of wealth. The Free Officers saw these inequalities as partly responsible for the relative backwardness of their society and for their own disastrous showing in the 1948 war with Israel. In Peru, the dominant social cleavages have had both ethnic and class aspects. Peruvian society is frequently portrayed as one in which a small aristocratic oligarchy (the "forty families") of pure European stock controls an overwhelming share of the country's arable land and wealth. At the bottom of the socioeconomic ladder is a huge mass of unassimilated Indian peasants, and in between is a fragmented and insecure middle class. In this century the changing political roles of the Peruvian military have reflected these cleavages in one way or another, first as the bulwark of the oligarchy and then more recently as the champion of the middle strata. Finally, in Thailand the army has been concerned with active and potential ethnic and religious conflicts—the insurgencies of Meo tribesmen in the north and Muslim minorities in the south, and the threat represented by a large and economically powerful Chinese minority. They have also had to combat communist-led guerrillas in the northeast. Both these factors influenced the army's decision to reassert its political primacy in the November 1971 coup.

In addition to conflicts related to the structural configuration of the economic system, the economic performance of the government in power is also a factor that influences the military's inclination to intervene. Proposition 17 suggests that the likelihood of intervention rises as prevailing economic conditions worsen, especially when the government is perceived to be responsible for or unable to control the situation. Our own analysis of Peru is consistent with this proposition. Economic deterioration leads to government belt tightening. Regimes with shallow public support are poorly equipped to withstand the protests of social groups from whom sacrifices are demanded. Austerity measures tend to affect the lower strata most severely, giving rise to strikes, demonstrations, and even riots. Actual outbreaks of violence or serious doubts about the government's ability to maintain order may prompt the military to intervene. Moreover, desperate presidents beset by economic crises may ask the armed forces themselves to sacrifice a part of their own budgetary appropriations. The Peruvian army, for one, has not responded positively to such suggestions.

The final three propositions are closely related to the social and economic factors just discussed, being concerned directly with

their political ramifications and with the general level of political institutionalization in a society. The social frustrations that result from people's
perceptions of injustice, or from their unfulfilled expectations of enhanced mobility, may cause them to make demands on the political system.
Where the level of political institutionalization is relatively high, these
demands may be absorbed and channeled within generally accepted rules
and procedures. Demands for change can thus be accommodated more
or less peacefully and "within the system." Where political institutions are
insufficiently resilient to absorb and respond to demands for change
the phenomenon of "political decay" or systemic breakdown may result.
Focusing on the need in any polity for agreed-upon "rules of the game,"
proposition 18 asserts that the likelihood of military intervention rises
in the absence or weakness of widely accepted procedures for effecting peaceful political change.

In one sense proposition 18 may appear tautological: by definition, military intervention in politics indicates a lack of agreement between
civilian and military elites regarding how political decisions should be
made and who should make them. Within the civilian sphere alone, however,
the degree of consensus among major contenders for power on the rules
and procedures governing their competition is crucial. The distinction
is whether prevailing rules are illegitimate (a) in the eyes of the military
alone, or (b) in those of certain civilian contenders, or (c) among both
groups. Where consensus among civilians is relatively high and the armed
forces alone are disaffected, the likelihood of successful military intervention remains low. Where the civilian consensus is weak and the armed
forces are inclined to support the government in power, the military may
nevertheless be drawn into interventionism by the unbridled nature of
conflict among civilian groups. Finally, where the civilian consensus
is weak and the armed forces are also alienated from the political system,
the likelihood of military intervention becomes great.

Examples of each of these three situations may be found in
the case studies we have presented. French citizens rallied behind de Gaulle
in the context of the crisis over Algeria, producing relatively high consensus among civilians. Despite the political disaffection of many military
officers as a result of de Gaulle's decision to permit Algerian independence,
the strength of this civilian consensus sharply circumscribed the options
of intervention open to the military. Nigeria's armed forces, notwith-
standing their socialization in the British tradition of respect for civil authority. were drawn into the politics of intervention when regional conflicts
dissipated the procedural consensus on which the survival of the federal
system depended. In Peru, finally, the various civilian contenders for
power were unable to agree on a single set of rules and procedures to decide
who should rule and which policies ought to be pursued by the government.
Coupled with the weakness or virtual absence of local traditions upholding civilian supremacy, the "legitimacy vacuums" of Nigeria and Peru

created conditions under which ambitious military leaders were able to expand the political role of the armed forces.

Where the procedural consensus among competing civilian groups is low, and where emerging contenders for power believe that prevailing rules favor the incumbent elites unjustly, these anti-status quo contenders may resort to conspiring with dissident military officers in order to drive their opponents out of the government. Proposition 19 argues that the likelihood of intervention rises as contending groups solicit support from the armed forces, thereby aggravating the fragmentation of civil and military institutional boundaries. The armed forces may thus be purposefully politicized by civilians, reflecting the absence or weakness of a civil consensus that the military should be kept out of politics. The course of Peruvian history provides numerous examples of this phenomenon. Representatives of the landed oligarchy, business elites (both domestic and foreign), the APRA party, and other contenders for power have all, at one time or another, allied themselves with the military or with factions within the armed forces.

The unifying element or common thread among all of these various environmental factors, whether primarily social, economic, or political in nature, is their effect on public support for civilian political institutions. Propositions 16 through 19 focus on factors that cause, or reflect, a weakening of those moral beliefs that validate the right of governing elites to exercise authority and power on behalf of the society as a whole. The depth and breadth of these moral beliefs determine the legitimacy of the government. According to proposition 20, the ease with which the armed forces can assume political authority varies inversely with the legitimacy enjoyed by the existing civilian government.

Political legitimacy is the most crucial factor affecting the likelihood of military intervention. Where public support for civilian institutions is strong, military participation in politics is unlikely to extend to the overthrow and outright supplantment of civil authorities. Where public support is weak, expansion of the military's political role seems probable. Military intervention is primarily a characteristic of a certain kind of political system, rather than an outgrowth of the personnel, ethics, or organizational imperatives of the military institution itself. For this reason, strategies for establishing civilian control that focus on reforming the armed forces are likely to fail unless they are accompanied by effective measures to strengthen civilian political institutions.

Military Rule and the Modernization Process

We have already argued that factors internal to the military institution are primarily useful as predictors of the form intervention is likely to take, and, in particular, of the kind of military or military-based regime that may result. One of the principal concerns of the preceding chapters has been to gain a more critical perspective for evaluating the impact of military regimes on the modernization process. If, as we suggest, the military will continue to play a central political role in the Third World, what can we now conclude about the likelihood of military success in confronting the challenges facing these societies? Are military-based governments more effective than civilian leadership in establishing the conditions that foster more rapid economic development? Are officer politicians better equipped and motivated to advance social integration and take the steps necessary to extend political participation to the masses? Does military rule appear better fitted to promote political order and maintain stability? Given the magnitude of the problems faced by Third World governments, are the armed forces more suited than civilian groups to create new and effective political institutions?

In formulating tentative answers to these questions, we believe it is helpful to maintain Huntington's distinction between modernization and political development. Modernization is viewed as synonymous with social mobilization, the complex process of social and economic change generated by the spread of urbanization, mass education and communications, and industrialization. Political development, on the other hand, refers to the process whereby political institutions are created or adapted to handle the growing volume of demands on the political system that accompanies modernization. The two processes are closely interrelated but far from identical. Modernization, especially in the Third World, has mounted a fundamental challenge to the stability, effectiveness, and legitimacy of political institutions. In country after country the post-colonial or traditional government has proven inadequate to the challenge. The weakness of civilian political institutions has created conditions under which expansion of the military's political role is almost inevitable. A central issue, of both theoretical and practical relevance, is whether the current wave of military regimes is likely to slow the pace of modernization or advance it even more rapidly. More broadly, are military rulers somehow better equipped and motivated to create new political institutions capable of integrating their societies and mobilizing them toward solutions to the problems of poverty, economic backwardness, and overpopulation?

In Part I, we saw that military interventions and resultant military-based regimes can be grouped analytically in three different political contexts, as defined by the extent and rates of expansion of political participation within the various societies. Low participation levels signify societies in which politics is the domain of a small elite, and in which an independent middle class has not become a significant political force. This setting we have exemplified by Thailand. Medium levels of participation prevail in societies where the urban middle strata have become politically dominant. Three of our cases fit broadly into this second category: Nigeria, Egypt, and Peru. Finally, high participation levels mean that the masses have in their turn become a significant factor in the political process, with France as the example given.

At the low and high extremes of this three-fold classification of political participation levels, the data on Thailand and France suggest that the roles likely to be filled by the armed forces are only indirectly related to the modernization process. Moreover, they are probably a destructive factor in the process of political institutionalization. Thailand's "bureaucratic polity" has generated a modest stimulus to modernization, especially in the fields of economic growth and education. However, these advances may well be explained more satisfactorily as byproducts of continuity in bureaucratic rule rather than as the results of purposeful policies on the part of the armed forces. In the absence of countervailing civilian political institutions, and lacking a strong sense of social responsibility on its own part, the Thai army has been an essentially predatory political actor. To be sure, the same charge is perhaps equally applicable to the civilian segment of Thailand's bureaucratic elite, which constitutes the only visible alternative to military rule at present. The growth of extrabureaucratic pressures for more responsible government has been retarded by a combination of factors, most notably by the homogeneity and passivity of Thai political culture, the fragmentation of the urban middle class, and the cloak of legitimacy worn by the present government through its continued identification with the traditional monarchy.

In the case of France, it appears that there are definite limits to the variety of activist political roles open to armed forces in societies with mass political participation. These roles, furthermore, are much more likely to be forms of guardianship than of activism in promoting programmatic modernizing change. Societies with mass participation tend to be economically and socially complex. The functions of government under these circumstances are too diverse, the technical and managerial skills required too specialized, the societal division of labor too intricate and interdependent, for the military to rule without extensive cooperation from civilian elites. Managing the daily operations of government in France is beyond the expertise of military elites alone. The task of formulating and implementing a comprehensive program for restructuring French society would be a virtually insurmountable challenge. In mass societies, in any case, the process of modernization is already well established. The goals of military intervention at this level tend to be far more closely related to narrow rather than diffuse policy grievances, to questions of promoting order and stability rather than structural change.

For these reasons, the relationship between politicized armed forces and the modernization–development processes is most significant at medium levels of political participation. In a recent study, Henry Bienen distinguished three types of military intervention that correspond roughly to the political roles we have described for Nigeria, Egypt, and Peru. Bienen's first type occurs when the military of a new state makes overtly threatening demands for the first time on the civilian government, either by asserting a moderating role among fractious civilian power contenders, or by assuming power directly as guardians of public order. This corresponds to conditions in sub-Saharan Africa in the postcolonial era. The second type involves systems in which the military is an established participant in the power equation, but where "there is a struggle for stability after the seizure of power." The principal criteria for this classification are: (1) a regime dominated by military officers, (2) the officers' leadership manifests considerable continuity with the original coup leadership, and (3) a situation not characterized by a sustained pattern of coups and countercoups signifying unstable military involvement in politics. This second type corresponds generally to the situation found in certain Middle Eastern and Asian countries, e.g., Egypt, Libya, Pakistan, Burma, and South Korea. Bienen's third type is defined as "institutionalized intervention," exemplified by a number of Latin American countries. In these particular systems the military's aspirations to rule and its coercive resources are powerful enough to deny control to civilian contenders, even though the latter may advance a much greater potential claim to legitimacy.[6]

Bienen's threefold classification scheme is useful because it highlights the very different immediate political problems faced by the military in each of the three situations:

> *In the first it must pick up the political pieces left by civilian regimes or by its own coup and must find allies and support from political groups. In the second it must build support, reach down into society, and maintain military cohesion. In the third phase the military is split, by definition, and must maintain some autonomy from civilian groups and keep military disputes within bounds. In all three phases in developing countries, the military invariably sets itself the task of providing political stability and public order and often tries to promote economic development.* [7]

In either phase, achieving compatibility among such diverse goals is difficult and requires great capacity in the form of political resources and skills. Command of coercive resources alone is not enough. To seek both modernization and political stability simultaneously is a formidable undertaking for any government, civilian or military. Economic development has unintended consequences in accelerating social mobilization and producing a rapid expansion of political demands. There may be widespread frustration if these demands are not accommodated, ultimately a deterioration of public order. In each situation, the military rulers face different kinds of problems in relation to their own internal politics and vis-à-vis the complex society they are seeking to manage.

In our assessment of civil–military relations in Part I, we suggested that military intervention in systems with medium levels of political participation will result either in a form of military guardianship, or in a reformist or radical military-based regime. The guardian role is, by definition, an indication that the military's central concerns are with the maintenance of public order and stability and with the pursuance of the officers' own corporate interests (not necessarily in that order). The great majority of the military-based governments currently in power fall in the guardianship category. As was the case with the guardian regimes in Peru following the coups of 1914, 1930, 1948, and 1962 (but not 1968), these soldier-politicians did not seize power in order to restructure their societies. As might be expected, their performance as rulers in responding to demands for economic and social reforms has not been impressive. On the basis of their sheer number, guardian regimes have been the focus of most scholarly generalizing about the consequences of military participation in politics. Eric Nordlinger, for example, employed statistical analysis of economic change under military regimes to conclude that:

> *At the level of descriptive generalization, when military officers occupy the highest seats of government, or when they have a good measure of control over the civilian incumbents, the officer-politicians are commonly unconcerned with the realization of economic change and reform, and where there are civilian organizations and strata pressing for such changes the officers purposefully oppose them.* [8]

However, Nordlinger later modifies this conclusion by stipulating that under certain conditions ("when there is hardly a middle class to speak of, and when workers and peasants have not been politically mobilized"), military rulers have allowed or even actively promoted economic modernization. In general terms, nevertheless, he sees the military's commitment to fundamental reforms as being of minor consequence compared to their preoccupation with political stability and with the advancement of their own corporate interests.

Since Nordlinger's findings are of direct importance to our own, a brief elaboration of his assumptions and procedures are in order. First, he utilized an index measuring the political strength of the military in order to classify seventy-four non-Western, noncommunist countries into three categories: (a) those "in which the military was in direct political control during some part of the period 1957–62"; (b) those "in which the military was an important political influence but was not in direct political control during most of (this) period"; and (c) those countries "in which the military had little or no political influence during (this) period."[9] This index of military political strength was then correlated with seven different indicators of modernization: (1) rate of growth of per capita GNP; (2) change in degree of industrialization; (3) degree of improvement in agricultural productivity; (4) rate of improvement in human resources (i.e., education); (5) gross investment rate; (6) change in effectiveness of tax systems; and (7) leadership commitment to economic development. The results of correlation analysis showed that military political strength was significantly related to only one of the seven indicators of modernization, —the measure of change in the degree of industrialization taking place during the test period. Nordlinger argues that even this single positive result is attributable not to military-induced reforms but to his assumption that industrial growth is "the one type of economic change that the military might undertake because of its corporate interests."[10] Thus, overall, the results suggest that the armed forces are socially conservative and uphold the economic status quo. The explanation for this, according to Nordlinger, is found in two motivations common to officer politicians. These are, first, "the officers' determined pursuance of their corporate interests in combination with their deeply inculcated military values that assign overriding importance to the preservation of a particular type of political stability," and second, "the officers' attachments to their middle class interests and identities."[11]

Nordlinger's findings lend support to the proposition that the role of politicized armed forces is closely related to the relative size and political security of the middle class. When the seventy-four countries he analyzed were broken down roughly according to levels of political participation (specifically, according to whether demands for modernizing change were articulated by both urban and rural populations, or by urban populations alone, or were not significant in either group—high, medium, and low participation levels, respectively), Nordlinger found that at high and medium levels of participation the conservative tendency of the military was especially pronounced. However, at low participation levels the data produced significant positive correlations between military political strength and all seven indicators of modernization.[12] These findings suggest that politicized armed forces in countries with established middle strata tend to oppose economic reforms and the social movements that seek them, presumably because reforms would threaten the privileged economic and political positions of the middle classes. On the other hand, in countries where the lower strata are politically quiescent and unmobilized, economic reforms are generally compatible with middle-class interests and may therefore be supported by the military.

These conclusions are consonant with our own assertion in Part I that only sub-Saharan Africa currently manifests the conditions necessary for the emergence of reformist military regimes. Throughout this region the urban middle strata have only begun to assert their potential for political leadership. For the most part the masses of black Africa have remained unpoliticized. With the important exception to date of the Nigerian military, the armies that have seized power in this region have established postcolonial guardian-type regimes. By contrast with this prevailing guardianship, Nigeria's military leaders have taken an activist role in promoting social and economic change. This role is compatible with the interests of the relatively more developed middle class of their country. However, following the logic of our typology of military political roles, it is likely that to the extent that the army reformers are successful in modernizing Nigeria, the growing political maturation of the urban middle classes and social mobilization of the lower strata will gradually produce a shift in the army's role, away from that of reformer toward some form of guardianship.

Some of the most significant (and difficult) questions for the researcher in the field of civil–military relations are related to transitions from one military political role to another. For example, under what conditions do military politicians reject guardianship in favor of active reformism or radicalism? Our own analysis suggests that the critical factors are a combination of internal and environmental variables. The most important environmental factors seem to be the nature and extent of class cleavages within the society and the role of the urban middle classes in existing political institutions. The critical internal factors appear to be the military's sense of mission and the extent to which its institutional boundaries are fragmented along the lines of the societal cleavages. The formula appears too complex and the number of empirical cases too few to support more precise generalizations. It seems probable, however, that the conditions are sufficiently narrow to militate against the appearance of more than a few African military regimes of the reformist type in the coming decade.

An even more intriguing question is raised by the radical military governments of Egypt and Peru. Presumably these represent deviant cases in the context of Nordlinger's findings, i.e., instances wherein military rulers actively promote socioeconomic reforms despite the presence of relatively established urban middle strata. Although again the number of cases is extremely small and generalizations are necessarily highly tentative, our analyses suggest that pre-1952 Egypt and pre-1968 Peru shared several broadly similar environmental factors. In both countries the legitimacy of existing civilian political institutions was weak, class cleavages were sharply defined, and the urban middle classes as well as the upper classes were threatened by the rapid social mobilization of the years immediately preceding the coups. Perhaps most significant, the articulation of demands by the lower strata had become a central element of political struggle in

both countries. But just why military leaders chose at these junctures to
lead rather than to obstruct lower-class demands is not clear. In the Egyptian case the leaders of the Free Officers apparently had no real program
of social change in mind at the time of their coup. The linkage of interests
with the masses came later, and the influence of a single leader, Gamal
Abdel Nasser, was probably decisive. In Peru, on the other hand, the coup
leaders of 1968 had their purposes clearly in mind when they resolved
to overthrow President Belaunde.

Despite their decision to align military institutional interests
with the satisfaction of lower-class demands, the military leaders of
Egypt and Peru have proceeded cautiously in promoting fundamental
change. Both groups of officer politicians are committed to modernization, but at the same time both have responded more readily and consistently to imperatives related to the more traditional institutional concerns
of military establishments. The ever-present threat of open warfare
with Israel is a complicating factor in the case of Egypt, but officers in
both Egypt and Peru appear primarily devoted to the preservation and
strengthening of their own organizations within a stable political order.
Their concern with order, stability, and control takes precedence over their
impulse to restructure their societies. Despite their frequent barrages
of revolutionary rhetoric that underscore their quests for legitimacy, traditional military values have been the central determinants of their behavior.
These values are also much more compatible in the long run with the
interests of the middle strata than with those of the masses.

It is clear that the armed forces have not fulfilled the predictions
of some social scientists, put forward during the early 1960's, that
their organizational modernity and nationalism would make them the
leaders of the modernization process in their countries. On the other hand,
their performance as rulers in this regard has possibly not been much
worse than that which might have been achieved by the available civilian
alternatives. Military intervention has often overthrown civilian regimes
that manifestly failed to promote either modernization or political
institutionalization. And to point out that military politicians are primarily
devoted to the pursuance of their particular corporate interests, placing
these above the best interests of society as a whole, is not to lose sight of
the fact that civilian politicians are often just as guilty of devotion to
particular special interests. Solutions to the pressing problems of Third
World countries demand the creation of new political institutions capable
of integrating newly mobilized social groups with already established strata.
As Huntington and others have argued, the creation of legitimate authority
in these circumstances has been most successfully accomplished by charismatic leadership and modern political parties, singly or in combination.
Despite the relative ease with which the military can seize power, it is in

this area of political institution building that military regimes have proven most inadequate.

Once having assumed power, military officers in the overwhelming majority of cases have opted to preserve the notion that they are somehow "above politics." Often this stance is a requirement if the armed forces are to maintain internal cohesion in the face of the divisive pressures of bearing responsibility for making difficult choices among alternative public policies. Nevertheless, it is an exercise in self-delusion. At times institutional cohesion can be maintained only by avoiding hard policy choices. The inevitable outcome for society is the political drift and stagnation that often characterize military guardianship. Occasionally, ambitious and charismatic leaders with political skills have risen from within the military. More often than not, however, their rise has signaled an end to rule by the military as an institution. The effect, as with Cárdenas in Mexico, Ataturk in Turkey, Mobutu in the Congo, and to a lesser extent with Nasser in Egypt, has been a growing distinction between the leader and the armed forces from which he emerged. These military governments gradually became increasingly "civilianized." Political institution building was advanced by new organizations put together by the leaders without the direct participation of the armed forces, who gradually return to the barracks. This pattern, however, is rare. More commonly, the imperative of maintaining internal cohesion makes the officers wary of colleagues who manifest ambitions to cultivate new bases of political support outside the military itself. As with Juan Peron in Argentina, the more professionally motivated officers may turn on their erstwhile colleague in a countercoup, realigning military rule along the lines of guardianship.

Because of their primary concern with institutional preservation, armed forces have not generally been motivated to engage in the kind of grass-roots political organization that is the business of modern parties. Lacking this motivation, they are ill-equipped to advance the legitimation of political authority on which the resolution of social issues ultimately depends. In most cases the prolonging of military rule leads to the gradual dissipation of whatever initial claims to legitimacy the military may have enjoyed. As society's consensual validation of their leadership declines, the officer politicians tend to fall back on the instruments of force and coercion in order to maintain control. And as a government's reliance on coercion increases, its command of information resources declines and hence its policy decisions become increasingly ill-suited to reality.[13] Military regimes often stumble into the snare that ultimately brought down their civilian predecessors. Confronted finally with the ineffectiveness of their command solutions to the complex problems of society, the officers may simply withdraw in disgust to the barracks (an alternative that is not open to their civilian counterparts). The civilian politicians are left to pick up the pieces as best they can, having no alternative to shouldering the responsibilities of office that military leaders can, if they wish, deny. With the fundamental problems of society unresolved and the military resuming its watchdog role over the choices open to civilian authorities, too often the cycle simply repeats itself as a new and less disillusioned generation of officers rises within the armed forces.

Failing the "civilianization" of a military regime and failing also the rise of a countervailing civilian institution in the form of a political party, the pattern of governmental ineffectiveness and alternating civilian and military regimes may conceivably be broken by social revolution. This is what occurred, for example, in China and Cuba where military-based governments were overthrown by social movements which ultimately established new political institutions and new bases of legitimation. Social revolutions, however, are rare. The 1960's have demonstrated that the Cuban and Chinese "models" are not readily transferable to other social systems. In Latin America, revolutionary insurrections in Bolivia, Peru, and Colombia have been soundly defeated by regular troops trained in counterinsurgency tactics. In their confrontations with armed forces whose cohesiveness and responsiveness to command are not in doubt, revolutionaries have fared badly in their applications of both rural and urban guerrilla tactics. Where the armed forces are internally divided, however, and where a massive foreign intervention on the side of the existing government (as in the Dominican Republic in 1965) is not feasible, a revolutionary solution may become possible. The Bolivian Revolution of 1952 was characterized by an urban setting (La Paz) in which the army's coercive resources could not be deployed with great effectiveness, and by the desertion of a substantial segment of the armed forces who went over to the side of the revolutionaries. A similar pattern developed in Santo Domingo in 1965, but the United States intervention probably prevented the emergence of a true revolutionary regime. On this evidence, a revolutionary alternative to military rule must overcome the relatively advanced state of military counterinsurgency techniques and the difficulties of promoting armed insurrection among rural masses. A success strategy of revolution for the present appears to depend on fomenting an urban mass uprising that splits the armed forces into pro- and antirevolutionary factions.[14] Considering the strength of the imperatives of professionalism and unity in military sociology, these conditions will not occur with great frequency.

A Final Alternative: The "Garrison-State"

More than thirty years have now passed since Harold D. Lasswell set forth his garrison-state hypothesis, centered around the proposition that a concatenation of social pressures and technological developments were leading toward a worldwide domination of politics by elites specialized in the management of violence. In its essentials, this militarization of world politics into garrison-states develops from assumptions about (1) the possibility of large-scale coercion as an effective means of structuring political relationships in nation-states, and (2) the willingness of entrenched elites to employ coercion against both internal and external challengers. In the context of civil–military relations, the garrison-state construct suggests that both economic and political elites are becoming increasingly dependent on the military as coercion becomes more and more central to how societies resolve the fundamental question of "who shall rule."[15]

From the evidence and arguments presented in the foregoing chapters, the authors must conclude, albeit reluctantly, that the garrison-state hypothesis provides a reasonably accurate image of the development of civil–military relations throughout much of the world. The burgeoning strategic arms race and the accelerating proliferation of the various means to organized violence continue to lend persuasive support to Lasswell's view of coercion as a political currency. World defense expenditures soared from $132 billion in 1962 to some $224 billion in 1972, with no letup yet in sight.[16] Military officers now occupy the highest seats of government in about a third of the world's states. Increasingly they define their rule, not as a stabilizing interregnum to the discordant civilian political processes of their countries, but as an open-ended necessity if national development and order are to be realized. Praetorianism in its various forms is a pervasive aspect of world politics at the outset of the 1970's. Political scientists as well as statesmen can no longer be satisfied merely to lament military intervention and rule as unfortunate retardations of democracy. The crucial question is how military values and the increasing sway of coercion can be reconciled with the consensual aspects of political legitimacy and the demands of human beings in society for the "political goods" of security, welfare, justice, and liberty.[17]

Clearly the technology of modern warfare and its implications for coercion as an augmented means of political control have vastly increased the bargaining power of military elites against other interest groups within their societies. Such is the extent and probable irreversibility of this phenomenon that the traditional distinction between military and civil spheres of authority seems no longer useful, and may even divert attention from questions of more fundamental research and policy significance.[18] The recent political evolution of the Third World suggests that the usurpation of the highest seats of power by military elites may not be viewed as particularly illegitimate, or necessarily more so than rule by corrupt or ineffective civilian politicians. The principle of civilian supremacy is uniquely Western in origin. There exists little evidence to support the assumption that it will flourish elsewhere as the modernization process unfolds.

Yet it is one thing to point out the relative ease with which the military may now seize power in the less developed countries and quite another to suggest that they, by virtue of their modern oganization and presumed dedication to the national interest, will necessarily be more successful than their civilian counterparts in promoting socioeconomic modernization and political development. Control of coercive resources provides a demonstrable advantage in struggles for power but, by itself, it grants no magic formula for effectiveness in governing beyond the mere preservation of order and the status quo. Today even most Third World societies are far too complex for naked coercion to be efficacious as a means of organizing and controlling processes of social change. If military elites aspire to do more than simply reign over stagnant or even politically decaying societies, they must somehow link their control over coercive resources with some principle of popular consent. The disposition and the political skill required to forge this link are rarely found in combination, for to be successful the military modernizer must shake off the contempt for politics that is characteristic of his institutional values in order to organize and channel the energies created by the process of social mobilization.

As these chapters suggest, both the scope and the character of the political role of the military are conditioned by a large number of interacting institutional and environmental variables. Whether or not the armed forces leaders in a particular country will choose to displace a civilian regime under a given set of circumstances is difficult to predict, and the various factors affecting the decision to intervene vary considerably in relative importance from country to country. Increasingly, however, the *outcomes* of military intervention and its implications for socioeconomic modernization and political development conform to a general pattern which might be called the "garrison-managerial state." As military institutions throughout the Third World have become more differentiated and specialized, and as their officer corps have become more professionalized, the performance in office of military politicians has tended to be more bureaucratic than political in motivation and in effect. Military rule focuses primarily on policies that serve the narrow interests of the armed forces, secondarily on the preservation of public order, thirdly on the promotion of stable industrial growth, and lastly (if at all) on policies designed to bring about fundamental social and economic reform.

The convergence of interests between the professional officer and the civilian technocrat is founded on a shared view of the role of government. Politics within this combined managerial elite becomes a matter of contending strategies and techniques in systems analysis and problem solving.

> *The technician sees the nation quite differently from the political man: to the technician, the nation is nothing more than another sphere in which to apply the instruments he has developed. To him, the state is not the expression of the will of the people nor a divine creation nor a creature of class conflict. It is an enterprise providing services that must be made to function* efficiently. *He judges states in terms of their capacity to utilize techniques effectively, not in terms of their relative justice. Political doctrine revolves around what is useful rather than what is good. Purposes drop out of sight and efficiency becomes the central concern. As the political form best suited to the massive and unprincipled use of technique, dictatorship gains in power.* [19]

Even in Latin America the era of the predatory and personalistic military caudillo appears to be drawing to a close. Current military regimes there and elsewhere are dominated overwhelmingly by organization men, relatively colorless administrators working together under varying structural arrangements of collegial decision making. Strong pressures internal to the military discourage the individual officer with ambition, charisma, and political skills. The new military officer deeply distrusts politics and especially abhors demagoguery that threatens to precipitate the mobilization of the masses. He is appalled by disorder, often is rather puritanical, and is committed to the vision of modernizing his country through economic planning and efficient administration. He justifies his interventions into politics by charging the civilian politicians with failure. He decries what he perceives to be the enervating waste of energies and resources resulting from the unregulated clash of special interests in the political arena. Above all, he is determined to preserve and foster his own military institutions as an integral part of his country's future modernization and development.

For the West, the traditional conceptualization of civil–military relations as distinct spheres of authority under civilian political supremacy continues to provide a useful framework for analysis. In the less developed countries, however, the armed forces seldom conform to the role of separate and dependent institutional actor posited by the model. With only a few exceptions, the Third World military is involved in the ongoing political processes of its country. Its control over a preponderance of organized coercive resources makes the military the critical "swing" group in most major policy decisions, especially those relating to the formation and termination of governments. Military intervention in politics is rarely the idealized Western image of military versus civilian, but rather is a matter of the armed forces coalescing with one group of civilians against another. Thus the coup d'etat is commonly the culmination of a military *and* civilian conspiracy, resulting in government by a new military–civilian coalition and generally supporting the interests of the urban middle strata.

Whereas a scant decade ago, politics in the Third World seemed to be becoming the domain of the mass-mobilization single-party state, today most of these movements have given way to bureaucratic rule by a middle-class managerial elite in which the military officer has a central and functional role. Military socialization and officer training, combined with expertise in the manipulation of coercion, are a crucial "ticket of entry" to the new governing elite. In concert with the urban middle classes, the military seeks orderly economic growth within a social order that changes only slowly, insulated as much as possible from new and potentially disruptive political techniques and ideologies.

Throughout most of the world the military appears to be in politics to stay, at least for the foreseeable future. Perhaps the "garrison-managerial state" is a transitory phenomenon, for if the widely accepted notion of "the revolution of rising expectations" is valid, then the military's disdain for political organization and ideology will possibly bring its downfall as pressures for greater mass participation and equality become irrepressible. Much will probably depend on how successfully the new managerial elite can promote steady economic growth. Certainly, as Lasswell suggests, coercion as a political currency has continued to ascend in importance, and the role of the military in politics will occupy the attention of political scientists for some time to come.

References

1. On the extensiveness and functions of civic action, see Edward Bernard Glick, *Peaceful Conflict: The Nonmilitary Use of the Military* (Harrisburg: Stackpole Books, 1967), and Hugh Hanning, *The Peaceful Uses of Military Forces* (New York: Frederick A. Praeger, 1967).

2. See José Nun, "A Latin American Phenomenon: The Middle Class Military Coup," in Institute of International Studies, *Trends in Social Science Research in Latin American Studies: A Conference Report* (Berkeley: University of California Press, 1965), pp. 55–99.

3. See Samuel P. Huntington, *Political Order in Changing Societies* (New Haven: Yale University Press, 1968), pp. 193–194; compare Morris Janowitz, *The Professional Soldier: A Social and Political Portrait* (New York: The Free Press, 1971), pp. 10–11.

4. Huntington, *Political Order in Changing Societies,* pp. 192–193.
5. William H. Brill, *Military Intervention in Bolivia: The Overthrow of Paz Estenssoro and the MNR* (Washington: Institute for the Comparative Study of Political Systems, 1967).
6. Henry Bienen, ed., *The Military and Modernization* (New York: Aldine–Atherton, 1971), pp. 5–7.
7. Ibid., p. 6.
8. Eric A. Nordlinger, "Soldiers in Mufti: The Impact of Military Rule Upon Economic and Social Change in the Non-Western States," *American Political Science Review,* Vol. LXIV, No. 4 (December 1970), p. 1134.
9. Ibid., p. 1138.
10. Ibid., p. 1139.
11. Ibid., p. 1134.
12. Ibid., pp. 1145–1146.
13. See David E. Apter, *The Politics of Modernization* (Chicago: University of Chicago Press, 1965), p. 40.
14. See Katharine Chorley, *Armies and the Art of Revolution* (London: Faber and Faber, 1943), pp. 241–247, 254–260.
15. Harold D. Lasswell, "The Garrison-State Hypothesis Today," in Samuel P. Huntington, ed., *Changing Patterns of Military Politics* (New York: The Free Press, 1962), pp. 51–69.
16. United States Arms Control and Disarmament Agency, *World Military Expenditures, 1971* (Washington: Bureau of Economic Affairs, United States Arms Control and Disarmament Agency, 1972), p. 9.
17. The concept of "political goods" is set forth in J. Roland Pennock, "Political Development, Political Systems, and Political Goods," *World Politics,* Vol. XVIII, No. 3 (April 1965), pp. 413–434.
18. Walter Millis, Harvey Mansfield, and Harold Stein, *Arms and the State* (New York: Twentieth Century Fund, 1958), p. 5.
19. Robert K. Merton, in his foreword to Jacques Ellul, *The Technological Society* (New York: Alfred A. Knopf, 1964), p. vii.

Annotated Bibliography

General Works

Abrahamsson, Bengt. *Military Professionalization and Political Power*. Beverly Hills: Sage, 1972. A theoretically provocative and empirically wide-ranging sociological study, *Military Professionalization and Political Power* attacks the belief that professionalism enhances civilian control. Abrahamsson shows that the power potential of the armed forces has grown considerably in the twentieth century, even though coups are rare in developed countries. He concludes that civilian control must attempt to restrict military autonomy.

Andreski, Stanislav. *Military Organization and Society*. Berkeley: University of California Press, 1968. This comparative sociological study of the influence of military organization on society focuses on the role of organized violence and the phenomenon of war. Andreski offers a fascinating analysis of militarism and "militocracy"—the phenomenon of military preponderance over civil officials and undifferentiated spheres of civil and military authority. The author's thoughts on the future should be compared with Harold D. Lasswell's "garrison-state" hypothesis.

Bienen, Henry (ed.). *The Military Intervenes: Case Studies in Political Development*. New York: Russell Sage Foundation, 1968. These geographically diverse case studies (Ethiopia, Korea, Turkey, Argentina, and Tropical Africa) were selected to challenge the notion that military elites are likely to be effective nation builders. Bienen doubts that the armed forces will be either a modernizing or a stabilizing agent in the developing countries.

Feit, Edward. *The Armed Bureaucrats: Military–Administrative Regimes and*

265

Political Development. Boston: Houghton Mifflin, 1973. Feit's emphasis is on coups d'etat in "segmented societies." According to Feit, military regimes pass through a cycle of seizing control, drawing on "apolitical" civilian bureaucrats, seeking a mass basis for legitimacy, and losing the cohesion necessary for governance. This provocative, abbreviated thesis is followed by case studies of Spain, Argentina, Pakistan, Burma, Greece, and Egypt.

Finer, S.E. *The Man on Horseback: The Role of the Military in Politics.* New York: Praeger, 1962. A profound and wide-ranging examination of military intervention, this work challenges the view that military professionalization and differentiated spheres of civil and military authority will lead to depoliticization of the armed forces. Finer offers a highly useful analysis of the circumstances, both internal and environmental to the military, that tend to lead to military overthrows of civilian government.

Huntington, Samuel P. (ed.). *Changing Patterns of Military Politics.* New York: The Free Press of Glencoe, 1962. This book contains a collection of essays dealing with the role of violence in international politics and patterns of civil–military relations, with emphasis on modern industrialized states. The editor suggests that the "distinction between intergovernmental and domestic wars may fade, with violence becoming more pervasive, more dispersed, and less within the control of governments." However, Huntington concludes on a more hopeful note by asserting that new forms of violence may well be the precursors of a new and more stable world political order.

Huntington, Samuel P. *Political Order in Changing Societies.* New Haven: Yale University Press, 1968. Huntington's thesis is that the pervasive violence and instability of world politics is the result of "rapid social change and the rapid mobilization of new groups into politics coupled with the slow development of political institutions." The armed forces are seen as promoters of socioeconomic modernization, but are generally ineffective as builders of stable political institutions. The author concludes that stability and order require Leninist-type political parties to stem further "political decay" in the less developed countries of Asia, Africa, and Latin America.

Huntington, Samuel P. *The Soldier and the State: The Theory and Politics of Civil–Military Relations.* New York: Vintage Books, 1957. In this work, Huntington presents a basic theory of civil–military relations as one aspect of national security policy. Huntington argues that military institutions are shaped by (1) external threats to the security of the society and (2) the complex of social forces, ideologies, and political institutions dominant within the society. A controversial element is the argument that military professionalization leads to (or is synonymous with) an apolitical role for the military.

Janowitz, Morris. *The Military in the Political Development of New Nations: An Essay*

in Comparative Analysis. Chicago: University of Chicago Press, 1964.
Janowitz has written a comparative analysis of civil–military relations in
the new states of Africa, Asia, and the Middle East, focusing on the
impact of technological changes and of the army's internal organizational
characteristics on the military's political role. Janowitz argues that social
and economic modernization is the overriding popular goal in these regions
and that the armed forces can contribute to this process. However, the
military's effectiveness is likely to be limited by its incapacity to develop
or to permit the development of a mass political base.

Janowitz, Morris. *The Professional Soldier: A Social and Political Portrait.* New York:
The Free Press, 1971. This is a revision and updating of Janowitz's basic
sociological study of the military profession. *The Professional Soldier*
is an indispensable source for the study of civil–military relations. Particularly useful are the discussions of military socialization and the effects of
technological changes on the profession of arms. Janowitz argues that the
use of force in international relations is in the process of being altered,
leading to the development of a "constabulary concept" with special
problems for controlling the career frustrations of the military officer.

Johnson, John J. (ed.). *The Role of the Military in Underdeveloped Countries.* Princeton: Princeton University Press, 1962. This collection of theoretical
essays and country studies deals with the emerging central role of the
armed forces in Asia, Africa, Latin America, and the Middle East. Now
somewhat dated, the volume remains a useful basic anthology.

Luckham, A.R. "A Comparative Typology of Civil–Military Relations." *Government
and Opposition* VI, 1, Winter 1971, 5–35. Luckham's typology of military political roles focuses on three summary variables: the strength or
weakness of civilian institutions, the strength or weakness of the military,
and the nature of the boundaries between the military establishment and
its sociopolitical environment. The author argues that a theory of civil–
military relations should account for both the organizational characteristics of the military and the influence of its social and political environment.

Luttwak, Edward. *Coup d'Etat: A Practical Handbook.* Greenwich: Fawcett, 1969.
A fascinating discussion of the mechanics of coups d'etat, this work details the prerequisites, dangers, and pitfalls of military conspiracy for
aspiring promoters of coups.

Nordlinger, Eric A. "Soldiers in Mufti: The Impact of Military Rule Upon Economic
and Social Change in the Non-Western States." *American Political Science
Review* LXIV, 4, December 1970, 1131–1148. Nordlinger has written
an interesting study of the policy consequences of military rule in the less
developed countries. He concludes that officer politicians are uninterested
in fundamental social change, and often employ their coercive resources
against those social groups or strata who actively press for social reforms.

van Doorn, Jacques (ed.). *Armed Forces and Society: Sociological Essays.* The Hague:

Mouton, 1968. This is a diverse collection of essays dealing with military professionalism, the armed forces and societal change in Western Europe, the role of the military in developing countries, and the future of international peace-keeping forces.

van Doorn, Jacques (ed.). *Military Profession and Military Regimes: Commitments and Conflicts.* The Hague: Mouton, 1969. Van Doorn has assembled a wide-ranging anthology of contributions covering the role of the military in some twenty countries representing all major regions of the world. The emphasis is on problems in the political control of the military.

Europe and North America

Ambler, John Steward. *Soldiers Against the State: The French Army in Politics.* Garden City: Doubleday, 1968. Guerrilla warfare in Indochina and Algeria pressed the French army toward a conception of "revolutionary warfare" that (given a vacuum of civilian leadership) resulted in greatly enhanced political activism among the military. Ambler asserts that professionalism can help to ensure civilian control only if coupled with both attention to the military's corporate interests and clear political directives.

Chorley, Katharine. *Armies and the Art of Revolution.* London: Faber and Faber, 1943. Can political revolution occur in a modern state with a highly trained army? Only if the control of the officer corps is broken, through the solvent of unsuccessful, large-scale war, Chorley asserts. Following the seizure of power, the leaders of political revolution must rebuild the armed forces in accord with revolutionary ideals.

Craig, Gordon A. *The Politics of the Prussian Army: 1640–1945.* New York: Oxford University Press, 1955. Prussia took the lead in developing a professional officer corps during the period of the Napoleonic wars. During the nineteenth century the Prussian officer corps was opened to all on the basis of education, discipline, and professional competence. Craig traces the antecedents and ramifications of military professionalism in Germany, with useful analyses of the Bismarckian era and the period between the two World Wars.

Giradet, Raoul. *La société militaire dans la France contemporaine: 1815–1939.* Paris: Plon, 1953. The outstanding analyst of the French army, Giradet sees the installation of the Vichy regime and Gaullist appeal as signaling the collapse of political subordination. Giradet concludes with this question: "How could one invoke the imperative of submission to legal authority when two or sometimes three governments simultaneously demanded the exclusive privilege of legitimacy?"

Howard, Michael (ed.). *Soldiers and Governments: Nine Studies in Civil–Military Relations.* Bloomington: Indiana University Press, 1959. The emphasis in this collection of essays is on civil–military relations in Europe, the

United States, and Japan. Howard argues that "in States where no orderly tradition of power and obedience has yet been established—or those where it has been destroyed—military force is the final and sometimes the only arbiter in government."

Kolkowicz, Roman. *The Soviet Military and the Communist Party*. Princeton: Princeton University Press, 1967. Kolkowicz focuses on the tension between military coercive strength and the totalitarian imperative of party control in the Soviet Union. He concludes that the impact of new technology in the art of warfare has increased the need for military professionals in the Soviet system and thus heightened the dependence of the party on the military experts.

Payne, Stanley G. *Politics and the Military in Modern Spain*. Stanford: Stanford University Press, 1967. Payne argues that the prolonged dictatorship of General Franco has led to a general reversion of the army to greater professionalization and apoliticization, paralleling the apolitical trend of Spanish society as a whole. The absence of strong and legitimate political institutions has made it virtually unavoidable that Spain, like much of Latin America, has fallen victim to the dominance of organized force.

Preston, Adrian. "The Profession of Arms in Postwar Canada, 1945–1970: Political Authority as a Military Problem." *World Politics* XXIII, 2, January 1971, 189–214. Preston has analyzed the interrelationships among political institutions, defense policy, and military professionalism in Canada. He is concerned by a twofold problem of social organization: "how, on the one hand, to develop armed forces necessary to external security without corroding internal liberties and how, on the other, to promote political economy and welfare without prejudice to the armed forces upon whose efficiency and valor that social order and prosperity ultimately rests."

Ralston, David B. *The Army of the Republic: The Place of the Military in the Political Evolution of France, 1871–1914*. Cambridge: M.I.T. Press, 1967. This is a detailed analysis of the period when French officers made obedience to civilian authority a pure and simple principle—based, in part, on the military's maintaining a sphere of unique responsibility.

Yarmolinsky, Adam. *The Military Establishment: Its Impacts on American Society*. New York: Harper & Row, 1971. Emerging out of concern for the growing influence of the "military–industrial complex" in the United States, this book investigates the intrusions of the military establishment in many nonmilitary areas of American society. Yarmolinsky writes partly out of personal outrage over the Vietnam war, and is especially concerned by what he perceives to be the ideological education of the American public through an extensive military public relations network. The author argues that the armed forces threaten the effectiveness of countervailing civilian groups to the point where the United States is in danger of becoming a militarized society.

Africa

Feit, Edward. "Military Coups and Political Development: Some Lessons from Ghana and Nigeria." *World Politics* XX, 2, 1968, 179-193. Feit asserts that although African officers possess several advantages in reconstructing an "administrative–traditional order," they make poor governors. He feels that the only meaningful political institutions in Africa are traditional ethnic groups and colonial bureaucracies; to avoid fragmentation, military governments must create strong central systems.

Feit, Edward. "The Rule of the 'Iron Surgeons': Military Government in Spain and Ghana." *Comparative Politics* I, 4, 1969, 485-497. According to Feit, officers must seek allies within the civilian bureaucracy. Despite claims to the contrary, military regimes cannot regenerate their societies. The regimes "break apart at the seams" because of lack of consensus, and confront strong pressures to leave.

First, Ruth. *The Barrel of a Gun: Political Power in Africa and the Coup d'Etat.* London: Allen Lane, The Penguin Press, 1970. A political exile from South Africa, First sees military intervention as the product of the "frailty of the power system," in which civilians have failed both to alter hierarchical styles of decision making and to develop a coherent ideology of development. Her case studies of Ghana, Nigeria, and the Sudan are filled with fascinating details and allegations of external involvement. She denies that most military-based governments can undertake radical modernization.

Lee, J.M. *African Armies and Civil Order.* New York: Praeger, 1969. In the absence of "civil order," which Lee defines as similar to Finer's "mature political culture," the armed forces will arrive at their own definitions of political legitimacy. Lee agrees with Feit and First that military regimes revert to the authoritarian, bureaucratic practices of the former colonial regimes. This is an excellent comparative study, though written in an occasionally obscure style.

Lofchie, Michael F. "The Uganda Coup—Class Action by the Military." *The Journal of Modern African Studies* X, 1, 1972, 19-35. Lofchie views the Uganda army as a type of economic class, protecting personal and institutional interests against equalizing policies pursued by an eventually deposed civilian government. Institutional weaknesses eased intervention, but the underlying cause of the coup remained corporate privilege.

Luckham, Robin. *The Nigerian Military: A Sociological Analysis of Authority and Revolt 1960-67.* Cambridge: Cambridge University Press, 1971. Luckham uses sociological data concerning the officer corps and its norms more sensitively than any other analyst of military intervention in tropical Africa. Despite the acute stresses of the 1966 coups, the strength of peer group cohesion, military norms, and organizational identities remained high. The interaction of these factors with political cleavages made it practically impossible for officers to adjust to political conflict once they became involved.

Miners, N.J. *The Nigerian Army 1956–1966.* London: Methuen, 1971. Under the British colonial government, the Nigerian army came close, according to Miners, to acting as a "passive instrument" free of political ambitions. Military loyalty could not be maintained after independence, despite higher pay and rapid Africanization of the officer corps; many political disputes spilled over into the military. Miners has written a concise, well-informed study, though it lacks the theoretical sophistication of Luckham's.

Price, Robert M. "A Theoretical Approach to Military Rule in New States: Reference-Group Theory and the Ghanaian Case." *World Politics* XXIII, 3, 1971, 399–430. The emulation of external models results in officers who are "non-nationalistic" and "non-puritanical," unable to mobilize popular sentiment around collective goals. Price's ideas, though controversial and based on suspect sources (the published apologias of officers who intervened successfully), merit examination in other settings.

Welch, Claude E., Jr. (ed). *Soldier and State in Africa: A Comparative Analysis of Military Intervention and Political Change.* Evanston: Northwestern University Press, 1970. A lengthy introductory chapter suggests that military intervention can be attributed to multiple economic, political, and social causes; it also asserts that intramilitary variables (with the exception of heightened awareness within the armed forces of their ability to displace civilian leaders) have little significance in seizures of control. Case studies of Algeria, Dahomey, Ghana, Upper Volta, and Zaire suggest the ease with which intervention can occur, and the difficulty with which the military returns to the barracks.

Zolberg, Aristide R. "The Structure of Political Conflict in the New States of Tropical Africa." *The American Political Science Review* LXII, 1, 1968, 70–87. Coups d'etat have become institutionalized in sub-Saharan states, with "conflict and disorder" the most prominent features of their political settings. Zolberg, like Welch, discounts intramilitary factors, focusing rather upon (1) growing gaps between aspirations for change and governments' capacities, and (2) an escalation of demands and politicization of ethnic ties that result in the widespread use of force.

Asia

Cohen, Stephen P. *The Indian Army: Its Contribution to the Development of a Nation.* Berkeley: University of California Press, 1971. This analysis is mostly historical in its outlook, with only one of its seven chapters devoted to civil–military relations since independence. The political role of the armed forces has been limited, Cohen asserts, by an alliance between politicians and civil servants.

Joffe, Ellis. *Party and Army: Professionalism and Political Control in the Chinese Officer Corps, 1949-1964.* Cambridge: Harvard University East Asian Monographs, No. 19, 1965. Joffe has written a detailed analysis of the "red versus expert" controversy as it affected the roles and expectations of officers. Professional officers developed views that brought them into conflict with the Chinese Communist Party over such issues as mechanization, centralization, and the nature of party control.

Kim, C.I. Eugene. "The Military in the Politics of South Korea: Creating Political Order," in Morris Janowitz and Jacques van Doorn, eds., *On Military Intervention.* Rotterdam: Rotterdam University Press, 1971, 361-386. The military government under General (later President) Park Chung-hee has been uniquely marked by a close alliance between military revolutionaries and leading intellectuals, and by an emphasis on building a political party. However, Kim deems the results "highly sophisticated instruments for control but no bold democratic experiments."

Moore, Raymond A. "The Army as a Vehicle for Social Change in Pakistan." *The Journal of Developing Areas* II, 1, 1967, 57-74. The Pakistani military participates significantly in modernization, Moore comments, because of its social prestige, skilled manpower, and cohesiveness—all factors that should be re-examined in light of the India–Pakistan war that resulted in the independence of Bangladesh.

Paget, Roger K. "The Military in Indonesian Politics: The Burden of Power." *Pacific Affairs* XL, 3 & 4, 1967, 294-314. The economic reforms carried out by the post-1965 military government have resulted in increased political domination by the military. According to Paget, the armed forces "by providing essential services of government fell into the habit of governing."

Rudolph, Lloyd I., and Rudolph, Susanne Hoeber. "Generals and Politicians in India." *Pacific Affairs* XXXVII, 1, 1964, 5-19. The armed forces of India, unlike those of Pakistan, have enjoyed relatively low prestige. Civilian control in India results from the strength of parliamentary and party traditions; the Rudolphs conclude that military rule "is more the result of civilian political failure than of the political ambition of military men."

Sohn, Jae Souk. "Political Dominance and Political Failure: The Role of the Military in the Republic of Korea," in Henry Bienen, ed., *The Military Intervenes: Case Studies in Political Development.* New York: Russell Sage Foundation, 1968, 103-121. Unlike Kim, Sohn gives scant attention to party organization by the military. The high costs of the 600,000-man army and the military's inadequate understanding of political and economic issues suggest that soldiers are not agents of modernization.

Wilson, David A. *Politics in Thailand.* Ithaca: Cornell University Press, 1962. Thai politics is limited to a closed bureaucratic system dominated by the military. Self-restraint of the military appears to be declining, with a corresponding upsurge of corruption and factionalism. Military rule is facilitated by the acquiescence of the king of Thailand, but political development probably depends on the growth of extragovernmental power centers.

Latin America

Barber, Willard F., and Ronning, C. Neale. *Internal Security and Military Power: Counterinsurgency and Civic Action in Latin America.* Columbus: Ohio State University Press, 1966. The United States, through its military aid programs and encouragement of military civic action under the Alliance for Progress, has strengthened the armed forces in Latin America. The effects of these programs may well be to stimulate rather than discourage military involvement in politics.

Brill, William H. *Military Intervention in Bolivia: The Overthrow of Paz Estenssoro and the MNR.* Washington: Institute for the Comparative Study of Political Systems, 1967. Almost decimated as a result of the Bolivian Revolution of 1952, the army gradually regained its strength and finally reasserted its political dominance in the coup of 1964. The military's resurgence was made possible by the failure of the MNR leadership to establish viable civilian institutions. Brill concludes that military internal factors were of secondary importance in promoting the coup.

Germani, Gino, and Silvert, Kalman. "Politics, Social Structure and Military Intervention in Latin America." *European Journal of Sociology* II, 1961, 62–81. A typology of the social structure of the Latin American political systems is used to explicate a variety of roles for the armed forces in politics. The presence of a self-identifying middle class, political and cultural participation levels, and the character of the economic system are seen as important environmental variables. The social origins of the officer corps and the role of the military as an avenue of social mobility are also considered significant indicators of military political behavior.

Imaz, Jose Luis de. *Los que mandan.* Buenos Aires: Editorial Universitaria de Buenos Aires, 1964. A systematic analysis of Argentina's ruling elite, *Los que mandan* is the best available treatment of military (and civilian) elite backgrounds by a Latin American social scientist. Imaz presents statistical data to show that military officers are drawn primarily from the families of military fathers, white-collar workers, and professional men.

Johnson, John J. *The Military and Society in Latin America.* Stanford: Stanford University Press, 1964. Johnson concludes that the military in Latin America is undergoing a social, economic, and political transformation that will lead to a divergence of interests away from conservative social forces. The army is likely to become the key institution in the promotion of modernization, especially in the critical rural areas of unrest. Johnson sees the growth of new civilian middle strata as the primary restraint against old-style Latin militarism, and ultimately as the basis of strong democratic institutions.

Lieuwen, Edwin. *Arms and Politics in Latin America.* New York: Praeger, 1960. Perceiving a trend away from Latin America's militaristic era, Lieuwen analyzes various factors—particularly internal professionalization and environmental socioeconomic changes—to support his conclusion that the region is moving toward civilian government. Lieuwen argues that the United States should assist this process by withholding economic and military aid from military dictatorships.

Lieuwen, Edwin. *Generals Vs. Presidents: Neo-Militarism in Latin America.* New York: Praeger, 1964. The secular trend toward civilian rule perceived earlier by Lieuwen is now seen to be reversed, and a new wave of military dictatorships is sweeping Latin America. A principal cause is the Cuban Revolution of 1959, which has prompted a new alliance between the armed forces and conservative groups. Lieuwen argues that the resurgence of militarism is "the greatest single impediment to democratic progress in Latin America today," and that the armed forces have become a serious obstacle to evolutionary social reform.

McAlister, Lyle M., et al., *The Military in Latin American Sociopolitical Evolution: Four Case Studies.* Washington: Center for Research in Social Systems, 1970. This work contains systematic analyses of civil–military relations in Peru, Argentina, Colombia, and Mexico—employing a combination of institutional (internal) and environmental factors to explain the political roles of these armed forces. Among its best features are the excellent discussions of the *estado militar,* officer recruitment and socialization, the military mission, and other institutional variables. The authors conclude that the political roles of the armed forces in these four countries are best understood in terms of the unique historical experiences of each.

Needler, Martin C. "Political Development and Military Intervention in Latin America." *American Political Science Review* LX, 3, September 1966, 616–626. Needler finds that military overthrows of governments in Latin America (1) are more likely when national economic conditions are deteriorating; (2) increasingly occur around the time of presidential elections and are accompanied by violence; and (3) result in a junta in which the senior officers are more likely than junior officers to try to restore constitutional forms. Pointing out that the pre-coup balance within the officer corps is often delicate, Needler argues that United States opposition can be a significant deterrent to military intervention in the region.

Nun, José "A Latin American Phenomenon: The Middle-Class Military Coup," in *Trends in Social Science Research in Latin American Studies: A Conference Report.* Berkeley: Institute of International Studies, University of California, 1965, 55–99. Nun challenges the prevailing assumption that the growth of the middle strata in Latin America will lead to a diminished political role for the military. These strata remain politically fragmented and insecure in the face of mass demands for broadened political participation and a more equitable distribution of wealth. The armed forces, acting on behalf of the middle classes, intervene to prevent a "premature democratization" of the political process.

Putnam, Robert D. "Toward Explaining Military Intervention in Latin American Politics." *World Politics* XX, 1, October 1967, 83–110. Using correlational analysis, Putnam argues that traditions of militarism are an important cause of military intervention; that social mobilization tends to increase the viability of civilian rule; and that "contagion" theories of military intervention do not seem valid.

Stepan, Alfred. *The Military in Politics: Changing Patterns in Brazil.* Princeton: Princeton University Press, 1971. Stepan's work is a systematic and highly useful analysis of the changing political role of the Brazilian military. Stepan argues that class analysis is of doubtful value to understanding the military's role. The armed forces constitute an institutional elite capable of opposing both middle- and upper-class interests if these are perceived to conflict with the vital interests of the military. The discussion of intramilitary politics, especially in terms of the conflicting demands of maintaining institutional solidarity while also governing the country, is excellent.

Villanueva, Victor. *¿Nueva mentalidad militar en el Perú?* Lima: Mejía Baca, 1969. The most prolific and best-informed author on the Peruvian military (*El militarismo en el Perú,* 1962; *Golpe en el Perú,* 1969), Villanueva expresses skepticism regarding the modernizing capabilities of the armed forces. His analysis of changing military attitudes and of the role of development studies at Peru's *Centro de Altos Estudios Militares* is especially useful.

Middle East

Be'eri, Eliezer. *Army Officers in Arab Politics and Society.* New York: Praeger, 1970. Be'eri, a former Israeli intelligence officer, presents by far the most detailed picture of Arab officers, particularly their social origins. His comparisons between Ataturk and Nasser illuminate the obstacles confronting the would-be modernizer, given the pluralistic nature of the Middle East.

Dekmejian, R. Hrair. *Egypt Under Nasir: A Study in Political Dynamics.* Albany: State University of New York Press, 1971. Charismatic authority provides the theoretical focus of this detailed examination of Nasser's rule. Crises such as the 1967 war result in enhanced military involvement in policy making; however, the creation in 1961 of the Arab Socialist Union may provide an alternative path to political influence.

Halpern, Manfred. *The Politics of Social Change in the Middle East and North Africa.* Princeton: Princeton University Press, 1963. Highly enthusiastic about the political role of the armed forces, Halpern calls the military "the instrument of the new middle class," serving as "the vanguard of national-ism and social reform." His book should be read in conjunction with the more critical observations of Be'eri.

Hurewitz, J.C. *Middle East Politics: The Military Dimension*. New York: Praeger, 1969. Largely a recounting of recent political history of 19 states (grouped into military republics, military–civilian coalitions, traditional monarchies, modernizing monarchies, and nonmilitary republics), this book is actually more descriptive than analytical or comparative.

Lerner, Daniel, and Robinson, Richard D. "Swords and Ploughshares: The Turkish Army as a Modernizing Force." *World Politics* XIII, 1, 1960, 19–44. An early example of the "military as effective modernizers" school of thought, this article praises Ataturk's support for the "mystique of civilian suprem-acy"—a mystique ruptured by a coup shortly before the essay's publication. Lerner and Robinson attribute the coup to failures of civilian leaders.

Ozbudun, Ergun. "The Role of the Military in Recent Turkish Politics." Cambridge: Center for International Affairs, Occasional Papers No. 14, 1966. According to Ozbudun, the 1960 coup resulted not from an explosion of political participation, nor from the supposed greater modernization of the armed forces; rather, it stemmed from the increasingly authori-tarian and conservative policies of the Menderes government. Military radicals pressed for intervention, but military moderates succeeded in restoring civilian rule.

Perlmutter, Amos. "The Arab Military Elite." *World Politics* XXII, 2, 1970, 269–300. This review article suggests that coup makers in the Arab world aim primarily at making the government strong and effective. "As a ruling class," Perlmutter asserts, officers "advocate the restoration of power, not the fulfillment of class ideologies and interests"—a rebuttal to the views of Be'eri and Halpern.

Perlmutter, Amos. *Military and Politics in Israel: Nation-Building and Role Expan-sion*. New York: Praeger, 1969. This is a highly detailed analysis of Israel's success in establishing and maintaining civilian control over the armed forces in the face of both external threats and a significant ex-pansion of the military's responsibilities.

Vatikiotis, P.J. *The Egyptian Army in Politics: Pattern for New Nations?* Blooming-ton: Indiana University Press, 1961. Published prior to the collapse of the United Arab Republic, Vatikiotis' book illuminates Nasser's diffi-culties in building responsive, mass-based parties. Generally speaking, Vatikiotis sees the Egyptian army playing a constructive role in trans-forming an agrarian society into an industrialized society; political and social conditions preclude more democratic forms of government.

Appendix

World Military Expenditures and Manpower

Country	Gross National Product (Million $)	Population (Millions)	GNP/ capita ($)	Military Expenditures (Million $)	Military Expenditures as % of GNP (%)	Total Active Armed Forces (Thousands)	Armed Forces as % of Population (%)	Military Expenditures per man ($)
North America								
United States	974,100	205.3	4,758	77,827	8.0	3,066	1.5	25,384
Canada	84,700	21.4	3,651	1,906	2.2	93	0.4	20,495
Europe (NATO)								
Belgium	25,700	9.7	2,649	697	2.7	95	1.0	7,337
Denmark	15,600	5.0	3,120	368	2.4	45	0.9	8,178
France	147,500	50.8	2,904	5,977	4.0	506	1.0	11,812
Germany (West)	183,300	61.6	3,019	6,167	3.3	484*	0.8	12,742
Greece	9,500	8.9	1,067	474	5.0	159	1.8	2,981
Iceland	500	0.2	2,500	—	—	—	—	—
Italy	93,200	53.6	1,739	2,499	2.7	413	0.8	6,051
Luxembourg	1,000	0.3	3,333	8	0.8	1	0.3	8,000
Netherlands	31,200	13.0	2,400	1,096	3.5	121	0.9	9,058
Norway	13,400	3.9	3,436	388	3.0	41	1.1	9,463
Portugal	6,200	9.7	639	435	7.0	185	1.9	2,351
Turkey	9,000	35.3	255	416	4.6	477	1.4	872
United Kingdom	121,000	55.8	2,168	5,865	4.8	390	0.7	15,038
Europe (Warsaw Pact)								
Bulgaria	9,800	8.5	1,153	310	3.2	166	2.0	1,867
Czechoslovakia	30,500	14.5	2,103	1,660	5.4	203	1.4	8,177
Germany (East)	32,300	17.1	1,889	2,200	6.8	202	1.2	10,891
Hungary	14,300	10.3	1,388	560	3.9	137	1.3	4,088
Poland	39,400	32.5	1,212	2,250	5.7	287	0.9	7,840
Rumania	22,300	20.3	1,099	610	2.7	231	1.1	2,641
Soviet Union	497,000	242.5	2,047	65,000	6-10†	3,535	1.4	17,878

Other European

Albania	800	2.2	364	95	11.9	54*	2.6	1,759
Austria	14,300	7.4	1,932	165	1.2	50	0.7	3,300
Finland	10,200	4.7	2,170	140§§	1.4	43*	0.9	3,256
Ireland	4,100	2.9	1,414	36§§	0.9	10	0.3	3,600
Spain	32,300	33.3	970	1,165	3.6	281	0.8	4,146
Sweden	32,600	8.1	4,025	1,129	3.5	82	1.0	13,768
Switzerland	20,500	6.3	3,254	422	2.0	28	0.4	15,071
Yugoslavia	19,000	20.5	927	667	3.5	257*	1.2	2,595

Latin America

Argentina	23,830	24.1	510	514	2.2	144*	0.6	3,569
Bolivia	976	4.7	989	19	1.9	17	0.4	1,118
Brazil	35,440	95.2	208	1,017	2.9	225*	0.2	4,520
Chile	6,670	9.3	372	169	2.5	64	0.7	2,609
Colombia	7,070	21.1	717	97	1.4	55*	0.3	1,764
Costa Rica	904	1.7	532	—	—	—	—	—
Cuba	5,200	8.5	612	290	5.6	200*	2.4	1,450
Dominican Rep.	1,500§§	4.2	357	30	2.0	19	0.4	1,579
Ecuador	1,800§§	6.1	295	26	1.4	17	0.3	1,529
El Salvador	997	3.4	293	11	1.1	6	0.2	1,833
Guatemala	1,786	5.3	337	29	1.6	9	0.2	3,222
Guyana	250§§	0.8	313	3	1.2	1	0.1	3,000
Haiti	360§§	4.9	73	7	1.9	5	0.1	1,400
Honduras	685	2.7	254	7	1.0	5	0.2	1,400
Jamaica	1,156	2.0	578	6	0.5	2	0.1	3,000
Mexico	33,000§§	50.7	651	224	0.7	71	0.1	3,155
Nicaragua	772	1.9	406	12	1.6	6	0.3	2,000
Panama	1,016	1.4	726	2	0.2	0	—	—
Paraguay	600§§	2.4	250	11	1.8	13	0.5	846
Peru	4,800§§	13.6	353	196	4.1	50	0.4	3,920
Trinidad/Tobago	850§§	1.1	773	15	1.8	1	0.1	15,000
Uruguay	2,145	2.9	740	44	2.1	16	0.6	2,750
Venezuela	10,300	10.4	990	204	2.0	31*	0.3	6,581

World Military Expenditures and Manpower (continued)

Country	Gross National Product (Million $)	Population (Millions)	GNP/capita ($)	Military Expenditures (Million $)	Military Expenditures as % of GNP (%)	Total Active Armed Forces (Thousands)	Armed Forces as % of Population (%)	Military Expenditures per man ($)
Far East								
Burma	2,080	27.6	75	120	5.8	143	0.5	839
Cambodia	760	6.9	110	126	16.6	124	1.8	1,016
China	120,000	836.0	144	10,000	8.3‡	3,100*	0.4	3,226
Taiwan	5,460	14.6	374	483	8.8	522	3.6	925
Indonesia	7,600	119.6	64	238	3.1	375*	0.3	635
Japan	197,180	103.4	1,907	1,522	0.8	250	0.2	6,083
Korea (North)	4,500	14.2	317	700	15.6‡	438*	3.1	1,598
Korea (Rep. of)	8,213	31.8	258	337	4.1	645	2.0	522
Laos	216	3.0	72	39	18.1	98	3.3	398
Malaysia	3,837	10.9	352	190	5.0	57	0.5	3,333
Mongolia	740	1.3	569	25	3.4‡	33*	2.5	758
Philippines	10,230	38.4	266	124	1.2	55*	0.1	2,255
Thailand	6,510	37.5	174	235	3.6	175	0.5	1,343
Vietnam (North)	1,500	20.1	75	300	20.0‡	452*	2.2	664
Vietnam (South)	3,200	18.3	175	1,087	34.0	100*	5.5	1,087
South Asia								
Afghanistan	1,500	16.9	89	15	1.0	70	0.4	229
Ceylon	2,117	12.5	169	16	0.8	10	0.1	1,600
India	52,920	553.8	96	1,788	3.4	1,200*	0.2	1,482
Nepal	885	11.1	80	5	0.6	15	0.1	333
Pakistan	17,500§	130.2	134	652	3.7	340	0.3	1,918
Near East								
Cyprus	540	0.6	900	8	1.5	1	0.2	8,000
Egypt	6,580	33.3	198	915	9.0	300*	0.9	3,050

Iran	10,180	28.7	355	833	8.2	238*	0.8	3,500
Iraq	2,693	9.7	278	297	11.0	98*	1.0	3,031
Israel	5,500§	2.9	1,897	1,382	25.1	85*	2.9	16,259
Jordan	575	2.3	250	118	20.5	60	2.6	1,967
Kuwait	2,750	0.7	3,929	73	2.7	7	1.0	10,429
Lebanon	1,525	2.9	526	52	3.4	14	0.5	3,714
Saudi Arabia	3,140	5.4	581	417	13.3	60*	1.1	6,950
Syria	1,590	6.1	261	220	13.8	70*	1.1	3,143
Yemen	600§	5.0	120	15§	2.5§	9	0.2	1,667
Africa								
Algeria	4,180	13.8	303	99	2.4	57	0.4	1,737
Cameroon	990	5.8	171	19	1.9	5*	0.1	3,800
Central African Rep.	200	1.5	133	6§§	3.0	1	–	6,000
Chad	259	3.6	72	8§§	3.1	1	–	8,000
Congo (Brazzaville)	233	0.9	259	6§§	2.6	2	–	3,000
Dahomey	235	2.5	94	4	1.7	2	–	2,000
Ethiopia	1,738	25.3	69	41	2.4	45	0.2	911
Gabon	309	0.5	618	3§§	1.0	1	–	3,000
Ghana	2,239	9.0	249	49	2.2	15	0.2	3,267
Guinea	315	3.9	81	15§§	4.8	5	0.1	3,000
Ivory Coast	1,424	4.2	339	20	1.4	4	0.1	5,000
Kenya	1,582	11.2	141	19	1.2	5	0.04	3,800
Liberia	352	1.5	235	3	0.9	4	0.3	750
Libya	3,140	1.9	1,653	45	1.4	15	0.8	3,000
Malagasy Rep.	878	7.3	120	12	1.4	4	0.05	3,000
Malawi	319	4.5	71	1	0.3	1	–	1,000
Mali	510	5.1	100	5	1.0	4	0.07	1,250
Mauritania	180	1.2	150	8§§	4.4	1	–	8,000
Morocco	3,341	15.9	210	9	2.8	60*	0.4	1,567
Niger	315	4.0	79	4	1.3	1	0.03	4,000
Nigeria	5,800	55.1	105	140§§	2.4	220	0.4	636
Rhodesia	1,427	5.3	269	25§§	1.8	5	0.1	5,000
Senegal	700	3.9	179	17	2.4	5	0.1	3,400
Sierra Leone	425	2.7	157	3	0.7	2	0.07	1,500
Somali Rep.	181	2.8	65	9§§	5.0	8	0.3	1,125

World Military Expenditures and Manpower (continued)

Country	Gross National Product (Million $)	Population (Millions)	GNP/ capita ($)	Military Expenditures (Million $)	Military Expenditures as % of GNP (%)	Total Active Armed Forces (Thousands)	Armed Forces as % of Population (%)	Military Expenditures per man ($)
South Africa	16,690	20.1	830	360	2.2	40	0.2	9,000
Sudan	1,890	15.8	120	116	6.1	28	0.2	4,143
Tanzania	1,332	13.3	100	17	1.3	10	0.08	1,700
Togo	267	1.9	141	3	1.1	1	0.05	3,000
Tunisia	1,225	5.2	236	23	1.9	26*	0.5	885
Uganda	1,297	9.7	134	19	1.5	6	0.06	3,167
Upper Volta	305	5.1	60	4	1.3	2	0.04	2,000
Zaire	1,947	17.8	109	60	3.1	38	0.2	1,579
Zambia	1,682	4.2	400	20	1.2	5	0.1	4,000
Oceania								
Australia	32,990	12.5	2,639	1,329	4.0	85	0.7	15,635
New Zealand	5,330	2.8	1,903	105§	2.0	13	0.5	8,077

Notes: *Includes paramilitary as well as military forces.
†Estimated range.
‡Since either or both military expenditures and GNP estimates are approximations, the resulting ratio should be viewed with particular caution.
§Rough estimate of the U.S. Arms Control and Disarmament Agency.

Source: United States Arms Control and Disarmament Agency, *World Military Expenditures 1971* (Washington: Bureau of Economic Affairs, U.S. Arms Control and Disarmament Agency, 1972), pp. 10–13.

Index